SHAPING INTERIOR SPACE

SPACE

SHAPING INTERIOR SPACE

Roberto J. Rengel

University of Wisconsin—Madison

FAIRCHILD PUBLICATIONS, INC.   NEW YORK

Executive Editor: Olga T. Kontzias

Assistant Acquisitions Editor: Carolyn Purcell

Editor: Sylvia L. Weber

Associate Production Editor: Amy Zarkos

Art Director: Adam B. Bohannon

Production Manager: Priscilla Taguer

Editorial Assistant: Suzette Lam

Copy Editor: Lorraine Schein

Interior Design: Ron Reeves and Adam B. Bohannon

Cover Design: Adam B. Bohannon

Proofreader: Douglas Puchowski

Library of Congress Catalog Card Number: 2002105407

ISBN: 1-56367- 221-9

GST R 133004424

Printed in the United States of America

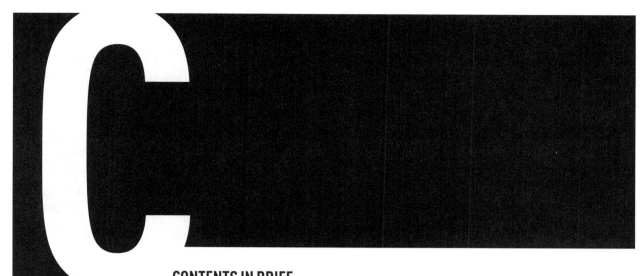

CONTENTS IN BRIEF

EXTENDED TABLE OF CONTENTS

PREFACE

Few professions can claim the kind of impact on the quality of our lives that the design professions have. We cannot escape the built environment. It is everywhere and affects us daily in profound ways. Particularly important are interior spaces. It is in them that we spend most of our time, whether working, shopping, dining, or sleeping. Interior space has become the focus of much attention among design professionals. On the one hand, interior designers, once preoccupied almost exclusively with the decorative aspects of design, have become active shapers of interior space. On the other hand, architects, normally more preoccupied with the complex requirements of designing a total building, are becoming more interested in interior projects and the particular sensibilities they entail.

Designing the built environment is difficult, certainly much more difficult than it is to just talk about design. Design students learn to "do" design while in school. The heart of the designer's education is the design studio, where design is done, not just talked about. Students tackle hypothetical projects that simulate real-life conditions with the assistance of the design instructor and, frequently, others who volunteer their time to provide valuable criticism. That way, they learn to do design. After a few of these design studios they are launched into the real world to do real design.

Despite the overwhelming importance of the doing, learning design also requires some degree of talking and reading about it. It is through these less direct ways that students gain valuable insights they can try out in the studio. This book is intended as a studio companion. It discusses design, but it does so while wearing a designer's hat. Consequently, the discussion is not historical, nor cultural, nor scientific, nor philosophical, but the talk of design. It is concerned with design's higher qualities and the ways to produce them, while not forgetting about the important and multiple contexts in which design takes place.

The book is intended for designers of interiors, with a primary focus on the particular realities of the interior design profession. The book is also intended to be helpful to students and instructors of architecture who have a special interest in the design of interior space. It has been conceived to complement the teaching of design studios and contribute in the design-teaching effort together with such other important paths to design insight and wisdom as learning by doing, learning from other students, and learning from the guidance of a conscientious design instructor. This book seeks to become part of the design instruction team and to make a strong contribution.

Specifically, this book is geared for students who are at least at an intermediate level of design. While it is written so that any design student can understand and benefit from its contents, it makes no attempt to cover many of the design basics necessary for the beginning design student. It is assumed, for instance, that the design student using this book knows about design fundamentals; can draft; and knows about materials, adjacencies, basic space planning, furniture, and other similar design elements and considerations. What this book attempts to do is take the novice designer to the next level. Inherent in this next level is an attitude that transcends the view of design as a vehicle for function and beauty alone and adopts an expanded view concerned with other significant contributions of design. Among these contributions are design's role in helping people make sense of their physical world, its role in enriching people's experiences inside buildings, and its role in affirming and expressing people's particular personalities and identities.

The designer is seen as a movie director. In this role, the designer is full of intentions beyond providing function and good looks and manipulates the qualities of both individual spaces and sequences of spaces to achieve specific results that enhance the sense of order, enrichment, and expression experienced by users. Successful implementation of this role is not easy. It requires familiarity with potential design approaches and strategies, the ability to diagnose the requirements of a project correctly, the ability to select appropriate design strategies, and the skills to execute the chosen strategies effectively.

The book is also concerned with the creative aspects of the design process, from the analysis stage, through to the resolution of all the physical issues about a project. The primary focus is on spatial issues. Because of this focus, it has been necessary to draw from existing architectural literature as opposed to interior design literature, where the topic of space has not been addressed extensively. In fact, because of the nature of the topic and its location at the point where architecture and interior design meet, much of the terminology used in the book goes back and forth between the two disciplines. It is not the intent to confuse or to show preference for one discipline over the other. It just happens that the topic addressed is equally part of both disciplines.

Other than the text, the book relies heavily on illustrations, most of them simple drawings and diagrams. Although many photographs are used as examples of the ideas presented, whenever possible, drawings have been used as the primary means to illustrate points. Drawings are the language of design, and the flow from idea to sketch or drawing is more akin to design thinking than is the flow between idea and photograph. Specifically, the drawings used are loose and design-oriented, not the rigid drawings used to represent the finished product. The goal is to emphasize a process that is creative, open-ended, and evolutionary, not one that is finished and immutable.

Writing a text for use in the design studio is a difficult proposition. It is hard to go beyond broad generalities and the often-repeated, elementary design elements and principles without going out on a limb and taking chances. Going beyond the usual generalities involves showing specific ideas and ways to implement them. It requires going beyond the usual neutral stance and stating do's and don'ts with belief and conviction. It involves the risk of encountering disagreement along the way. However, a strong position is never unproductive. It establishes a definite point of departure. One can fully agree, partially agree, or disagree, but surely, it always elicits a reaction and makes one think. That's precisely what is being attempted here, to present ideas and promote critical thinking.

The book is organized around 10 core principles introduced in Chapter 1. Chapters are divided into four general sections: General Principles (Chapters 2–4), Establishing the Design (Chapters 5 and 6), Developing the Design (Chapters 7–9), and Completing the Design (Chapters 10 and 11). Chapter 2 addresses what users do in buildings. The important role of place and its elements are explained in Chapter 3. Chapter 4 is a review of the many aspects of architectural space: how it is defined, enclosed, shaped, manipulated, combined, and composed into entire projects. The early tasks of the design process are covered in Chapters 5 and 6. Chapter 5 explains the importance of proper understanding in design and covers the different variables for which understanding is necessary. The process of early ideation and concept development is covered in Chapter 6. Chapters 7 through 10 get to the core of the design virtues advocated in this book: order, enrichment, expression, and resolution. Chapter 11 rounds out the book by discussing the important role of the design elements that modify how space is experienced.

Chapters in the book contain several important pedagogical features. Each chapter opens with a list of instructional objectives. Most include a short capsule that highlights commentary about a relevant topic from important sources in the existing design literature. The capsules aim not only to supplement the chapter but to encourage students to become aware of and seek these other valuable sources of design information. At the end of Chapters 6 through 11, short case studies discuss built projects designed by prominent designers, focusing on aspects of the design relevant to the chapter topics. Finally, an end-of-chapter review includes a summary, chapter questions, and, in some cases, exercises to promote understanding and discussion.

The text concludes with two appendices. Appendix 1 includes various segments covering miscellaneous supplementary topics about interior architectural elements and decorative patterns. Appendix 2 includes supplementary information relevant to the design of offices, stores, and restaurants, three common interior project types assigned in design studios.

Acknowledgments

My gratitude goes to the entire staff at Fairchild Books for their help in making this book a reality. Special thanks go to Mary McGarry, who was enthusiastic about the book from the beginning and Sylvia Weber for her editorial help and for keeping me on track. Finally, I would like to acknowledge the valuable feedback received from the following reviewers selected by the publisher, who provided much useful advice about both style and content:

Sharon Anderson, Moorpark College; Mary Anne Beecher, University of Oregon; Glen Currie, Art Institute of Pittsburgh; Anita Henson, St. Mary's University; Jerry Neilson, University of Florida; LuAnn Nissen, University of Nevada-Reno; Rachel Pike, Wentworth Institute of Technology; and JoEllen Weingart, Illinois Institute of Art-Schaumburg.

The final product owes much to their valuable input.

GENERAL PRINCIPLES

CHAPTER 1

Mastering Interior Design

INSTRUCTIONAL OBJECTIVES

Explain the crucial role of the design studio in design education.

Present several important sources of design knowledge.

Explain the role of intentions and strategies in design.

Introduce the concept of total design.

Describe the evolving role of interior designers as shapers of space.

Explain the close interrelationship between architecture and interior
design in interiors.

Introduce the ten design principles that guide this book.

You employ stone, wood, and concrete, and with those materials you build houses and palaces. That is construction. Ingenuity is at work...

But suppose that walls rise towards heaven in such a way that I am moved. I perceive your intentions. Your mood has been gentle, brutal, charming, or noble. The stones you have erected tell me so. You fix me to the place and my eyes regard it. They behold something that expresses a thought. A thought that reveals itself without word or sound, but solely by means of shapes which stand in a certain relationship to one another. These shapes are such that they are clearly revealed in light. The relationships between them have not necessarily any reference to what is practical or descriptive. They are a mathematical creation of your mind. They are the language of Architecture. By the use of raw materials and starting from conditions more or less utilitarian, you have established certain relationships which have aroused my emotions.[1]

Design students know there is more to design than mere utility. In fact, many choose to become designers because they enjoy being creative and because of the prospect that their creations will arouse the emotions of those who come in contact with them. There are important differences between the contributions of interior designers and those of other professionals related to design and the building process. Engineers use their knowledge to provide practical and efficient solutions based on the physical laws of nature. Builders use their knowledge to construct projects that are structurally sound and well crafted. The dominant trait of designers is their knowledge and ability to create designs that touch the human heart in ways that neither the engineer's design nor the builder's construction can. A good interior design reflects a design solution conceived by and for human beings. It holds in high regard not only their physical well-being, but also their emotional and spiritual well-being.

When clients hire interior designers, they know they are getting more than just a practical design solution; they are also buying style and substance. While practically all designers are sincerely interested in creating special interiors, some do a better job at it than others. This is due to a number of reasons, including level of skill, level of motivation, and most important, level of awareness. Many skilled and motivated designers fall short of being great designers because they are not fully aware of the range of possibilities available to arouse human emotions. Many designers still believe interior design consists of just providing functional and good-looking environment. While this view is not incorrect, it is certainly incomplete. Design, as we will see, has much more to offer than function and good looks. It is when we go beyond these two basic necessities that we start practicing total design.

The Difficulty of Design

Designing good interior spaces is difficult. The number of design problems, and their complexity can be staggering. These alone make interior design one of the most difficult fields in design. Designers are required to make sense of the realities and needs of a given client; translate them into collections of spaces subdivided in special ways in response to their optimal relationships; shape and finish the enclosing surfaces of those spaces; select and design furnishings, accessories, and fixtures that match and reinforce the particular style used; and make it all work together and look good. Ultimately, full **synthesis** is the goal of every project. All the parts and pieces need to work together, but still be flexible to accommodate change over time.

One of the aspects of design that makes it so hard is the way parts of a project have precise and delicate interrelationships between them. Designing interiors is like solving a giant table puzzle. What makes the interior design puzzle harder is that pieces can fit in not just one, but many locations, some better than others. To make matters worse, when solving the design puzzle, you may find that resolving one side of the puzzle

a certain way will weaken or clash with a part you already had resolved successfully somewhere else.

Design requires the resolution of a multitude of problems at many different levels and scales. The solutions to these design problems (adjacencies, privacy, connections, enclosure, views, details, furnishings, lighting, and so on) are layered next to and over one and other in intricate ways that create specific effects. On any given job, the designer needs to manipulate, control, and, ultimately, resolve these combinations, pushing, pulling, and twisting to achieve engaging and evocative designs.

While many of the practical tasks of design involve rational decision making, much about design, especially its artistic and poetic aspects, relies on intuition and good design sense. Stanley Abercrombie has referred to the discipline of interiors as being, "so subjective and so intimate, so immune to the calculations of science, so special to a singular circumstance and therefore so often ephemeral."[2] While many of the elusive qualities of design make the application of exact rules and formulas unrealistic, the use of guidelines, principles, and strategies are helpful for those studying design. This book will offer many.

Becoming a Designer

At its most general level, design requires two things to be successful: a fitting response to the design problem and its skillful execution (Figure 1.1). Proper response requires that the design problem (and subproblems) are understood correctly and that an appropriate design strategy is formulated to solve them. Choices have to be made about how to distribute space, assemble spatial sequences, determine levels of enclosure

$$\text{DESIGN} \quad = \quad \frac{\text{Response}}{\text{Understanding}} \quad \text{Plus} \quad \frac{\text{Execution}}{\text{Developing}}$$
$$\text{Establishing} \qquad\qquad \text{Completing}$$

Figure 1.1 Design requires proper response and proper execution. Proper response requires accurate and insightful understanding of the design problem and establishing a corresponding responsive design solution. Proper execution involves the tasks of design development and final resolution.

and articulation, and so on. The choices made by the designer need to be responsive to not only the particular utilitarian requirements of the project, but also the client's particular character. Once a design direction is established, designers need to be able to execute the design with skill. This means developing the design ideas in detail, and, ultimately, resolving and completing all aspects of the design. Particular shapes and articulations are given to all the design elements and compatible furnishings and miscellaneous nonpermanent pieces are specified. The result, if responsive and well executed, will contribute much to the day-to-day experience of the client and other users.

The Importance of the Design Studio

The inherent complexities of design make its mastery a lifelong process. So intricate and inexact is the discipline of design that many years of conscientious design practice are needed to fully understand all the levels of intricacy and nuance involved. Learning design starts in school, specifically in the design studio. In the studio, students learn to design hypothetical projects, similar to the ones encountered later in real practice. The best way to learn design is by doing. Design is not learned by memorization or the application of formulas. You learn design by solving design problems. The tangible outcomes required to communicate designs leave little room for "faking it." The drawings used in design force designers to show, explicitly, both the design intent and the specifics of the solution. Either the solution is shown and developed on paper or it is not. And if it is, it usually speaks for itself, with its virtues and shortcomings reflected in the drawings.

The design studio is the most important component of your design education. It is in the studio that you first learn to assess design situations that simulate real life and to make judgments that lead to a limited number of viable solutions. You have to commit to certain choices and make them work, resolving each chosen strategy to the best of your abilities within tight time constraints.

Not only the doing is critical. Equally important is the process of review and critique. It is imperative to get beyond the fear of criticism and seek design feedback from peers, design instructors, and, most importantly, from yourself. You need to constantly question your design choices. What is right or wrong about this design approach? Is the overall approach appropriate? Is anything not working? Are there any good ideas not resolved properly? Are there any bad ideas resolved brilliantly? What needs further development? These are the important questions you need to ask constantly.

Only through this kind of ongoing questioning will you be able to develop the reasoning skills necessary to isolate the basic issues of a design problem, understand their implications, and develop fitting design approaches for testing and development. These are skills that need reinforcement even beyond the school years. It is then that design problems become most intricate as they involve all of the complexities and problems inherent in reality. After school, you are faced with situations that require probing and detective work instead of the fully digested and convenient summary of needs and requirements you are handed for most school projects. Developing a habit of critical questioning will develop your mental agility to solve problems. The more you do this in school and then later in practice, the sharper you'll become.

In addition to good reasoning skills, proper response in design requires proper perspective. This has to be developed over time. Early on, it is hard to make certain decisions because it seems you have no basis on which to anchor them. It is therefore important to start acquiring a personal sense of what is correct and appropriate in your own view. A good way to start is by learning from other designers and design professors. By asking questions and studying how other designers have responded to real design problems, you start to acquire a sense of what is doable. Developing an alert set of eyes and a good design memory that recalls characteristics of environments is also valuable. Once you gain some experience, you'll start developing and trusting your own personal sense of propriety.

Sources of Design Knowledge

There are many sources of knowledge and information available to designers. These include design history, current design trends, design theory, and observations made while traveling to new environments. Studying past and present design solutions helps you develop your sense of appropriateness and fit. Design history is an excellent way to gain design perspective. When studying design history, one of your principal aims should be to understand the conditions that were present during specific times and to evaluate the kinds of design solutions conceived within the context of those conditions. By seeking to understand what made certain design approaches fit a specific set of circumstances in the past, you develop your sense of judg-

ment, refining your sense of fit and nuance even further.

In addition to studying past design solutions, you need to become an avid follower of current design trends. There are a number of excellent trade journals, including specialized ones for specific sectors of the industry. There are good design books available too. By following the work being done by today's designers, you can get a sense of the breadth of recent trends and start developing your own opinions about what is most appropriate.

Another important source of information for designers is the rapidly growing body of interior design research. You should become familiar with ways of accessing this important information. It can give you valuable insights about the effects of certain types of environments or their environmental attributes on users. While many areas of design have not been researched, others enjoy a good amount of published material. At present, there are countless educators worldwide, engaged in research that is expanding the available knowledge base. Although it is normally not possible to utilize research findings directly in the form of rules and formulas, research findings establish a sound point of departure, especially in areas that have established conclusive findings about specific aspects of design.

Although research findings can provide useful information, you must remember that in design every case is new and needs to be looked at with fresh eyes. You can think of and use research findings in the same way you think of and use advice from people possessing expertise and wisdom—what they have to say may be perceptive and truthful. How you decide to use the information is up to you, but at least you have some important ideas to consider. One thing to realize when using research information is that the information will merely establish an approach, a direction. Giving it specific form for the application at hand will still be your responsibility.

One last source of design knowledge we want to mention is travel. Travel, whether abroad, to a neighboring town or city, or to a local tavern, can provide invaluable insights to designers. Keeping a notebook of observations or taking pictures is also helpful. When you travel, things are fresh and you notice them. There are design lessons everywhere. Whether you visit places known for their design quality or just ordinary places, you will notice many examples of elements or combinations that either work, don't work, or could work. You will also notice examples of things you had never thought about or things you didn't think possible, and yet, here they are, and they seem to work!

Intentions and Strategies

There are important design considerations beyond the basic ones of function and aesthetics. These occur at different hierarchical levels, from broad overall goals to narrow considerations about how to treat a niche on a wall. It is important to expand your own personal scope of design possibilities. The more possibilities and variations you have in your personal repertoire, the more intentionality you can bring to your projects. Intentionality is crucial to make projects come alive; every design move should be justifiable. Nothing in a project should happen by chance. The more you become aware of the possibilities, the broader and deeper your intentions will be and your designs will acquire new layers of meaning.

Distinguishing between design problems, design intentions, and design strategies, can be confusing. They are part of one common string of thought that progresses sequentially from the identification of a problem to the implementation of a solution. **Design problems** usually involve specific needs and issues requiring a design solution. An example is the identification of the need for a friendly and inviting reception area. This design problem already comes with the requirement that the space be friendly and inviting. Two general intentions have been declared from the outset. **Design intentions** are precise goals related to a design problem. They can be concerned with practical or experiential aspects of design. Possible design intentions for the design problem above (more specific than just "friendly and inviting") are such ideas as having a bright, cheerful room with a clear, prominent receptionist desk and a cozy, comfortable waiting area off to one side, including a local focal wall and perhaps an exterior view. These are more specific ideas and start to introduce potential design strategies.

Design strategies are specific means of implementing design intentions by using particular physical materials, compositions, finishes, and so forth. For our example, determining design strategies would require devising specific means to achieve a bright and cheerful room, a clear and emphasized reception desk, and so on. These might include using contrasting levels of light, varying the height of ceilings, using an unusually shaped reception desk, creating a focal wall, or incorporating a view of the exterior into the design of the waiting area. The thing to remember is that problems, intentions, and strategies progress in their level of specificity, getting more and more detailed.

Every intention in design needs to be followed by a corresponding strategy. It would be frustrating to pursue even general intentions such as, say, modern formality, or evocative simplicity, or an engaging sequence, without first explicitly articulating what is meant by them, and, second, being equipped with a repertoire of specific strategies to achieve from. You don't need to have an exact mental picture of the way it is going to look when it's done, but having a general strategy to begin with helps. You can draw mental pictures from something you saw while traveling, or from a magazine, or even from an idea you doodled on a napkin one day. The more of these you have stored in your subconscious design library, the faster your own ideas will pop up when thinking about design strategies.

Ideas in your collection of personal strategies can also come from your own designs and those of your peers. Look around and become aware of what is possible and how it can be made to work, always keeping the two thoughts in mind. There may be cases where you see a brilliant design that happens to be the wrong solution to the problem to which it was applied. Yet some of the particulars may be especially well executed, so make a mental or written note of the particulars and perhaps a note about what kind of application they would be more appropriate for.

Eventually, you will assemble a collection of design moves that work in response to specific design problems, similar to a chess player having a collection of strategic moves ready to respond to any situation during a match. It is important, though, to always stay fresh and to avoid having those moves become automatic formulas. For that reason, it is useful always to have some consciousness of your current preferences and convictions. These tend to evolve over time as you gain experience and insight; as you age; and as the times, conditions, and styles change.

Achieving excellence in design requires conscious effort, resolve, and hard work. Competence comes with exposure and experience, but excellence requires more. It is quite common for designers to become adequate and coast through their careers producing acceptable, ordinary design. If you truly want to become good, you need to develop a commitment to design. If it is not ingrained in you during the early years, it is easily lost. The real practice of design is full of mundane requirements that will consume much of your effort, making it very tempting to aim for ordinary, acceptable design and never progress from there. If you choose to aim for excellence, you need to start now. The first thing you need to do is develop a desire to go beyond the basics. Good function and good looks are important, but they are just the beginning. Good design requires total design.

Aims of This Book

The goal of this book is to help make you a better designer. It is assumed that you have some design studio experience under your belt, have been exposed to the basics, and are ready to move into the advanced levels of design nuance and sophistication necessary for total design.

We will present important aspects of both the design process and design content. Related to the design process, we will particularly stress the important tasks of analysis, ideation, and resolution. Related to content, we will touch on many aspects and elements of interior design. However, the focus of this book is on **spatial design**. This is an aspect of increasing importance in the field and one with which many interior design students and practitioners seem to struggle.

As interior design has become a more prominent and recognized profession, the role of the interior designer has expanded considerably. Once relegated to the selection of finishes, furnishings, and other additive aspects of design, today's designer is not merely a completer of interior designs but a shaper of interior space. Once the exclusive province of architects, when it comes to interiors, today's interior designer frequently has total control over the design. Yet many interior design students, and even many practitioners, experience difficulties with spatial design, and seldom go beyond the most simplistic and unimaginative plans with minimal three-dimensional exploration.

The view we hold of interiors is an inclusive one. Interior designs work as a unity that includes spaces, surfaces, barriers, openings, sequences, furnishings, finishes, accessories, artwork, and other elements, and the skillful manipulation of interior space is crucial to establishing the kind of place the project becomes. True, it is possible to have a gigantic undifferentiated shell and to determine all the subspaces, functions, and tone only by the furnishings and other nonpermanent elements, but even that undifferentiated shell would be making a statement and strongly influencing the overall tone of the project. Most projects, however, have the benefit of more differentiated space with changes in volumes and all the kinds of twists and turns that give projects their drama and excitement. Space and its related elements are too crucial to leave to others or treat blandly; interior designers need to become adept at working with, manipulating, and controlling them.

There is a fine line between architecture and interior design in this book. In terms of the subject matter of interior environments, these disciplines become one and the same: elements present in the design of interiors, whether architectural or decorative, contribute to the qualities of the same place. The lessons of this book can be equally helpful to architecture students interested in interiors and to interior design students. There are a few basic and important differences between the realities encountered by architects and designers when they face the design of interior space. The most crucial one is that architects, for the most part, shape interior space in the process of designing an overall building, and interior designers almost always design projects in existing interior spaces, usually starting from empty building shells without internal construction or existing spaces to be altered or completely redesigned and rebuilt. The examples in the book are aimed at the interior designers who encounter existing shells as their points of departure.

Above all, this book hopes to teach you a way of thinking about design that fosters the pursuit of high ideals and to show you design strategies and concepts to help you understand the ideas presented. This, hopefully, will make a contribution to your personal library of design intentions and strategies. When, where, and how you apply the ideas presented is up to you. Judging whether the way you apply a certain strategy is appropriate for the circumstances or whether the execution is successful is beyond what the book can offer. That's where the design studio, your peers, and your instructor come in. The appropriateness of design is such a subjective matter, governed by the individual peculiarities of each situation, that constant evaluation and critique pertaining to the specific application at hand is necessary to ascertain the merits of any design attempt.

The book, then, is like a bridge between you and the design studio. It presents you with new information to consider and use, but you will have to try it within the context of the studio and learn by doing. Whether the design problem interpretation is sound, whether the strategies devised are appropriate and fitting, and whether the execution of the design ideas is carried out skillfully will need to be evaluated by you and others on a case-by-case basis.

Ten Design Principles

The contents of this book are based on ten principles about interior design. These are:

General Principles
1. Buildings are for people.
2. Place is the basic unit of interior design.
3. To master place you must master space.

Principles to Establish the Design
4. A good design solution requires good understanding of the problem.
5. A good design starts with a simple and powerful organizational idea.

Principles to Develop the Design
6. A good design produces order.
7. To satisfy, projects need to have enriching qualities.
8. In order to have deeper meaning, projects need to incorporate a fitting expression.

Completing the Design
9. The obligation to balance and unify all the physical components used in a project is an inherent aspect of the design task.
10. Spatial design is not complete with space alone. It requires the effects of key modifying elements that contribute to the way it is perceived.

General Principles

The first three principles lay the basic ground for the view of interior design advocated throughout. They reflect a basic attitude about the interior environment and its purpose.

1. Buildings are for people.

The fundamental purpose of all interior environments is to support people and their activities (Figure 1.2). Some buildings and individual projects may command considerable attention due to their grand-

Figure 1.2 Even when burdened by the many physical details and problems of a project, designers need to remember that buildings are for people. Every design effort should have as its goals the utility, convenience, comfort, safety, and delight it produces for people.

Figure 1.3 The basic unit of interiors is place. Interior environments need to be looked at as assemblies of multiple places for people. These vary in size, character, and function, but are always distinguishable as discrete locations where specific activities take place.

ness or beauty, but their most basic functions are to support the functions and dreams of those who use them.

Designers need to cultivate an appreciation and understanding of the types of rituals and events associated with different project types. By listening, observing, and most of all, by experiencing directly the realities of those who use specific project types, designers can acquire the insights and sensibilities necessary to inform their designs.

The many activities associated with the use of buildings need to be analyzed and understood. These are the subplots of the total building experience. The experiences of people approaching, arriving, moving, interacting, performing tasks, and leaving a project are all important events with important design implications. The rituals performed routinely in given types of projects, the specific occasions that vary from time to time, the people involved, and the effect of the surroundings all affect the total experience people have in buildings. Although the physical design is only one of the components, it acts as part of the total mix and needs to be considered in relation to the other factors present at the scene.

An important consideration to remember is that different users of a project have different perceptions of a given situation depending on their role in it, their level of affinity with what is taking place, their familiarity with the place and the occasion, how challenging their involvement is, and how much control they have over what is going on. Designers have to be sensitive to all these considerations, for they affect the experience of the different types of users of a given facility.

2. Place is the basic unit of interior design.

Interior design is a unique and complicated discipline. Comparing it to other art forms is very difficult. The basic units of interior design are not points, lines, shapes, planes, or even space. Of course, these all are factors in the process of assembling interior environments, but none of them is the basic unit of lived-in environments. The basic unit of interior design is place (Figure 1.3). Designers need to learn to think about environment in terms of place, each place having a unique character of its own depending on the choices made in putting it together. The concept of place implies that the environments we create are complex totalities that function as real and coherent locations where life takes place. This is a different way of looking at it compared to the abstractions we tend to use when we think of environments created by the addition of walls and other building components, or worse, when we think of environments as drawings on a piece of paper.

The unit of place needs to be the first and last yardstick with which we measure projects. In the process of creating places of particular qualities, individual elements automatically suggest themselves as belonging together to achieve the desired effect. The more detailed individual considerations such as colors, textures, and shapes have to be fine-tuned and given individual consideration. But the overall picture has to return to the basic unit of place, as a totality, to really be evaluated properly.

There are not too many different generic types of places in interiors. Basically, in most interior projects there are identifiable locations such as rooms and cir-

Figure 1.4 The manipulation of interior space, including its distribution, composition, and sculpting, is one of the most basic and important requirements of design.

culation paths to get around. Some places, because of their function or location, are more important. Some of these are arrival spaces or the locations where main paths converge. Important attributes of places to consider are the way they are enclosed, connected to each other, and arranged so that people can sit, stand, and move in ways appropriate to the project.

The task of design is such that, at some point, designers have to spend considerable time dealing with the smaller components that constitute place. Our judgment of all these components, however, has to be made in relation to the place of which they are a part.

3. To master place, you must master space.

The mastery of space and its many components is essential in the design of interior places (Figure 1.4). Most of us have spent considerable time during our formative years in enclosed rooms, either at home or school. Consequently, there is a natural tendency to equate architectural space with rooms. While in many cases space is defined as a room, in other cases it is not. Designers need to make special efforts to understand the many variations and subtleties of space.

Space can be explicit (like a room with four walls, a floor, and a ceiling) or it can be implied. In between there are many possible combinations. The level of enclosure is a crucial variable, as space can be defined with different degrees of enclosure. Defined space can be totally encapsulated or totally free. Variations in the treatment of the edges as well as the size, number, and placement of openings will create very different effects.

Space, although most often composed of regular, simple volumes, can be irregular. Sometimes the solid masses inside space can be the ones having the regularity of form, and space can be the leftover shape. Space comes in all sizes and shapes. Depending on its proportions, it acquires forces of its own and starts either to suggest stability or to induce movement. Many different manipulations can be performed when designing spaces. Individual basic forms can be added to, divided, and distorted. Additionally, the physical elements in space can be arranged to reveal or conceal views ahead, to control movement or to free it.

Equally as important as creating good individual spaces is composing sequences of spaces, and entire projects. There are many possible arrangements of spaces in relation to the paths that feed them and in relation to adjacent or nearby spaces. Eventually, decisions have to be made about how all the spaces work as a system, with choices ranging from simple utilitarian compositions to elaborate classical ones.

Principles to Establish the Design

The next two principles are related to the task of establishing a basic design direction early in the design process.

4. A good design solution requires good understanding of the problem.

Good design is responsive to particular needs, is appropriate to the circumstances in substance and style, and fits within its context. In order to achieve this kind of congruence between needs and solutions it is imperative for designers to understand the requirements of a project. Aspects to be understood include, but go beyond, the programmatic requirements of the project (Figure 1.5).

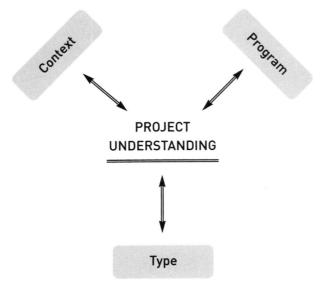

Figure 1.5 To respond appropriately to the particular realities of a project, the designer needs to understand its context, its program, and the type of project it is a manifestation of.

There are often important historical, cultural, and regional realities that become important contexts to be considered and responded to. The local neighborhood with its physical and environmental features and movement patterns represents a more immediate and important context. The building in which the project is housed also constitutes an important context. It comes with a set of suggestive attributes and patterns of use that need to be understood and responded to.

Usually, the most direct needs of a project are associated with the requirements outlined in the design program. Most projects come with a program listing the specific requirements to be addressed. Functions, as well as their space requirements and relationships, are included. Although most of the project requirements are likely to be included in the program, some important considerations are sometimes omitted. It can take some detective work and perceptive questioning by the designer to get to the heart of some issues not articulated in the program.

It is important to realize that most types of projects are examples of a particular kind of institution or entity having specific characteristics and needs based on its function. Every project is a specific type of facility. Whether a restaurant, store, or office, all projects have unique requirements characteristic of their type. Designers need to really understand the inherent requirements associated with specific kinds of projects. Some of these will not be reflected in the program and will surface only if the designer is familiar with the specific nuances of the project type through study or experience.

Potential levels of understanding vary widely. A doctor may say she knows how you must be feeling, but if she has never had your disease, she really doesn't know how you feel. Only through proper questioning and a good dose of empathy can she begin to get a sense of what you are feeling. The same is true in design. You may feel you understand how a place functions, but if you have not spent time in a similar place before, your understanding will be superficial. The people who really know how a place functions, at least in their corner of the world, are its users. For complex projects, designers need to make every effort possible to get to the users if they sincerely hope to understand how things are supposed to work.

Proper understanding takes effort. Designers need to develop the habits of proper questioning and proper listening, as well as develop effective ways of recording the information collected in ways that are useful for the design. These efforts should not be limited to the beginning of a project. Although most information is collected at the beginning of a project, this information evolves, is expanded, and even changes during the life of a project. Therefore, processes used to solicit and record this information throughout the life of a project will ensure proper understanding of the project at any point during its duration.

5. A good design starts with a simple and powerful organizational idea.

The most basic design response to a given project is the organizational structure it is given (Figure 1.6). Of all the many needs and realities that must be understood about a project, the most fundamental one is a

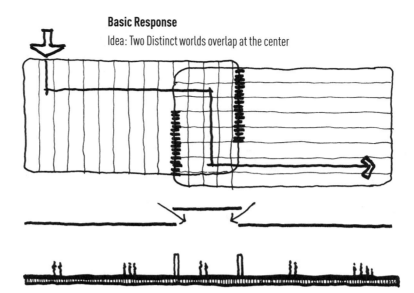

Basic Response
Idea: Two Distinct worlds overlap at the center

Figure 1.6 A simple and powerful organizational idea endows a project with a solid foundation on which to rest. This requires proper response at its most fundamental level.

good grasp of the basic essence of the project, with as little detail as possible. This may take some effort, but once you understand a project's basic organizational essence, and whether it suggests a large central space or many small sequential units, you are prepared to make your first design move, like the first stroke on a blank piece of canvas. Keep in mind however, that having a good grasp of the essence of the design problem will facilitate, but not guarantee, an appropriate response.

A simple organizational idea (also known as organizational concept) is the start of a good project. Its success depends on its appropriateness—how well it responds to the basic design problem. The idea may be bold or jazzy, but does not need to be. Its main goal is to establish an overall organizational system that gives coherence and clarity to the project.

The generation of fitting concepts requires a good understanding of the basic behaviors that take place in the facility, the relationships of different units, the hierarchy of parts, and the flow of people, goods, or information. The process of concept generation requires the identification of dominant issues, the generation and evaluation of workable alternatives, and the selection of one to develop. This sometimes requires the painful discarding of other workable alternatives.

Principles to Develop the Design
The next three principles are concerned with specific goals initiated early and pursued in full during the development stages of the design process. During development, the basic design idea established earlier is given precise form and refined.

6. A good design produces order.
The need for order is one of the most basic human needs, especially in unfamiliar environments. A sense of correctness and confidence comes with order. Proper order provides points of reference to help people feel oriented and have a sense of where they are. It operates at many levels. Order is produced by strong and clear organization. A sense of order is also perceived when things appear to be where they belong, producing a tidy environment, where everything is in its proper place. Visual harmony produces a sense of order too. Order is also sometimes associated with situations that have good correspondence between needs and conditions, as in cases where there seems to be an answer every time a functional need arises.

At the project level, a sense of order is perceived when the project's organization and structure are understood. Projects with clear organizational structures, readable links between parts, and memorable spaces or elements become rich in order and are easier to understand. People seem to have a sense of where they are in relationship to the whole. Logical, well-structured sequences, clear intersections and groupings, distinctive parts, and the use of a hierarchical design approach are the kinds of attributes you can incorporate to contribute to a project's sense of order.

Providing healthy levels of order is sometimes not as straightforward as it appears. Every increase in order will not necessarily translate into a corresponding increase in preference. In fact, sometimes too much order can be undesirable. Designers need to learn to provide the optimal level of order for the na-

Figure 1.7 Rich physical qualities bring projects to life. The shapes, patterns, textures, rhythms, and details of this bar contribute to its playfulness and richness.

Figure 1.8 Projects need to express qualities that their users will relate to and support. These become the project's personality. Many businesses, like this coffee shop, make conscious efforts to portray very specific personalities targeted to their audiences.

ture of the project and for the different kinds of users of a project. The optimal level of environmental order for a clinic and a discothéque is going to be different. The same is true if you compare the desirable level of order for a first-time visitor to a large hospital to the desirable level for a staff member. In this case, the problem of providing a clear, straightforward environment for the visitor, and an interesting environment for the regular user presents a unique design challenge.

7. To satisfy, projects need to have enriching qualities.

While the main function of a project is to support and enhance the activities that take place in it, projects have a significant physical presence. Other than providing spaces for functions with the desired levels of connection and separation between them, the physical parts of a project have the capacity to delight humans by providing enriching physical qualities and experiences (Figure 1.7). Enriching qualities and experiences can be bold or subtle depending on the circumstances and the desired effect.

Not all enriching experiences need to provide stimulus with the intent to excite and motivate. Enriching experiences can also help to relax and restore one's emotional equilibrium. Variety and complexity can be used to stimulate and create interest. Novelty and picturesqueness can provide momentary vacations and relax the busy mind. They both have their place in design. The appropriate type of enrichment for any given space depends on the circumstances.

Circulation areas present special opportunities for

enrichment. They can be dramatic and full of pleasant surprises. Sequences can be made interesting; events can take place along the way; surfaces can incorporate engaging details, colors, and textures; and views can provide pleasant distractions and interesting information. Areas for tasks involving mental concentration benefit from the type of environmental qualities that promote a sense of stability. Establishing meaningful visual connections with the surroundings and providing views for relief and distraction also enrich the busy mind at work.

8. In order to have deeper meaning, projects need to incorporate a fitting expression.

The qualities provided to enrich a project also carry with them inherent expressions of particular attitudes. Designers need to give projects the right expression. The way of allocating and dividing space, the shapes of the architectural and decorative documents used, and the colors, furnishings, and accessories incorporated in a project all carry connotations of particular attitudes and stylistic tendencies (Figure 1.8). Care has to be exercised by the designer so that the expressions manifested are the desired and appropriate ones.

The way design elements are arranged and shaped, and the characteristics of the products selected for a project can be expressive of universal human manifestations, such as constraint or freedom. They can also express significant historic or cultural associations, or important programmatic requirements, such as connection or segregation. Furthermore, and quite importantly, design can express dominant traits about

Figure 1.9 All physical aspects of the project need to be resolved. This view of a simple transition in the circulation spaces of an office shows thoughtful consideration and integration of walls and their placement, of the ceilings and their articulation, and of lighting, art, and plants.

the personality of the project's owners and users. Manifestations of qualities related to status, control, hierarchy, sophistication, and extroversion are all possible through design.

The expressions manifested in a project can also speak to the designer's own stylistic inclinations and personal preferences, as well as reflect the particular design tendencies of a specific location at a particular time in history.

Completing the Design

The final two principles are related to the important tasks of completing the design. In the end, all the design issues and problems need to be fully resolved and finalized.

9. The obligation to balance and unify all the physical components used in a project is an inherent aspect of the design task.

So many are the parts and pieces of typical interior projects that solving the functional puzzle alone is quite a challenging task. Additionally, designers are asked to make projects look good, balanced and unified. The process of total resolution of the many components into a single unified entity is one of the greatest responsibilities of design (Figure 1.9). It starts with the resolution and refinement of the floor plan in order to make it work right and eliminate all awkward or wasteful spots.

Beyond that, parts need to be sized and balanced to look right. The relative size of things in relation to humans and to other parts needs to be addressed and resolved. The proportions of parts and sections in rela-

tion to other parts and the compositions they are a part of also must be resolved. Parts seen together or experienced sequentially have to be balanced for proper equilibrium. Additionally, despite the inherent or intentional variety of a project, ultimately it has to read as a unified totality, conceived and produced by a single hand, while avoiding the dullness that comes with excessive regularity and repetition.

10. Spatial design is not complete with space alone. It requires the effects of key modifying elements that contribute to the way it is perceived.

While space and its enclosing surfaces establish the basis for spatial design and experience, the complete space experience includes other important environmental elements such as lighting, color, details, and sounds. The blending of all these elements becomes one of the biggest challenges and opportunities for the designer. When the many elements that comprise the spatial experience work together in coherent, synergetic fashion, the result is much more powerful than the result of merely adding their individual effects. It is when this happens that space is experienced in full, resulting in rich, evocative environments that strike a chord in those who use them (Figure 1.10).

Beginning the Journey

The following chapters of this book are organized in the same order as the ten principles just introduced. Chapter 2 addresses what users do in buildings. The important role of place and its elements are explained

Figure 1.10 The spaces we create require the important modifying effects produced by lighting, colors, materials, details, furnishings, and so on. It is as a totality that we perceive them through our senses and minds.

in Chapter 3. Chapter 4 is a review of the many aspects of architectural space: how it is defined, enclosed, shaped, manipulated, combined, and composed into entire projects. The early tasks of the design process are covered in Chapters 5 and 6. Chapter 5 explains the importance of understanding the requirements of a project properly. The crucial process of early ideation and concept development is covered in Chapter 6.

Chapters 7 through 10 get to the core of the design virtues advocated in this book: order, enrichment, expression, and resolution. Chapter 11 finishes with a brief look at the important role of the interior elements that help give interior spaces many of their special characteristics.

We are ready to begin our journey. Open your mind and get ready to experiment and travel beyond function and good looks. Enjoy!

Review

Summary

Good interior design projects offer more than just utility. The designs of interior environments have the capacity to delight and inspire. Design requires, at the most fundamental level, proper response to the specific problems of the project, and that the execution of the response be carried out skillfully.

The design studio is the most important component of a design education for it is there that students perform the act of designing. Also important is the practice of reviewing and critiquing design solutions. It is

through proper questioning that students develop the reasoning skills necessary to become good design thinkers. It is also important for the young designer to expand his or her range of design ideas and strategies so they grow over time, expanding the designer's collection of potential design solutions.

Today's designers are responsible for the distribution and shaping of the interior environments they design. It is therefore crucial that they become adept at working with interior space and be able to conceive, establish, develop, and complete space and its many components.

This book is organized around ten design principles. These address concepts students need to know regarding the realities of interior space and its design, and specific design issues concerned with the tasks of establishing, developing, and completing design solutions.

Endnotes

[1] LeCorbusier. *Towards a New Architecture*, (Dover Publications: New York, 1968) p.153.
[2] Abercrombie, S. *A Philosophy of Interior Design*, (Harper and Row Publishers: New York, 1990) p. 165.

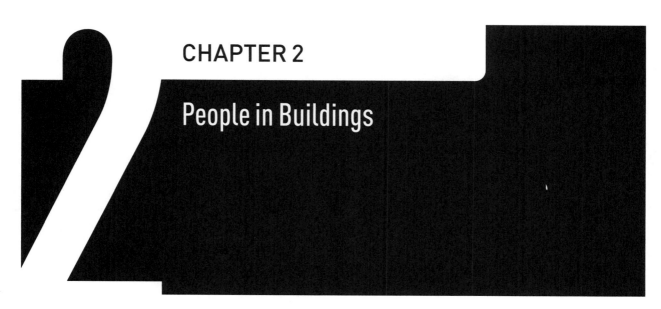

CHAPTER 2

People in Buildings

INSTRUCTIONAL OBJECTIVES

Describe typical events during building visits.

Highlight the importance of events preceding the main activity in buildings.

Highlight the importance of secondary events in buildings.

Highlight the distinction between stationary and transitory activities.

Explain how situational factors affect users' experiences in buildings.

Explain how certain variables affect how users react to situational factors.

Explain how the various events people go through when visiting buildings add
up to the total experience of the visit.

Architecture is more to do with making frames than painting pictures; more a matter of providing an accompaniment to life than the dance itself.[1]

Our experience is made up largely of the activities we do to satisfy our human needs and the societal rituals we perform daily. Learning, working, playing, and connecting are some of the things we do. Although some of these could take place outside, it seems like most of what we do, we do inside. We seem to spend a lot of our time going from building to building. In fact, the majority of us can, most often, be found either inside a building or in transit between one building and another.

As the quote at the beginning of this chapter suggests, architecture serves as an accompaniment to the dance of life. Our conscious awareness, however, is usually more preoccupied with the dance of life itself, than the surroundings in which the dance takes place. As we move from activity to activity and from goal to goal, our mind is focused on the meeting, the purchase, the meal, or the dance. People, goods, food, and dancing partners are our primary objectives. Despite its seemingly secondary status in our lives, architecture is a crucial ingredient in the mix. It represents the setting in which the various dances of life take place and, as such, it plays a vital supporting role. It supplies not only a roof over our head, warmth, and safety, but also favorable conditions for an effective meeting, a smooth sale, an unforgettable meal, and a flowing dance. True, the other meeting members, the merchandiser, the salesperson, the cook, the waiter, and the dance partner, all have to do their share for their activities to be successful and meaningful, but architecture, and specifically, its interior spaces, needs to do its share too. Human experience is a seamless phenomenon, involving people, their rituals, and the settings in which they occur.

To design beyond function and good looks, we have to start by knowing the human rituals we perform inside buildings and the mix of ingredients that constitute these. These ingredients make up a given activity, acting as forces that push and pull in many directions, sometimes in complementary, and other times in conflicting, ways. Understanding this mix and what role the spaces we design play in the whole picture will allow you to respond with fitting solutions that supply the right amounts of particular enhancing attributes.

Our first task is to learn about people and their rituals in buildings. We may start by asking: What exactly do we do in buildings? The full answer to this question is likely to be quite long and complex. There are countless activities that we perform in buildings. However, despite the fact that we do so many different activities inside buildings, such as eating, shopping, studying, or working, there are several sequential events that occur most of the time. The purpose of this chapter is to explain these events so that we can learn to design with those events in mind. Additionally, this chapter will cover some of the main ingredients that form the mix of human activity and suggest how people's experiences in buildings will vary depending on these.

Basic Events of the Building Experience

The basic events that take place during building visits seem to be consistent and repetitive. Many of these events take place before or after the main activity associated with the visit. By gaining awareness of these events, we can identify opportunities to provide design features to enrich the experience of those who visit our projects. Let's start with a scenario of a person's trip to the theater to see a live play, taken from Martin Bloom's book *Accommodating the Lively Arts*. In one of the chapters Bloom describes, in detail, the requirements of the spaces and places of a theater. Below is a description of one patron's experiences and observations as he visits the kind of theater described by Bloom. We take it from the exterior approach to the moment preceding the start of the show.

A patron approaches the theater on foot. The approach sets the tone for the experience. The ambience surrounding the theater is festive, creating a mood of anticipation of the event to come. The marquee projects, protects, and announces the current show. It welcomes, lures, and dazzles with light. The entranceways beneath the marquee welcome him to the attraction and feature promotional signs, posters, and photos on either side. Just beyond the entranceways, the box office allows sufficient space so that the long lines of ticket buyers do not impede the flow of patrons already ticketed and entering the theater. A staff member goes back to the administration area through a door accessible from the outer lobby, but located inconspicuously. The ample space in the outer lobby allows for discrete circulation, avoiding congestion from the crowd. Patrons not yet ready to enter the theater wait in allotted spaces away from the main paths of circulation.

Figure 2.1 The marquee of this modest theater strongly announces both the presence of the theater and the particular events showing. Its outward projection makes the theater location visible among the adjacent row buildings.

Figure 2.2 The outer lobby features the box office area. There are three windows for ticket purchases plus an attractive stand promoting the event currently playing.

Although businesslike and efficient, the lobby space serves as a prelude to the performance, enhancing the anticipation for the event to come. As the patron approaches the entrance to the inner lobby and passes through the control point, he surrenders his tickets and receives a stub indicating his seat assignment. At this point he begins to sense his relationship to the theater as a whole. The locations of checking facilities, restrooms, and public telephones become quickly apparent, and the pathway to the particular portion of the theater where he will eventually be seated is clearly disclosed.

Having unburdened himself of coats and parcels, he moves freely into the highly structured environment that begins to prepare him for the coming event. Having some time to wander, he contemplates images of past events in the theater, as well as historic artifacts related to the building. The main lobby is spacious, enabling the large audience to circulate freely and facilitating social interaction. The main lobby also provides glimpses of the immediate surroundings through window openings and through doors leading onto terraces, contributing a dynamic quality and aesthetic amenity. The grand stairway to the mezzanine contributes to the overall character of the lobby, providing viewing positions from the upper level that overlook the lobby below. The overall height and breadth of the space is monumental.

The lobby has established the patron's mindset for the ensuing event, transforming him into a participant in the event about to take place in the theater. Meanwhile, the patron becomes an actor in a secondary act, the drama created by the spectators in the lobby. As the patron approaches the entrance of the auditorium, he proceeds through a transitional zone in which the lighting and sound levels of the lobby are gradually diminished. Once inside, he takes measure of the totality of the space, gaining a sense of his relationship to it.

Understanding his position in relationship to the whole gives him a sense of security within the environment. After being conducted to his assigned row, he negotiates the space between the rows and gets to his seat. The seat, clearly identified by letter and number, is comfortable, with enough height, width, and elbow room to accommodate a wide range of physical types.

There is enough ambient light to allow him to grasp the size, shape, and appearance of the room. The colors and textures of the walls and ceilings relate harmoniously to the seating areas and tie the whole composition of the room into a cohesive whole. Narrowly focused downlights complement the ambient lighting, facilitate the reading of the programs, and provide adequate lighting levels for aisles and exits.

The focus of the auditorium lies within the performance space and the seating arrangement reinforces that focus. It provides good sight lines and acoustics so that the audience is able to see and hear the performance with ease. As the time for the event nears, individual members of the audience settle in their separate locations, begin to focus their attention on the performance space and, as they do, become a coherent and attentive body,

Figure 2.3 The inner lobby includes a restaurant and a bar. A prominent stairway leads to the inviting mezzanine upstairs.

Figure 2.4 The mezzanine of this theater lobby features some of the best spots for standing or seating before shows and during intermission. From it one can, comfortably, see the procession of people arriving downstairs.

ready to react to the stimuli of the production. As the house lights dim, the environment of the audience space gradually loses its identity and begins to yield to the reality of the stage. In it, shortly, the audience will witness a presentation of a heightened reality, one more focused and more persuasive than anything that can be experienced outside the theater.[2]

The description above provides a rich account of all the minievents that take place even before the start of the big event, the theatrical production itself. In the case of a theater show, the production is the main activity. Actors act on stage and the audience looks on attentively from their seats. Behind the scenes, countless workers perform their roles with scenery, costumes, lights and other crucial backstage activities to make the production smooth and flawless. During intermission, our sample patron my take a trip to the restroom and then proceed to the lobby for a beverage and, perhaps, conversation with friends about the first half of the show and what may be in store for the second. At the end of the production, the entrance sequence is reversed. The patron proceeds from the auditorium to the coat checkroom, to the various lobbies and, finally, exits the building. This may be done in ceremonious fashion, as when arriving, although exiting often tends to be a bit more chaotic because of the large number of people leaving simultaneously. Figures 2.1 through 2.4 show four views likely to be experienced by a theater patron while in the public areas. These are only a few of the many the visitor will experience during the entire experience of attending a

function at the theater as illustrated by our example above.

The trip to the theater above incorporates all the events a person is likely to go through in a building. These are approaching, arriving, waiting, moving towards the destination place, arriving at the destination, performing the intended activity, taking side trips, engaging in peripheral activities, departing from the destination, moving towards the exit, and exiting. Although the specific nature of these experiences will vary from occasion to occasion, and from building type to building type, they are, essentially, the rituals we do in buildings. Below, we examine them more closely.

Approach

Our journey to a place begins the moment we decide to go there. In most cases, the decision we make is a decision to engage in a certain activity, be it eating out, shopping, going to work, or meeting with friends. Although in some cases people visit a building to see the building, such as in a building tour, the majority of times the building (and its interiors) is a secondary component of the activity. It is, however, a crucial one.

Even before we can see the building, we may start thinking about it; where we will park the car, which entrance we'll use, and so on. At some point, we see the building. It ceases to be a memory and becomes real. We start approaching it and recognize it as our destination. Depending on our familiarity with the building, we may have to think hard, or not so hard, about the eventual entrance sequence. It may be challenging to the first-timer if it's a complicated building. For others it will be business as usual.

Figure 2.5 These two exterior views show the approach to a restaurant (a) and to a medical clinic (b).

Figure 2.6 A common arrival space in buildings housing more than one entity is a public lobby. The image shows the lobby for a downtown office building.

The building surroundings and general circumstantial conditions will have an effect on how we react to the act of entering. If it is a beautiful day, we may be reluctant to go in; if it is cold and windy, we will welcome the building's warmth; if the scenery is flat, open, and undifferentiated outside, we may welcome the building's sense of structure and enclosure. The building may be handsome, ordinary, or ugly. Depending on how apparent these qualities are and on our state of mind, we may or may not pay attention to them.

The approach to the building is full of anticipation. The first sight of the building leaves an important first impression on the visitor. Depending on the type of facility, its outward appearance may need to be bold or subtle, plain or adorned, formal or informal. In most cases, designers of interiors inherit a building with a given exterior character that cannot be changed. Whether it can or not, though, it will be part of the visitor's experience. Many commercial businesses, such as office facilities and retail stores, make decisions about where to lease space depending on, among other things, the quality and image of the building exterior. Figure 2.5 shows views of a restaurant and a dental clinic as seen when approached from the exterior.

Overall Arrival 1

At some point we reach the building's front door, open it, and step inside, a significant event. The act of entering itself (opening the door and proceeding in) is usually straightforward and performed automatically. Few people stop and think: Wow, what an entrance! However, we may become more aware of an entrance if the door is excessively heavy or if it unexpectedly

opens automatically. The resulting experiences would be annoying in the first case, and surprising in the second. We may also notice particularly well-composed and inviting entrances.

At this point, if we are familiar with the building, we may proceed automatically towards our goal. Otherwise, it may take a few minutes, depending on the building's complexity and internal arrangement, to get oriented and figure out where to go next. It is also at this point that we get our first impression of the building's interior. Depending on what the space has to offer and our state of mind, we may notice this first space and its qualities to a greater or lesser degree.

Our goal destination may be a short distance away, way in the back, or on a different floor altogether. Accordingly, we proceed the short distance, to the back, or towards the stairs or elevators to reach our next destination. If we take the stairs or elevators to go to a different floor, we go through a similar sequence to the one on the original floor at the new level (proceeding or stopping to get oriented).

Arrival gives us a partial sense of accomplishment. It represents meeting a partial objective of the overall goal of arriving at the final destination. For the designer, there are opportunities to make the arrival memorable, to reveal the whole cohesively, and to make the path to follow clear for visitors, among others.

Figure 2.6 shows an image of the arrival space at a fancy office building, a public lobby space.

Overall Arrival 2

As we get closer to the front door of the space we are going to, the level of excitement (or apprehension) we

Figure 2.7 In buildings containing more than one facility, a second arrival takes place when we transition into the specific facility we are visiting. The two views above show the first views seen upon entering a dental clinic (a) and a multitheater civic building (b).

have in anticipation of whatever will take place there is sure to increase. As we open the door (if there is one) and proceed to enter we go through an entrance experience similar to the one of entering the building except here the transition is between two interior spaces, and we are actually arriving at the destination space. Again, we will have first impressions, perhaps more noticeable here since the burden of finding our way around is behind us, leaving more room in our mind to attend to other things.

Depending on the type of space, there may or may not be someone to greet us. An office, clinic, and a restaurant are likely to have a person greeting us; a store is not. Here, similar to when we entered the building and arrived at the destination floor, we may take a moment to glance around and get oriented. If we are familiar with the space, we just proceed ahead.

This arrival, more than the others, is sure to give us a sense of accomplishment and relief. In these kinds of spaces there are opportunities for the designer to make a strong first impression with the arrival space itself, and the spaces seen beyond as well. Figure 2.7a and b show the arrival spaces of a dental clinic and a multi-theater civic building.

Waiting

In many facilities, such as offices, clinics, and restaurants, visitors have to wait their turn. A waiting room or area is supplied in these facilities for that purpose. Waiting is one of those rare instances when we are neither engaged in the target activity nor traveling to it. We are at the general destination but must now wait before we engage in the main ac-

tivity. Any potential anxiety related to finding the right place, getting there on time, and so on may have subsided considerably. We now have some time on our hands.

Depending on the length of the wait and what else we have scheduled, waiting may or may not be a relaxed experience. Even if we are rushed, we have to wait. Oftentimes, there will be other people waiting too, strangers in close proximity. This could be pleasurable for the extroverted person who likes to talk and meet people, and stressful for the introverted person who dislikes talking, much less to strangers. Frequently, waiting rooms will provide a solution to this problem: reading materials. The magazines provided in offices and clinics, and the menus at the restaurant provide relief and comfort to those who would rather avoid strangers. If you have company, this could become a welcome opportunity to talk. Eventually, the person you are there to meet with, or the waiter, or the nurse, arrives and calls your name. You are getting closer to your real goal!

A couple of exceptions to the experience described above occur in some restaurants and most stores. Some restaurants have a bar and encourage patrons to wait there. The resulting waiting experience is different since you begin to use the facility; in this case, you may start to consume a beverage, something different from waiting passively. Stores are still different. Stores, except by-appointment specialty stores, require no waiting; you proceed right in and start looking around. Interestingly enough, many stores, notably grocery stores and convenience stores, have some waiting at the end. A different kind of waiting

Figure 2.8 Waiting is an unavoidable reality for visitors of many facility types. Shown above are views of the waiting areas in a dental clinic (a) and a corporate office setting (b).

from the one described here, waiting in line is nevertheless a waiting experience. Retailers make attempts to make this idle time productive by placing small merchandise close to the registers for last minute impulse purchases. Some include magazines and miscellaneous tabloids for our browsing pleasure and potential purchase. This kind of waiting, however, occurs at an entirely different time in the sequence and it represents the consummation of the shopping activity, rather than the waiting-at-the-gate kind of experience at the restaurant, office, or clinic.

One final kind of waiting occurs at the theater. There, you can wait outside in the lobby where you are free to move about at will, a much more active waiting experience. Part of what makes the typical waiting room experience uncomfortable for many is the lack of control and freedom of movement. There is usually nowhere to go, plus the close proximity to strangers is uncomfortable for many.

Waiting experiences are full of anticipation and expectation. They are instances of suspended attention, sort of a limbo between one place and another. People are not burdened with the logistics and challenges of finding the place and are still not engaged with, maybe not even thinking about, the upcoming activity. This is an excellent opportunity to make an impression and provide meaningful engaging detail. Figure 2.8a and b show waiting areas for the dental clinic, and an office suite.

Moving to the Destination

The route taken to, and the experience of moving to the principal destination, is often different for first-

timers, frequent visitors, and the insiders of a given facility. Insiders will proceed ahead and often use the back way in. Visitors, whether alone or escorted, will be limited to the public corridors intended for them.

The walk to the destination can be straightforward and utilitarian, or it can be involved and eventful. While in transit, we can often look around and get a better sense of the overall environment, even if we don't get to see it all. We form impressions based on what is revealed in the corridor and the views from it to the spaces beyond. Insiders know the environment well and are not as likely to focus on and be affected by it. They are harder to impress but still deserve to be.

Moving to the destination is often the most revealing experience of visitors to a facility. The opportunities to make an impression and provide enriching experiences are enormous. Circulation used to move around the facility can be experientially stimulating at different levels. At the most basic level, it can orient and provide rich experiences to the visitor. At a second level, it may provide a not readily apparent interest, the kind you notice after repeated exposures, such as intricate details about the carpet or fabric pattern or a distant view seen through a window on the way to your final destination. This second level of stimuli could be geared to the regular visitor. At yet another level, it can contain a more intricate level of interest and even elements that change over time, to provide an additional level of engagement to the daily visitor who might otherwise get bored with it from repeated exposure. Figures 2.9a and b show routes to the destinations of the clinic and restaurant projects, respectively.

Figure 2.9 The road to our destination can be an eventful and expressive journey in itself. The views of the main paths to the dental clinic's main examination area (a) and a restaurant's dining room (b) start to reveal the features of the spaces beyond.

Figure 2.10 The heart of any facility is the place where the principal activity is conducted. Examples of these are the workstation in the office (a), the conference table in the meeting room (b), the dining table in the restaurant (c), and the dental chair in the dentist's office (d).

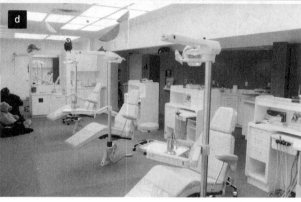

Arrival at the Activity Destination

The experience of arriving at the final activity destination varies depending on the role of the person getting there. In a restaurant, the cook will arrive in the kitchen, the food server will move around her area, the cashier will arrive at the front cashier station, and the customer will arrive at the table. Depending on the facility type and the target activity, the destination place may be a desk, a conference room, a doctor's examination room, a dentist's chair, or a dining table, among others.

The common denominator of all these cases is a sense of arrival at the heart of the activity. It will be here that we, in our specific roles, will engage in the activity we came to perform. These activities may range from a couple of minutes to longer periods of time, depending on the activity.

Our experience in stores as customers, however, is usually different. The experience there is one of constant movement from one place to the next with no specific place of arrival as described above. Museums and galleries offer a similar kind of experience, featur-

Figure 2.11 Once stationed in the right place, facility users can engage in whatever their target activity is. Shoppers are an exception. They seldom settle down or linger much since most shopping involves exploration and movement (a). Others, like restaurant kitchen personnel (b) and bar visitors (c), usually conduct their businesses within the specific settings designated for their activities.

person. The activity may be dining at a table, working at a desk, meeting in a conference room, shopping somewhere in a store, being examined in an examination room, or watching a show in a theater. The activity may also be serving the customer in the above dining table, selling merchandise at the store, examining the patient in the examination room, or being the lead actor of the theatrical production in the theater.

Many activities are done while stationary, either standing or seating, although some, like shopping as mentioned above, involve locomotion and exploration. Some activities require both. A library experience may involve considerable amounts of both stationary and locomotive activity. We may spend as much time searching for books in the stacks as reading them at the table or carrel.

Target activities represent the functions of the facility. They require functional provisions as well as ambient ones. Spatial qualities should take all aspects of the function into consideration and respond in ways that facilitate desirable experiences and avoid undesirable ones. Figures 2.11a–c show people performing their target activities in various settings.

ing a sequential and locomotive experience from space to space rather than one involving one principal activity place. Nevertheless, there can be an experience of arrival in stores or museums when we go to them to get (at the store) or see (in the museum), one specific item. The moment we get to where that item is, we arrive.

Figure 2.10a–d show views of the final destination places for an office worker, a visitor attending a meeting at the office facility, a customer in a restaurant, and a patient at the dental office.

Engaging in the Target Activity

Once we arrive at the target destination we engage in the target activity. The nature of the activity will vary widely depending on facility type and the role of the

Side Trips

Side trips are usually short-term visits to other spaces in the facility for personal or other reasons. These trips are not necessarily an essential component of the target activity per se. The best known is the trip to the restroom. Whether at work, at a restaurant, or at the theater, there comes a time when most of us have to pay a visit to the restroom. This, in itself, becomes a miniexperience requiring us to leave the target destination,

Figure 2.12 The places we go to during our side trips can also be attempts to entertain and arouse curiosity.

Figure 2.13 Secondary activities require us to leave the principal setting to visit a related setting. An example of these is the individual examination and X-ray room in a dental facility.

travel to the restroom, conduct our business there, and return. In too many facilities, unfortunately, the spaces leading to, and from, the restrooms are not given proper design attention and do not make a favorable impression. Figure 2.12 shows the unexpected and eclectic approach used for the vanity mirrors to enliven the restroom experience in a restaurant.

Another well-known side-trip destination is the concession stand in theaters and stadiums. As a designer, you should think of the circulation to side-trip destinations and these destinations themselves as worthwhile secondary experiences deserving proper design attention.

Secondary Activities

Some building experiences are limited, once you reach the destination, to the activity performed there and, perhaps, one side trip to the restroom. Other experiences, however, involve additional meaningful events as part of the total experience. A day at the office may involve a principal meeting in the board room, another meeting with staff, and a training session. In addition, there will usually be a time for lunch, whether taken in the lunchroom or outside the office. These are all examples of what we call secondary activities, instances when functions related to the main activity take one temporarily away from the main destination place and into another space for a related activity.

For many, the typical work day at the office is loaded with these types of events. For others in the office, the entire day may be spent at the desk with side trips to the restroom and the copy room, but without any special occasion other than lunch. A visit to a clinic may involve important stops at the lab and the X-ray room. A

trip to a museum may involve a talk before the show opens and the usual stop at the gift shop on the way out. The point is that many building experiences involve secondary activities in addition to the main one.

One example we brought up earlier is the case of the bar in a restaurant. Waiting at the bar for a table to be ready doubles as a waiting experience and a secondary activity too. The activity no longer involves the typical waiting room experience, but becomes a meaningful experience in its own right. Once your name is called, however, you leave the bar and proceed to your main destination and activity: dining in the dining room.

Secondary activities, obviously, deserve as much design attention as the main target destinations in a facility. Figure 2.13 shows an examination room in a clinic, an example of the kind of secondary activity places people go to.

Departing the Destination

At some point it is time to leave. This is an important transition. The reason for leaving may be because the activity has been completed (dinner is finished) or because it is simply time to leave (the store or office is closing at the end of the day). We stop doing the activity we were doing and start gathering our belongings to head out. At this point we may be preoccupied with things such as the last details of the activity (such as paying the bill after dinner) and gathering our possessions, and may begin to anticipate and prepare for the next activities (getting the car, acquiring some change to pay the attendant, making it to the movies on time, and so on).

Figure 2.14 Leaving a facility usually involves a sequence similar to the arriving sequence, except in reverse. The three views seen here show the experience of leaving the dental clinic: the corridor leaving the examination area (a), the path through the waiting area leading to the exit door (b), and the exit doors from the building's public lobby (c).

We may be rushed or relaxed, depending on what the next destination is and how much time we have to get there. There are usually enough concerns running through our minds that, most times, we will be mentally performing the physical actions of getting up and leaving. The departure from the target destination starts the overall departure process. It is followed by movement towards the exit and the eventual exit.

Moving towards the Exit

After getting up and gathering our possessions we proceed towards the exit. We may go alone or be escorted. If not escorted, we may need to concentrate to find the way out, depending on the complexity of the building and our familiarity with it. The walk towards the exit may be hurried or relaxed, and with or without much awareness of the surroundings depending on the level of rush, mental preoccupation, or engagement with others. Nevertheless, it is a time of movement through the premises and has the potential, once again, for meaningful engagement with the surroundings. Therefore, serious consideration should be given to the experience offered as one travels back from the destination space. It has the opportunity to be as engaging as the experience we had when traveling to the destination place at the beginning of the journey. It may be the same route taken to the target destination or, perhaps, a different one. Figure 2.14a–c shows views of the exiting sequence from the dental clinic.

Final Departure

Eventually we go through the last space and then exit through the door. The last space and the last wall may or may not attempt to make one final impression on us. At this point the building experience is complete and starts to become a memory. The collection of impressions has been made and is recorded in our minds. It is stored away to free up our minds to start planning our next building experience, perhaps minutes away and substantially different.

These are, then, the generic rituals we perform in buildings. They occur time and time again in different settings, and in slightly different ways and provide a context of sequential events useful for design. This is not to say that design should consist of a series of fragmented responses to these events. That would hardly work, resulting in choppy projects lacking flow and unity. What is meant, rather, is that designers should take into account these events, become aware of inherent design opportunities, and respond to them whenever possible and appropriate.

Users' Response to Interior Spaces

In addition to becoming familiar with the above rituals, we must become aware of the situational factors that affect our experiences in buildings and some important variables that influence how we react to them. We start with the situational factors.

Situational Factors Affecting Users' Experience in Buildings

Many have tried to study the relationship between human beings and their environment, often reducing the experience of life to people, functions, and environments. Unfortunately, the experience of life is much more complicated than that, consisting of many more variables that interact in complex and changing ways. The goal of this section is to increase your awareness about the situational factors that affect experience in buildings and the role the spaces we design contribute to the overall experience. As stated in the opening quotation to this chapter, architecture is "more a matter of providing an accompaniment to life than the dance itself." Here we take a look at some of the important aspects of "the dance itself."

The things people do in life ("the dance") can be analyzed in terms of specific events or occasions that take place in specific places, where we play specific roles, utilize given resources, and are surrounded by certain people, objects, and building parts. All these combine in complex and intricate combinations to become unique contexts for our activities. In order to think of ways spaces in buildings can contribute to the enrichment of our experiences in them, we need to have an understanding of how these factors typically interact in the specific kind of setting we are designing for. These situational factors consist of occasions, players, resources, and surroundings, the latter consisting of architectural features, people and objects.

Occasion

The occasion is a particular instance of an activity, such as a formal dinner for the members of upper management of a corporation. Here, the generic activity is dinner. However, it is a specific kind of dinner with specific connotations and requiring particular behaviors.

Players

The people involved in the occasion are the players. These can be locals or visitors. Both the mix of players and the characteristics of individual ones will have an effect on the occasion. Are they lively or subdued? Formal or casual? Important or ordinary? Some of the key players in our example are the members of upper management attending the dinner, but also the wait staff servicing the group.

Resources

Resources include physical ones, such as space, equipment, and the like plus other important intangible ones, such as time and money. Our dinner example, for instance, may be taking place in a comfortable banquet room with ample space and tables. Say, for example, that this particular corporation is going through difficult economic times and its members are holding a retreat the following day starting early in the morning. As a result, the budget for the dinner this year may be low, and they will not be able to spend the evening in as leisurely a fashion as in past years because of the activity the next morning. Let's also say that this year's dinner may be somewhat rushed because they couldn't get the room on time and they started late.

This year's dinner, in all likelihood, will not be as pleasant as those of other years, although none of it will be the fault of the interior physical environment.

Have you ever wondered how a person will react to a particular environment? Or what type of environment is most suitable for a particular person? In order to be able to make these predictions, we need a workable model that links specific emotional reactions to the load (complexity, intensity) of a given environment. Fortunately, Albert Mehrabian and James Russell have devised a practical framework we can use to make reasonable predictions to these challenging questions. Their research has led them to conclude that people's reactions to environments are based on just a few emotional dimensions, which in turn can produce many different behaviors. The basic chain of events consists of a given environment experienced by a person, the person's processing of the conditions presented by the place and situation, and the person's behavioral reaction, be it jumping with excitement, or running in disgust.

Three basic emotional dimensions determine how a person reacts to a situation in the environment. They are the level of arousal, the level of pleasure, and the level of dominance experienced by the person in relation to the conditions presented. Keep in mind that although our focus here is man's reaction to the built environment, there are, as we have seen, other factors at play, such as the influence of other people, the specific occasion, and so on. Arousal refers to the overall level of stimulation experienced. The qualities of an environment may excite you and increase your blood pressure and heart rate. A different environment may have the opposite effect and may cause you to feel relaxed, or even sluggish and sleepy.

The second emotional dimension is pleasure. It refers, as the word suggests, to the amount of pleasure derived from a particular environment. Some environments may cause contentment and an overall good feeling, while others annoy or depress. The third dimension, dominance, refers to the degree of control or influence one feels in relation to a specific situation. This depends on both the setting and the event. For example, working at home may be more relaxing than working at the office. The familiarity of home and the fact that you don't need to be on your best behavior give you greater control over the situation. You could be wearing your cutoff jeans and singing loudly and no one will complain. Even within the office, though, different events will produce different levels of dominance. If you are, say, a midlevel manager, you will feel more in control in a meeting with the people you supervise than in a meeting with the top executives from upper management.

According to Mehrabian and Russell, just these three dimensions of emotional reaction, in different combinations, produce all possible feelings. For example, high displeasure, high arousal, and high dominance equate to anger. Anxiety, on the other hand involves high displeasure, high arousal, but low dominance. Every feeling known, from joy to anguish, may be described as some combination of the three basic emotional dimensions.

Our emotional reaction to any given environment, then, can be measured as a certain combination of arousal, pleasure, and dominance. Depending on our particular reaction we will be more or less inclined to approach, or avoid, the environment. The graph in Figure C2.1 shows the approach/avoidance behaviors produced by different combinations of arousal and pleasure. In general, conditions of neutral pleasantness will be avoided at low and high levels of arousal and approached at some level of moderate arousal. Pleasant situations and environments will generally be ap-

C2.1 **Figure C2.1** Approach/avoidance behaviors for different combinations of pleasantness and arousal.

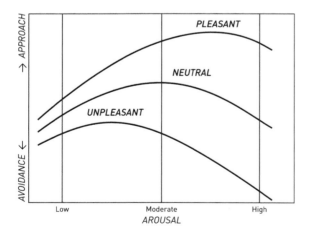

Source: From Public Places & Private Spaces: The Psychology of Work, Play, and Living Environment *by Abert Mehrabian. Copyright © 1976 by Basic Books, Inc. Reprinted by permission of Basic Books, a member of Perseus Books, L.L.C.*

proached increasingly as arousal increases up to some level of very high arousal, which will begin a downward trend in the degree of approach. Unpleasant situations and environments will be increasingly avoided as arousal levels increase. It is no surprise that an ugly but mild room is less offensive than an ugly and intense one.

The third dimension, dominance, also plays an important role in the overall effect produced by an environment. For example, an environment that produces low arousal, mild pleasure, and some dominance, will be cozy and enjoyable, and produce a relaxed and comfortable overall effect. Conversely, an environment that produces low arousal, mild displeasure, and low dominance (submissiveness) will cause boredom and avoidance.

Having established the basics, we can now address the important consideration of differences among people. The authors propose that the same three basic emotional dimensions be used to describe the particular emotional traits and temperaments of people. Thus, we have people of generally pleasant or unpleasant dispositions, people whose personality and/or role make them more or less dominant or submissive, and people who innately tolerate more or less arousal. This last one is the trickiest of the three dimensions.

It works like this: People, according to personality and temperament, screen out more or less of the stimuli presented by the environment in order to reduce the actual environmental load perceived. Some people screen a lot of the stimuli (screeners) and others don't (nonscreeners). Nonscreeners tend to pay attention to most of what the environment offers without attempting to discard nonessentials. As a result, they experience environments as being higher in arousal levels. Screeners, on the other hand, are selective in what they pay attention to. By subconsciously prioritizing the components of a complex situation and attending only to the relevant ones, they effectively reduce the total environmental load perceived. Therefore, the same amount of environmental stimulus will cause greater amounts of and longer lasting arousal for nonscreeners than for screeners. That is why some people feel right at home in the loud, colorful, and blinking discotheque and others feel more at home sipping decaf tea at the muffled café in the bookstore.

If arousal serves as a magnet in neutral and pleasant environments and situations, at least up to a certain point, then the nonscreener, who is more susceptible to environmental stimulus, will feel attracted to a scene with progressively ascending arousal sooner than the screener. We have said, however, that all people tend to avoid situations when the load level gets too high. Predictably, the nonscreener will reach the point of avoidance earlier than the screener. As Mehrabian explains, the higher susceptibility of the nonscreener to become "more aroused in high load settings causes them to exhibit more polarized approach-avoidance behaviors to pleasant and unpleasant situations: compared to screeners they have a stronger approach to high-load and pleasant places, and a stronger avoidance of high-load and unpleasant ones."[1]

While designers may be able to create a good match between the personality of a single client and the qualities produced for, say, an apartment designed for that specific person, most projects are designed for multiple, in some cases hundreds of, people. In those cases, obviously, it is impossible to please everyone. Nevertheless, what is possible, and makes this type of information highly useable, is to determine the collective ideal levels of the three variables that a certain environment should stimulate or offer. A good office setting would likely stimulate a low to moderate level of arousal (at least in areas requiring high concentration), and offer a pleasant environment that allows a moderate amount of control. An ideal store may strive to stimulate a moderate to high level of arousal (depending on the store), offer high pleasantness, and, at least, moderate levels of control and freedom (except for the full-service store). A fancy, intimate restaurant may want to stimulate a low to moderate level of arousal, offer high pleasantness (all restaurants want to be pleasant), and low to moderate control. A tavern, by contrast, wants to stimulate high arousal and offer a high level of freedom and control.

We know you like pleasant environments. How about the other two variables? Are you either dominant or submissive by nature? Are you a screener or a nonscreener? How does your personality match the types of places and situations you typically approach and avoid?

---

[1] Mehrabian, Albert, *Public Spaces and Private Places*, (Basic Books: New York, 1976). p. 27.

Surroundings

The interior physical environment, of course, is more than just a resource. It also has a presence of its own as an entity, as do the other people and objects in the room. We refer to these here as the surroundings. In this group we can distinguish between surroundings directly related to the occasion and those peripheral ones in close enough proximity to be perceived, even though they play no direct role in our occasion. Examples of the first group would be the room and its features plus all the other furnishings, objects, utensils, and the like. Examples of the second group would be the people having a dinner next door and all the sights, sounds and smells emanating from them and their activities.

The evening's experience will be a combination of complex dynamics involving all these factors and is likely to be different for the various attendees. Some factors will be experienced in approximately the same way by all, such as consistent, prompt and courteous service, and a fantastic view. The experience of other factors may vary from person to person, such as seating assignments and the quality of the dish ordered. In some cases, the same factor will be experienced differently by different people, such as one person liking and another disliking the same dish, or someone being more annoyed than others about the rushed nature of this year's dinner.

Variables Affecting Users' Reactions to Situational Factors

Human beings, despite their similarities, are different because of their personalities and backgrounds. Some people like quiet environments and others loud ones. Some like public over private places. Some people like old styles over contemporary ones. Some people like involvement; others are more restrained. Additionally, everyone brings with them the context of the recent past. A modest-sized room may seem splendid to someone moving in from tiny quarters, while it may seem insufficient for someone accustomed to large spaces. At an entirely different level, someone may have heard some good news and be in a happy mood, but the person next door may have just been laid off and be experiencing tremendous emotional pain.

In addition to personal traits and the recent past, a few other factors affect the way we react to events. These include our role in the occasion and the degrees of affinity, familiarity, demand, and control with the situational factors described above.

If you are part of the occasion, you have a role in it. You may be one of the people attending the dinner or you may be one of the people servicing those having dinner. Among members of upper management you may be an old member or a new member; you may be the CEO or a treasurer. Furthermore, you may be the member who helped coordinate the event and might be attending to all kinds of details during the evening.

For many reasons, usually associated with our personalities, backgrounds and other circumstances, we all have unique personal affinities. Not everyone likes the same settings, people, and so on. Certain occasions, players, resources, and surroundings may be enjoyable to some and not to others. A member of the dinner example above may not like going to formal dinners; another may like them but dislike her role as the event coordinator. Another person may like both the formal dinners and her role, but have a real problem with rushed dinners. Still another person may find everything else agreeable except the style of the furniture and paintings in the room and the person he has to sit next to, whom everyone else likes.

We may or may not be familiar with the occasion, players, resources, and surroundings associated with an activity. In our management dinner example, some members may be familiar with the occasion of the yearly dinner, their role in it, the usual setting for the event, and even the occasional shortage of money and time. Newcomers may not be familiar with some or all of these factors so they will have to work harder to participate and make sense of the event. The level of familiarity, then, is one of the variables that determines the stress level associated with a particular occasion.

The demand of a situation is the degree of difficulty associated with it. Depending on the particular circumstances of an event, it may be more or less demanding of us as participants. A casual family dinner is likely to be considerably less demanding than the formal business-type dinner in our example. Some roles will be more demanding and require more concentration than others. The management member in charge of co-ordinating the event will have a more demanding evening than the others. This, in turn, may be nothing compared to the demands of the cook in the kitchen. Inadequate resources will usually increase the level of demand of any task. Finally, people and environments can also be more or less demanding to relate to.

The degree of control we have over a given activity also affects our reactions to it. This also is related to the four factors of occasion, players, resources and surroundings. Issues of freedom and power come into play. In our example, people had no control over the occurrence of the event. It was going to happen and they had to attend. Once there, they have to play their role. For some it may be the artificial corporate persona many executives play in order to be like the rest of the crowd. They have no control over the time and budget limitations. Some may have some creative ideas on how to deal with these problems but may be reluctant to bring them up since it may be inappropriate. Additionally, they certainly have no control over the setting, the group next door, and maybe even the choice of dish (they have only two main dish choices). Compare this with the control you have over a casual, relaxed lunch with your best friend on a Saturday.

People in Buildings and Design

The context of our lives' activities is, indeed, complex. Although physical setting is an important component of any experience, much of our satisfaction or dissatisfaction at home, work or play is the result of factors unrelated to the setting in which they occur. The dance of life is very intricate. As designers we need to learn about the particular nuances of every project we do in order to support them with the environment and its qualities.

As a designer, you have no control over most of the factors that influence experience, nor should you try to take responsibility for them. It would be impossible to predict the infinite number of possible combinations of personalities, preferences, and chance occurrences that take place. However, it is possible to get an understanding of the general overall factors present in a particular application of a project through familiarity with the building type, the typical roles associated with it, and some of the idiosyncrasies the current user group may share with you. Then you are equipped to use the environment as a balancing and enhancing act to do its share in the complex mix of activity components. Depending on the project and the particular setting within it, you may decide to reinforce some physical characteristics and downplay others in order to enhance the experience of as many users as possible.

Providing enhancing environmental conditions goes beyond the production of merely functional and pleasant solutions. It takes more work too, but it is richly rewarding for users and designers alike. Although you as a designer may have little control over who is and isn't familiar with the interior environment of a facility, you can, if you are aware that there will be people with different degrees of familiarity, provide adequate provisions for the satisfaction of the greatest number. Knowing the various roles involved in a particular type of building, you may make special efforts to create enriching and satisfying environments for all, regardless of role. For instance, you may attempt to provide meaningful events for not only the customer in the restaurant dining room but also for the food preparation staff in the kitchen. Of course, the magnitude of these will be different, but so will the expectations. In other words, a small gesture that may go unnoticed in the main room may be enough to cheer about by the kitchen crowd.

If the customary activities of a given environment are intense and demanding you may want to seek a balance by providing a soothing environment and vice versa. On the other hand, if it is a nightclub, you may want to actually reinforce and magnify the experience by providing an intense, charged physical environment too. If the tasks performed are routine and monotonous you may want to compensate by providing a lively environment.

In terms of control, if the atmosphere at a particular enterprise, such as an office, is very hierarchical and employees feel powerless, you could compensate by providing environments that offer choices and some control, thus empowering them to some extent. If, on the contrary, the atmosphere is excessively loose and unstructured, a healthy supply of formal structure may be adequate, unless, of course, management desires to reinforce the sense of looseness.

These are just some examples to illustrate the kind of thinking involved in using the environment as a balancing force in interior environments. Obviously, the correct response will depend on the exact circumstances of the project and the goals of both the people controlling the project and the eventual users, as well as the insights of the designer after considering the possibilities.

One of the most significant ways in which the mood of a physical environment can be altered is by controlling its sensory load. Environments can be classified as high or low load depending on their degree of complexity, novelty, and intensity. A dense, busy, unpredictable environment with multiple bright colors would be considered a high-load environment. A simple, ordered, predictable one, with white paint everywhere, would be a low-load one. In addition to the physical qualities of the space itself and their relative degree of complexity, intensity, and so on, it is possible to have an effect on load by planning and manipulating spaces to generate different degrees of inherent activity. Very active, high-density environments, for instance, will generate high levels of motion and sound coming from various sources and directions. This, even in an otherwise plain environment, will result, most likely, in a high-load environment. For more about the effect of the environment's load level see the capsule (People and the Environment) in this chapter.

The design of environments always allows great degrees of intervention and involvement, sometimes in subtle ways. It is up to us as individual designers to decide to what level we want to take our designs. Many designers stop after function and good looks, because they have never been encouraged to think beyond them. We invite you to become aware of the possibilities and seek meaningful, deliberate design interventions aimed at enriching people's experiences in buildings. As we have said before, there are no hard rules, just the willingness to become familiar with strategies and possibilities and to exercise good, insightful judgment during the design process.

If we compare the game of life to a dance, or series of dances, then it is your responsibility as an individual designer to know the stages of the dances, the people involved in them, and the particularities of each dance. Only then will you be able to design appropriate accompaniments.

Review

Summary

Knowing the basic rituals people perform in buildings gives the designer valuable information useable to provide engaging experiences at every step of the process. These activities can be categorized into 12 generic activities we perform in buildings. These start with our approach to and arrival at a building. Next comes the process of moving towards and arriving at our target destination, including any necessary waiting periods. Target destinations include primary and secondary ones. Additionally, we may need to make side trips to the rest room or other similar destinations. Once finished, we begin a departure sequence that eventually leads to the exit from the building.

In addition to these rituals, this chapter explained that the spaces we design are one of many factors affecting our experiences in buildings. These spaces are part of the surroundings, which provide a setting for our activities. Also affecting the experience will be the type of occasion, the other players associated with it, and the resources at our disposal. How we react to a particular experience depends on our relationship to the mix above. Most notable are the role we play in the occasion, our degrees of affinity and familiarity towards the other factors, the level of demand imposed by the circumstances, and the degree of control we have over them.

While designers have little or no control over many of the nondesign factors that make up experience, they do control one of the most important ones, the setting in which the dance of life unfolds. The environments we design can often act as a balancing force providing the right kinds and amounts of order, enrichment and expression to optimize the conditions around the rituals of life enacted in buildings.

Chapter Questions

1. Name and describe the basic building events that involve arrival.
2. Name and describe the basic building events that involve movement from one place to another.
3. Name and describe the basic building events performed while stationary.
4. As a visitor to an office on the tenth floor, how many total transitions would you go through if you went there for a meeting and also made one trip to the rest room and one trip to the break room? Count from the moment you would approach the building on foot to the moment you would leave the building.
5. What makes a visit to the grocery store or to a museum different from visits to other building types in terms of the 12 basic events described in this chapter?
6. What 4 factors that affect our experiences in buildings were discussed in this chapter? Explain your understanding of them.
7. What 5 variables affect the way you react to the 4 factors of Question 6? Explain how they affect your reactions.

Exercises

1. Increasing your awareness of the way the basic events occur in different building types requires consciously thinking about them and analyzing how the built environment contributes to the various events. In order to get some practice, try dissecting the visits to the following settings in terms of the 12 events discussed in this chapter. You may respond to Exercises 1 through 3 in either outline or essay format. Check with your instructor.

   A nightclub
   The movies
   The design studio
   The library
   A coffee shop
   The bookstore

2. For the settings above, analyze potential scenarios related to the occasion, the players, the resources and the surroundings.
3. For each of the scenarios proposed, analyze possible reactions by you and some of the other players depending on role, affinity, familiarity, demand, and control.

Endnotes

1 Unwin, Simon, *Analysing Architecture*, (Routledge: London, 1997) p. 75.
2 Bloom, Martin, *Accommodating the Lively Arts, An Architect's View*, (Smith and Kraus: Lyme, NH, 1997) pp. 12–20.

CHAPTER 3

Interior Place and Its Components

INSTRUCTIONAL OBJECTIVES

Describe the differences between function, space, and place.

Present and describe the basic components of place.

Explain the different levels of prominence of domains.

Describe the components of circulation systems: arrival spaces, paths, and nodes.

Explain the hierarchical distinction of paths.

Explain the role and importance of nodes in interior circulation systems.

Show and describe various levels of openness of barriers.

Explain the various levels of invitation provided by different types of connectors.

Explain the role of project ends in providing a connection to the rest of the world
outside the project.

Explain the role of furnishings as spatial modifiers in interior environments.

Explain the role of interior landmarks in interior environments.

n Chapter 2 we reviewed the basic events of our experiences inside buildings, starting with the moment we approach the facility and ending with the moment we leave. A sequence of events precedes arrival at the final destination place. Once there, we conduct our business and then begin another sequence of events leading to the final exit from the facility. We also looked at other considerations that affect our experience in buildings.

In this chapter we begin to focus on place as the basic unit of interior design. More specifically, we will explain the basic components of the projects we design in terms of place. You will see that there are not too many types of places in buildings when we generalize them into our basic categories.

We will first explain the concept of place, a central one in this book. We will see that buildings are collections of places, not of functions. Certain activities or functions occur in spaces of certain shapes and proportions. The mental pictures we form of environments are those of spaces that have very specific qualities and serve very specific functions, the kind of space we call a place. The basic components of place are explained as a system we can use to conceptualize projects.

Function, Space, and Place

In design we commonly use the terms function, space, and place. We need to understand the differences between these three concepts and how they are related.

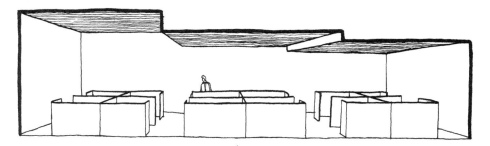

Figure 3.1 The same container can house several groupings or functions. Within this place, three distinct areas are defined by the articulation of ceiling heights. The three subareas occur within the same overall place.

You are most likely familiar with the idea of **function** as used in the environmental design disciplines. It simply refers to the things people (or animals, plants, or machines) are supposed to do within a specific environment. These translate to specific arrangements of spaces, furnishings, and equipment and particular placements of the people within the required spaces. To use an analogy from theater, function involves the actors (users) using props (furnishings and equipment) to perform certain roles. In the theater, this occurs on a stage that provides a certain amount of space.

Space is all around us, on the exterior as well as the interior of the buildings we occupy. When we design and build projects, we claim space and subdivide it in particular ways to suit the needs of the project. The spaces so defined have specific boundaries, shapes, and dimensions. This act of definition and shaping transforms generic space into the kind of space designers work with: **architectural space**. But designers do more than just define space. These defined spaces usually correspond to specific functions that occur in them. Their design is also developed further and given particular characteristics to suit those specific functions and to reflect the general character of the project. Openings are placed strategically, surfaces are articulated, and subareas defined during this process of customization in order to reflect the particular requirements of the people who will occupy it and the rituals that will take place in that space. The resulting environment ceases being merely architectural space (although it can still be described in terms of boundaries, shapes, dimensions, and so on) and now becomes a place.

Of all the space in the theater, the space occupied by the stage has been claimed for the functions performed by the actors. It has some recognizable limits and it is on this stage that the functions of the actors occur. During a play, the stage scenery portrays distinct places that often change from scene to scene, each having unique physical qualities and related activities. In the interior projects we design, the settings within a particular space don't generally change that much, and defined places tend to have consistent qualities and related functions. Thus, the bar in a restaurant or the waiting room in a dental clinic remains distinguishable as a specific and unique place from day to day and from week to week.

Spaces become **places** when they are clearly recognizable as discrete entities separate from adjacent ones and have an identifiable purpose. They become recognizable as particular spaces with limits within which specific events or functions take place (Figure 3.1).

A project having dozens of different functions performed by different people will acquire a particular form based on the number and relationship of places created by the designer for the project. As a designer, you always have a choice of how to break the functions into discrete compartments and how to assemble these compartments. Delimitation and differentiation become powerful tools with which to achieve place. How many places you create and what size, proportion, and shape you give them becomes crucial. When they are well conceived, clear, and well placed, they give environments a strong sense of identity and make a strong impact.

To understand the relationship between function,

Figure 3.2 Centers refer to important domains rather than spaces located at the geometric center of a project. Because of their status as special destinations, their placement requires special consideration.

space, and place, remember that functions occur within available space. This available space can be one encompassing space or can be subdivided into smaller units. When the units established are strongly defined architecturally and can be identified with particular uses and activities, they acquire the status of place.

In this chapter we are not concerned with properties of space such as size, proportion, geometry, and level of definition. Our intent here is to discuss the generic types of places that occur in interior projects. Specific properties of space will be discussed in the next chapter.

Basic Components of the Environment (Place Elements)

At the most basic level, interior environments can be reduced to places we go to, to do something (destination places) and places that help us get there (circulation systems). The spatial characteristics of these two types of places are defined by the boundaries around, and the objects within, these places. With these four categories (destination places, circulation systems, boundaries, and objects) and some elaboration we can establish a group of ten elements useful for conceptualizing interior space.

The group is a combination of Kevin Lynch's five elements of urban imageability,[1] Christian Norberg-Schulz's elements of existential space,[2] and some minor additions that address aspects specific to interiors. Lynch's studies revealed that people make sense of urban surroundings by making mental maps that consistently feature five kinds of elements: districts,

paths, nodes, edges, and landmarks. They are defined below, where they occur. Norberg-Schulz's model of existential space features three core elements: centers, paths, and domains. For an explanation of these, see the capsule in this chapter.

Destination Places

Destination places can be categorized as domains or centers, depending on their degree of prominence.

Domains

Domains are recognizable regions or areas. They are analogous to what Lynch called *districts*. Lynch defines districts as "medium to large sections of the city, conceived of as having two-dimensional extent, which the observer mentally enters inside of, and which are recognizable as having some common identifiable character."[3] Norberg-Schulz's concept of domain is better suited for interior spaces since domains don't carry the large area connotations of districts. Despite the difference in scale, however, the concepts are nearly interchangeable. A district is usually some neighborhood (residential or otherwise) with recognizable boundaries and a particular character based on the kind of people who inhabit it and the things they do. You may not be familiar with the neighborhood, but you are likely to have at least some idea about its general extent. In some cases there may be more than one adjacent neighborhood, and, even if you are not familiar with these neighborhoods, you may have a general mental picture of the area they occupy, even though you lack a clear sense of where one ends and the next one begins.

Figure 3.3 This room is one of many similar rooms inside a teaching/meeting facility. Is it a center? Despite its special function, in this context it is a fairly ordinary component. A center designation in this facility would be reserved for the few large and truly dominant assembly rooms.

Figure 3.4 This room is a center. It is one of the most prestigious spaces of this particular building and is used exclusively for very special events.

The concept is the same for interior projects, although the scale is smaller. The departments in an office or retail shop, the units in a health care clinic, and the different dining rooms in a large restaurant are all examples of domains in interiors. Domains are the basic destinations in a facility. They are the places where people go to do whatever they do in a given facility, be it work, shop, or eat.

Projects usually consist of a collection of domains accommodated based on the requirements of the program. They are important because they constitute the greatest area of a project. They are, typically, the spaces where users spend the most time.

Centers

Centers are special destination places. You can think of them as very special domains. The term comes from Norberg-Schulz. Centers are well-known places where particularly meaningful activities and social interactions take place. They are both the goals toward which we move and the points of departure from which we orient ourselves in relation to the rest of the environment.

Of all the places people visit inside buildings, these are the most special. In public projects, they are usually the places where important group activities happen. Examples of centers include the principal conference room in an office, the main dining hall in a restaurant, and the main lounge of a hotel. In some cases these important locations require clear and direct access; in other cases, a ceremonial approach.

Centers are important during planning because they require strategic placement. You should consider their locations before those of other, less important, places. In many projects, users will orient themselves in relation to these centers. Whether they become the great big space at the entrance, the sacred space in the middle, or the prestigious (or mysterious) destination at the end of an important path, centers always demand prominent placement. Figure 3.2 shows the main auditorium in a training facility, truly one of the centers of that project.

It is important to note that not all projects have or need centers. It is quite common to find restaurants where all dining areas are of similar importance and retail stores with no dominant departments. Another important aspect of centers to note is that it is their relative importance that makes them a center. Figure 3.3 shows a photograph of one of many meeting rooms in a teaching/meeting facility. Despite the relative importance of the function, there are so many similar rooms in the facility that, relatively speaking, the room's prominence can be considered average. Figure 3.4, on the other hand, shows a large and prestigious public meeting room of a building, leaving little doubt that it is, indeed, a center.

Circulation Systems

Circulation systems control the way you move around a building or facility. To a great extent, your impressions of a particular interior environment will depend on your experience while moving from place to place through the circulation system. Here we distinguish among three basic components of these systems: arrival space, the paths themselves, and nodes.

Figure 3.5 This reception area is the arrival space of an office facility. It serves as a transition between the outside and what lies beyond within the facility.

Figure 3.6 Arrival spaces such as this one are relatively informal, with no checkpoints. Notice, however, how the special decorative treatments at the ceiling help to define it as a location of above-average importance.

Arrival Space

The place you arrive at when visiting any facility is of such importance that it deserves its own category as an element. At the city scale there are usually many access points, but in buildings and their interiors, there is usually only one main entrance. Therefore, in interiors, much more than in cities, it is possible to control the first impression of visitors.

The **arrival space** serves to make an initial overall impression on the visitor and also serves as a departure point to the rest of the facility. It is often the place where we are greeted and where we check in and/or get directions on how to reach our destination within the building or project. Its importance and potential are enormous. Figure 3.5 shows the reception area of an office facility, very often the arrival space to such office suites. Figure 3.6 shows the arrival space to an academic building displaying some special articulation and lighting fixtures at the ceiling to highlight its importance.

The design of arrival places can contribute greatly to the sense of order, enrichment, and expression in a facility. Arrivals are occasions of transition between the inside and outside of the project as well as between themselves and the rest of the project. The impact of these transitions and the need to make route decisions produce greater than average levels of stress, and, therefore, a state of heightened awareness.

Paths

Paths are the channels of movement that we use to get around. Lynch defines them as the "channels along which the observer customarily, occasionally, or potentially moves."[4] Paths connect spaces, allowing users to get from one to another. All architectural spaces need paths for movement, whether they are separated from, or integrated with, the places they serve. They can be autonomous paths occurring outside the areas they serve or integrated paths occurring within the spaces they serve. Figure 3.7 shows examples of an autonomous path (a) and two integrated paths of different degrees of explicitness (b and c).

Not only do paths serve the function of transporting us to our destination, but they are also, to a great extent, the vantage points from which we perceive the totality of a project, its spaces, and their sequences. So important was this secondary function for the great Swiss architect Le Corbusier that he developed the notion of **promenade architecturale**,[5] a carefully orchestrated route that revealed a building's spaces and their overall organization.

Paths are the heart of the circulation system. Note, however, that while the circulation system refers to the total system of movement within a building or project, a path refers to a specific segment having specific characteristics. You could think of paths as channels of movement of distinctive character that allow movement towards particular destinations.

Paths are hierarchical. Not all paths move as many people or share the same degree of importance. A major corridor in a busy airport would be an interior space analogous to a freeway. A highly articulated corridor in a modern office with one or more places to stop, sit, and talk would be analogous to a pedestrian street. Designers should understand the conceptual and functional differences between main and secondary paths.

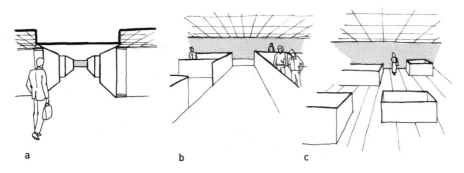

a   b   c

Figure 3.7 The degree of explicitness of a path can vary. It can be very explicit (a), clear but unaccented (b), or rather loose and ambiguous (c).

Figure 3.8 This segment of a main path is made extraspecial by its volume, forms, details, and materials.

Figure 3.9 This is a main path in an institutional building. Its generous proportions and elegant materials set it apart from other paths in the same building.

Main Paths ❖ Main paths are equivalent to avenues in cities. They define the main overall movement structure and often get us to prominent destinations. Similarly, in interiors, the main paths are used to define the principal movement system and to get us to the most important places. They, like avenues, tend to be the most public thoroughfares for movement, the channels through which visitors move. As such, they not only get us places, but also provide visual and other types of sensual experiences that make certain impressions on people, especially on visitors and new users. Additionally, they help provide a sense of sequence and so are partially responsible for the sense of unity and cohesiveness (or the opposite, chaos) of a project. Figure 3.8 shows an example of a main path featuring above-average finishes and details.

Main paths are often important contributors to the perceptions people form of built environments. It is while moving through and looking from them that visitors collect impressions of facilities and their people. A main path's shape, proportion, degree of openness, level of detail, and number of events will communicate in important ways with users and visitors alike. This will be discussed in Chapter 4. The rhythms, details, and materials of the path shown in Figure 3.9 are also above-average for the conferencing facility shown.

Secondary Paths ❖ Secondary paths are equivalent to the streets and alleys of our cities. In interiors, they are often narrow and less formal than the main paths. Large facilities like office complexes and large department stores usually have a network of main and secondary paths. The secondary paths tend to be more

utilitarian, although there is no reason why some of them should not delight the user. There are instances when it might be appropriate to convert a particular minor path into an experientially rewarding one.

It is not only the functional importance of a path segment that accounts for its level in the hierarchy. In a project of fairly even functional hierarchy, the designer often decides to put higher perceptual importance on a particular path or segment of a path, distinguishing that segment as principal and more important than the rest. Perceptual hierarchy, then, becomes at least as important as functional hierarchy.

Distinguishing between main and secondary paths and designing spaces that physically show the difference between the two will produce clearer, easier to navigate projects. Figure 3.10 shows diagrams of three circulation systems combining main and secondary paths.

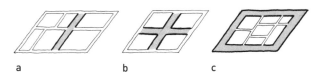

Figure 3.10 Maintaining a clear hierarchy between main and secondary paths helps users feel oriented and understand the building better. Three diagrammatic schemes of circulation systems show various main and secondary path arrangements.

a   b   c

Figure 3.11 Nodes often occur at important junctions (a). They can also occur anywhere along a path (b), or at the end of a path (c).

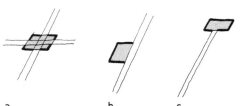

a   b   c

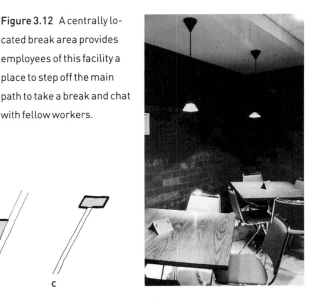

Figure 3.12 A centrally located break area provides employees of this facility a place to step off the main path to take a break and chat with fellow workers.

In terms of configuration, there are not many path varieties. A single path can go from one point to another, it can start at one point and branch out into more than one destination, and it can also start from and return to the same point. While performing these functions, paths can have a variety of shapes. They can be straight, curved, segmented, undulating, or any combination of these. Paths can also be combined in many ways. They can join as well as intersect. Additionally, as we know, paths are not always level: they can also ascend or descend to higher and lower levels via ramps and stairs.

As we have said, many of our perceptions of environments are experienced while we navigate the paths of the project. Later chapters will elaborate on ways paths contribute order, enrichment, and expression in interiors.

Nodes

Nodes are focal points. We have said that centers are domains of particular importance or significance. Nodes serve a similar function in relation to paths. They are not paths themselves, but, rather, places at given points of the paths. Lynch explains that they can be junctions, like a convergence of paths; or concentrations, like an enclosed square. Nodes can occur at significant intersections, off to one side along the route or at end points. Space usually expands at these locations, and places or miniplaces are created. These remain public and are more of an appendix to the path than a domain. Figure 3.11 shows three diagrammatic examples illustrating how space expands at the junctures. Intersections are good strategic points since

they require a choice of direction to be made, thus heightening awareness and increasing the conscious attention given to a spot.

Both the distinction and the relationship between nodes and centers are helpful for design purposes. Centers are related to place, nodes to path. Nodes become in-between places: not quite a domain or a path. They typically become either a temporary place to stop and step off the path or an expanded and emphasized location along a path. An example of a temporary place would be a well-placed break/coffee area along the circulation route in an office setting (see Figure 3.12). An example of an emphasized location is a place where several paths converge and that is made prominent by a combination of an increase in size and the addition of special features for emphasis. These treatments generally make the location a memorable junction. Figure 3.13 shows an example of paths from different directions and elevations converging in a powerful node.

Nodes are important architectural enhancers. They provide relief, encourage social contact, accentuate transitions and entrances, and create memorable spaces along the way. Like paths, they are important components that contribute to order, enrichment, and expression. If we lived in a totally utilitarian world there would be no need for nodes. Paths and domains would be sufficient. This would produce what might be called an architecture of deprivation. Figure 3.14 shows a photograph of a node off the path outside a series of meeting rooms. It successfully provides a break space for people before, after, or between meetings, supplying some welcome relief.

Figure 3.13 Paths converging in a powerful and expanded center create a major node in this educational building. Although this space may seem more like a center, in our definition it is a node, because it is not a destination place but a prominent juncture within the circulation system.

Figure 3.14 Nodes can be small space appendices such as this small waiting area.

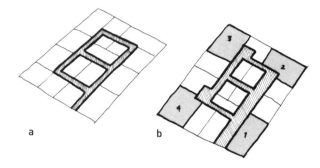

Figure 3.15 Projects without differentiation are seldom memorable. The differentiation between domains and centers and between main and secondary paths, together with the addition of nodes along the circulation route greatly enhance the clarity and memorability of a project.

The architectural program you are given during the early stages of a project is not likely to ask for any nodes. Nodes happen because designers make them happen. They are a strategy utilized by designers to enhance projects through the creation of spaces for informal human contact.

Destination places (domains and centers) and circulation systems (arrival spaces, paths, and nodes) comprise the most basic place elements of interior environments. Any interior space system can be reduced to these elements. Figure 3.15a shows a diagram of a hypothetical project expressed in terms of these elements but without differentiation. Figure 3.15b shows the same space, but this time centers, main circulation segments, and nodes are included. Notice how the clarity of the project, even as seen as a plan diagram, is enhanced by the addition of hierarchy.

Boundaries

Now that you are familiar with the most basic and fundamental place components we can look at some important elements that help determine how places relate physically to one another. We will present three important elements related to boundaries: edges, connectors, and ends. While edges are the only one of these addressed by either Lynch or Norberg-Schulz, connectors and ends are important basic elements inside buildings and deserve special attention.

Edges

So far we have considered places and the circulation systems that provide access to them. Now we'll look at how paths relate to places, and how places relate to other places in terms of the levels of separation and/or connection their edges allow. **Edges**, according to Lynch, are often boundaries between two places. They can be more or less penetrable barriers, closing off one region from another, or seams, relating and joining two regions.[6] We will focus on barriers here. This topic is closely related to the topic of enclosure addressed in our next chapter. For now we will focus on the basics.

Once you have decided that two places are going to be adjacent to one another, you have to think about the degree of separation between them. The same is true between routes and places. We rely on barriers to separate adjacent spaces. Between the extremes of having no barrier and having a full barrier are many levels of potential separation. For convenience we will categorize the possibilities into four levels of barrier: solid, mostly solid, mostly open, and open. Solid

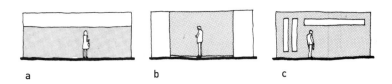

a   b   c

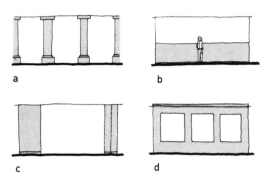

a   b

c   d

Figure 3.16 (above) Mostly solid barriers come in many configurations. Three are shown here. Note that the solid area (shaded) is greater than the open area.

Figure 3.17 (left) Mostly open barriers also come in many configurations. The amount of openness, and therefore, connection to adjacent spaces, is increased to more than half of the barrier's area.

means having a full solid wall representing a total barrier. At the other extreme, open means having no obstacle whatsoever between two spaces. The other two categories are less straightforward and require illustration.

Mostly solid refers to a barrier having some openings that provide visual, auditory, haptic, and physical connection between one space and the next. The solid portion is greater than the open one. Examples include a full-length partial wall seven feet high; a partial-length full-height wall; and a full-length full-height wall with a few punched openings. Figure 3.16 shows elevation views of these examples.

Mostly open barriers are similar to the mostly solid ones except the ratios are inverted and the open portions constitute a greater area of the plane than the solid ones. Examples include anything from a colonnade to examples similar to the ones in Figure 3.16, but with larger open areas. Figure 3.17 shows some examples.

Glass is a unique material that is hard to classify but falls somewhere between mostly solid to mostly open. It is a solid material. You cannot walk through it. However, glass allows light to penetrate from one space to the next and clear glass allows one to see through from one space to the next. Given the sophistication of manufacturing techniques today, it is possible to manufacture glass of various degrees of opacity. While clear glass allows you to see through it, etched glass does not. Consequently, using glass, a designer can create the desired level of transparency to fit the occasion.

Even as early as the concept generation stage of design you should begin thinking about the desired nature and degree of separation between places and between paths and places. Being aware of the many ways to separate areas will enable you to be more responsive to the optimal level of separation and more creative about the means you utilize to achieve it.

Depending on their number, size, and configuration, barriers can have immense effects on how much of the visual field is disclosed at one time, thus influencing our sense of order and orientation. They influence the sense of drama as one moves about the project. Their shapes, placement, and arrangement serve to communicate a portion of a project's expression.

Connectors

Contrary to the idea of barrier is that of access. The points of connection between adjacent spaces are important determinants of the character and flow of those spaces. Options range from the well-known (and often overused) doorway to full-width openings between spaces. Here, we distinguish between two broad categories: gateways and passages, each with a multitude of variations. Gateways suggest and even precipitate penetration, while passageways often allow penetration without demanding it.

Gateways ❖ A **gateway**, as the name implies, is a clearly defined point of entry. The most common one is the doorway. So strongly do we associate the symbol of a cased opening having a swinging door with the ideas of entrance and exit that the doorway has be-

Figure 3.18 The colossal colonnade (a) and the generous arched entryway (b) are examples of inviting grand gateways of different scales. Retail stores usually feature inviting grand gateways (c) to lure outsiders in.

come the quintessential example of a gateway. For our purposes, we'll distinguish between grand entryways and ordinary entryways.

Ordinary entryways have single or double doors, or cased openings of comparable size, that invite us to enter. We are all familiar with these. Grand entryways are more formal and monumental. They are unmistakable gateways that draw you in and are usually reserved for prominent entrances. The size of the door and frame as well as the size of the surrounding casing and the depth of the passage all contribute to their grandiosity. In interiors, grand entryways often consist of a specially detailed door or opening, usually oversized, and often placed in an extradeep cavity. Figure 3.18 shows three examples of grand entryways in interiors.

Passageways ❖ **Passageways** are not framed openings like the more formal gateways discussed above. They can be either tunnel-like adjoining passages between spaces or merely openings on the wall that allow movement between spaces. In the first case, they invite movement, in the second, they allow it. Many modern interiors rely on wide passageways as a way to move between spaces. Openings allow movement between spaces, but the user relies on other directional cues from the furnishings or other objects to know which way to go. Figure 3.19 shows two examples. Notice how these act as gateways, although they are much more casual and don't include doors or cased openings. Figure 3.20 shows a scene where passage is allowed to the space off the main path in a very unstructured way. The invitation is produced by the high accessibility to the space. Movement between

Figure 3.19 In both of these interiors the combination of the opening, the short stairs, and the prospect of what lies beyond entices users to go through the passageway.

areas in this case is more flowing because of the generous openings on either side of the center column.

Connectors also contribute much to a project's sense of order, enrichment, and expression. Their placement controls patterns of movement and the exact points of entry to the different parts of a project, affecting both our senses of orientation and stimulation. Their placement and detail also communicate certain types of expression.

Scholars in the design disciplines have pursued diverse avenues in search of a better understanding of the built environment. One notable scholar who has contributed much to our understanding of the significance of the man-made environment is Christian Norberg-Schulz. His primary aim, he explains, has been "to investigate the psychic implications of architecture rather than its practical side."[1] Norberg-Schulz has pursued architectural insights from every angle possible. After initial attempts to analyze art and architecture scientifically, he turned to other methods. Although a believer in the contributions of scientific methods, he found them limiting, noting that "when we treat architecture analytically, we miss the concrete environmental character, that is, the very quality that is the object of man's identification."[2] His diverse explorations into the minds of artists, philosophers, historians, and psychologists led him to phenomenology as a vehicle for architectural inquiry. It provided a mode of inquiry compatible with his desire to study architecture as a concrete phenomenon.

Phenomenology is an approach within the field of philosophy initiated by Edmund Husserl as a reaction to what he perceived as modern science's incapacity to help us understand the concrete "life-world." As Norberg-Schulz puts it, "the life-world does not consist of sensations, but is immediately given as a world of characteristic, meaningful things, which do not have to be 'constructed' through individual experience."[3] He further explains, "Phenomenology was conceived as a 'return to things,' as opposed to abstractions and mental constructions."[4] Encouraged by the potential contributions of phenomenology to architectural thinking, he embarked on the mission of developing a phenomenology of architecture.

Much of Norberg-Schulz's efforts have focused on the topics of place and dwelling. Below, we summarize some of his thinking on these topics to give you a sample of his views.

Place

The place is the concrete manifestation of man's dwelling, and his identity depends on his belonging to places ... [by place] we mean something more than abstract location. We mean a totality made up of concrete things having material substance, shape, texture and colour. Together these things determine an "environmental character," which is the essence of place ... A place is therefore a qualitative, "total" phenomenon, which we cannot reduce to any of its properties, such as spatial relationships, without losing its concrete nature out of sight.

Because of their qualitative nature and levels of complexity, Norberg-Schulz believes places cannot be properly described by methods that rely on abstractions of concrete phenomena to arrive at neutral, objective knowledge. Lost by such approaches "is the everyday life-world, which ought to be the real concern of man in general, and planners and architects in particular."

Places have a specific concrete presence. They can be either natural or man-made, and are experienced as environments having a particular set of qualities, that is, particular characters. Concentration and enclosure are the properties of man-made places, be they cities, towns, or individual buildings. At any of their scales, man-made places are collections of things grouped together and somehow bound. Norberg-Schulz analyzes them in terms of "space" and "character." Space refers to the three-dimensional organization of the elements that make up place. He looks at space not as a mathematical concept, but as an existential dimension. Character refers to the general atmosphere of a place. While spatial organizations may have different characters, space and character operate as a unit, and specific spatial organizations limit the possible characterizations within them.

The elements of existential place are center, path, and domain. At the heart of the notion of place is the center. The ultimate environmental center is the home, the center of each individual's personal world. Centers are known places where meaningful activities and social interactions take place. They are both the goals toward which people move and the points of departure from which they orient themselves in relation to the rest of the environment.

Beyond the home, other places become centers in our lives. Friends' houses and the meaningful public buildings of our lives such as the school, community center, and church become centers. At different scales, certain specific rooms and spots within those buildings also become centers. Regardless of scale, a center, because it is a place, has recognizable limits. There is a definite sense of inside and outside defined by a physical or symbolic boundary between here and there.

The next basic property of human existence is the path. Any center, or place, exists within a context, never in isolation. As such, a place is physically related to the rest of the world around it. Thus, starting from the very center of a place, we can identify directions such as up and down, and left and right. As Norberg-Schulz explains, "the simplest model of man's existential space is, therefore, a horizontal plane pierced by a vertical axis. But on the plane man chooses and creates paths which give his existential space a more particular structure." The path connects the known with the unknown and its presence sets in motion a cycle of departure and return. Contrary to the center, which is static and contained, the path is continuous and dynamic. Paths represent a direction to follow towards a goal, but, as Norberg-Schulz explains, "during the journey events happen and the path is also experienced as having a character of its own. What happens along the way, thus, is added to the tension created by the goal to be reached and the point of departure left behind."

The last basic property of existential space is the domain. As we travel regularly along the same path towards a meaningful destination, the areas we pass on either side become somewhat well known, even if we don't enter them directly. Norberg-Schulz calls these areas domains and distinguishes them from the areas beyond them, the real unknown. Domains are not just the "everything else," but are distinct from one another and identifiable because of their boundaries or some other unifying characteristic, such as grouping of parts or common visual characteristics. The difference between domains and centers is that each person belongs in certain centers, and, therefore, these become his or her particular, personal goals. Despite the cohesiveness they may enjoy, domains are not destinations or goals, although they might very well be for someone else. For us domains are "relatively unstructured 'ground' on which places and paths appear as more pronounced 'figures.'"

Places, paths, and domains form the basic schemata

for man's orientation, and thus, according to Norberg-Schulz's view, constitute the elements of existential space. Depending on where we find ourselves, a certain environment may be dominated by one or another of these three properties. The experience of driving towards a familiar destination may be dominated by paths and domains. Then, all of a sudden, one enters familiar and meaningful territory and the experience gets transformed into a progression of centers at different scales starting with the entrance into the familiar neighborhood and culminating with the final arrival at the dinner table.

The elements of existential space exist at different levels. The first and smallest level is determined by the hand and what it can grasp. It is the level of small things and objects. The next level is determined by the body. It is the level of the furniture on which we can sit, recline, or lie down. The third level is the house, or individual building, which allows movement and comprises defined territories. Beyond these, and less useful for the purposes of people concerned with interiors, are the urban, landscape, and regional levels.

The levels of house (meaning also familiar individual buildings) and things are the most relevant to the designer of interiors. The house represents the very center of human existence. It gives man a place to be, a place in which to stay and spend time in safety and comfort. Within it, of course, there are also rooms, each a place having a unique character. As we get into the smaller objects of life, the furnishings and other items of our lives, we get into objects of very precise forms that we come to know intimately. These are the objects with which our hands and bodies come into the most intimate contact. The fireplace, the dinner table, the bed, and even the chest of drawers become true foci in our lives and are known in the most direct ways. In fact, it is the progressively smaller levels of the hierarchy that give the larger ones their character. Thus, the character of the neighborhood is determined largely by its buildings, the character of the buildings by their details and objects, and so on.

Dwelling

By tracing its linguistic evolution, Heidegger uncovered the meanings associated with the word dwell. Combining these meanings, he defined dwelling as "to be at peace in a protected place." To this, Norberg-Schulz adds some linguistic derivations of his own, and adds that through dwelling the life-world becomes habitual and "known." He goes on to distinguish among four modes of dwelling related to their scale, level of development, and how collective or individual the interactions occurring within are. The four modes are: natural dwelling, collective dwelling, public dwelling, and private dwelling. For our purposes, the last two are the most significant. Public dwelling occurs within a community with shared common values and beliefs, such as the employees of a given company. In fact, it usually takes place in a public building. Private dwelling refers to the private and personal kind of dwelling required to develop one's individual identity. It finds its most pure expression in the home.

True dwelling requires a meaningful relationship between a person and a given environment. In other words, one has to establish a meaningful relationship with both the space and the character aspects of the given place. Where a person is and how he or she is in a given place have to be understood. Norberg-Schulz labels these two required psychological functions orientation and identification. "To gain an existential foothold," he explains, "man needs to orientate himself ... he also has to identify himself with the environment." Orientation is concerned with the spatial relationship of things, while identification is concerned with the qualities of places. The two are always present, although they don't necessarily have to correspond. In other words, it is possible to feel oriented in a place and not identify with it and vice versa.

Orientation ties directly to our previous discussion of the three properties or elements of existential space: centers, paths, and domains. The designer's task becomes to translate these into physical form in a way that produces a good environmental image likely to facilitate the process of feeling oriented. For this, Norberg-Schulz uses Kevin Lynch's influential ideas on environmental imaging and his concepts of districts, paths, nodes, edges, and landmarks, which work nicely with the existential space concepts of center, path, and domain. The place elements introduced in this chapter, in fact, are a combination of the concepts from both Lynch and Norberg-Schulz.

Perhaps more important than orientation is the func-

tion of identification with a given environment. Identification means to relate meaningfully, to truly belong. It requires proper correspondence between the interior and exterior worlds of the individual, where the environment embodies aspects of existence meaningful to the person. This is the aspect that Norberg-Schulz feels has not been given proper attention in modern society, where "attention has almost exclusively been concentrated on the 'practical' function of orientation, whereas identification has been left to chance."

Proper dwelling requires the proper alignment of interior self, body, and exterior world. The interaction between internal and external things can be tricky to decipher. Norberg-Schulz believes that the identities of man and environment feed off each other. He explains: "identity ... consists in an interiorization of understood things, and ... growing up therefore depends on being open to what surrounds us. Although the world is immediately given, it has to be interpreted and understood, and although man is part of the world, he has to concretize his belonging to feel at home."

1 Norberg-Schulz, Christian. *Genius Loci: Towards a Phenomenology of Architecture*, Rizzoli: New York (1980) p. 5.

2 Ibid., p. 5.

3 Norberg-Schulz. *The Concept of Dwelling*, Rizzoli: New York (1985) p. 16.

4 Norberg-Schulz. *Genius Loci*, p. 8.

5 Ibid., p. 6.

6 Ibid., p. 8.

7 Norberg-Schulz. *Existence, Space and Architecture*, Praeger: New York (1971) p. 21.

8 Ibid., p. 22.

9 Ibid., p. 23.

10 Norberg-Schulz. *Genius Loci*, p. 22.

11 Ibid., p. 19.

12 Ibid., p. 21.

13 Ibid., p. 20.

Figure 3.20 Passageways can also be very wide and unstructured. The thick column above provides enough separation between areas but still allows for two generous openings on either side.

Figure 3.21 An important end of a retail store is its front side. It represents the main opportunity to entice shoppers in. A generous and inviting gateway and a mostly transparent front dissolve the barrier, revealing the merchandise inside.

Ends

Ends are special kinds of edges. We make the distinction to differentiate between internal separations (edges) and interior/exterior separations (ends). Ends occur at the limits of a project's allotted space. These are the boundaries within which you design a given office, store, or restaurant. They may or may not be important, depending on the circumstances. In a high-rise building, the outside walls are ends that relate to the exterior context and are thus important. Exposure to views, the sun path, or important visual or symbolic elements outside rely on the proper placement of spaces in relation to these ends. Similarly, while the exterior edge of an intimate—and therefore introverted—restaurant may not be that important, the opposite is true at a sidewalk café, where an important goal is to connect with street activity. Ends are significant because they dictate the limits of your space and the type of relationship with adjacent spaces. For a retail store, for instance, it is important to use the main front end, such as the storefront, to entice potential buyers. See Figure 3.21.

Ends at a project's perimeter often feature some level of transparency, allowing us to see beyond. They are important in providing a sense orientation. They also provide daylight and views, important stimulators and enhancers.

Objects

Finally, we will now inspect the role of objects in the orchestration of place. Objects in space are a very important aspect of interior environments and their composition and characteristics have a significant impact on movement and access. Some objects are fairly ordinary, yet some are quite special and memorable.

Furnishings

Under the general term **furnishings** we refer to fixtures, furniture pieces, and equipment of sufficient size to influence the experience of space. Designers of interiors often rely heavily on these to choreograph the interior experience, and therefore, they represent an important category among our place element groups.

Examples of influential furnishings are freestanding fixtures or display cases in stores, tables in restaurants, and systems furniture in open office spaces. These types of furnishings tend to work more as space modifiers than space creators except in cases where they are tall enough to provide a real sense of enclosure. In these cases they have an effect on the visual lines of a space and become important screening devices; their placement becomes critical, and a tug-of-war between placement for function and placement for effect is common.

Perhaps the main attribute of furnishings in interior environments is how their placement affects the use of space and controls movement. The placement of furnishings dictates which areas of the floor remain open for human occupation as well as become circulation patterns in space. Figure 3.22 shows six different furniture arrangements in a simple waiting space and the resulting use patterns.

The way furnishings are grouped can also contribute to the definition of place. A group of furnishings can help define regions, and, when used repetitively, can

Figure 3.25 The high furniture panels act like walls in this tall space, hiding the work areas behind them.

Figure 3.22 These six furniture scenarios divide the same space in very different ways. All the arrangements consist of a group of four chairs. Their placement in the room, along with their spacing and orientation in relation to each other, produces the different results.

Figure 3.23 The furniture arrangement above complements the overall effect of this waiting area, defining two very distinct seating areas that become focal points in the space.

Figure 3.24 The high density of the workstations above is one of the principal factors that give this space its character.

contribute a sense of continuity and rhythm (Figure 3.23). Furnishings can also have a strong effect on the general density of a space. Depending on their size, number, and spacing they can produce various effects, from spare to crowded. In Figure 3.24 the furnishings, although low, have a major impact on the use and overall density of the respective spaces. The tall office cubicle panels in Figure 3.25 act as walls, defining the corridor strongly and reducing the sense of clutter, since the contents of the desks on the other side are hidden.

Furnishings contribute to order, enhanced experience, and expression. The paths dictated by their arrangement affect our experiences as we move around them. The layout's level of balance and harmony and the disclosure of more or less clutter greatly influence the project's sense of order.

Landmarks

Lynch defines **landmarks** as "simply defined physical object[s]. Their use involves the singling out of one element from a host of possibilities."[7] Their key physical characteristic is singularity, some aspect that is unique or memorable in the context. Landmarks are more clearly identifiable if they have a clear form, if they contrast with their background, and if there is some prominence of spatial location. At the scale of interior space we rarely encounter the plazas with memorable monuments or the distinctive high-rise buildings that frequently become the landmarks at the city scale. The designer of interiors relies on other, less grandiose, types of landmarks. Possibilities include special details, accent walls, art niches, and special displays. They, like landmarks in cities, help to make certain areas of proj-

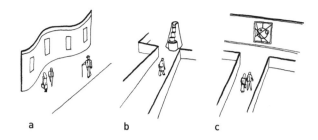

Figure 3.26 Special walls (a), sculptures (b), and artwork (c) are examples of potential landmarks in an interiors project.

Figure 3.27 Statues and prominent sculptures, so effective as landmarks outdoors, are also effective inside (a). Artwork, in this case an oversized stained-glass window placed low on a wall, can also be memorable and, thus, effective as a landmark (b).

ects memorable and distinctive. Figure 3.26 shows three conceptual examples of landmarks.

Landmarks give people points of reference around which to get oriented and contribute to both the experience and sense of expression of a space. Landmarks can be especially effective if they can be seen from multiple locations, even from a distance, and if they occur at key intersections where our sense of perception is stimulated, making us more aware of the environment. Figure 3.27 shows two examples of interior landmarks: a prominent statue in a lobby area and a magnificent stained-glass window in a library.

Landmarks, like nodes, mark important locations of projects. As such they contribute much to order and orientation. Whether seen from a distance as goals, or discovered suddenly as surprises, they can serve to enhance users' experiences. Furthermore, their specific character, form, and occasional symbolism can contribute to expression.

Review

Summary

More than a collection of spaces, the interior environments you design are collections of places. Although the parts and elements of a project are always numerous, there are only a few basic components of place. Being aware of these will help you understand the main parts of a project.

The main activity of interior environments usually occurs in their destination places. Most of these are what we call domains. Centers are domains of special importance by virtue of their functional or symbolic prominence. Circulation systems provide networks of movement to get to the destination places. These include the project's arrival space, the network of paths to move around the facility (main paths and secondary paths), and nodes. Nodes are special events along the paths that provide relief, mark specific locations, and serve as collection spaces.

Projects, their places and paths, are confined and defined by boundaries. These include edges, barriers, connectors between spaces, and ends. Barriers provide separation, connectors passage between areas. These can be formal and strongly defined gateways or informal and less defined passageways. Ends are the outermost boundaries of a project. This is where a project meets the rest of the world, be it the suite next door, a public corridor of the building, or the exterior.

Interior places contain objects of different kinds. Furnishings are important spatially. The number, size, and placement of large pieces of furniture, fixtures, and equipment, have a major impact on interior space and how it is perceived. Finally, landmarks are prominent objects used to mark a spot in space. These can be pieces of artwork or specially detailed building elements or fixtures. Their main attribute is singularity. They stand out and are remembered.

Chapter Questions

1. Think of important buildings in your life, past and present. What special domains, that is, centers, can you recall? Can you recall special nodes along the circulation system? Describe them.

2. How would you introduce nodes in an office project? How about in an educational setting or clinic?

3. Try to recall some prominent, main interior paths. Were they appropriate for the occasion? Describe them.

4. What memorable arrival spaces have you experienced? What made them good or memorable?

5. How would you make a secondary path experientially rich? Could you do it without spending too much money?

6. Can you recall successful partially solid or partially open barriers? Describe them.

7. Where would you use a partially solid barrier?

8. Where would you use a partially open barrier?

9. Recall and describe grand gateways you have experienced.

10. Can you describe effective passageways that invited passage without demanding it?

11. Can you describe effective passageways that didn't necessarily invite passage but allowed it?

12. Recall and describe successful transparent project ends you have seen.

13. Can you recall projects with tall furnishings that created a corridorlike effect as you moved between them? Describe them.

14. Can you recall instances where the furnishings enhanced or disturbed order due to their level of density or the level of order or disorder of the smaller objects placed on them? Describe them.

15. Describe interior landmarks you have seen. How are they effective? How are they memorable?

16. In what ways, which have not already been mentioned, would you create interior landmarks?

17. Diagram your current academic building in terms of the ten place components covered in this chapter.

Endnotes

1 Lynch, Kevin. *The Image of the City*, (MIT Press: Cambridge, Massachusetts, 1960).

2 Norberg-Schulz, Christian. *Existence Space and Architecture*, (Praeger: New York, 1971).

3 Lynch, p. 47.

4 Ibid., p. 47.

5 Leupen, B., Grafe, C., Köinig N., Lampe, M., & de Zeeuw, P. *Design and Analysis*, (Van Nostrand Reinhold: New York, 1997).

6 Lynch, p. 47.

7 Ibid., p. 48.

CHAPTER 4

The Basics of Space

INSTRUCTIONAL OBJECTIVES

Explain different ways to define space.

Present the hierarchy of spaces.

Explain the related concepts of containment and encapsulation.

Demonstrate the impact of openings and edges on enclosure.

Demonstrate the role of edges on the definition of positive and negative space.

Describe four-room size scales useful for interior design.

Describe five basic geometric forms used to design space.

Explain different approaches to manipulate spatial form.

Explain the concept of disclosure in design.

Describe basic approaches to the design of movement in design.

Describe basic types of path-to-space and space-to-space relationships.

Describe basic organization systems for interior projects.

Present four basic spatial approaches commonly used in interior projects.

Chapter 3 was devoted to the idea of environments as collections of places. We talked about the differences and relationships among the concepts of function, space, and place, and explained the elements of place. These elements were discussed in terms of their role and significance, but our presentation did not elaborate on specifics concerning the treatment and manipulation of spaces. This chapter focuses on fundamental aspects of space. The aim is to learn to define and manipulate both individual spaces and systems of spaces.

A key to the success of a project is the proper orchestration of its parts according to function and hierarchy. Additionally, it is necessary to properly manipulate spaces to make them come alive and have engaging effects. The manipulation of spaces for desired effect requires the control of space; its shape, size, degree of enclosure, and its relationship to other spaces. Space inside buildings can be defined, enclosed, and orchestrated in a variety of ways. Possibilities are limited only by the designer's level of knowledge and skill. The more you know about the properties of spaces and ways to manipulate these properties to create specific effects, the better equipped you'll be to enhance the experience of users in your projects.

Interior design projects require responses to complex physical needs and processes. Decisions about the subdivision, placement, and composition of spaces respond primarily to the basic functional requirements of the project. A customer service office facility intended for the processing of telephone inquiries is likely to require different spaces than, say, an accounting firm. The customer service facility will require large open spaces furnished with clusters of small cubicles where workers can receive calls from customers. The accounting firm, in turn, will need many private offices where accountants can work privately with a high degree of concentration.

In the two examples above the ratio of enclosed space to open space will be very different, the accounting office having a far greater area of enclosed space. Let's suppose the accounting firm has a floor in its building devoted to training that consists of several large training rooms. Even if the total ratio of enclosed to open space were similar, the nature of their arrangement would likely be different. The training floor would need a few large rooms with easy public access. The typical office floor would consist of many small private rooms.

Whether a project is more or less open, more or less rigid, or more or less innovative will depend greatly on its own set of circumstances. It is up to the designer to understand these and determine what type of arrangement is most responsive to the particular set of requirements at hand. In all these cases, it is the project that suggests the appropriate organization and treatment of spaces. A designer must be able to interpret the needs of the project and know how to shape and manipulate space.

We will look at individual spaces and their spatial properties first. Then we will look at some basic relationships between adjacent spaces and, finally, spatial organizations for entire projects. For much of the information contained here we are indebted to the contributions of previous authors who have tackled the subject of architectural space, particularly Francis Ching,[1] whose work has helped us understand its many manifestations.

Properties of Individual Spaces

It is important to acquire an awareness of spatial design choices for single spaces and their implications first, before dealing with the orchestration of complex spatial organizations and sequences. We will devote the first parts of this chapter to the examination of the issues of spatial definition, enclosure, degree of visual disclosure, and freedom of movement in individual spaces.

Spatial Definition

Space, whether claimed (as a spot claimed with a blanket for a picnic in the park) or allocated (as the kind of space distribution designers perform) is usually marked or defined in some way. For the picnic example, you lay a large blanket over the desired spot, add the picnic basket and perhaps a few other personal items, and the space in the park becomes yours for the afternoon. In interiors, spaces are demarcated in order to differentiate them from neighboring spaces and create different territories. A variety of architectural and interior design elements are used to define space. Depending on the choice of elements and their composition, space can be explicitly defined or simply implied. Furthermore, various layers of a spatial hierarchy usually operate simul-

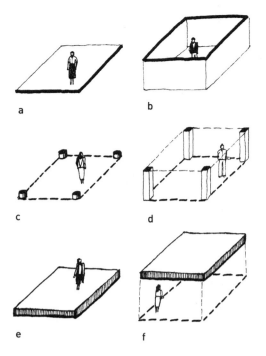

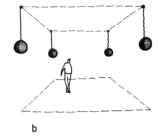

Figure 4.1 Space can be defined by marking the boundary on the floor (a), by erecting walls at the edges (b), by marking strategic points along the edges with objects or columns (c and d), by raising the floor area inside the boundary (e), and by dropping the ceiling plane over the space (f).

Figure 4.2 The suspended spheres at the corners help to complete the volume suggested here by defining its height.

taneously in interior spaces, creating opportunities for multilayered arrangements. We will look at space-defining elements first.

Space-Defining Elements

Space is defined by the marking of its boundaries. This is done by establishing and marking the lines that represent the limits between inside and outside. Designers use various devices to accomplish *space-definition*, the most recognizable being a vertical plane (usually a wall) placed along the boundary. This can be a solid wall or some sort of permeable screen. It can be full in height or a partial wall. Another way to define space is to just mark its corners with an object such as a column (or any other device), and, thus, define four (or more) corners that establish a particular space. Furthermore, one can distinguish a space by differentiating its floor and/or ceiling plane from its surroundings through changes of level and/or material between adjacent areas. Figure 4.1 shows examples of these basic space-defining methods.

Space can be defined two- or three-dimensionally. *Two-dimensional definition* is achieved by claiming an area through the marking of its limits on a two-dimensional plane, usually the floor or the overhead plane. The extent of space demarcated is mentally extended (upwards or downwards, depending on the case) and the implied volume of space is understood. In the picnic example above, the blanket demarcates an area using the floor plane. Note that you can demarcate territory two-dimensionally by marking the limits of the boundary only (fully or partially), or by changing the entire surface treatment of the floor or ceiling plane inside the territory through variations of material, color, texture, or pattern.

Three-dimensional definition is more explicit about the vertical extent of the defined volume. It not only defines the territory claimed but also indicates its vertical dimension. A minimal way to achieve this in a square space would be to place four objects (such as suspended spheres) on the four corners at the desired height. See Figure 4.2. This would complete the "box," suggesting the full extent of the space defined.

The issues of height and mass are important in establishing the precise character of a boundary. Points at corners and markers along a boundary line on the floor merely establish the boundary. If the line is solid and has some height, it becomes a partial wall and partial separation is created. If the line is of full height and reaches the ceiling plane, complete separation is accomplished.

We have mentioned four common ways of demarcating the limits of defined space: marking the corner points, marking the boundary lines, articulating the floor plane, and articulating the overhead plane. In interior projects, three types of space-defining elements can

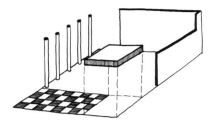

Figure 4.3 This space is defined by a combination of full and partial walls, a row of columns, a partial ceiling plane, and two types of contrasting floor patterns.

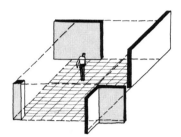

Figure 4.4 Even though all the walls continue beyond the limits of the defined rectangular space, their placement on the boundary lines, together with the strong corner demarcation achieved by the two foreground walls, helps to define the rectangular area shown.

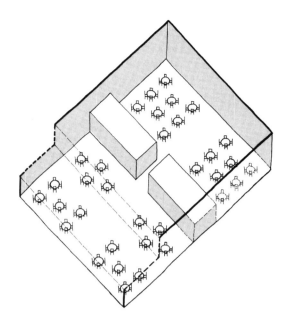

Figure 4.5 Spaces such as this hypothetical restaurant often have many levels of spatial definition defined by grouping or common enclosure.

be placed strategically on these locations: objects (furnishings, columns, accessories), permeable barriers (colonnade, glass, partial walls), and full barriers (solid walls). In practice, these can be used to create different configurations of furnishings, columns, suspended objects (light fixtures and such), full and partial partitions, overhead and base planes, and solid masses to define space. See Figure 4.3.

Literal and Implied Space

Space definition can be literal or suggested. It varies, depending on the defining elements used and their placement. Solid, full-height walls at the boundaries define space most strongly. They help define the edge assertively with a physical barrier that provides separation from one space to the next. When spatial shape is implied by objects at the corners or on overhead planes, the resulting definition is not as strong, although it is still effective and even preferable when some degree of openness is desirable. A wide range of possibilities exists between the extremes of fully-explicit and fully-implicit space. Figure 4.4 shows an example of implied space where a rectangular area is defined by partial planes and a corner column.

Hierarchy of Space-Definition

Space-definition can occur at different levels simultaneously. Inside a building, say, a restaurant, you may be sitting at a table (space 1), which is part of a well-defined group of tables (space 2). The group of tables may be part of several groups of tables under a section defined by a lowered ceiling (space 3). This lower area, in turn, may be open to, and part of, a larger overall dining area in the restaurant (space 4), which may represent one-half of the total dining area (space 5). See Figure 4.5.

Knowledge of the various ways of differentiating space can help you create separations in bold or subtle ways. In the example above, differentiation is achieved as follows:

Space 1: Object - A single recognizable object—the table

Space 2: Group - A group of closely spaced tables reading as a discrete region

Space 3: Section - A collection of several groups of tables under a space defined by a lowered ceiling

Space 4: Volume - Two sections within the same overall volumetric space

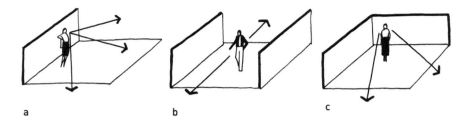

Figure 4.6 Containment is related to the perceived sense of enclosure. You can think of containment as gathering without spilling. Of these examples, c shows the best ability to contain without spilling.

Space 5: Overall project - Two sides of a restaurant, each with its own volume but linked as one overall project.

An advantage of multilevel space definition is that it gives a sense of being part of various "spatial groups" simultaneously, and thus helps to maintain a sense of place at the various levels of the hierarchy.

Enclosure

Closely related to levels of spatial definition are levels of enclosure. As we saw above, a space can be defined strongly without having to be enclosed. Some spaces, of course, need to be fully enclosed for functional or practical reasons. Those spaces require, not only definition, but also a sense of separation and containment. Private offices, conference rooms, changing rooms, and restrooms all demand enclosure, some more than others. Other spaces, like open retail or office areas, do not require enclosure and can remain open within themselves and in relation to adjacent spaces.

There are many levels of definition between the two extremes of full enclosure and full openness. The choices made by designers regarding the openness or enclosure of spaces greatly determine the spatial character of a project. In this section we will examine various levels of enclosure, the characteristics of their space-defining edges, and the effect of different kinds of wall openings. We will begin with containment and encapsulation, two important concepts related to enclosure.

Containment

Some spaces are not only recognizable as well-defined areas but actually provide a strong sense of **containment**. Containment is a concept that refers to a space's ability to gather people and/or objects. You can test the containment capabilities of any given space by thinking of it as a container with more or less ability to hold its contents without spilling them. The three spaces shown in Figure 4.6 provide some degree of containment. The example with the L-shaped corner walls provides the strongest containment because of the sealed corner it offers. If you were to pour its "contents" into these three shapes, only the L-shaped configuration would be able to contain them without spilling.

This concept is important in living environments because it translates into a sense of shelter and protection. The potential of the L-shaped configuration in Figure 4.6 to give us both a sense of protection and visibility because of its open sides appeals to our innate sense of self-preservation. The inside corner shown provides a space that affords protection from two sides. Only the front sides are open, but they are visible straight ahead when looking diagonally from the sheltering corner. There are configurations that provide stronger containment than the L-shape. Examples include U-shaped configurations and completely "boxed" rooms.

Encapsulation

Encapsulation is another term related to enclosure. It refers to the degree to which the enclosure of a space creates a seal from adjacent spaces. Until the early

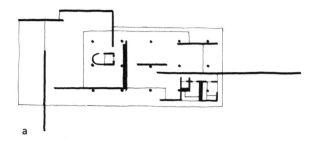

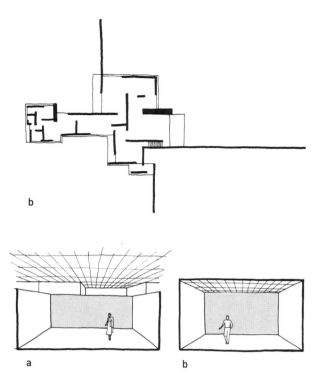

Figure 4.8 Contained space contains without creating a complete seal (a). Encapsulated space is sealed on all sides (b).

twentieth century, the norm in spatial design was to subdivide an overall space into many smaller encapsulated rooms. You always knew when you were entering a new room as soon as you approached it. In some cases, you walked through the actual rooms to go from one space to another. The location of the doors established the path. Later on, corridors were added and one could move between spaces without disturbing intervening spaces. Still, the actual habitable spaces remained encapsulated, autonomous rooms separated from one another.

With the modern movement and its new technologies came new ways of thinking about space. Space was not to be encapsulated as in the past. Instead, space was thought of as a continuum of infinite space that could be defined by minimal means in order to distinguish one area from the next while maintaining flow and continuity. Edges were ambiguous and loosely defined by the strategic placement of a few nonaligning walls. Encapsulation was avoided except when absolutely necessary for privacy. Some of the projects by Mies van der Rohe represent the best examples of this approach to space planning. See Figure 4.7 and the capsule "Destruction of the Box."

Today, architects and designers employ many different levels of spatial definition. These range from the fully encapsulated to the barely differentiated. Although no strict categorization of the levels of enclosure exists, it is useful to distinguish among four general levels.

Loosely defined space is implied or suggested space. No visual, acoustic, or haptic separation is required between it and the adjacent spaces. It relies on providing enough spatial clues to make the space readable. Strategies may include definition of corners, that is, marking enough spots along the periphery of the space or providing planar definition from above or below through floor or ceiling changes to demarcate limits.

In *strongly defined space* edges are explicit in at least two, preferably three sides. Space also starts having a moderate degree of containment. Some visual separation may be desirable depending on the application, although it is possible to achieve strong definition with partial-height elements that allow strong visual connection between spaces.

Contained space has maximum containment capacity by having walls on all sides. It provides visual separation, no acoustic or haptic separation is necessary. Therefore, it can have some openings that achieve containment with partial height elements that do not provide a complete seal at the corners or overhead.

Encapsulated space not only has walls on all sides, but the overhead and floor planes are connected to create a sealed space, a totally enclosed room. Visual, acoustical, and haptic separations are required. Figure 4.8 shows examples of a contained and an encapsulated space with the front wall removed.

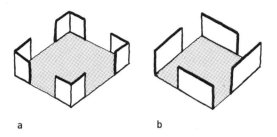
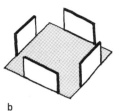

a   b   b

Figure 4.9 Closed corners facilitate readability and increase the sense of containment of a room (a). Partially open corners (b) and fully open corners (c) can define and contain a space, but with some degree of ambiguity.

successful definition of the space, doesn't contain the room as strongly because of its open corners. The room in Figure 4.9b has a sense of containment that falls somewhere in between.

The location of openings also affects the first impression of a room's degree of enclosure, depending on the view offered as you enter. In general, spaces with an opening straight ahead that reveals what lies beyond will produce a strong sense of openness; spaces with a solid mass straight ahead as you enter will produce a stronger sense of enclosure. See Figure 4.10.

Spatial Edges

We have seen how important spatial edges are in determining the degree of enclosure. We have also seen how edges can, but don't need to be, defined by physical barriers. They can, alternatively, be defined by changes in the materials or levels of ceilings or floors, by the strategic placement of freestanding objects, and by strategic alignment with adjacent elements. In considering spatial edges next, we explore the physical barriers that define and shape space. They tend to be of three kinds: vertical walls or screens around the sides, the horizontal base plane on which we stand (the floor), and a horizontal (although sometimes sloped) plane overhead (the ceiling).

Vertical Edges Walls or screens of various heights and thicknesses, whether free standing or part of an adjoining room, are the most common vertical edges. Important design considerations include the relative degree of openness or closeness achieved by them, as well as their figural and textural character. The degree of openness is affected by the horizontal conti-

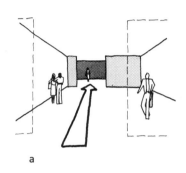

a

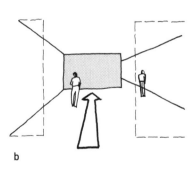

b

Figure 4.10 An opening placed opposite a room's entrance produces a sense of openness and continuity. A wall placed opposite a room's entrance will contain the space.

Openings

The size and location of openings have a strong impact on the sense of containment of a space. Figure 4.9 shows the impact different opening configurations have on the perceived level of enclosure in a simple square room. The room with the strongest integrity at the corners (Figure 4.9a) has the strongest sense of enclosure. The room in Figure 4.9c, despite a somewhat

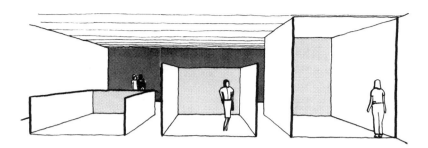

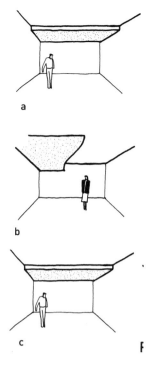

Figure 4.11 Below eye-level, above eye-level, and full-height enclosing planes produce dramatically different perceptual effects when seen in space.

Figure 4.12 Ceilings are very effective in differentiating adjacent areas. Ceiling height changes (a), ceiling shape variations (b), and material changes (c), can all be effective ways to define edges.

nuity of the barrier (it may be continuous or have gaps), the number and size of openings, and the barrier's height. Openings and horizontal extent will be discussed later, so we will focus here on the issue of heights.

A vertical solid barrier can range from a low baseboard a few inches high to a full height partition reaching the ceiling plane above. It is useful to distinguish among three different heights: below eye level; above eye level, but partial; and full. Each produces a distinct effect.

Edges that are below eye-level include low partitions, furnishings, or fixtures. These provide physical separation, but visual, auditory, and haptic connections are maintained. They are useful in instances where both definition and a strong sense of connection are desired.

Edges that are above eye level but of partial height also include partitions, furnishings, and fixtures. They provide not only physical but visual separation while maintaining auditory and haptic connections. You can still hear sounds from the adjacent space and feel the same air and temperature. These edges are useful when visual privacy as well as a sense of connection are desirable.

Edges that are full in height are most often walls and other partitions. They provide physical, visual, auditory, and haptic separation between spaces and are commonly used where a full separation is desired. Figure 4.11 shows examples of these three types of vertical edges.

Horizontal Edges Base planes (floors) and overhead planes (ceilings) are the two types of horizontal edges

that help to complete the spatial definition of enclosed space. Ceilings are not always horizontal but are included under horizontal edges for convenience since they are commonly horizontal in interior spaces.

Floors are limited in their capacity to enclose and define space. They are always level (except at ramps) and for commercial applications require minimal changes in height because of issues of accessibility. Material, color, texture, and pattern variations are the most common ways of treating floors for space definition and differentiation.

Although floors are limited in their ability to differentiate space, ceilings offer many opportunities to do so. They offer two advantages. First, there is no issue of accessibility with ceilings since we don't walk on them. Second, being overhead, they are highly visible. Variations are commonly achieved by level changes or shape changes. See Figure 4.12.

Although elevation changes at the ceiling are most effective, changes of ceiling material, color, texture, and pattern can also be used to distinguish between adjacent areas. The range of surface manipulations is not as wide as it is with floors, given the fairly neutral treatment normally provided for ceilings. Nevertheless, transitions from a monolithic, smooth ceiling system to a grid and tile system at the same elevation, for instance, is often enough to achieve a subtle separation between areas. See Figure 4.12c.

Scientific developments in the early twentieth century revolutionized the way people thought about the universe. It was seen as having four dimensions, time being the fourth dimension. Space and time became part of a relational continuum, with space changing as one moved in time. Artists, writers, and filmmakers started to adopt this new way of thinking about space, a radical departure from the perspectivism of the Renaissance, which perceived space from a single fixed point. This new idea soon influenced architects and designers. After all, of all the arts, it had the potential to affect architecture and interior design the most.

In addition to the new thinking, the development of new construction techniques utilizing steel and concrete made it possible to use slender skeletal support structures, thus providing the freedom necessary to revolutionize interior layouts. Perhaps the most significant design-related outcome resulting from these changes was the destruction of the box. Until then, interior environments consisted of collections of contained spaces arranged in various configurations. All of a sudden, corners opened up, walls disappeared, dividers and partial walls were introduced, and a freer way to design came about. While the use of open flowing space has been prominent for many years, many design students still tend to design in boxes. They need to learn to stop relying on the box! The information contained here should help.

Frank Lloyd Wright was one of the most important catalysts for the destruction of the box, something that consciously preoccupied him as early as 1904, while designing the Larkin Building. However, it wasn't until later that this idea started to flourish. Said Wright, "Unity Temple is where I thought I had it, this idea that the reality of a building no longer consisted in the walls and roof.... In Unity Temple you will find the walls actually disappearing; you will find the interior space opening to the outside and see the outside coming in. You will see assembled about this interior space, screening it, various free, related features instead of enclosing walls. See, you now can make features of many types for enclosure and group the features about interior space with no sense of boxing it."

Wright's destruction of the box entailed the opening of the corners, the use of walls as independent screens, and the detachment of the wall-to-roof connection. He explained: "I knew enough engineering to know that the outer angles of a box were not where its most economical support would be, if you made a building of it. No, a certain distance in each way from the corner is where the economic support of a box-building is invariably to be found.... Now, when you put support at these points you have created a short cantiliverage to the corners that lessens actual spans and sets the corner free or open for whatever distance you choose. The corners disappear altogether if you choose to let space come in there, or let it go out." In this way the corner was opened up: lesson number one.

The next task was to manipulate walls to open up space. "These unattached side walls," continues Wright, "become something independent, no longer enclosing walls. They're separate supporting screens, any one of which may be shortened, or extended, or perforated, or occasionally eliminated." So, walls started to acquire a new meaning. They were no longer continuous, uninterrupted enclosures placed exactly at the boundary of each room and sealed hermetically at the corners. They were now screens full of possibilities. Not only was it possible to free up the corner, but now, by moving and shortening walls, it was possible to really open up a space and make the inside and outside continuous: lesson number two.

Next, Wright continued the liberation by transforming the connection between the horizontal plane and the vertical plane. "No one has looked through the box at the sky up there at the upper angle, have they? Why not? Because the box always had a cornice at the top. It was added to the sides in order that the box might not look so much like a box, but more classic." According to Wright, it was possible to do more than just free up the four, or however many, corners of a room and move the walls within the room. By shortening the top of a wall along its length, and using a transparent material such as glass to join the wall and roof so it appeared to float, it was possible to fully liberate space and do away with the box: lesson number three. Figure C4.1 shows representative sketches of the evolution from box to free plan.

Not only did it become important to break the box between interior and exterior, but also the boxes within buildings in order to create more flowing arrangements symbolic of the times. Wright was not the only one concerned with the destruction of the box and the general opening up of interior space. Other well-known architects followed suit and experimented with various approaches to the same problem. The de Stijl movement in the Netherlands offered its own antibox theories involving dismembering via the disjointment of planes and their strategic positioning. Some of the best examples of such an approach can be found in the work of the German-born architect Mies van der Rohe. Some of his early designs employed a minimal number of strategically placed wall planes to achieve openness, flow, and connection to the exterior. A great example of this approach is his German Pavilion for the 1929 International Exposition in Barcelona, Spain (Figure C4.2). Mies, whose slogan was "less is more," succeeded in giving us one of the purer examples of free-flowing space unimpeded by structural walls and also provided one of the earliest examples of unadorned richness. His design relied on the purity, beauty, and texture of the chosen materials. Another notable example from Mies was the Tugendhat House in Czechoslovakia (1930) shown in Figure C4.3. This house employs an approach similar to that of the German Pavilion (lightweight skeletal structure and independent screens) to maintain a similar sense of openness and sparseness, despite the more demanding programmatic requirements of a real house.

In a similar vein as these two designs by Mies is Philip Johnson's well-known Glass House in New Canaan, Connecticut (1949). See Figure C4.4. It features an all-glass envelope and three masses, two linear masses providing storage, and one cylindrical mass containing the bathroom and a fireplace. These serve to subdivide the open space into three areas, a large living and dining area, and two smaller areas, the bedroom and the kitchen. In this example, it is not thin screens, but functional masses that serve as screens and perform the dividing task.

Other good examples of functional masses serving as screens can be found in Mies' Farnsworth House in Plano, Illinois (1950) and Wright's Robie (1909) and Zimmerman (1950) houses. See Figure C4.5. These offer illuminating examples to the designer of interior space about how a single interior mass, strategically placed and carefully articulated, can screen, house, and divide, while helping to keep the rest of the space free and open.

By using these simple approaches, designers can produce simple and pure designs. Most interior design projects occur in empty open shells where the structural concerns have already been established. The designer is given a clean space on which to plan the new project. Partitions and masses don't have to support any loads. They are free. They can be thin, curved, or movable. Spaces can overlap with and flow into one another. Imagine the possibilities!

Suggested Exercises:

1. Pretend you are Wright. Start with a boxlike floor plan, and destroy the box. Concern yourself only with the relation of the room to its exterior. Open up the room to achieve inside-outside continuity, by moving or shortening walls, freeing up corners and any other devices you can think of.

2. Put on Mies van der Rohe's cap for a while. Using grid paper, take a rectangular area and subdivide it into subareas using thin planes as Mies did with the German Pavilion. Try at least two versions.

3. Similar to the examples shown in Figure C4.5 above, in an otherwise open rectangular room, design a single mass that incorporates some function, and, because of its strategic location and shape, helps to divide the room into various zones.

4. Pretend you are given a hypothetical store space to design. Without getting into design specifics, use one or more masses and one or more screens to define and subdivide several spaces in the store. Pretend the footprint of the space is approximately 40 by 120 feet.

---

[1] Kaufmann, Edgar & Raeburn, Ben (ed.). *Frank Lloyd Wright: Writings and Buildings*, (Meridian: New York, 1960) p. 284.
[2] Ibid., p. 285.
[3] Ibid., p. 286.
[4] Ibid., p. 286.

Figure C4.1 Evolution of the destruction of the box: enclosure at boundary, supports at four corners (a), partial enclosure at boundaries, supports "in" from corners (b), minimal enclosure, strategically located "free" walls act as supports (c).

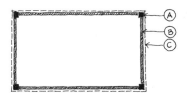

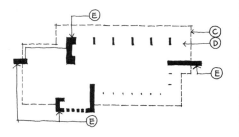

Figure C4.2 Floor plan of Mies' Barcelona Pavilion.

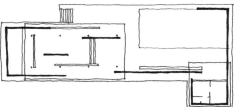

Figure C4.3 Floor plan of Mies' Tugendhat House.

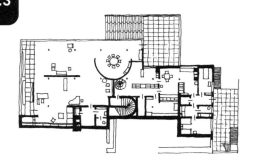

Figure C4.4 Floor plan of Johnson's Glass House.

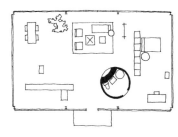

Figure C4.5 Floor plans of Mies' Farnsworth House (a), Wright's Robie House (b), and Wright's Zimmerman House (c).

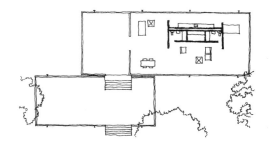
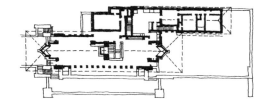
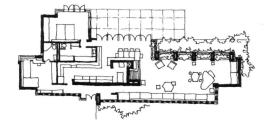

Figure 4.13 Articulation of walls and ceilings helps to produce spatial texture. It occurs on a much larger scale than surface texture of certain materials and finishes.

Textural and Figural Aspects of Edges

In addition to helping separate and contain spaces, edges contribute to their textual qualities. We normally think of texture in relation to surfaces. Yet space can also be thought of as having texture. It is called **spatial texture**. The Random House College Dictionary defines texture as "the characteristic physical structure given to a material (or space) by the size, shape, density, arrangement, and proportions of its elementary parts."[2] While spatial texture is often determined by the objects (furnishings, suspended lights, and so on) in the space, the defining surfaces can also play an important part in supplying texture.

Enclosing walls can be smooth and plain but they can also be highly articulated, thus adding textural qualities to the space. Ceilings and floors also offer opportunities to add spatial texture. For instance, ceilings can be subdivided into modules, rhythmic bands can be used, and so forth. Figure 4.13 shows a space with a textured side wall and ceiling. Spatial texture also occurs when spaces are left open to the structure above, such as in a room without a ceiling. The structural members and other elements normally hidden by a ceiling establish a texture of their own. Mechanical ducts, sprinkler lines and electrical conduits, boxes and fixtures become visible and can add texture, although sometimes a chaotic texture.

Positive/Negative Spaces and Masses

An important contribution of defining edges is their role in defining the shape of space, both positive and negative. In **positive space**, space is the figure (recognized shape) and the surface is the background (left-over space). In **negative space**, space is the background and the surface is the figure. You cannot give geometric figural shape to a space without the contribution of the surrounding edges. A round room needs concave walls, an octagonal room needs eight wall segments, a domed space needs a domed ceiling plane. We rely on the shapes we give these edges in order to give the space its shape. We will talk about the basic shapes of rooms later in this chapter. For now we will concentrate on issues of positive and negative spaces.

It is the enclosing surfaces of rooms that define their shape. In general, at any one time, either the enclosing plane or the shape of the space it defines has a more regular shape. Sometimes an enclosing wall takes on a figural recognizable shape and the leftover space in front of it ends up with an irregular, sometimes unrecognizable shape. In these cases the wall, and not the shape of the room, is seen and recognized as a shape and becomes dominant. In some cases, a certain wall may fluctuate back and forth, alternating between being the recognizable shape and being the background and letting the space in front of it have the recognizable shape. Figure 4.14 shows this phenomenon. A portion of the wall shown defines a circular space in front of it, and a little bit further ahead, the wall takes on the shape of a cylindrical mass.

Size

It may seem as if designers have relatively little influence on the size of spaces. After all, most project programs prescribe the floor areas required by the different project functions, leaving you little flexibility in the matter. This is only partially true. While designers

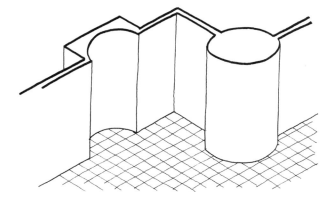

Figure 4.14 The enclosing planes are by turns a mold that shapes space and the shape itself. Where the wall recedes in, it acts as the mold that gives shape to the space in front of it. Where it projects out, it becomes the cylindrical shape itself.

are often given area breakdowns for the spaces needed, they do have opportunities to influence the perceptual size of spaces.

Designers can sometimes influence the size of the spaces they design to accentuate or downplay the perceptual size of the space. This is done by manipulating a room's plan and height dimensions. By manipulating the scale of a room slightly it can attain special qualities related to size, such as grandeur or intimacy.

When we say room scale we mean the overall relative size of the space or room. While room scales range within a continuum of varying degrees of spaciousness, we may think of spatial size in terms of four broad and useful categories. These are monumental scale, generous scale, functional scale, and intimate scale. Designers should be familiar with the connotations of each and become adept at designing in any of them.

There are no specific guidelines that prescribe specific dimensions for these various room scales since they depend on the specifics of the situation and are therefore relative. More important than thinking in terms of specific dimensions is understanding the traits of these different scales, the appropriate time to use them, and the experience they produce. A brief explanation of each follows.

Monumental Scale

Monumental scale is the scale of grand cathedrals and palaces. It is usually conceived of as part of the architecture, used on very special buildings, and very infrequently. It was used in the past much more than

now and is always easily recognized. Its key traits are verticality and spaciousness on a grand scale.

Achieving monumental scale in interior projects is sometimes impossible due to the limited size of most existing interior building sites. Yet multifloor lobbies in some new office buildings and spaces in older buildings with large volumes sometimes present opportunities to achieve monumental space. This grand scale often presents design compositional challenges related to the large amounts of empty space overhead and the usually expansive surrounding surfaces high up. Decisions about the modulation and general treatment of these surfaces and spaces must be considered carefully to achieve satisfying and balanced results. See Figure 4.15a.

Generous Scale

Generous scale is the scale of very comfortable office and hotel lobbies, spacious dining areas in restaurants, and generous shopping areas in stores. It is more easily achievable than monumental scale as it doesn't require as much volume. It is often up to the designer to push the limits of space and make otherwise ordinary spaces more generous. As with monumental scale, the feeling of spatial generosity relies heavily on the extension of the vertical dimension. Change an 8-foot-high, 5-foot-wide corridor to 10 feet high and you will create a generously scaled corridor. Give a low lobby space a 14-foot-high ceiling and you will have a generous lobby. Generous scale is important in design and is often achievable. All that's required is the awareness to recognize potential opportunities for it, the desire to do it, the willingness

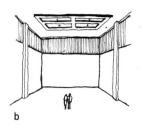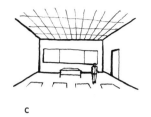

a   b   c   d

Figure 4.15 Space comes in many sizes. Depicted here are representations of four basic scales: monumental (a), generous (b), functional (c), and intimate (d).

to make it happen, and the ability to justify it. Figure 4.15b shows an example of a generously scaled room.

Functional Scale

Functional scale provides an adequate amount of space to fulfill the basic requirements of a room or space. All of us see it every day and know it well. It ranges from sizes that are minimally acceptable to sizes that are slightly more comfortable but not generous. An example of the minimal approach is a project designed to meet the minimum requirements stated in the building codes. This is often the direction followed for projects requiring maximum efficiency and economy. In these cases, room sizes and corridor widths are minimal. In multilevel buildings, the floor to ceiling heights are kept as low as possible to permit the stacking of as many floors as possible. The functional scale does not need to be minimal. It can be, and often is, more comfortable.

The functional scale will often do the job but will rarely motivate or inspire. However, this is the scale of everyday normal design and can not be totally avoided. A good strategy to follow is to learn to use functional scale selectively and to balance it when possible with other more generous spaces that provide relief and comfort. See Figure 4.15c.

Intimate Scale

Intimate scale is the scale of small spaces for one individual or a few people. Tighter spaces and lower ceilings are not only allowed but desirable. This is the scale of niches, alcoves, and inglenooks. It is also the scale of small but comfortable conference rooms and

theaters. The difference between spaces of intimate scale and spaces on the minimal end of the functional scale is that intimately scaled spaces are used when intimacy is appropriate. When designing intimately scaled spaces, care is taken not to oppress the users or make the use of the space oppressive.

You should not limit your idea of good spaces to comfortable, generous, and grand spaces. You also need to learn how to create purposely cozy spaces and to use them where necessary. The library study carrel, the small break room in an office, and the dining table in an intimate restaurant become better spaces when supplied with the coziness of intimate scale. See Figure 4.15d.

Form

Another important property of space is its **form**. By form we mean the basic configuration of the space, such as rectangular, circular, or square.

The form of space has important implications concerning the dynamics of the space and its centers of energy. It is possible to classify spaces into one of two broad categories: those that are narrow and linear and induce movement and those that are wider and promote habitation. Our discussion below focuses on rooms and spaces belonging to the second category.

The Square Space

Square spaces are pure, formal, and static. They are spaces to be occupied and normally do house a function. Square spaces have a strong sense of definition because of their strongly defined and uniform corners. They also

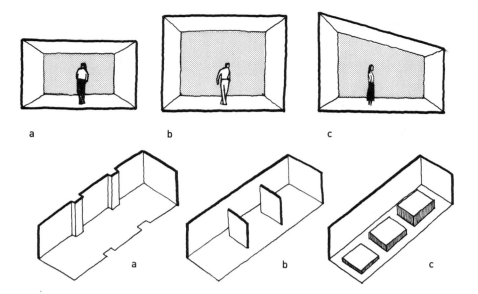

Figure 4.16 The extent and shape of the vertical dimension can produce dramatically different spaces with the same floor area. Here we see how they affect three rooms with equally-sized square floors.

Figure 4.17 Long rectangular rooms are often more comfortable when subdivided. These illustrations show divisions created by articulations on the side walls (a), actual dividing screens (b), and the grouping of furnishings and/or fixtures in the space (c).

provide a strong sense of enclosure because of their four prominent walls. Furthermore, a square space possesses a strong sense of centrality. Although the only plan variation possible for square spaces is their size, square spaces can acquire different characteristics depending on the treatment of the third dimension. Different heights and ceiling shapes will give similarly sized rooms a substantially different feel. See Figure 4.16.

The Circular Space

The circle, like the square, is pure, formal, and static. The circle, however, more than the square, is a highly memorable shape. Circles can be places for habitation as well as circulation spaces. Unlike the square, the circle has no corners. However, it does possess a strong center and a very readable surrounding envelope that, like the square, provides a strong sense of containment and enclosure.

The Rectangular Space

Rectangular spaces have different properties depending on their size and proportions. For that reason it is useful to divide them into two categories: short and long rectangles. The short rectangle is any rectangle whose long to short side ratio does not exceed two to one. When a square space is elongated, it becomes linear in nature and its dynamic properties increase, suggesting movement along the long dimension. Still, the proportions of the short rectangle are such that it retains a strong sense of place because it is not too long. Depending on their intended use, these spaces can be left as one space with one center or subdivided into two or more zones, each having its own center.

In a long rectangular space, the long side exceeds its short one by a ratio greater than two to one. The long rectangle is very dynamic. It suggests movement along the long axis. Very long rectangular spaces sometimes become perceptually uncomfortable unless they are subdivided into smaller units. When they get very long and narrow, they start to acquire the qualities of a corridor. Subdivision can be accomplished by the articulation of the enclosing surfaces to suggest subcompartments, by the addition of physical edges between sections, or by the arrangement of the contents into subgroups. See Figure 4.17.

The Triangular Space

The triangle, such as the equilateral triangle, is generally not a good shape for interior spaces because of its functionally problematic acute angles. Nevertheless, it can sometimes be used successfully. In fact, one type of triangular shape can be used successfully in interiors to create dynamic areas while maintaining adequate functionality: the right triangle.

The right triangle is a dynamic shape because of its long diagonal side and the tension created between the right-angle sides and the diagonal side. All objects within the space can be placed either parallel or perpendicular to the two sides forming the right angle, or placed diagonally in relation to the diagonal side. See Figure 4.18. Circulation can follow either the diagonal or the two sides of the right angle. In most cases, however, it will be more efficient to have circulation moving along the diagonal.

The triangle, even the equilateral triangle, can be used selectively for impact. Like the circle, the triangle

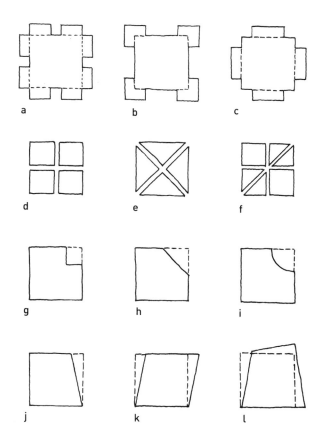

Figure 4.19 In this example, a square is subjected to manipulation techniques including aggregation (a–c), fragmentation (d–f), segmentation (g–i), and distortion (j–l).

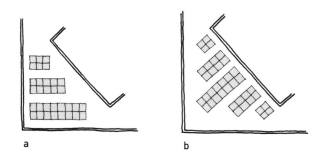

Figure 4.18 The right triangle is the most functional triangle for design. Notice the two basic variations possible for the placement of furniture.

is very memorable when kept pure. It is possible to truncate the sharp corners for increased functionality, although this will have the undesirable effect of compromising its purity and reducing its impact.

Manipulation of Form

All the basic shapes described above can be used in pure form or can be manipulated a number of ways for effect. Below is a brief description of four common manipulation techniques: aggregation, fragmentation, segmentation, and distortion. These are derived from Rob Krier's studies of form manipulation.[3]

Aggregation consists of the addition of smaller, ancillary spaces to larger spaces, such as the pure shapes described above. The art of creating the side niche or alcove is something every designer should learn and practice. In the case of aggregation, the main form remains dominant and recognizable and the ancillary spaces read clearly as additions. See Figure 4.19a–c.

Fragmentation occurs when a pure shape is broken up into smaller fragments in such a way that, by virtue of their proximity and configuration, the overall shape remains recognizable. See Figure 4.19d–f. It is also possible to achieve fragmentation by modulating a given spatial envelope into smaller compartments, as long as the overall shape is maintained. This is similar to aggregation, but in the case of fragmentation the total shape defined by the subspaces is the basic form without any protrusions.

Segmentation occurs when incomplete shapes (segments of a known shape) are complete enough that the shape is recognizable. The level of definition of the

segment needs to have enough resolution to make the form readable. If this is done appropriately, the mind will complete closure of the shape suggested. See Figure 4.19g–i.

Distortion is achieved by inflecting the edges of a known form in order to alter it while keeping it somewhat recognizable. This is normally done for effect, based on specific design intentions such as the addition of texture or the creation of a more dynamic composition. The level of distortion is up to the designer and the circumstances. The key is for the basic shape to remain readable. Otherwise the shape gets transformed into an entirely different shape. See Figure 4.19j–l.

Permeability

As we have noted in some of the earlier examples from this chapter, one of the principal aspects of interior architectural space is its degree of **permeability**. Most projects require important decisions concerning the extent to which air, smells, views, and paths are open

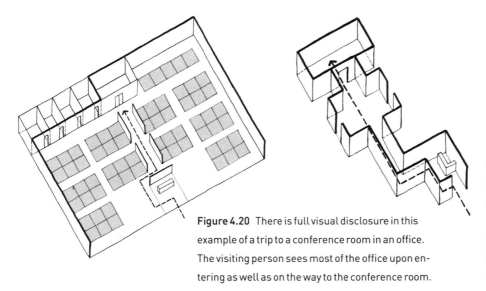

Figure 4.20 There is full visual disclosure in this example of a trip to a conference room in an office. The visiting person sees most of the office upon entering as well as on the way to the conference room.

Figure 4.21 There is very little visual disclosure in this version of a trip to a conference room. The high degree of compartmentalization prevents the visitor from seeing beyond the high walls.

from one space to the next. Designers have control over these variables, and, in most cases, are able to fulfill the functional requirements of the program with any number of scenarios of different degrees of permeability.

In this section we concentrate on two aspects of permeability: disclosure and mobility. **Disclosure** refers to how much of a space, and the other spaces beyond, are revealed as you walk around. **Mobility** refers to the relative degree of restraint and control a particular spatial arrangement affords those who move in it. As a designer, you can play the role of movie director controlling movement and the kinds of things seen along the way to create specific experiences.

Disclosure

Imagine that on a given day you visit two offices for business meetings. You arrive at the first one, open the door, and find yourself in the reception area. From it, you can see a good portion of the facility. To the right are clusters of systems furniture with low dividing panels that let you see all the way to the end of the space. To the left are more low workstations. If you move to the side, you can see all the way to the back of the room where a group of private offices is located against the end wall of the space. Straight ahead is the reception desk with a partial height-dividing wall behind it. Behind the wall is the route leading to a particular room with a central formal entrance: the conference room, your destination.

The second office space is quite different. Upon entering, you arrive at an enclosed reception area with high walls on all sides except for an opening to the left.

From that room you get a glimpse beyond, but can't really see what's going on. Once your contact person arrives, she takes you to the conference room. To get there, you go through the opening on the left and enter an enclosed corridor. You cannot see much except for what's straight ahead. At one point, the corridor opens up into a large square area, an intersection. From there, you get a quick glimpse to either side, barely making out what lies beyond. You continue straight and arrive at a small anteroom, walk through it, and arrive, finally, at the conference room.

Figures 4.20 and 4.21 show schematic views of these two spaces. It is evident that the level of visual disclosure is remarkably different between them. The first space is very open; the second, enclosed and quite controlled.

These two examples illustrate one of the basic distinctions of interior space: the distinction between open plans and compartmentalized plans. The first category features large main spaces, which can be apprehended as a whole, with the parts and subdivisions acting as freestanding objects. The amount of visual disclosure in these projects is substantial. The second category describes projects that are subdivided into compartments that are experienced sequentially, one at a time. Visual disclosure in these projects is very restrained.

Levels of visual disclosure are determined by the number, type, and placement of view-obstructing elements, whether they are permanent architectural elements, or less permanent elements such as furnishings, pieces of equipment, or even plants. Elements higher than eye level will provide substantial

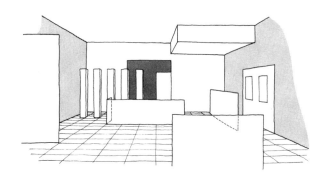

Figure 4.22 Planes, objects, and screens layered in space control what is seen within a space as well as what is seen beyond the immediate space.

blockage. Nonpermanent elements (furnishings, fixtures, and so on.) also serve an important role in regulating disclosure as one walks through a space. Their heights dictate whether uninterrupted views of the space are permitted or just an occasional glimpse. Views range from panoramic views to glimpses and vary depending on whether what's seen is a wide general view or a carefully planned and focused vista.

We talked earlier about edges of different heights and the kind of enclosure they afford. Now, as we begin to focus on the issue of disclosure, it is helpful to expand those categorizations to include additional techniques you have at your disposal. One of them is to manipulate the placement of visual barriers on different planes and at various distances from the observer. Most spaces will have combinations of architectural elements, furnishings, and other objects positioned at various depths in space and producing numerous combinations of disclosure, depending on their height and placement. See Figure 4.22.

Additionally, these barriers can have different degrees of transparency. They can be completely solid, mostly solid with some openings, translucent, transparent, closely spaced solids that form screens (closely spaced columns, for instance), or isolated single or grouped objects such as plants.

Disclosure within the Space

Disclosure within the space is concerned with the level of disclosure inside the immediate space you occupy. It is determined by the objects, furnishings, masses, and architectural elements within the space.

Disclosure, whether within the space or beyond it, should serve three important functions: provide orientation, focus attention, and provide relief.

Orientation The level of disclosure provided within a single space can help or hinder the users' ability to feel oriented. You may choose to make the understanding of both the project as a whole and its component parts immediately crystal clear by providing full disclosure. This is desirable in a large space of a project serving many first-time visitors. Conversely, in other instances, you may choose to make this understanding more of a gradual process as one moves through the space. Small rooms are easy to grasp all at once. Larger spaces, especially those with tall elements within, have the potential of being either interesting and engaging or confusing and discouraging. This depends on the composition of view-obstructing elements within them.

The extent to which and the rate at which spatial information is revealed creates unique and specific experiences regarding orientation. If you provide clarity based on visibility, you will make the process of understanding a particular space easy. Large or complex spaces will demand more clarity while smaller, simpler spaces may welcome some intentional complexity, as long as an acceptable degree of clarity is maintained.

Focus Most spaces have a functional focus. Depending on their nature, they may have one or more functional foci. In most teaching classrooms, for instance, there is one main focus: the front of the room, where the lecturer stands. A restaurant, in contrast, may not have a single communal focal point, and instead may be designed to highlight each seating section so that each becomes an individual foci. An office space may have both individual foci at the workstations and a central team-oriented area. It is part of the designer's responsibilities to emphasize some views and de-emphasize others in order to focus attention where it's needed. Guiding the eye towards focal areas can be done in subtle ways with elements such as lines, or more boldly, through room shapes and other techniques.

Relief In contrast to the idea of functional focus is that of relief. While a functional focus tends to be task oriented, relief is usually distraction oriented. You can think of relief as intentional distraction for the purpose of restoring tired or bored minds. Few designers think consciously about providing relief to space users. However, many interior places can benefit from foci created for the purpose of relief. Try to remember, for instance, those times you have been inside a crowded elevator, surrounded by strangers. There are two basic ways you can find some relief. One is to look straight ahead at the back of the person in front of you (boring and awkward). The other is to look at the changing floor numbers displayed on the dial above the door (better). The number display provides not only helpful information (letting you know how close you are to your destination floor) but also an acceptable area you can direct your attention to for relief.

Similarly, you may find opportunities to provide relief in settings like waiting rooms, office work areas, restaurants, and clinics. This type of internal relief usually translates into some sort of focal area, focal surface, or focal object. These, when supplied, are the areas where we direct our attention to get a momentary mental vacation. A focal area may be as simple as an open space amidst an otherwise enclosed area. A focal surface can either provide information or something pleasant or stimulating to look at. A focal object can be an enclosed room strategically located amidst an otherwise open area or a memorable freestanding object like a nice kiosk, a display, or a piece of sculpture.

Not all spaces require internal relief, but many benefit from it. Designers sensitive to this need will make an effort to provide some kind of visual relief and encourage those useful mental vacations we all need.

Disclosure beyond the Space

Disclosure beyond the space is concerned with what is revealed beyond the immediate occupied space. It can be what is seen when looking towards an adjacent space or while looking outside. Like its internal counterpart, disclosure beyond can serve the three functions of providing orientation, focus, and relief.

Orientation There are different ways in which you can gain orientation while seeing what lies beyond, whether looking inside or outside. Even though what lies outside or in the next room is there for you to see sooner or later, you, as the designer can control the experience by manipulating the rate and nature of the disclosure. You can reveal everything at once, gradually, or piece by piece, to elicit some specific desired response, be it suspense or surprise.

The exterior provides important informational clues that help our general sense of orientation. Seeing

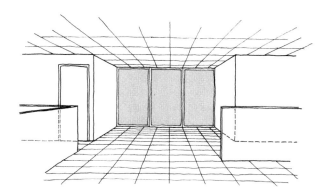

Figure 4.23 Large spaces with long window walls can become monotonous. Sometimes it is advisable to strive for variety by alternating runs of windows with enclosed masses.

outside gives us a sense of the approximate time of the day, the weather conditions, and what side of the building we are on.

The degree of control you have over disclosure of the exterior varies depending on the circumstances. Oftentimes, you have no control over the kind of windows you inherit with your project's building or the degree to which you can modify them. Most office buildings have windows all around the perimeter, and in an effort to maximize natural lighting and views, we leave them untouched. How we arrange the masses of enclosed spaces inside can, however, produce different experiences in relation to external disclosure. It is usually how we treat the foreground that will determine how much of the outside we can see at any given point in a place. Figure 4.23 shows an example of two perimeter rooms framing an exterior view. This strategy can accentuate the view by virtue of the contrast between the rooms' solid walls and the openness of the view.

Internal disclosure beyond the immediate space provides important internal orientation that helps users get a clear mental picture of where they are in relation to the overall footprint of the facility. In general, the orientation provided by a clear view of what lies beyond is helpful in promoting a sense of order, although a totally given disclosure provides no suspense and can become boring. However a designer chooses to do it, manipulating the rate of disclosure to adjacent spaces is sure to have an emotional effect on the users, as they become more or less clear about what lies beyond. The appropriate rate of disclosure depends on the circumstances and can only be judged on a case-by-case basis.

Focus Focus between spaces calls attention to important features or destinations on the other side. You can highlight a nice feature of the next space to provide a pleasurable experience or you can reveal a key destination ahead to give people the proper direction in which to move. A proper orchestration of spaces and a helpful level of disclosure from one space to the next can provide the rewarding experience of moving from one goal to the next.

Relief As with disclosure within, you can also provide relief, and brief mental breaks, with views to other interior spaces or to the outside. Techniques for providing relief through other adjacent interior spaces are similar to those for providing them within the same space. They include using contrast (open versus closed) or focusing on special objects or surfaces that provide relief. Relief is also achieved by exposure to and disclosure of the exterior. Here, relief is associated with the feeling of spatial expansion one has when looking at the open space beyond as well as the picturesque qualities of certain views.

As important as the decision is to reveal the exterior of a space is the decision on how to achieve it. How do you reveal, for instance, a particular side of a building that has a magnificent view? Can the view be seen as you approach that side of the building, thus generating a sense of anticipation? Do you reveal a glimpse, arouse the user's curiosity, then hide it momentarily before finally revealing it in full? Do you reveal it in chunks? Or, do you keep it hidden until the last possible moment and then, all of a sudden, surprise the user with the magnificent view? These are all viable options. The solution depends on the particular circum-

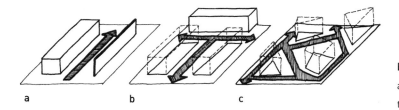

a   b   c

Figure 4.24 Movement in space can be controlled
and unidirectional (a), controlled and multidirec-
tional (b), or free (c).

stances and your sense of what is appropriate and desirable.

Mobility Patterns

One of the ways building interiors affect our experience is by controlling the freedom we have to move
about. When we start to think about circulation as
more than a utilitarian commodity and consider its
role in creating experience, we quickly become aware
of the kind of control designers have over the experiential qualities related to movement. A project may have
strongly prescribed paths or a somewhat freer system
to move about in. The goal of the thoughtful designer is
to reach a compromise between the need for economy
and clarity, on the one hand, and manipulations for
particular experiential effects, on the other.

As a designer, you control whether or not people
will have access to move in certain directions, and
when they do have access, the level of relative constraint and freedom inherent in the route to get there.
A place may only have one route that leads to it and it
may be a direct and clear route. Another place may
have three alternate routes leading to it and they may
be indirect and meandering. Below we discuss three
common ways of designing a path for movement: a
controlled route with only one choice of travel direction, a controlled route with more than one travel direction, and a free route with many travel directions
and loose boundaries.

Controlled Mobility: Only One Way to Go

Controlled mobility occurs when there is a well-defined route (usually some sort of corridor) that every-

one must follow to move around a given space. You
move only within this corridor and there is little or no
chance to improvise. In the case of a controlled mobil-
ity/single direction route you have only one way to
move back and forth between any two points. See Figure 4.24a and b. The center aisle in an airport terminal
is a perfect example of this scenario. This linear aisle
represents the only way of moving back and forth between the spaces in the terminal.

Controlled Mobility: Multiple Direction

This type of route features controlled movement
but in this case offers a network with more than one
single way to move around and get to a destination.
The paths may be tight and controlled, but at least you
have more than one to take. Having choices is not necessarily better. In some instances, you will want to
provide multiple routes; other cases will be better
served by having only one.

Free Mobility

Free mobility occurs when routes are not explicitly
differentiated by hard elements and simply become
(or at least they seem to be) the leftover "space between things." See Figure 4.24c. There is usually some
sort of implied route preconceived by the designer but
its definition is left loose and often somewhat ambiguous. Usually, you want enough differentiation so the
user feels that it's okay to go down a suggested path. In
areas that serve locals only, you can have a higher degree of intentional ambiguity. The users will be familiar with the space and will know it is okay to move in
the suggested circulation spaces.

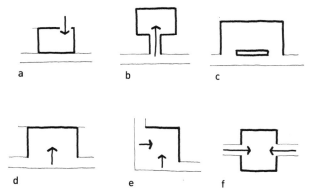

a   b   c

d   e   f

Figure 4.26 Space to space relationships involve issues of proximity and access. Two adjoining rooms do not necessarily need direct access between them (a and b); they may have an opening between them for a direct connection (c).

Composing Multiple Spaces

So far we have focused on characteristics of single spaces, such as ways to define space, different levels of enclosure possible, and, more recently, levels of visual disclosure and patterns of movement within single spaces. Now we turn our attention to multiple spaces, starting with basic relationships between spaces and paths, and concluding with ways of organizing entire projects.

Space/Path Relationship and Level of Autonomy

Depending on the relationship between a space and the path providing access to it, different levels of spatial autonomy can be attained. Degrees of spatial autonomy range from fully autonomous spaces to fully integrated spaces. Figure 4.25 shows a range of possibilities. Figure 4.25a represents high autonomy. Despite the space's adjacency to the path, one enters it on the side opposite the path, therefore providing no easy linkage. Figure 4.25b shows another autonomous space. In this case access is straight from the main path, but it is through a transitional route, thus affording separation between the path and the space. Figure 4.25c and d show spaces right off the path, the only difference being the added wall in 4.25c, which provides increased separation and some autonomy. Figure 4.25e is similar to 4.25d, but entry occurs at a corner intersection with paths occurring on two sides of the space. Finally, Figure 4.25f shows an integrated configuration in which the paths go right through the space and provide no separation between path and place.

Figure 4.25 Space/path relationships involve issues of proximity and access. A path may be adjacent to a space, but access may not be direct (a). Conversely, a space may be somewhat offset from the path, but may enjoy direct access through a secondary space (b). The designed relationship may also combine both proximity and convenient direct access, (c, d, and e) and, in some cases, the path may go right through the space (f).

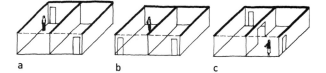

a   b   c

In cases where paths are kept physically detached from and outside the spaces they serve, the spaces remain autonomous and experience no intrusion from users going to other destinations. This type of arrangement is useful for major thoroughfares serving spaces requiring at least a moderate level of privacy.

These paths are usually adjacent and parallel to the spaces they serve. Depending on the circumstances, they can either stand out physically or blend in. Differentiation can be achieved through subtle strategies, such as minor ceiling height variations or through bold ones such as the use of totally different decorative approaches with strong physical barriers between them.

In the case of paths that pass through the served spaces, there is a planned, intentional intrusion. In these cases you, as the designer, have determined that the resulting integration between the path and the served space or spaces is desirable or, at least, acceptable. This is sometimes the case with secondary thoroughfares that tend to have local traffic, thereby not causing objectionable levels of intrusion. In most of these instances the path blends spatially and decoratively with the served space or spaces.

The Art of Joining Spaces

There are only a few ways to join adjacent spaces. Here we're talking about composition between major spaces as opposed to assemblies featuring a dominant space plus ancillary ones or the space/path relationships as discussed above. We will point out five types of relationships between adjacent spaces you should

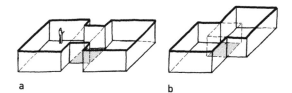

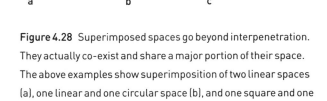

Figure 4.27 Adjacent spaces may be joined by an intermediate space that provides access between them (a) or, in the case of interpenetrated spaces, by the common space they share, in which case one can occupy both simultaneously (b).

Figure 4.28 Superimposed spaces go beyond interpenetration. They actually co-exist and share a major portion of their space. The above examples show superimposition of two linear spaces (a), one linear and one circular space (b), and one square and one circular space (c).

know about. These vary in their relative degree of connection and integration.

Adjoining Spaces with No Physical Connection

In these cases, two spaces are attached as shown in Figure 4.26a but have no direct connection between them. In fact, the points of access are on opposite ends. Although they are close in proximity, the spaces are far apart in mutual accessibility.

Adjoining Spaces with an Off-Side Connection

Here spaces are attached, and, as above, lack a direct connection. However, in this case both spaces are open to the same circulation spine, making it relatively easy to move from one to the other. See Figure 4.26b.

Adjoining Spaces with a Direct Connection

In these cases, spaces are attached and also have a direct connection through the common plane providing direct passage between them. This connection may range from a standard door to a wide and generous opening. See Figure 4.26c.

Proximate Spaces with an In-Between Space as Connection

Here spaces are adjacent, although not quite attached. They are connected by a third, smaller space providing direct linkage between them. This arrangement is useful when a strong and somewhat formal sense of transition is desired. See Figure 4.27a.

Interpenetrated Spaces

With **interpenetrated spaces**, both spaces overlap partially, sharing a common area of ambiguous ownership. With this type of arrangement access is direct and flows from one space to the next, especially as one approaches the territory in the ambiguous common area. See Figure 4.27b.

Superimposed Spaces

In the case of **superimposed spaces**, two (or more) spaces are literally superimposed over one an other, creating a new spatial definition and geometry. Depending on the treatment of the surfaces and ceiling planes, both spaces can have equal dominance or one can dominate the other. Figure 4.28 shows some examples of superimposed spaces. The relationships between the spaces can be orthogonal, symmetrical, rotated, and so on. Also, it is possible to superimpose multiple shapes on top of each other, creating increasing degrees of complexity.

Composing Systems of Spaces

Most projects consist of more than two rooms joined together. The connection of adjacent spaces remains a common theme throughout all the design phases. Questions about the relationships between project parts have to be resolved for larger parts of a project and, ultimately, the entire project to become an organized system.

The ways of combining these elements for a specific project are seemingly endless. The realities of the project and the specifics of context help to narrow down the possibilities. Also influential are the preferences of the user as well as your personal ones as a designer. The synthesis of all these factors gives shape to a project. Ultimately, the final project includes some kind of organization as well as a particular spatial approach.

Here, we will look at some of the basic choices you have as a designer to address the overall organization of the project. We will discuss several ways to arrange a project based on the circulation system as well as four distinct spatial approaches that represent the basic directions you can take as the compositional rules for a given project. We will start with arrangement alternatives based on circulation, an approach suggested by Stanley Abercrombie who analyzed plan types based on their circulation.[4]

To devise organization systems for entire projects it is possible, theoretically, to begin with the circulation system as an organizing force and then plug in the spaces where appropriate. In reality, both the spaces and the routes feeding them are part of an inseparable system and need to be considered together. Once you have a feel for the required spaces in a project you will have to think of arrangements that will work for the project within the site configuration (container) given. This inevitably will force you to make some decisions about how you will move people around. For that reason, thinking of project organization in terms of its circulation system makes a lot of sense.

Below we present six movement-based models you can use to organize projects. Each is illustrated with examples of different geometries that work within that particular system.

Linear Systems

You may choose to use a **linear system** consisting of linear circulation with spaces on one or both sides. If there are spaces on both sides you can balance them equally with the circulation bisecting the two sides or make one of the two sides wider than the other. The circulation spine of linear systems can also go through the spaces it feeds, becoming part of those spaces. See Figure 4.29a–c.

There may or may not be special goals (destinations) at the two ends of linear systems. Additionally, special spaces can occur near the center or even at more than one point along the route if the path is long enough.

Linear organizations may undulate and the linear paths may twist and turn. As long as the general character remains linear, we can still describe them as having linear circulation. Whether L-shaped, U-shaped, or linear segments at random angles, the system is still linear if its character remains linear. Where you have corners in L- and U-shaped configurations, these become potentially important junctions reserved for special destinations. Figure 4.29d–f shows additional variations of linear organizations.

Loop Systems

When a linear system closes itself up, forming a loop, it takes on a different character both geometrically and functionally, to become a **loop system**. A loop can also be circular, segmented, or free-form. Its distinguishing attribute is that it is a closed system with no loose ends. A loop can be single- or double-loaded. An inner loop feeding outwards and

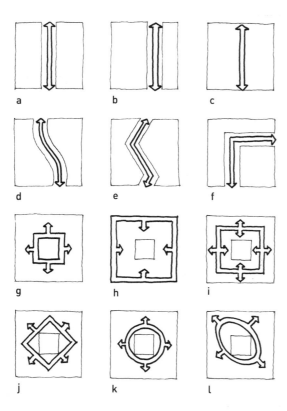

Figure 4.29 Linear and loop organizations have many possible variations.

an outer loop feeding inwards are both examples of single-loaded loop systems. See Figure 4.29g and h. Double-loaded loop systems feed both an interior zone (inwards) and an exterior zone (outwards) as shown in Figure 4.29i. With a double-loaded loop system, the decisions to be made on the placing of spaces are many. They can be tailored to the specifics of the project. The central inner zone, for instance, can be either a space of great importance, or a utilitarian space. As with linear systems, the corners in loop systems have the potential of being special strategic destinations, and thus, loop systems can have diverse geometries. Figure 4.29j–l shows some examples of alternative geometries.

Axial Systems

Axial systems consist of routes arranged around an axis; typically, these routes intersect at right angles. They often feature a main linear axis intersected by a secondary one. These configurations tend to be formal because of the linearity of the routes and their often perfect intersection at or near the center of the space. Oftentimes this center coincides with an important central space. The ends in both directions are all potential strategic locations as are the four corners defined by the right-angle intersections.

While the traditional use of axial circulation systems tends to be formal and symmetrical it is entirely possible to use this approach with asymmetrical compositions or even non-right-angle configurations. These, of course, would instantly transform the formality and décor usually sought from and provided by axial arrangements. Figure 4.30 a–c shows some examples.

Radial Systems

Radial systems are characterized by linear routes that emanate radially from a common center. The common center can be a major place or an important node. It does not need to be at the geometric center of the project, although it often is. Other potential locations for the central space are edges and corners, whether inside or outside. See Figure 4.30 d–f. One drawback of this type of arrangement is the difficulty of using the wedge-shaped areas between the circulation spines efficiently.

Free Movement Systems

Free movement systems are characterized by a free flow and at times an apparent lack of coherent geometry. Their success relies on the compositional balance achieved by the placement of project elements around which one circulates. These can be linear elements, like the walls of Mies van der Rohe's houses, or free-floating masses acting as islands. Given the many free-form configurations possible it is difficult to generalize about specific attributes of these configurations. Free movement systems are viable and appropriate organizations

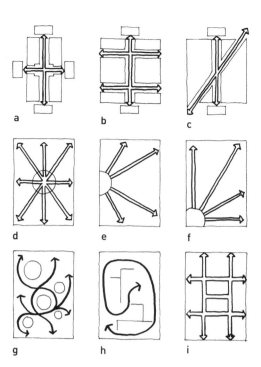

Figure 4.30 Variations of axial (a–c) and radial organizations (d–f) are shown above. Also shown are two examples of free organizations (g and h) and one of a network system (i).

used in many interior settings that do not require the strict geometry or formality of the other systems described here. See Figure 4.30g and h.

Network Systems

Network systems are characterized by fairly complex circulation systems that are interconnected and form a network. They usually occur in large complex projects or smaller ones with intentionally intricate circulation systems, as is common with some retail projects. For large projects with many circulation segments, maintaining a sense of hierarchy among the parts will help to ensure a sense of legibility and order. In contrast, in many retail settings, the segments are undifferentiated to achieve intentional disorientation. Figure 4.30i shows an example of a fairly straightforward network system.

Spatial Approaches

Project particularities such as size, complexity, client type, and site configuration will begin to suggest to you some of the above organizations more than others. We just described six basic types of spatial organizations based on patterns of movement. You also need a clear direction about the general compositional approach to be used for the project. This requires not only route configuration but decisions about the character of spaces and the type of spatial model dominating the approach. Earlier we talked about different approaches to space definition, enclosure, and disclosure. When you consider all the variables, the number of possible compositional combinations can seem staggering.

Although the many ways of combining different circulation systems and spatial approaches yields a great number of different solutions, we would like to suggest four basic approaches to the orchestration of space. They are the functional approach, the classical approach, the modern approach, and the loose approach. Using these four approaches as a point of departure may facilitate your efforts to arrive at a model suitable for your project. However, do remember that these are only points of departure and variations and combinations are often desirable. Descriptions of each follow. Figure 4.31 a–d shows representative simple diagrams for each approach.

Functional Approach

This approach is, perhaps, the most common. The time and budget pressures experienced by both clients and designers tend to produce, by default, projects that follow the **functional approach**. This model uses an efficient, engineered approach that frequently features a highly efficient loop or network type of circulation system with spaces efficiently organized on both sides of the circulation.

You will have to adopt the functional approach for many projects during your career. They can be boring projects, although there is no reason why they can't be made stimulating. As long as you are aware that the functional approach is what a particular project requires you can avoid wasting time

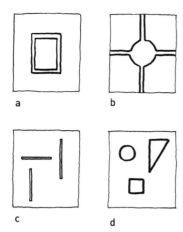

Figure 4.31 These four diagrams represent four basic spatial approaches: functional (a), classical (b), modern (c), and loose (d).

with other unrealistic approaches, and focus on making the best of the project despite the limitations of the approach. Occasionally you may be able to compensate for the limitations by producing a functional plan enhanced by one or several design features. You may also find clever ways to differentiate space and treat important spaces (centers and nodes) in special ways.

Classical Approach

The **classical approach** is formal and features a high degree of compartmentalization. It is likely to be symmetrical and ceremonial. Possible circulation organizations are the linear, the axial, and the radial. Formal offices, restaurants, hotels, and retail stores can use this approach. With the proper accompanying finishes it can convey class and sophistication.

Modern Approach

The **modern approach** is based on modernistic principles. It features simplicity and clean lines. General spaces are often loosely defined, not encapsulated. Movement tends to flow from space to space. Open spaces, even if not enclosed, are well defined and shaped in geometrically so that they become positive spaces. Arrangements tend to be asymmetrical but balanced.

Loose Approach

In the **loose approach,** solids float in space in well-balanced arrangements. These solids tend to stand out as figures. The leftover space around them is often irregularly shaped and includes circulation and other adjoining open spaces. These spaces tend to be casual and are often playful as well.

Review

Summary

The definition and manipulation of space is essential to the production of designs that go beyond function and provide order, enrichment, and expression. This chapter reviewed some basic considerations necessary for the composition of single spaces and systems of spaces.

Important spatial properties of individual spaces include their level of definition, the type of enclosure they provide, their size, shape, and form, and the degree of disclosure and movement they afford. Space can be articulated many different ways, some literal and others implied. It can be highly contained and even totally encapsulated. The perceived degree of enclosure varies with the position of openings such as doorways and windows in the space. Walls sometimes act as backgrounds to the shape of space and at other times become the shapes themselves.

Spaces come in different sizes and shapes. As a designer, you have considerable control over these variables. They all have specific enclosure characteristics and their form can be manipulated by techniques such as aggregation, fragmentation, segmentation, and distortion.

Levels and patterns of disclosure can be manipulated by you to create specific effects. Disclosure, whether within a space or beyond the space, effects a user's sense of orientation; it contributes a sense of focus and relief.

When designing adjoining spaces, whether a space-to-path or a space-to-space relationship, issues of proximity and connection come into play. Spaces can be proximate without being directly accessible. They can have moderate or high levels of accessibility between them, depending on the location of openings and the geometry of the spaces. Some spaces are literally superimposed onto one another.

As you go from designing a couple of spaces to the design of the entire project, certain organizational systems will appear more appropriate than others. Based on movement patterns, potential systems include linear, loop, axial, radial, free, and network organizations. You may stick to one approach for a project or use a combination of two or more.

Finally, to help you think of approaches to the organization and spatial character of interior spaces it is useful to think in terms of four basic models that represent four different stylistic directions. These are the functional approach, the classical approach, the modern approach, and the loose approach.

Chapter Questions

1. Explain the related concepts of space definition, containment, and encapsulation. When does a space go from definition to containment or encapsulation?

2. Recall monumental spaces you have visited. What was your reaction to them?

3. Can you recall a corridor, room, or open space you have experienced that had a very generous scale?

4. Recall intimate scale spaces you have seen. How did they feel?

5. As a designer, you will often be faced with decisions about whether to make a certain space a little more generous or more intimate. Depending on the space, its setting and use, you may favor one approach over the other. What kinds of spaces would you make more generous? Which ones would you make more intimate?

6. Think of at least two instances where you would use each of the following:
   a) An off-the-path room with a short direct path to it
   b) A corner space completely open to both side paths. Would you differentiate the path from the space or have it blend with the space?
   c) A path running through the heart of a space

7. Sketch and briefly describe at least two instances where you would use each of the following:
   a) Two adjoining spaces with a prominent opening on the common side
   b) Two adjacent spaces with an intervening connecting space
   c) Two interpenetrated spaces
   d) Two superimposed spaces

8. In what types of applications would you consider the following systems?
   a) A linear system

b) An axial system

c) A radial system

d) A free system

9. Describe two ideal types of projects for each of the following approaches:

a) The functional approach

b) The classic approach

c) The modern approach

d) The loose approach

Exercises

The recommended type of drawing for these exercises is a three-dimensional drawing, such as an axonometric or a perspective. In some cases, however, a floor plan will work. Check with your instructor to determine the type of drawings you should use.

1. Draw two minimally defined rectangular spaces, one straightforward and literal, the other implied.

2. Draw three rectangular rooms enclosed by walls. Add openings (number, size, and placement are up to you) to achieve the following:

a) A very open space with minimal enclosure.

b) A space with an open feel but a moderate sense of containment.

c) A strongly contained space with as much openness as possible.

3. Draw at least two similarly sized spaces with enclosing edges of different heights and different levels of transparency (using screens) to produce two very different effects.

4. Draw one space in which you use the ceiling to define:

a) A subspace in the center

b) A path along one side

5. Draw a space using the floor to define an area near the center.

6. Draw two square, two circular, and two short rectangular spaces in which you use the placement of doors to achieve different circulation patterns. These will be rooms that users must go through so the rooms will all need at least two doors—an inlet and an outlet.

7. Draw two long rectangular spaces and subdivide each into three compartments by using a combination of different techniques, such as wall articulations, dividing planes, furniture arrangements, or placement of doors.

8. Draw three rooms in one of the basic forms we studied and manipulate their form by using:

a) aggregation

b) segmentation

c) distortion

9. Using the concept of disclosure, draw a large space where the view within the space provides a general sense of orientation. This can be achieved by providing a constant (or periodic) view of a central prominent element, by providing a view of a set of regular elements that indicate a route, by providing an extensive disclosure that allows you to see the whole, and by using other techniques as well.

10. Draw a portion of a retail space where the disclosure provided helps to focus attention on one particular display area.

11. Draw either an office or restaurant space where disclosure is planned in such a way that users get at least one instance of internal relief from their work station or dining table.

Endnotes

1 Ching, Francis D.K. *Form Space and Order*, (Van Nostrand Reinhold: New York, 1979).

2 Berg, Stuart. *The Random House Dictionary of the English Language*, (Random House: New York, 1987).

3 Krier, Rob. *Elements of Architecture*, (Academy Editions: London, 1992) pp. 26–33.

4 Abercrombie, Stanley. *A Philosophy of Interior Design*, (Harper and Row: New York, 1990) pp. 17–25.

PART 2

ESTABLISHING THE DESIGN

CHAPTER 5

Understanding

INSTRUCTIONAL OBJECTIVES

Explain how a project occurs within a given historic, cultural, and geographic context.

Explain the contextual impact of the surroundings on interior projects.

Explain the contextual impact of the building in which the project occurs.

Present the concept of types and show its relevance to interior projects.

Present the roles played by a project's internal players.

Present examples of external context analysis.

Present examples of internal context analysis.

Present an approach that seeks to understand a project's most basic realities.

Present approaches that seek to distinguish among projects of the same type.

Present a format to acquire specific detailed information about important

project spaces.

Present a format to collect detailed information about relationships between

project spaces' aspects.

efore we can begin to design a project, it is necessary to collect pertinent information about the project and its needs. This information is collected during the programming (data collection) phase through conversations, surveys, group sessions, and observations. Successful design solutions rely on decisions based on accurate and complete information. Otherwise, no matter how thoughtful and skillful the design efforts, the project could easily provide good solutions to the wrong set of problems.

At some point towards the end of programming, or immediately after it, the information collected is sorted out and analyzed to get an overall understanding of the project and its particular requirements. The process of shaping interior space starts with the understanding gained during this important stage. Only when a project is based on accurate and well-understood information can we know for certain the stages that follow (ideation, development, and resolution) will be addressing the right design problems. The diagram in Figure 5.1 shows the progression through the basic stages. Each stage is based on information gained or arrived at during the previous one, allowing design ideas to become more detailed and refined as we move forward.

Understanding requires a considerable amount of analysis. During this stage all the project's evident realities, both inherent and contextual, are considered. The following aspects of the project need to be understood properly in order to produce a responsive design.

Figure 5.1 Design involves a series of stages that progressively solve the problem with greater accuracy and detail. The diagram represents the four basic stages. These are: analysis of data to achieve understanding (a), ideation to generate potential approaches that solve the basic design problem (b), development to articulate the concept chosen in more detail (c), and resolution to refine and resolve all aspects of the project (d).

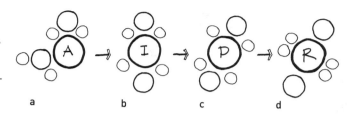

Context

1. the project's general context
2. the project's surroundings
3. the building in which the project will take place

Internal Players

4. the project's client
5. the project's users

The Project Itself

6. the type of project being designed
7. the project's parts and their functions
8. the relationship among the various parts
9. the relationship of the parts to the whole

The better the above considerations are understood, the better position you are in to supply a solution that responds well to them. It all starts, however, by making sure you are responding to the appropriate needs of the project.

The analysis stage, particularly for large or complex projects, can be overwhelming. While collecting data and starting to think about project needs and strategies, it is important to remember that design needs to fulfill, first and foremost, the project's functional purpose. This is the most basic requirement of design. While some of the higher aims of design advocated in this book are important, their pursuit would be empty if it was not carried out in the process of responding to functional purpose. Order, enrichment, and expression complement and enhance function but they are never a substitute for it. Even a designer's own artistic purposes need to be carried out in the process of pro-

viding function. Cesar Pelli makes this point eloquently when he states: "the artistic purposes of the architect need to somehow combine with the many purposes and functions of clients and users. Skillful architects manage to achieve their personal artistic goals while respecting the goals and needs of those for whom the building is being designed. This balance is simple to propose and difficult to achieve."[1]

While purpose and its related functions shape a project from the inside out, physical context shapes a project from the outside in. Responses to this collection of internal and external forces determine the arrangement of project parts and are, therefore, a critical aspect of the process of shaping interior space. This chapter will focus on the task of gaining proper understanding about both the project's functional purpose and its contextual circumstances. We will look at context first.

Context

General Context

A project is part of many contexts. It takes place at a certain time in history (historical context), within a certain culture (cultural context), and in a specific location (regional and local contexts). These contexts all come with their own set of rules within which designers need to operate. Designers are usually familiar with the contextual rules within their geographic area of operation, such as stylistic tendencies related to cultural and historic issues. The situation is different, however, any time the designer steps into a different culture, re-

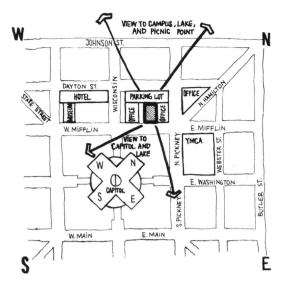

Figure 5.2 External features, mainly the characteristics of neighboring buildings and their users, can inform design decisions. In this example, a prominent civic building across from the building site becomes a significant presence that demands a design response. The selection of which areas will have access to views of this building becomes an important design consideration.

gion, or neighborhood. In these cases the rules change, thus requiring different design responses.

Designing in a historic district, a foreign culture, or within a neighborhood of a particularly strong stylistic character are all instances requiring proper care in order to ensure proper response. When confronted with these unfamiliar circumstances we need to carefully study and understand what their contexts suggest and respond accordingly.

Surroundings

A project's immediate physical context, its surroundings, is the most tangible context and requires proper understanding by you as the designer. For convenience, we can divide surroundings into two categories of different scales: the neighborhood and the specific site. Neighborhood characteristics usually have a greater impact on the designs of new buildings than on interior spaces. They can, however, be relevant to interiors when they have dominant tendencies, as in the case of an old historic neighborhood. It is, however, the project's immediate site that provides the most significant information requiring a design response.

The immediate site can significantly influence the placement of a project's parts. Contextual realities from the site often play a major role in determining a project's plan. Unfortunately, the realities outside the project's bounding walls are frequently ignored in interior projects and many opportunities to take advantage of or avoid problems associated with the context are missed. Designers must realize that exterior realities present both amenities and problems

that need to be taken seriously if a project is to have a harmonious and complementary coexistence with its setting.

Response to context in interior projects is somewhat different from response in architectural projects. In architectural projects, architects consider the site's location, orientation, and configuration in order to make proper decisions about where the building should be placed on the site, as well as how it is to be oriented, two of the most important decisions in building design. Based on the particular realities of the site for a given project, the building is located on a given spot, oriented a certain way, and configured to fit the location.

In contrast, most interior design projects occur in buildings that either already exist or, if new, are designed by others. The designer is therefore confined by the given boundaries and geometry of a predetermined building and must work within its constraints, taking advantage of its strengths and downplaying its weaknesses. This presents a unique architectural condition. On the one hand, the designer cannot change the building in response to the site since the building has already been shaped. On the other hand, the building itself now becomes another layer of the context since it is the container within which the interior design will take place.

Even when the building already exists, the exterior context needs to be acknowledged and responded to by the interior designer. It will become one of your tasks to locate interior rooms and spaces according to what the exterior has to offer. Significant immediate contextual considerations are the neighborhood, existing natural

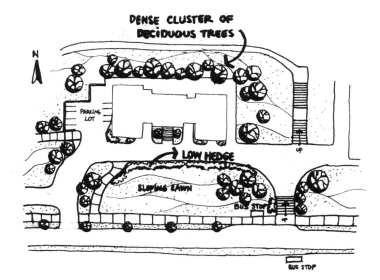

Figure 5.3 This diagram shows a survey of natural features outside the project site for an academic building. The most significant natural feature in this example are the trees on the north, behind the building. These provide pleasant, filtered views to rooms located on that side of the building. The lawn in front of the building slopes away from the building, resulting in expansive views, even from the lower floors.

features, circulation around the site and access points to the buildings, and environmental issues.

Immediate Neighborhood

The immediate neighborhood consists of those surroundings close enough to the project building to have an effect on it. Depending on the project, this may be anywhere in extent from a segment of a street to an area of several blocks. The main things to look for are the surrounding buildings (size, character, proximity) and patterns of use. Figure 5.2 shows a diagram of an office building with observations about significant aspects of the immediate neighborhood that will need to be considered during design.

Natural Features

There are three natural features that require analysis: single natural elements such as significant trees and other plants; regions of particular character such as woods, lakes, and clearings; and topographic characteristics of the site, such as slopes, peaks and valleys. Some natural site features, like a lake, may provide visual relief. Others, like a group of trees, may provide shade to cool the building.

Charles Moore wrote about the importance of outlook, a concept related to the relationship of interior spaces and the exterior "in which something outside the room attracts the attention of the inhabitant without requiring him to give up those advantages enclosure brings. Outlook occurs through openings, generally windows, and is, in effect, another kind of focus."[2] Put simply, it refers to pleasant features outside that can serve as focal points for the people in-

side. Such instances of favorable outlook usually demand a design response; thus, a room or space should be located on the side that faces the desirable feature. "The distinguishing characteristic of rooms enfronting the outside," adds Moore, "is that they are arranged in relation to something beyond themselves, and the chief advantage of this arrangement is that it allows the rooms to have an outlook over whatever they face and share its qualities. By the same token, it is only useful if there is something worth facing: either something already there; or something made and shared."[3]

Figure 5.3 shows a diagram identifying significant natural elements around an academic building.

Circulation and Access

The analysis of circulation patterns and building access (both vehicular and pedestrian) provides useful information about patterns of movement adjacent to the building. It provides information about how people get to the subject building (by car, bus, bike, or on foot), and which side they approach it from. Additionally, information about general patterns of movement outside helps determine what parts of the building people walk by the most, providing insights about where to place internal functions that need more or less visibility and exposure. Figure 5.4 shows the circulation and access diagram for the school building previously introduced. It identifies, among other patterns, two important parallel arteries, one intended primarily for pedestrian circulation (adjacent to and parallel to the building's long dimension), and one further down dedicated to vehicular traffic.

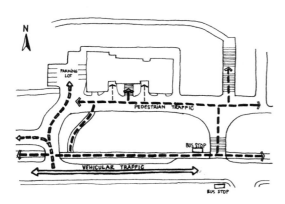

Figure 5.4 This kind of diagram shows the analysis of circulation and access points to the building, displaying both vehicular and pedestrian circulation and giving the designer useful information for design.

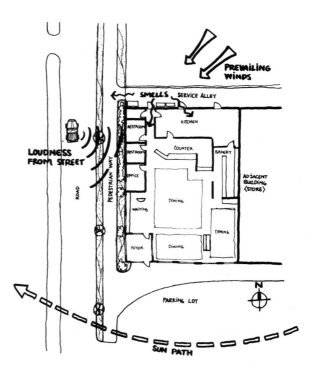

Figure 5.5 Conducting an analysis of environmental factors, such as this one for a restaurant site, helps to identify sources of light, glare, noises, winds, and smells.

Environmental Features

Environmental features include factors such as general climate characteristics and the sun path, as well as prevailing winds and sources of external sounds (including noise) and smells (including offensive ones). These factors are often influential in the zoning of interior functions. Exposure in relation to the sun path determines which spaces will get the morning sun (and the resulting light, heat, or glare it provides) and which will get sun in the afternoon.

Concerns for the proper placement of interior functions in relation to the outside are not anything new. As early as the first century B.C., the Roman architect Vitruvius wrote about the virtues of giving proper exposure to the different rooms in buildings according to climatic considerations.

Winter dining rooms and bathrooms should have a southwestern exposure, for the reason that they need the evening light, and also because the setting sun, facing them in all its splendor but with abated heat, lends a gentler warmth to that quarter in the evening. Bedrooms and libraries ought to have an eastern exposure, because their purposes require the morning light, and also because books in such libraries will not decay. In libraries with southern exposures the books are ruined by worms and dampness, because damp winds come up, which breed and nourish worms, and destroy the books with mould, by spreading their damp breath over them.[4]

While much has changed since Vitruvius' days, such as the advent of sophisticated heating and air conditioning systems, designers have a responsibility to consider a room's placement in relation to the outside. Issues ranging from functional needs to energy conservation will influence decisions of room placement.

Awareness of the source of winds, sounds, and smells is also important and rooms should be placed in appropriate proximity to them. Figure 5.5 shows an environmental feature diagram for a restaurant having sights, sounds, and smells to contend with.

Building

Beyond its surroundings, the building that houses an interior project presents a context of its own. It has its own geometry, circulation, modularity, column placement, core to perimeter distance, and, in

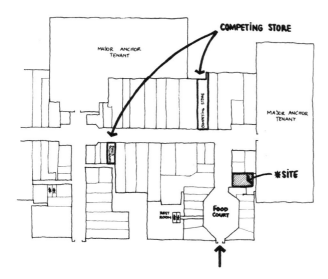

Figure 5.6 The interior of large, multiuse buildings act as homogeneous neighborhoods. These, like exterior neighborhoods, feature miscellaneous functions and neighbors that can have an impact on your project. In this example of a store site inside a shopping center, the analysis reveals two nearby stores with similar merchandise (competition) and the location of a food court near the site (good exposure).

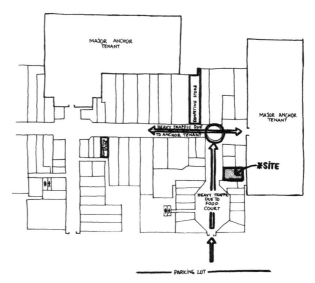

Figure 5.7 Similar to an external circulation analysis, this internal version identifies patterns of movement inside. In our example, the proximity to the food court and a major anchor tenant is likely to ensure substantial pedestrian traffic nearby.

some cases, unique configurations or characteristics. Depending on the project to be accommodated and the building's features, these may be seen as assets or liabilities. Significant aspects of a building's context include the interior context, the circulation patterns, and the features of the actual project space, the site.

Interior Context

The analysis of **interior context** considers the space to be occupied in relation to the rest of the building. The pertinent factors include the location of the space within the overall building, the neighbors within the building, the location of building systems and features, the adjacent building's activities, and the surrounding sounds and smells. Is the space in a corner, in the middle, on the perimeter, by the entrance? Is it on the sunny or the shaded side? Who are the neighbors in adjacent suites? What do they do? Do they generate noise or offensive odors? Performing this kind of analysis will provide useful insights to help you make appropriate design decisions. Figure 5.6 shows a diagram analyzing the interior context of a site in a regional shopping center. This tenant is located near the food court, mean-

ing employees and customers will have to contend with distracting noise and tempting smells throughout the day. It also means the store will be seen by a great number of people.

Circulation

Analyzing circulation patterns provides insights about movement systems within the building, points of access to and egress from the space or suite, and egress from the floor or building. Circulation patterns are crucial for any business that relies on proper exposure such as restaurants and retail stores. Locating such businesses in strategic areas of high exposure is paramount to their success. Points of access are important both for the ease of the visitor and the convenience of the locals. Appropriate egress patterns are necessary to ensure safe exiting during emergencies. All these factors will affect the choice of location within a building and design strategies once a location has been chosen. Figure 5.7 shows a circulation analysis diagram for the store near the food court introduced above.

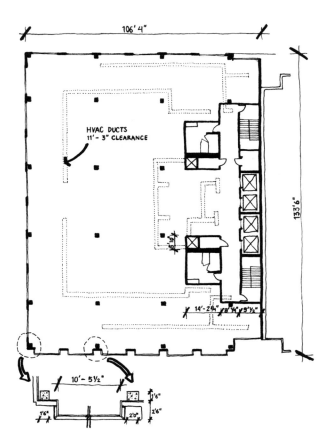

Figure 5.8 along with HVAC DUCTS 11' - 3" CLEARANCE

Figure 5.8 This diagram focuses on the internal space features of a floor in an office building. Existing conditions are surveyed and notes made of key dimensions and locations of significant elements such as overhead ductwork.

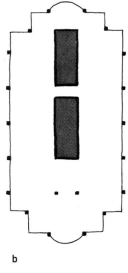

a

b

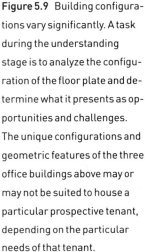

c

Figure 5.9 Building configurations vary significantly. A task during the understanding stage is to analyze the configuration of the floor plate and determine what it presents as opportunities and challenges. The unique configurations and geometric features of the three office buildings above may or may not be suited to house a particular prospective tenant, depending on the particular needs of that tenant.

Features of the Space

Here the concern is with the project space itself. Whether the client is occupying the entire building, an entire floor, or a portion of a floor, the aspects needing attention are the same. Among them are the size of the floor area to be occupied; the space's shape and overall geometry; significant features, such as the size, location, and spacing of columns; the characteristics of the perimeter wall; window spacing; light penetration and exposure to outside views; and the location of miscellaneous building components, such as mechanical equipment, ducts, and sprinkler systems.

Figure 5.8 shows a space feature diagram for a floor of an office building. It shows some of the internal aspects of the site that will impact the design of the space, such as column locations and sizes, perimeter window characteristics, and clearance heights to existing mechanical ductwork overhead.

We turn our attention now to some basic differences among floor plates to understand the significant variations one encounters from building to building. Figure 5.9 shows three of the many configurations possible in office buildings with central service cores. We will concentrate on the geometry of the buildings and the use of space they allow. Figure 5.9a features a rectangular floor plate with a two-part building core. The configuration provides usable space in the very center of the building as well as space around the two core masses. Articulations on either end of the building, behind the cores, provide special spaces for potentially special functions. The designer will have to work around rows of interior columns on either side of the core when rooms or furniture workstations are laid out in those areas. Figure 5.9b also consists of a rectangular floor plate. The linear core occupies most of the center spine and is pushed towards one side of the

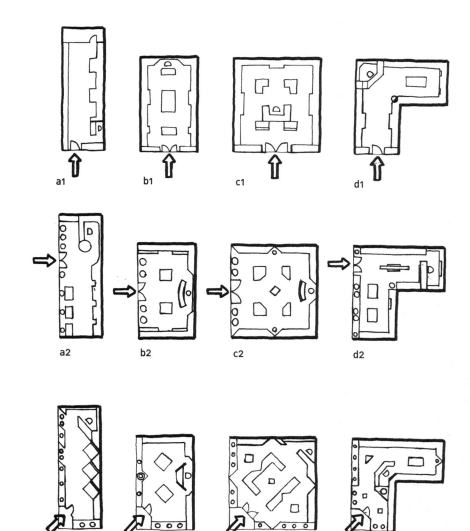

Figure 5.10 In addition to geometry, factors such as which side is in front and which has the entrance, will have an effect on design. Notice the different configurations these stores assume as the location and number of exposed sides, and the entrance location, change.

a1 b1 c1 d1

a2 b2 c2 d2

a3 b3 c3 d3

building, opening space on the opposite end. The zigzagging at the four corners produces eight corner locations instead of four, a welcome feature for any organization requiring many corner offices for its executives. Figure 5.9c is another predominantly rectangular plan with a central core. Like the previous example, its core is also off-center resulting in one tight, and one generous, end. Its most distinctive feature is the curving wall on one end. This feature can present planning challenges. It may be a blessing or a curse depending on the requirements of the project to be accommodated, although most competent designers would be able to put it to good use in any case, even if some efficiency is lost.

We will now examine some basic configurations of simple spatial geometries and see the effects of shape, exposure, and point of entry on the resulting space layout. These are the kinds of spaces you may en-

counter as sites for a small office, a retail store, or a restaurant. Figure 5.10 shows four basic shapes for a retail store: the narrow rectangle, the normal rectangle, the square, and the L-shape. A basic diagram is shown for each of the shapes for two scenarios: one with access on the narrow side and one with access on the wide side. Additional diagrams show the effect of visual exposure (glass) on a second side. Notice the way the schemes change depending on configuration, orientation, point of access, and the number of sides visually exposed to the outside.

Figure 5.11 shows the floor plates of two more office buildings. The service cores of these two buildings occur along one end and not at the center of the building as is more customary. Figure 5.11a occurs in a large multistory office building. It offers a large usable central area. The service core elements occur along one of the long sides, thus providing freedom in the

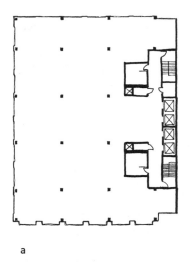
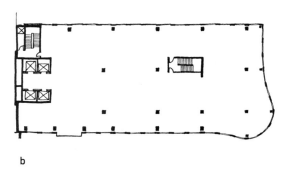

a   b

Figure 5.11 These two floor plates of office buildings reveal some information about their size and geometry. It is not until we have the details of the surrounding context that some of the real opportunities here can be understood and project parts located appropriately.

center but also potential challenges when planning for multiple tenants on one floor. Additionally, one side features six bay windows and overlooks a magnificent civic building and related grounds across the street. The opposite side has a panoramic view of the downtown in the foreground and of a lake in the background. Finally, there are eight large free-standing interior columns in the space that will require careful planning around them.

Figure 5.11b occurs in another office building. It features a narrow rectangular floor plate with elevators on one of its short ends and minimal core elements elsewhere. Distinctive features of this building include a high perimeter-to-area ratio, and a short distance from the perimeter to the center. Additionally, it features two areas of special architectural articulation: one bay window on the wall near the entry side and an outward-expanding, curved area on the far end. Looking over a vacant lot, there are some good views of the civic building, although there are plans for an adjacent building which will likely block some of these views.

Understanding what the building and its surroundings have to offer is an essential part of the analysis task. Good analysis and understanding will increase the likelihood that project parts are placed in the most appropriate locations and that the configurations used are complementary to the building's geometry.

The following are design considerations to keep in mind:

- Orient spaces in response to what's outside, seeking or avoiding outside features as appropriate.
- Take advantage of the building's geometry.
- Plan your modules carefully if the building has many interior columns. Use a module that works with the column spacing.
- Carefully plan modules along the exterior perimeter to work with the existing module of window mullions and solid elements.
- When planning tall spaces, consider limitations posed by existing elements overhead.
- Decide which characteristics of a building you want to adopt, feature, ignore, downplay, or hide.

Internal Players

The internal players that most affect decisions of a project are the client and the users. By client, we refer to the owner or the designated representative in charge of the project. By users we mean the actual people who will spend time in it, either locals or visitors. Often, the client is also one of the users, such as when the president of a company is the project's client in addition to being one of its users.

Clients

The client is the person controlling the project on the owner's side. This is often the owner, although sometimes a designated representative is in charge of managing the project. In any case, the client is the person or group of persons who make important decisions about the project. Clients decide, first of all, that there is a need for the project. They tend to be practical people and are responsible for the feasibility of the project. As such, they are always deeply concerned about issues of function, cost, and schedule. Clients have a tremendous influence on the projects they control. They decide how money will be spent, approving or rejecting design proposals from you as the designer.

The client's influence can be either beneficial or detrimental to the project, depending on the client. "A good client," says Cesar Pelli, "used to mean the supportive patron, one who would approve all proposals and agreed on whatever direction the architect wanted to give the design. Such patrons are now very rare. Good clients are needed more than ever, but today that means people who care about the building and the art; are involved through the whole design process; are explicit in their needs and goals, likes and dislikes; and make clear and timely decisions. We can learn much from our clients and depend on them to keep us on track as we move toward the most appropriate, functional, and exciting buildings for their needs."[5]

Users

If clients set the tone for projects, users shape their content. Buildings and their interiors are for users. The client may or may not be one of the active users of the building. As we saw in Chapter 2, the outlook of users varies depending on their role within the building or project. In a restaurant, for instance, the roles of the maitre'd, the chef, the bartender, the food servers, and the cashier are different and this influences their individual opinions about the needs of the project. The view of a patron who comes in to dine is, likewise, quite different from those of the group above. The patron's opinion will be colored by impressions gained while entering, waiting for a table, proceeding to the table, ordering, consuming the food, visiting the restrooms, and paying the bill. The staff's opinion of their experience will be influenced by how much the facilities, as well as other factors, ease the execution of their roles. For the cook this will mean a functional kitchen, an adequate supply of ingredients, and a competent help staff. For the food servers it will mean a manageable workload, comfortable traffic paths between tables and kitchen, and functional waitstations.

In Chapter 2 we mentioned the difference between locals (those people who work in a facility) and visitors (those people who visit the facility but don't spend much time there). Clovis Heimsath makes a similar and useful distinction by dividing user roles into served and service roles.[6] The restaurant example above serves to illustrate this point. All the players in the first group above, such as cooks, food servers, and busboys, perform the role of service. The patrons are the ones served. Another useful distinction is the one between "front-of-the-house" and "back-of-the-house" functions. Front-of-the-house functions are public ones, such as those performed in the dining area of a restaurant or in the main hall of a theater. These functions tend to be performed in the more image-conscious areas of a facility, areas where a facility's purpose is consummated, be it eating, shopping, or watching a movie. Back-of-the-house functions are support functions, usually highly utilitarian in nature. Some workers never leave the back of the house while others operate strictly up front. Still others, like food servers in a restaurant, go back and forth between these two worlds. Hotels, restaurants,

Figure 5.12 The people shown here are performing service roles in restaurant settings. Fig. 5.12a shows the hostess in a front-of-the-house service role. Fig. 5.12b shows cooks performing back-of-the-house functions.

hospitals, and theaters are service-oriented institutions involving massive behind-the-scenes efforts in order to produce desirable experiences for those being served in the front of the house. Figure 5.12 shows individuals performing service roles in an eating establishment.

Understanding users and their roles is crucial for a project. Users perform the usual functions associated with their roles, but they often perform them in distinct ways. In some cases, workers of a company may have a specific style because of their collective personality, a certain tone set by the owner, particular company traditions, or some other reason. This accounts for differences among groups performing similar roles in different establishments. This sense of unique tone and attitude becomes a consideration that influences the expression given to the project. The food servers at a formal, exclusive restaurant are likely to have a different collective personality than a group of servers at, for instance, a school cafeteria, although both groups perform a similar role.

The Project Itself

The project itself is the central concern of all predesign and design activities. In this section we examine five key aspects of projects: the project type, the project's essential purpose, the parts of a project, their relationships to each other, and their relationship to the whole.

Project Type

Most projects are a specific application of a project **type** that has been done before. Whether a retail store, a restaurant, a theatre, a clinic, or an office, projects share commonalties with similar projects done previously. Therefore, it is usually unnecessary to invent ways of solving old design problems, as long as the existing solutions work. Studying these old solutions can teach invaluable lessons and provide insights. The practice of analyzing prototypical solutions to common project types, with all their variations, is a good habit for designers to adopt.

Whenever you find yourself working on a type of project never encountered before it is critical to spend some time studying past projects of the same type (called precedent studies). This can be done by visiting similar projects and/or by reading the literature available on this type of project. Information is widely available in reference books as well as in specialized books and magazines. Both are useful, although better still are the insights gained by actually visiting similar projects and spending time observing them and using them. These insights are deeper and have more impact than the experience gained from books and magazines.

Projects of a common type share a basic purpose, a number of core elements essential to their function, and some recurring issues that always have to be addressed. Following is a cursory analysis of a few common project types. The intent is to give you a basic idea of the kind of information useful in understanding a certain type of project. The informa-

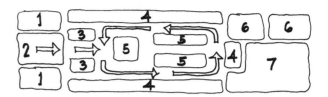

Figure 5.13 Prototypical diagram of a store. The following basic elements are included: window display (1), entry (2), checkout/cashier (3), perimeter displays (4), freestanding displays (5), employee areas (6), and merchandise storage (7).

tion given is, therefore, representative and does not attempt to present a full analysis of all the types. Detailed information about different project types is readily available in reference books for architectural and interiors standards. When carrying out a project it will often be necessary for you to consult these guides to get more detailed information.

A Retail Store

Essential Purpose ❖ A retail store brings consumer and merchandise together.

Means of Achieving Purpose ❖ The goal is to bring the consumer in and entice him or her to buy. Presenting merchandise at every turn will increase the chances of the customer buying.

Dominant Features ❖ The most important physical presence in a store is the merchandise. Everything else is secondary. Merchandise rules.

Basic Components ❖ Storefront display, merchandise, fixtures, cashier, provisions for trying on merchandise, such as shoes or clothing. Also, merchandise stock in the back.

Common Issues ❖ Stores require proper merchandise display with appropriate customer service and surveillance. The staff, sometimes limited, needs one or more strategic central locations from which to oversee all the public areas of the store to monitor customers.

Crucial Aspects ❖ The way merchandise is displayed (the fixtures, lighting, and so on), how the design moves the consumer around the store and presents the merchandise, and how the staff can monitor customers, both to assist them and to prevent theft.

Particularities of the Experience ❖ Retail stores can offer simplicity and clarity in applications where the customer wants predictability and efficiency (such as in a grocery store). At the other extreme, they can offer complexity and ambiguity to disorient and entice. In most cases, the shopping experience is performed in transit. Whether in a grocery store or a fashion boutique, the customer is on foot moving from aisle to aisle or from rack to rack. Sales staff spend their day attending to customers, arranging merchandise, and conducting transactions at the cashier desk. They are usually on their feet all day long.

Opportunities ❖ Retail stores offer design opportunities to use strategies related to order, enrichment, and expression. Depending on the type of store, greater or lesser levels of order may be appropriate. The experience of customers can be enhanced by providing creative circulation patterns as well as creative merchandise placement and display. Strategies can be explored to help bring merchandise and customer together. There are also opportunities to devise ideas to enhance the experience of those who work in stores by increasing the comfort of their stations and providing visual relief in overly busy environments.

Prototype ❖ Retail stores come in all shapes, sizes, and styles. There are many variations on the theme, depending on the industry, the intended audience, and the level of service offered. Figure 5.13 shows a prototypical diagram for a simple generic store.

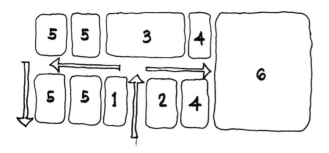

An Office

Essential Purpose ❖ People come together in offices to perform work related to their line of business: the work is part of the process of performing some service (medical, legal, design, and so on). The nature of the work is typically administrative and involves the production and communication of information through documents transmitted by manual and electronic means.

Means of Achieving Purpose ❖ Typical tasks include talking on the phone, reading and producing letters or documents, and holding meetings and presentations.

Dominant Features ❖ People, furnishings, and equipment dominate the visual field in office settings.

Basic Components ❖ The workplace consists of private offices, large open areas shared by many workers, conference rooms, and miscellaneous support areas for arriving, waiting, copying, storage, and so on.

Common Issues ❖ The amount of floor area occupied, the ratio of open to enclosed areas, and the amount of flexibility desired are some of the common issues encountered.

Critical Aspects ❖ Space efficiency, the interface with technology, and the accommodation of changing needs are some of the critical aspects.

Particularities of the Experience ❖ Most activities are performed at a workstation, a desk, or a conference table. There is a marked increase in the use of computers. Workers do most of their work while sitting, except when in transit between areas or when standing and presenting. Work is performed individu-

ally as well as in teams. Depending on the type of office, a number of visitors (clients or customers) will stop by every day.

Opportunities ❖ Office environments can easily be boring because of the constant repetition of elements and tasks and the need for economy. There are many opportunities for designers to manipulate the sense of order to achieve an appropriate level for the office's size and level of complexity. Design interventions provide enrichment and can be explored for both circulation and stationary areas to add interest and variety for workers. Given the wide variety of corporate personalities, it is also possible to manipulate expressive components to seek a proper fit between the company and its environment.

Prototype ❖ It is somewhat difficult to describe a generic office without discussing subtypes since offices vary significantly from subtype to subtype. Even among generic offices there are major differences between the open office plan and the closed plan. For the purposes of generating a workable prototypical plan we will use a combination of open and closed areas (Figure 5.14).

A Restaurant

Essential Purpose ❖ The basic purpose of a restaurant is to provide the patron with a meal. The experience of dining out, however, can satisfy more than the need for food. Other potential benefits include the convenience of not having to prepare the meal, the quality of the meal (sensual gratification), the quality of the service (pampering), and the quality of the overall experience (entertainment, shared activity, and so on).

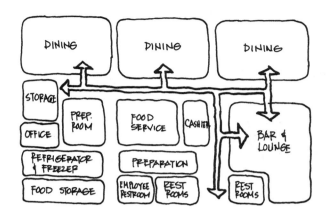

Figure 5.15 Prototypical diagram of a restaurant. Notice how the functions are divided by the circulation into front-of-the-house functions (top and right), and back-of-the-house functions (bottom left quadrant).

Means of Achieving Purpose ❖ A meal selected by the patron is prepared on the premises and served at a table or counter.

Dominant Features ❖ Tables and chairs dominate a restaurant. There is often a bar as well. Amount and type of decorations vary from case to case.

Basic Components ❖ Despite the differences, there are common factors in restaurants. As we saw earlier, they feature front- and back-of-the-house activities. The most important components are the kitchen and the dining areas. Other components include bars, an entry foyer with a waiting area, a cashier station, and restrooms.

Common Issues ❖ Issues include decisions about the kind of restaurant, and thus, the kind of experience to provide. What's the menu? What's the atmosphere like? Important decisions need to be made about the levels of privacy, sound, and light to be offered. Other issues involve the subdivision of space and traffic patterns.

Critical Aspects ❖ Restaurants are tricky businesses and often fail. Many of the critical aspects for success (such as location, target population, number of tables, menu choice, and quality of food and service) are outside the control of the designer. Providing an appealing, comfortable, and efficient backdrop to the show performed by the cast of employees is the contribution of the designer.

Particularities of the Experience ❖ For the patron, the majority of the experience takes place while sitting at a table. The patron's focus can be directed at the table and its contents, towards accompanying guests, or towards views away from the table, either within the restaurant or outside it. For the staff, the experience varies widely depending on whether they are kitchen staff, wait staff, bar staff, or management staff.

Opportunities ❖ Spatially, the biggest opportunities in restaurant design are those involving the subdivision of space and the placement of tables to create desired levels of privacy as well as connection. Additionally, there are above-average decorative opportunities given the thematic character of many restaurants.

Prototype ❖ The experience in a restaurant can vary depending on whether one is there to get a quick, inexpensive, practical meal or to experience an unforgettable meal in a luxurious setting while being pampered by the wait staff. As with retail stores, there are many variations depending on the type of food served, the location, the clientele, and so on. Figure 5.15 shows a prototypical diagram for a generic restaurant.

A Library

Essential Purpose ❖ A library is a building where recorded knowledge is stored and made available to the public. The public sometimes looks at the materials in the library. However, materials are often borrowed and taken home for limited periods of time at the end of which they must be returned. A strict control of materials leaving the facility is necessary in order to avoid theft.

Means of Achieving Purpose ❖ Knowledge finds its way to users through various media. Information is stored in books and other media such as audio, video, and CD-ROMS. Computer usage is becoming widely

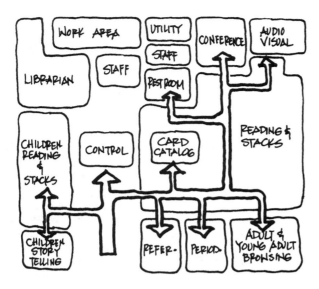

Figure 5.16 Prototypical diagram for a small community library.

prevalent and is already transforming the way we store and distribute knowledge.

Dominant Features ❖ Dominant elements in public areas are book stacks to store books, carrels and tables for people to use, and computers to perform searches.

Basic Components ❖ These include a prominently situated control desk, staff areas, search areas with computers, and public areas with stacks and tables. In public community libraries, there is often a division between the adult and childrens' sections. Specialized areas include a section for periodicals and one for audio/video materials.

Common Issues ❖ A challenging issue with libraries is distributing zones in order to achieve a good balance between stacks and reading areas as well as between quiet and loud areas.

Critical Aspects ❖ The back-of-the-house activities in libraries are essential for their proper functioning. Adequate facilities to receive, catalog, and distribute books are imperative. Environmental and sunlight controls to protect books and a proper control point near the exit to monitor people leaving the facility are also important.

Particularities of the Experience ❖ For the library user, activities include searching for materials (first at a computer and then physically searching for the material in the aisles), reading or studying the materials within the library, and checking out materials. A library scene involves a combination of transitory patrons looking for materials, settled ones enjoying the materials found, and others returning books or checking out new ones.

Opportunities ❖ Libraries require orientation and clarity. For that reason, order is paramount in libraries. Subtle design gestures to enhance experience are adequate as long as they don't dominate and distract the user. The same is true of attempts to provide expression.

Prototype ❖ Figure 5.16 shows a prototypical diagram for a community library.

A Theater

Essential Purpose ❖ The theater brings audience and actors together. The actors dramatize aspects of reality and present them in focused, heightened ways that help the audience experience them much more intensely than in real life.

Means of Achieving Purpose ❖ The theater achieves its purpose via live performances of theatrical productions.

Dominant Features ❖ Theaters are examples of functions dominated by a central principal space. Although there are a series of spaces (often prominent) leading to them, and many crucial spaces behind them, there is little doubt that the combination of stage and auditorium represent the heart of any theater facility.

Basic Components ❖ Like restaurants, theaters have front-of-the-house and back-of-the-house functions. The back-of-the-house functions can be quite extensive, housing dressing rooms, rehearsal rooms, costume storage rooms, workshops, and the stage itself. Front-of-the-house functions are public and include entry foyers, lobbies, and the auditorium itself.

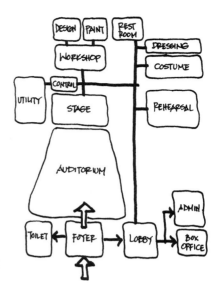

Figure 5.17 Prototypical diagram for a community theater

Common Issues ❖ The proper design of back-of-the-house spaces is always a challenge in theater design. Although not public and prominent, these need to facilitate smooth back-of-the-house operations if productions are going to be successful. Also important are all aspects of crowd management and control including means of egress in case of emergency.

Critical Aspects ❖ Because of the nature of live performances, all aspects of production (back-of-the-house activities) need to be coordinated and executed flawlessly. There are no second chances. Although the execution of the production relies heavily on the skill and preparation of the actors and the production staff, a well-functioning back-of-the-house facility is essential.

Particularities of the Experience ❖ Preshow and intermission are times when the activities of the crowds become a show in itself. Theaters are prominent public places in which to see and be seen. Once in the hall, the spatial volume of the auditorium is often impressive but when the lights are dimmed, everything vanishes except the production itself. Theater audiences experience the production while seated. There may be several thousand pairs of eyes focusing on exactly the same thing on stage at once.

Opportunities ❖ Theater design, because of its complexity, is often done by specialists. There are opportunities to make the public spaces outside the auditorium a stage of sorts where the drama and excitement of the patrons become the event, enhancing the theatricality of the whole experience. There are also opportunities to build anticipation through the progression of spaces leading to the main hall. In the main

hall, there is always the challenge of making the immense space rich and dignified when the lights are on and giving patrons something worthwhile to look at while they wait for the show to start.

Prototype ❖ Figure 5.17 shows a prototypical diagram for a community theater.

As these simple descriptions show, there are always a few essential functions intrinsic to a particular project type. Before one embarks on the design of an unknown type of project it is necessary to study and understand its type and its basic characteristics. Having this knowledge will provide a solid foundation for you from which to start to design.

Understanding the basic type is only the beginning, though. Types occur at various levels of specificity and detail. In addition to belonging to a basic type such as "store" or "office," projects are usually a **subtype** of a general type, such as "shoe store" and "interior design office." Consequently, even though the spirit of retail is similar from store to store, the requirements for, say, a shoe store and a candy store are very different. Even within the same subspecialty there are variations. A shoe store that sells exclusive Italian footwear, for instance, is likely to be organized differently than a budget family footwear store. It is necessary to think beyond the basic type of a project and consider the particularities of a project, its specific niche, approach, or philosophy. A handful of factors define the varieties within types. These include product or service offered, target customer profile, particular style or kind of product or service, level of quality, type of service or delivery, image or theme projected, and, in some instances like restaurants, type of experience

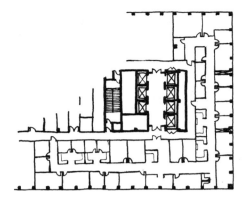

a

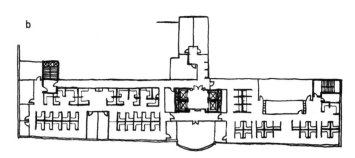

b

Figure 5.18 Two office subtypes. The investment firm on the left (a) is made up, primarily, of enclosed private offices, while the design firm on the right (b) consists, almost entirely, of open office spaces.

promoted. Let's apply these to retail stores and restaurants as examples. Consider, first, the two stores profiled below.

Store A	Store B
Product: Fashion	Product: Fashion
Store format: Small Boutique	Store format: Large Warehouse
Customer: Young Females	Customer: Entire Family
Style: Chic and Trendy	Style: Traditional
Quality and Price: Moderate	Quality and Price: Low
Service: Full-Service	Service: Self-Service
Image: Irreverent, Urban	Image: Rugged, Country

Clearly, the two profiles shown for these stores suggest different design directions, the urban boutique needing to be small, articulated, and to have some flair; the country warehouse needing to be large and rustic.

Let's now consider two restaurants.

Restaurant A	Restaurant B
Product: American Food	Product: Italian Food
Store format: Stand-alone restaurant	Store format: Leased space downtown
Customer: Family	Customer: Young Professionals
Style: Steakhouse	Style: Trattoria
Quality and Price: Moderate	Quality and Price: Moderate
Service: Table Service	Service: Table Service
Image: American Prairie	Image: Urban Casual

Here, again, the different profiles of the two restaurants are likely to result in two spatially and visually different restaurants. Despite their differences, they will both have the basic components of all restaurants, such as a waiting area, perhaps a bar, one or more dining areas, and all of the back-of-the-house spaces such as a kitchen and a storage area.

Sometimes two different subtypes imply substantially different arrangements, almost different typologies. Let's consider two different office types. A financial investment firm has different requirements from an interior design firm even though they are both office types (Figure 5.18). The investment firm consists of perimeter offices with support staff on the inside; in the interior design office the perimeter is occupied by systems furniture clusters housing the workers in a more democratic fashion.

Let's compare three different jewelry stores now. The three small stores in Figure 5.19 all share the basic components of a jewelry store: window displays up front, display cases inside, an area to complete transactions, and several back-of-the-house rooms. Yet they are different from one another in their spatial organization. What at first may appear to be differences in the designers' interpretations of a jewelry store are actually insightful responses to three slightly different approaches to selling jewelry.

Figure 5.19a features a store with a linear arrangement leading to a transaction counter centered in the back. The arrangement is simple and straightforward. Customers stand in front of the display cases at either side and move from front to back and are assisted as needed by someone standing behind the counter. Sales take place at the counter and the transaction is completed at the counter in the back. Figure 5.19b also shows a store housed in a long and narrow space. In

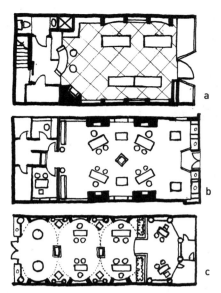

Figure 5.19 Three variations of the jewelry store. The way of conducting business transactions varies from one example to another. The store shown in (a) is the most informal. The store in (b) is a bit more formal. The store in (c) is the most formal and ceremonial.

this case, however, the linearity of the space is de-emphasized. Instead, a somewhat static space is created in the center of the store as defined by four wall protrusions and the furniture arrangement. Here the customer is encouraged not only to stand in front of a particular display case but to sit down in one of the provided chairs where they are assisted by a salesperson sitting opposite the display case. The center space reinforces the invitation to get comfortable and stay for a while. Unlike the first case, the sale occurs, and is also completed, at the display cases.

The approach to the customer/salesperson interaction in the store shown in Figure 5.19c is similar to the one in Figure 5.19b. They sit across from one another at one of the display cases. The difference here is that the store consists, not of one main space, but a progression of four spaces culminating in a formal and climatic closing area at the end. The sales transaction takes place and is completed ceremonially in a raised circular space that features two small desks; there are no transaction counters. This approach is much more formal than those of the first two stores.

Projects, then, despite forming part of a type, are specific applications of that type. Their particularities need to be known and understood. It is these particularities that give projects the nuances that make them different, and in some cases, special. They have important implications for the use, subdivision, and expression of space.

The Project's Parts and Their Functions

Few tasks are as important during the understanding stage than accounting for all the required functions, un-

---

PRESENTATION ROOM

Function
- To accommodate staff meetings and client meetings.
- The time spent in this room can range from one hour to a whole day.

Occupancy | Activities | Time

Space
- 400–500sf
- Open feel but controlled acoustically
- Basic rectangular shape to accomodate a large conference table and chairs.

Area | Height | Configuration

Relationships
- Close to the entrance and to the stairs to the e floor
- Has one wall of all windows to the outside as well as some visual access to the office insde.

To other rooms | To outside

Light & Air
- Natural light will pour in through the windows, especially because of its southern location.

→

- Adequate down lighting should be supplied to make up for lack of natural light at night and on cloudy days.
- Accent lighting shold alsol be applied to enhance the image of the office.

Natural Light | Electric | Light

Special Elements
- The focus will be the back wall seen when you walk in. It will portray the image of the company.
- A coffee area will be located inside or near the conference room.

Focus | Edges | Machines

Materials and Details
- Soft floor coverings will be used in th e conference room
- Ceiling will have an interesting cut out pattern—a kind of cove.
- The walls will be drywall with wood accents
- It will have the over all affect of an innovative and very professional room.

Character | Floor Wall | Ceiling

Figure 5.20 Design criteria for a presentation room. These requirements outline desirable features for one of the important rooms of a project and give the designer early detailed information.

derstanding how they work, and determining what kind of space and layout they require. Some functions occur only once, others repeat themselves; some are large and some small; some are really important and others not so important. Yet, they all have to be included and worked into some kind of cohesive system.

Despite a designer's familiarity with the parts of a given project type, it is only by working with a project's client and users that a list of complete requirements can be generated. The goal is to account for all functions and to learn the particular application for the given project. The type and number of spaces need to be identified and desired qualities described.

Beyond accounting for all spaces, however, it is also useful for you to set specific criteria for important and unique spaces. Figure 5.20 shows a list of requirements for the main presentation room of an advertising agency. It gives specific information about content, relationships, qualities, and so on. This programmatic

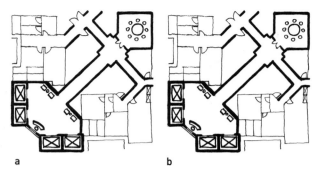

a   b

Figure 5.21 Entry sequences to two office spaces in the same building. Sequence (a) utilizes the elevator lobby space for the office's modest reception area, while sequence (b) brings the reception area inside into a grand, two-story lobby space at the heart of the office.

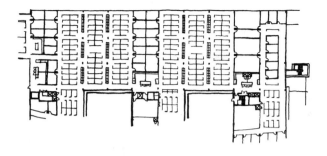

Figure 5.22 This large office space is arranged in repeated patterns of open and enclosed spaces. The design relies on the repetition of standard modules that work for the various groups of workers.

information goes beyond the minimal space names, quantities, and sizes usually given in a program. Having this kind of detailed qualitative information will fuel the search for thoughtful and detailed design solutions.

Finding out how a certain client wants to treat a given part of a project is important. You may believe that you know how to design a certain project part. Yet unless you understand the client's intentions and the particular realities of the project, you may be off target. Let's take two entry sequences to two office projects to illustrate this point.

Figure 5.21 shows entry sequences to two office suites. They occur in the same building. Both clients are relatively formal and conservative; in one case, a law firm, in the other, an accounting firm. The main difference between the two office suites is that one suite (Figure 5.21a) is a satellite office of a larger firm and the other suite (Figure 5.21b) is a one-of-a-kind main office. The client in the latter suite wants a grand reception area. The design of the elevator is not suitable to become a tall and grand space. Consequently, the lobby is used as an arrival space only, and the fancy reception area for the main office of the accounting firm is elsewhere. From there, a short formal corridor leads to the center of the suite where a grand two-story space serves as the reception area. It, in turn, serves as a gateway to the rest of the office, completing the entry sequence. The reception area for the law firm, in contrast, occurs within the elevator lobby itself. The modest reception space is appropriate for the client's modest intention. From it one proceeds through a formal corridor, similar to the one shown in Figure 5.21b,

that leads to an internal conference room straight ahead and to the rest of the office on either side.

Collecting detailed project information can be an arduous task. Few clients will have it available and ready to use. The existing facilities of the client may not be a good or complete example of what is desired for the new facility. It often takes a multitude of meetings, needs surveys, field observations, and several checkpoints to compile an acceptable list of project parts and their requirements. The process of collecting this information occurs during programming. You may or may not be involved in the process. In cases where you have not been involved, it is a good practice to check the validity of the program. A program may have been done several months (or years) earlier and requirements may have changed, or a program may have been hastily put together to get a general idea of the project and may not be totally accurate.

Projects do not always consist of unique parts. A project's overall scheme is often the result of the repeated occurrence of typical parts. These parts are usually specific sections or departments within a project. Sometimes it is the aggregate created by the addition of many units of the same part that determines the overall layout of the project. An example of this would be an office project composed of the repetition of typical neighborhoods. Such is the case in the two office projects shown in Figure 5.22 and Figure 5.23. The layout of the office in Figure 5.22 consists of neighborhoods comprised of rows of workstations forming three successive groups of 8 to 12 workers separated by banks of files. These neighborhoods are bounded on either side by bands of enclosed spaces

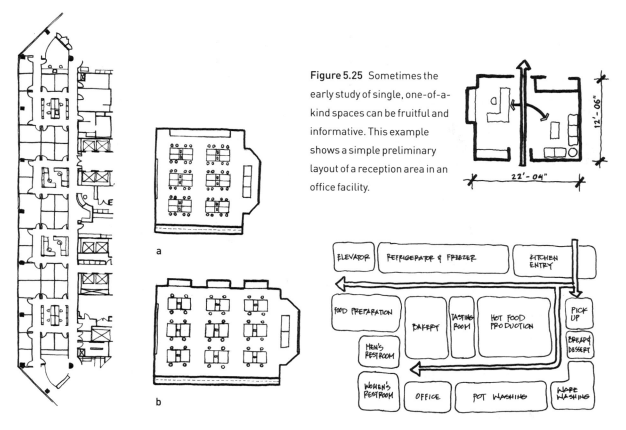

Figure 5.25 Sometimes the early study of single, one-of-a-kind spaces can be fruitful and informative. This example shows a simple preliminary layout of a reception area in an office facility.

12'-06"

22'-04"

ELEVATOR   REFRIGERATOR & FREEZER   KITCHEN ENTRY

FOOD PREPARATION   BAKERY   TASTING ROOM   HOT FOOD PRODUCTION   PICK UP

BREAD & DESSERT

MEN'S RESTROOM

WOMEN'S RESTROOM   OFFICE   POT WASHING   WARE WASHING

a

b

Figure 5.23 This office is also arranged in modules, although quite different from the ones shown in Figure 5.22. Here the scale of the space is smaller and private enclosed offices predominate.

Figure 5.24 Two typical modules of teaching laboratories to be used (and repeated) in the planning of a science academic facility.

Figure 5.26 Another example of a single space worth understanding early on is the kitchen of a restaurant. Its importance lies in the need of optimal relationships among its various parts to facilitate a smooth and productive operation.

consisting of offices, conference rooms, and miscellaneous support spaces. This arrangement represents the basic neighborhood unit, which is then repeated.

The typical module of the office in Figure 5.23 consists of a U-shaped arrangement of offices with workstations for secretarial staff inside the space created by the configuration. Here again, the module repeats itself. It is subject to some modifications at the ends and near the center where two office spaces are combined to create a conference room. In both these cases we see how modules, or neighborhoods, are assembled from the repetition of basic units and these, once determined, are themselves repeated giving the plan its basic configuration.

Sometimes, understanding project parts early on is necessary even when the total plan will not be made up of their repetition. Such is the case, for example,

with specialty teaching labs for a science building. Figure 5.24 shows several layouts for the teaching labs which suggest certain optimal arrangements and dimensions for these rooms. These arrangements, once optimized, become critical for the development of the section of the floor plan where they occur.

Other times, a highly specialized part, occurring just once, is important enough to merit the designer's detailed attention during the early stages of a project. Such is the case of the reception area in an office (Figure 5.25) or the kitchen in a restaurant (Figure 5.26). The reception area is an important component of an office's public side and, thus, one the designer wants to address early in the project. The kitchen is the hidden heart of a restaurant operation. It needs to be conceived appropriately from the beginning, as it represents a large area of the total restaurant footprint.

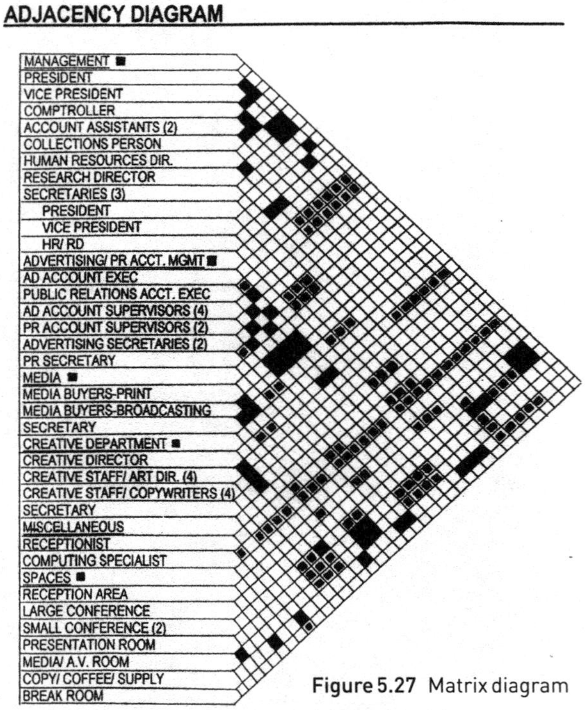

ADJACENCY DIAGRAM
MANAGEMENT ■
PRESIDENT
VICE PRESIDENT
COMPTROLLER
ACCOUNT ASSISTANTS (2)
COLLECTIONS PERSON
HUMAN RESOURCES DIR.
RESEARCH DIRECTOR
SECRETARIES (3)
PRESIDENT
VICE PRESIDENT
HR/ RD
ADVERTISING/ PR ACCT. MGMT ■
AD ACCOUNT EXEC
PUBLIC RELATIONS ACCT. EXEC
AD ACCOUNT SUPERVISORS (4)
PR ACCOUNT SUPERVISORS (2)
ADVERTISING SECRETARIES (2)
PR SECRETARY
MEDIA ■
MEDIA BUYERS-PRINT
MEDIA BUYERS-BROADCASTING
SECRETARY
CREATIVE DEPARTMENT ■
CREATIVE DIRECTOR
CREATIVE STAFF/ ART DIR. (4)
CREATIVE STAFF/ COPYWRITERS (4)
SECRETARY
MISCELLANEOUS
RECEPTIONIST
COMPUTING SPECIALIST
SPACES ■
RECEPTION AREA
LARGE CONFERENCE
SMALL CONFERENCE (2)
PRESENTATION ROOM
MEDIA/ A.V. ROOM
COPY/ COFFEE/ SUPPLY
BREAK ROOM

Figure 5.27 Matrix diagram for an advertising agency.

NURSING
HEALTH CENTER
NURSERY
SERVICE
ADJUNCT DIAGNOSTIC FACILITY
SURGERY
DELIVERY
OUT PATIENT DEPT.
EMERG.
ADMIN.

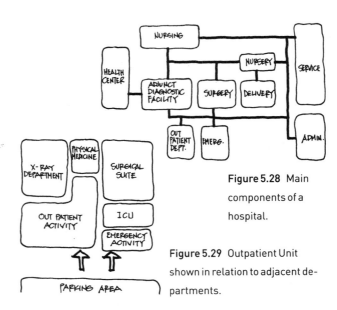

Figure 5.28 Main components of a hospital.

X-RAY DEPARTMENT
PHYSICAL MEDICINE
SURGICAL SUITE
OUT PATIENT ACTIVITY
ICU
EMERGENCY ACTIVITY
PARKING AREA

Figure 5.29 Outpatient Unit shown in relation to adjacent departments.

Relationship among the Various Parts

The next thing to understand about project parts is how they relate. Project parts need to be accommodated in the project site in such a way that they fit and work together, sort of like a puzzle. In order to assemble the project's puzzle, it is necessary to combine parts into groups. These groups, in turn, are assembled as a project. In this section we will focus on parts and groups.

One of the basic ways to structure a system of parts is by analyzing desired adjacencies. This is done by determining which parts a particular component needs to be in close proximity to, and which ones it should maintain some distance from. You can think in terms of three basic relationships between parts: attraction, indifference, and repulsion. You probably are familiar with this practice and have some experience using the adjacency matrices and diagrams normally used to illustrate adjacency information graphically. These graphic tools can be useful and convenient. In fact, one of the first things young designers learn is how to apply them.

However, you need to be cautioned that these tools, if used incorrectly, especially in large and complex projects, can also burden and confuse. The potential danger with the use of adjacency matrices and bubble diagrams is one of unnecessary fragmentation. It is common practice, especially among young designers, to indiscriminately list every single space given in the program on both axes of an adjacency matrix and start indicating desired relationships between spaces. This is problematic for two reasons. First, it creates an unnecessary burden in projects other than the most simple. Second, it tends to promote a myopic view of the project encouraging the analysis of fragmented parts only in terms of how any two parts relate to each other. While the relationship of many pairs of spaces or project parts to each other is important, not every pair of parts needs to be examined against each other, as you will see. See Figure 5.27.

The unit used for the analysis of adjacencies does not need to be the individual space. Although this will work well for small projects, it will be unsuitable for large ones. The advertising agency example of Figure 5.27 shows how the use of the matrix can become cumbersome when projects are not small. Adjacencies of large projects are best done hierarchically. Early on, your goal is to understand the project in terms of its systems or groupings. This approach will accelerate your understanding of the project and save you valuable time. The size of the beginning unit will depend on the size and complexity of the project. The initial search for relationship between parts should be for these groupings. The first question asked should not be about the relationship between any two parts. Instead, the questions should be what are the basic groups in this project? And then, what are their parts?

A hospital, a project of considerable complexity, should serve to illustrate the points made above. If you were to list all the components of a hospital on the two

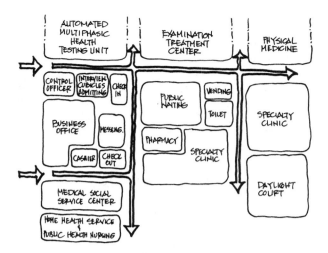

Figure 5.30 Intradepartmental diagram of Outpatient Unit.

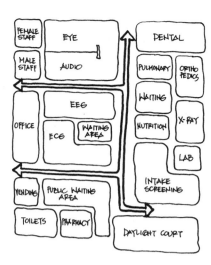

Figure 5.31 Components and relationships within Specialty Clinics area in the Outpatient Unit.

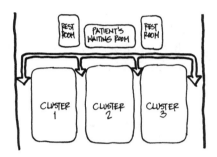

Figure 5.32 Outpatient Unit's Examination Treatment Center components and relationships.

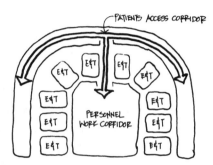

Figure 5.33 Examination Treatment Center clusters' components and relationships.

axes of an adjacency matrix and get information from hospital experts about ideal adjacencies, two things would happen. It would take a very long time to make sense of all the information and you would find out that many pairs of spaces or functions have no relationship. It would be difficult to arrange many spaces in relationship to everything else due to ambiguous data. Approaching the search hierarchically would help you make sense of the project. Several levels of hierarchy are necessary for such a complex building type.

Let's start with the basic components of a general hospital. Data at this general level would produce a diagram, as shown in Figure 5.28, that seems manageable. Every one of the components shown, however, has a complex internal organization of its own. Let's take the outpatient unit next to the emergency area to illustrate this. Figure 5.29 shows its relationship to the other units of the hospital. Figure 5.30 shows a diagram of the components within the outpatient unit and their relationships. If we focus on the specialty

clinics a new set of relationships at another hierarchical level is revealed (Figure 5.31). Similarly, if we go back to Figure 5.30 and focus on the examination treatment center we see it is subdivided into various clusters as shown in Figure 5.32, which, in turn, are assembled of the components shown in Figure 5.33. Investigating relationships between components of this outpatient unit is necessary and relevant, but seeking relationships between the detailed components of this unit and those of say, the administration of the hospital, would not be. Taking small parts out of context (without regard to their departments) and trying to understand their relationship would be highly unproductive and confusing.

At the appropriate level in the hierarchy, determining desired adjacencies between pairs of spaces is both necessary and useful. Here, again, matrices and bubble diagrams can be both helpful and limiting. They are helpful because they give us a general idea of desired adjacency between any two spaces. They are

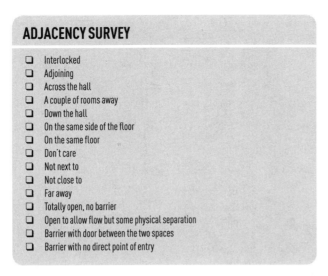

Figure 5.34 Adjacency Survey form.

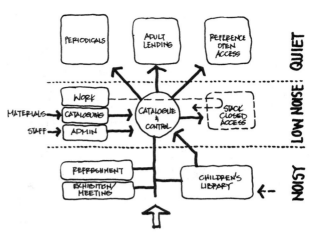

Figure 5.35 Acoustical zoning diagram for a library based on noise levels.

limiting because they lack detail and nuance, and, therefore, fail to tell the full story.

Most adjacency matrices and diagrams distinguish the various levels of adjacency desirability among spaces such as high priority, medium priority, and low priority. While this is helpful, it will seldom give us enough information to introduce specificity and nuance in our designs. A more complete and helpful approach would be one expressing desirable relationships between spaces utilizing three kinds of data: the level of proximity desired, the importance of achieving that level of proximity, and, for adjacent spaces, the nature of the desired connection/separation between the two spaces.

In addition to proximity, determining a desire for distance is also important. Figure 5.34 has a useful list of these possibilities. It lists a range of possible relationships between units. These relationships range from a desire for close proximity to a desire for great distance. Figure 5.34 also incorporates a way to express the degree of importance of the request as well as a means of indicating the degree of connection between adjacent spaces.

Issues other than the functional adjacency needs between project parts are also helpful to determine how to group the parts. These issues arise because of common characteristics or needs of spaces otherwise functionally unrelated. They include grouping according to privacy needs (public vs. private), according to degree of acoustic quality (loud vs. quiet), according to degree of accessibility (accessible vs. remote), according to need of exposure to exterior (internal vs. external), and according to enclosure extent (open vs. enclosed). These criteria will frequently bring together spaces that otherwise don't need to be together, unless, of course, doing so creates other functional problems. Figure 5.35 shows a diagram of a library organized by acoustical zones.

Synergy: Efficiency and Impact

Good projects achieve efficiencies and effects that go beyond the additive result of their individual components. Three important strategies that help achieve this are creating spaces that serve more than one function or can be shared; creating meaningful use of space between the programmed spaces; and creating spaces that add up to more than the sum of their parts in ways other than function.

Spaces that can be shared include conference and workrooms shared by departments in office settings and classrooms shared by different units in schools. Spaces that serve more than one function can include theater lobbies, community rooms in offices and civic facilities, and the well-known cafetorium (cafeteria/auditorium combination) in some school settings. This sharing results in economies for all the groups involved.

Meaningful in-between spaces can sometimes be added to projects to enhance the experience of their users. This is often the case in large projects where pockets along the circulation and off main public areas provide spaces for users to congregate, rest, or just stop for a moment to reflect or perform a secondary activity. You may recall our discussion of nodes in Chapter 3.

The principle of spaces adding up to more than the sum of their parts was eloquently expressed by Charles Moore while talking about house design. "A good house will have resonances that extend beyond a set of discrete elements. The principle is that, in the assembly of parts, one plus one must equal more than two … to make one plus one equal more than two you must, in doing any one thing you think important, (making rooms, putting them together, or fitting them to the land) do something else that you think important as well (make spaces to live in, establish a meaningful pattern inside, or claim other realms outside)."7 The way to give special qualities to otherwise plain and utilitarian spaces and functions requires purpose and resolve beyond the mere assembly of parts in functional ways. That's where order, enrichment, and expression come in. These start to emerge during ideation, the topic of our next chapter.

Affordances | CAPSULE

You may wonder, with good reason, to what extent the built environment can influence human behavior. This is a difficult question, but we can provide an acceptable answer with the help of James J. Gibson's concept of affordances.[1] This term is derived from "to afford" but does not exist as such in the dictionary. As conceived by Gibson, it refers to the way the particular configuration or arrangement of an object or setting makes it suitable for some overt activity. The horizontality of a concrete slab on the ground together with the natural law of gravity afford the possibility of walking on it with ease. The covered shelter at the park affords a good refuge when it rains. One does not necessarily have to run towards the shelter when it starts to pour outside, but the potential for refuge is there for those who desire it.

A good amount of what designers do is to create environmental opportunities and constraints. As seen from the examples above, the presence and arrangement of certain features encourage and facilitate certain actions and behaviors. Similarly, the absence or specific arrangement of certain features eliminate or discourage certain actions or behaviors. If the slab mentioned above was on a very steep incline instead of being flat, walking on it would be made difficult for most people. Incidentally, the neighborhood's young and daring skateboarders would probably be delighted with the possibilities created by the inclined arrangement. At the park, if the shelter was not provided, one would not have the potential for refuge against the rain. Cover from the rain would be impossible, not because of imposed difficulty, but because of the omission of a sheltering structure.

Designers have great control over the provision or omission of features. They also enjoy considerable control over the specific arrangements of a project's parts and pieces. By manipulating these variables they encourage certain behaviors and discourage others in response to the needs of the project. The environments they design, with all their inherent affordances represent an environment full of potential. However, just because certain affordances are provided does not necessarily mean that they will be used, or even noticed. Perception of the possibilities offered by the environment varies depending on the straightforwardness of the affordance as well as the needs and motivations of the people using it. Motivations are particularly significant in determining whether and how a presented affordance is interpreted. As a result, sometimes the same condition is interpreted differently by different people. The half-open window in the house kitchen, for example, affords exposure to fresh air for the occupant, but it also affords a potential burglar an opportunity to get into the house.

Affordances occur at various levels of explicitness and sophistication. Many affordances are direct and obviously related to the requirements of the program, such as the provision of a desk, a chair, and four solid walls for someone who works in an office and needs privacy. Others are less tangible but work in subtle ways to influence behavior, such as the act of progressively widening a corridor to encourage movement in a particular direction. Still others serve secondary, and even nonprogrammed desirable activities. These are often the most rewarding ones and the ones responsible for creating great environments. Just by being conscious of human nature and tendencies, the thoughtful designer can add meaningful gestures to a project. A place to rest somewhere in the middle of an excessively long path is likely to be used and appreciated by many users. It would be good to have it whether the program asked for it or not.

Other affordances can allow secondary activities in certain places, or even the transformation of those places in order to perform double duty. The introduction of comfortable lounge seating in many bookstores has transformed them from places to browse, buy, and leave, to places where lingering in comfort is strongly encouraged. Likewise, providing a strategically placed pivoting or otherwise moving panel can, on demand, transform two moderately sized rooms into a large one suitable to host the periodic all-staff meeting or annual open-house party in an office setting. Window sills of such construction, height, and depth as to permit sitting may help increase the seating capacity in the new "great room"

during those special occasions.

Therefore, it is through the ability of built environments to invite certain activities and discourage others that they often exert their strongest influence on behavior. The concept of affordance is a useful one. You may start thinking of different ways of arranging or detailing parts of projects in order to add humanizing gestures, support secondary activities, and create areas that serve double duty. You may also want to look at your designs and see how they can discourage undesirable or inappropriate behaviors. You may also check for unintentional invitations or denials. The concept of affordance implies that there are many different degrees of a space's permissiveness related to any specific behavior. At one extreme, you can create conditions that not only allow, but actually mandate a certain behavior, such as when entering a corridor with turnstiles that will not let you go back, thus imposing one particular type of action, forward movement. At the other extreme, you can deny access to an area from a given side by having a solid wall between the two areas. In between these extremes, affordances can exhibit different intermediate degrees of invitation or denial, such as strong invitation, subtle encouragement, possibility without encouragement, possibility with some difficulty (discouragement), or very difficult possibility (strong discouragement). As the designer, you are the permission granter. Think hard and choose wisely.

---

1 James Gibson. *An Ecological Approach to Visual Perception*, (Houghton Mifflin: Boston, 1979).

Review

Summary

Designers need to understand the specific realities of the projects they design. The basic understanding of a project should be acquired during the predesign process. In general, you need to get a good understanding of the realities of the context, the internal players, and those of the project itself.

All projects occur within, and are influenced by, specific historic, cultural, and geographic contexts. Additionally, and varying from project to project, are the contextual realities of both the immediate surroundings of a project and the building in which it occurs.

The immediate neighborhood provides an important context with specific adjacent buildings, important long-standing patterns, and so on. The site and nearby surroundings provide specific natural features, circulation patterns, and points of access to the building. Environmental features such as the sun path, climate, sounds, sights, and smells are also crucial considerations.

The building in which the project takes place also offers an important context at an even more immediate scale. Particular aspects to be analyzed include the other neighbors in the building and the public circulation inside the building. Additionally, it is necessary to analyze the physical features of the space designated for the project. A thorough understanding of the space's size, geometry, internal components, perimeter conditions, views to the outside, and so on always provides essential information.

Another important aspect requiring proper understanding is the nature of the project's internal players, usually the client and the users. The users are those people the building is intended for. The building must, by all accounts, work for them and their own particular circumstances.

Perhaps the most important aspect requiring understanding is the project itself. All projects are instances of project types that have been designed and built before. Therefore, there is a substantial body of examples and knowledge about most building types, as well as built examples, often nearby. Every type also has different applications, or subtypes. Even among different subtypes, there are specific variations like those among different kinds of clothing stores.

The specific requirements of the project must also be understood. Each part and its role in the overall scheme needs to be identified and understood. Additionally, the relationships among parts and their hierarchical status need to be analyzed.

Chapter Questions

1. Name and describe the four contextual aspects discussed under surroundings.
2. Name and describe the three contextual inside-the-buildings aspects discussed.
3. Explain the difference between clients and users.
4. Think of as many subtypes as you can for different kinds of retail stores, restaurants, and offices.
5. Name the various adjacency categories mentioned in this chapter.

6. What factors other than adjacencies can assist in grouping project parts besides adjacencies?

Exercises

1. Analyze the building that houses your design department. Use diagrams to illustrate significant factors for the building's interior and the building's surroundings.

2. Analyze the building that serves as context to the project you are currently working on in your design studio. Use diagrams to illustrate significant exterior and interior factors.

3. Perform a typological profile study similar to the ones shown in this chapter for a church, your school building, a movie theater, and a sky club.

4. Produce a series of detailed bubble adjacency diagrams for your current project. Proceed hierarchically. First, do one diagram of the main project parts, and then proceed to do one for each major department or section.

Endnotes

1 Pelli, Cesar. *Observations for Young Architects*, (Monacelli Press: New York, 1999) p. 126.

2 Moore, C., Allen, G. & Lyndon, D. *The Place of Houses*, (Holt, Rinehard, & Winston: New York, 1974) p. 102.

3 Ibid, p. 173.

4 Vitruvius. *The Ten Books of Architecture*, translated by Morris Hicky Morgan, (Dover Publications: New York, 1960) pp. 180–181.

5 Pelli, C. p., 181.

6 Heinsath, C. *Behavioral Architecture: Toward an Accountable Design Process*, (McGraw-Hill: New York, 1977) p. 52.

7 Moore, pp. 147–148.

CHAPTER 6

Ideation

INSTRUCTIONAL OBJECTIVES

Explain the meaning and function of concepts in design.

Explain the difference between different types of concepts.

Identify the stages of concept development.

Present an approach to spatial organization using the place elements.

Explain how to select a design idea among dominant issues.

Suggest ways of formulating concept ideas.

Explain how to draw parti and functional concept diagrams.

Explain how to prepare graphically strong concept diagrams.

n Chapter 5 we looked at some of the variables that make each project unique such as the users, context, and program. We also explained the importance of making sense of large amounts of information and reviewed some of the graphic tools designers use to account for project requirements and their relationships.

At the conclusion of the analysis stage you should have a good understanding of the client's nature, the project's parts, how these relate, and the context (physical, cultural, and historical) in which the project will take place. In some cases, you may even have a preliminary vision for a potential design solution.

The design stage that follows, **ideation**, is one of the most critical for successful design. It is also one of the most challenging. After all the project entities have been accounted for, their relationships understood and diagrammed many times over, designers have to come up with the project's concept, a paralyzing moment in the design process for many of them. Chapter 6 is about the process of going from an understanding of the project and its requirements to the production of one or more insightful concepts that respond to its unique circumstances. The chapter focuses on the importance of achieving a proper fit between the realities of the project and the chosen organizational structure for the project. The main topic is the design concept, with a particular focus on the organizational concept. As you will see, early decisions made during this stage of design become the foundations upon which the rest of the design is built. It is essential, then, that they are sound and fitting.

The Search for Fit

Contemporary interior design practice has changed dramatically, evolving from a primarily decorative discipline to one responsible for the solution of an ever-increasing number of design problems. Designers, especially commercial designers, are hired to provide solutions to projects with complex and often conflicting requirements. An office may want to reduce the amount of leased space while increasing morale and productivity; a store may want to emphasize certain merchandise without a decrease in sales of the de-emphasized merchandise; a restaurant may want to increase seating capacity while preserving a sense of intimacy. Good solutions to these types of problems require imagination and insight on the one hand, as well as balance and compromise on the other.

The concept of fit in design refers to the appropriate correspondence between a set of requirements or needs and the design solution that addresses them. It is analogous to the well-known correspondence between clothing and our bodies. Using this familiar analogy you can easily recall instances of great fit, adequate fit, and tight fit related to comfort. You may also recall instances when a dress or a pair of jeans were comfortable, but were not the right style, or when they fit comfortably and were stylistically appropriate, but were not appropriate for the occasion for which you needed them. Similarly, the concept of fit in interior design is concerned with issues of comfort, style, and occasion. One of its unique challenges, however, is that with interior design, concepts start

with no predetermined form. Where in fashion you always know you are designing for the human body with its predictable form and structure (despite the infinite small particularities within this structure), in contemporary interior design you not only dress the "body," you shape it!

Despite the fact that interior projects always occur within a predetermined enclosure, the number, size, and distribution of parts vary, depending on the requirements of the project. Instead of always designing for the same body, you arrange and distribute parts in custom-made ways to fit the particularities of each project. A big part of a designer's challenge, then, is to determine what this form (body) needs to be to fulfill the requirements of the project.

The ideation stage, more than any other, is responsible for establishing the project's basic fit. It is during this stage of design that the basic overall decisions concerning placement, shape, and orientation of places are made. Also decided are issues of the proper relationship of parts to their enclosures and of parts to each other. The process of assembling places and functions, as you will see, involves much more than transposing relationship diagrams to the given floor plan and drawing walls at the edges. This rarely produces a satisfying design. A successful design requires the inclusion and organization of all required functions within a coherent yet varied structure that will make users' experiences both orderly and engaging. This is seldom accomplished without an insightful and fitting overall basic strategy, also known as the **design concept.**

The main outcome of the ideation phase is, not sur-

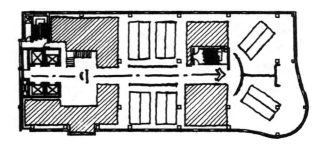

Figure 6.1 Functional concept diagram for an office space.

prisingly, a design concept for the project. It is eventually developed, refined, and articulated to achieve the desired balance between fit, order, enrichment, and expression.

The Concept

Successful projects are not made from a summation of places that fulfill functional requirements. A successful design possesses a structure that is uniquely derived from the requirements of the project and a character that reflects its nature and personality. These are the attributes that give the project a real sense of identity.

The first basic ingredient you need for a congruent and meaningful design is a strong and fitting design concept. Yet the notion of design concept remains one of the most misunderstood among interior design students. Part of the blame for this can be attributed to the myriad of existing definitions for the concept as well as the mystical connotations implied by some of them. Furthermore, no clear explanation of the process of generating concepts exists to help students learn how to devise them.

What is a Design Concept?

The American Heritage Dictionary defines concept as "a general idea or understanding, especially one derived from specific instances or occurrences."[1] Based on this definition, a concept in environmental design could be a general strategy or approach for the solution of a design problem having specific circum-

stances. A design concept aims to define appropriate responses that help generate a specific approach to solve a design problem. Projects, however, are made up of many problems of different scopes and levels of importance. Solutions to each of them require the use of strategies that will produce fitting solutions. Each one of these ideas or strategies is a concept. There can, in fact, be dozens of concepts for a single project!

In order to work with concepts, then, you have to be able to understand their hierarchy. There are big concepts and little ones. It's the big concepts that we are most concerned with here, although the smaller ones are important to resolve design issues at more detailed levels. Figure 6.1 shows a functional concept diagram for an office project. It conveys the overall scheme. The sketches in Figure 6.2 show more detailed functional concepts for a specific area at the rear of the space. These are concepts too, but on a smaller scale.

Every project needs a concept at the overall project scale to give the design approach some coherence. This **main concept** helps to tie the entire project together by providing a dominant structure or idea that all other design ideas adhere to. While the distinction between major and minor concepts and the need for one big concept may seem plausible enough, there are still some nuances that need to be understood in order to grasp how to use concepts in design. The main questions that need to be answered are: What does the main project concept consist of? How did it come about? And, is there only one kind of main concept?

A major misconception about design concepts is the belief that they consist of one single big idea. While

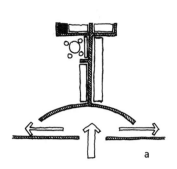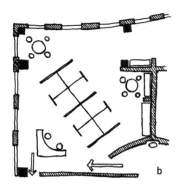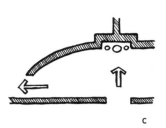

Figure 6.2 Localized concept ideas for the rear of the office project shown.

some main concepts may consist of a single idea, most consist of a handful of ideas that, together, constitute a single approach. Students are often paralyzed by the difficulty of having to synthesize an entire project into one idea. A concept consisting of a single idea is not realistic in most cases. Thinking in terms of a series of ideas pointing to one dominant approach is a more realistic proposition.

Another misleading notion is the thought that concept ideas arise out of spontaneous flashes of inspiration. Again, this is far from the truth and neither students nor practitioners should sit and wait for such flashes to strike. The generation of concept ideas involves a great deal of systematic thinking and analysis. Although it is true that after a thorough analysis of the design problem and a period of incubation ideas may arise spontaneously, there are no guarantees this will happen. The best advice is to approach the process systematically and rely more on rational thinking than on flashes of inspiration.

There are several kinds of main concepts, and this can further confuse the student trying to understand how to use design concepts. Concepts can be philosophical (less is more; equal amount of space for all, and so on), thematic (a western bar), functional (a two wing configuration separating two distinct groups), artistic (a balanced composition of bold colors), mood-related (a place that induces tranquility), or stylistic (a space that projects a futuristic outlook while remaining rooted in past tradition). Which kind does one choose? Does one adopt them all? These are all important considerations. How can one arrive at only one dominant concept then?

You may begin to realize the challenge of working with and selecting "the concept among concepts." How is it done? First, it is useful to divide interior design concepts into two broad categories: organizational concepts and character concepts. **Organizational concepts** are those that guide the arrangement of space. They provide an approach for the placement of, division among, and relation between spaces and parts in a project. These tend to be the more straightforward of the two. **Character concepts** are those related to style, image, or theme. They involve decisions about the stylistic approach for the project and the selection of related surface treatments, furnishings, and miscellaneous objects. They can also, to some extent, influence the arrangement of space. Character concepts are less pragmatic, and, consequently, more elusive.

Both these types of concepts are crucial for the project, and certainly interrelated. Of the two types, the organizational concept is the most useful for generating floor plans, their organization and sequence; in other words, organizational concepts are the ones directly linked to the shaping of interior space.

Given our focus on spatial design, we will concentrate our discussion on organizational concepts. Chapter 9, on expression, deals with some of the considerations that help shape the more elusive, and subjective, character concepts.

Goals of Concepts

We have made an important distinction between organizational concepts, those which inform the organization and layout of a project, and character concepts,

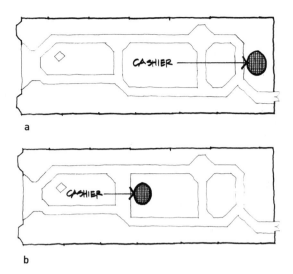

a

b

Figure 6.3 Two cashier schemes for a small retail store are shown here. Plan (a) fails to fulfill a basic functional requirement of stores: to have a central cashier location from which to monitor customers.

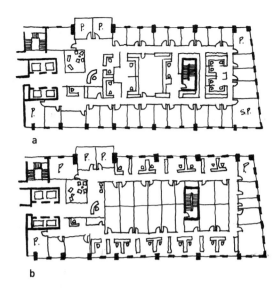

a

b

Figure 6.4 Scheme (a) is a better response to a given programmatic requirement to arrange private offices along the exterior perimeter of the building.

those which inform the image and identity of the project. The former help you to establish a scheme, the latter give it a personality. What exactly should you try to achieve through the organizational concept?

A good organizational concept does several important things. First and foremost, it establishes a responsive scheme to be developed. It is the organizational idea behind the scheme. Additionally, it provides a strong foundation for order, enrichment, and expression. We will examine each of these separately.

Establishing a Responsive Scheme

The **scheme** you develop from your concept must represent an appropriate response to the project type, its particular programmatic requirements, and the context in which it occurs. The fundamental organizational issues of a project (as opposed to the more detailed ones) are resolved at this stage. The examples below show both successful and unsuccessful early schemes in response to type, program, and context. Figure 6.3 shows two schemes for a small retail store. One of the basic functional requirements of a store as a type is that the cashier station be located centrally in order to visually monitor shoppers. Therefore, one of the most important functional considerations in developing a scheme for a store is the proper location of the cashier function. The plan in Figure 6.3a does not solve this requirement because the cashier is placed too far back in the store. The plan in Figure 6.3b is

more successful, placing the cashier centrally and closer to the front.

Figure 6.4 shows two designs for a law firm. The user has clearly stated a programmatic requirement that all the private offices be on the perimeter by a window. The scheme in Figure 6.4b, however considerate to the support staff, is wrong for this application. The scheme in Figure 6.4a is more responsive to the request of perimeter offices.

Figure 6.5 shows two schemes for a casual restaurant in a northern climate. The restaurant faces a pleasant pedestrian alley on the eastern side, a lively street with shops on the northern side, and a service alley on the western side. Both schemes shown are workable. However, Figure 6.5b takes better advantage of the desirable exposure to the northern street and the pedestrian alley to the east and, thus, responds better to the particular contextual realities of the site. These examples, however simple and obvious, help to illustrate fundamental design responses to basic but crucial project requirements concerning type, program, and context.

The processes of establishing an organizational concept and accommodating detailed requirements into a given floor plan are related but require different approaches. These need to be synthesized by the designer into a single solution. To establish the scheme you have to think of the project as a puzzle of small but essential pieces that must be arranged with insight and preci-

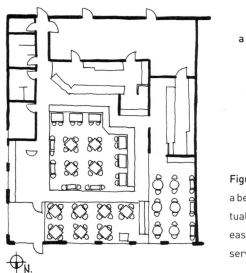

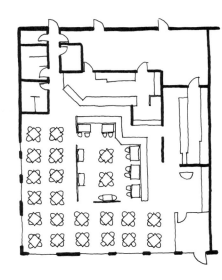

Figure 6.5 Scheme (b) provides a better response to the contextual amenities to the north and east and turns its back on the service alley to the west.

sion. This must happen at the start of a project, before the many little problems at the microlevel bog you down. The incorporation of specific functions and their respective interrelationships at the microlevel requires looking at the project differently because there are more parts, and, thus, more complexity. Once a basic scheme has been devised, these more detailed parts can be tested within its structure. At that point, the basic scheme generated from the organizational concept goes through a fine-tuning and calibration process as all the detailed parts are plugged in.

The process of allocating specific functions informs the development of a scheme. The addition of extra requirements forces you to give the scheme more definite form and to solve the puzzle of fitting pieces into their ideal locations. This initiates a process of give-and-take in order to make the scheme and all the project parts work with each other. This process, in turn, usually changes as you reach new understandings in the process of superimposing the detailed parts over the basic scheme.

Establishing a Coherent Scheme

If a project is going to be ultimately coherent, it needs to be based on a solid foundation. This is why organizational concepts are so important. They force the designer to make explicit decisions about an organizational structure based on the particularities of the project. One of the necessary requirements to produce a basic scheme is to think about the project in terms of a few essential components. As stated above, detail and elaboration are added as you go, but to generate the basic scheme, you should be concerned with finding a

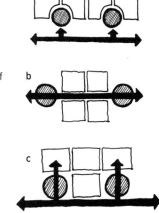

Figure 6.6 There are many possible schemes composed of four districts and two centers. Three are shown here. It becomes apparent that after distilling the main fundamental parts of a project, it is necessary to decide how to best arrange them as a system.

basic arrangement for the few fundamental components. Reducing the parts to a minimum requires some abstraction. Thinking in terms of the place elements introduced in Chapter 3 becomes extremely helpful. For instance, you may be able to abstract a complex project into four distinct domains and two centers of equal importance connected by a circulation system. For the purposes of the scheme, the project is reduced to six main components and a circulation loop. This makes it simple and focused. The aim is not to negate all the detailed pieces that will eventually be incorporated into these six parts but to focus on the main parts.

Next, it is necessary to arrange these parts in response to the realities of type, program, and context. The main concerns are placement, sequence, and separation. Issues such as public versus private, the physical fit of parts within the site's geometry, and the hierarchical value of the domains and centers play a major role. Figure 6.6 shows three possible schemes for the

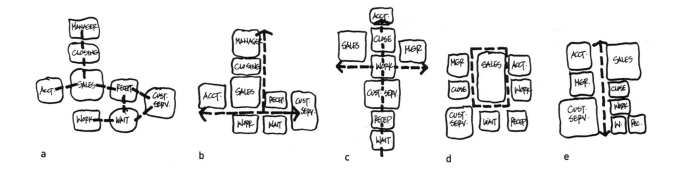

a   b   c   d   e

Figure 6.7 It is possible to convert any particular set of adjacency requirements into a variety of organizations. The scheme for a project does not need to be a literal translation of the adjacency diagram. It is up to the designer to convert the adjacency diagrams into a responsive structure.

hypothetical four domains/two centers scenario described above.

Many designers dismiss the recommendation to start with just a few parts as a gross oversimplification; they jump into design, attempting to solve all the problems, big and small, at once. After all, one of the most important contributions of interior design is the way designers account for and synthesize complex relationships of systems having many parts. We are not trying to deny the importance of this synthesis. It is essential to establish where parts are placed and how they relate to each other. The point here is that devising a basic structure for a project's organization is very useful, and dealing with a few large chunks makes the exercise of developing a scheme clear and focused. More layers of detail will be added before too long.

One of the most common mistakes made by novice designers is to literally transpose the adjacency bubble diagram, a diagram produced earlier in the process, into the site and call it the scheme. This is where many projects lose their sense of coherence, becoming an agglomeration of parts rather than a unified structure. While in some lucky cases this practice may produce a good scheme, in most cases it is unlikely to do so.

Figure 6.7 helps to illustrate this point by showing how the adjacency diagram for a small sales office can be given different form to fit the circumstances. Figure 6.7a shows the diagram, Figure 6.7b a literal translation, and Figure 6.7c–e three different schemes based

on the diagram, demonstrating the adaptability of adjacency diagrams. Some configurations will address the project's circumstances better than others and it is up to you as the designer to select the most responsive configuration.

Establishing First-level Order

The beginning of order in a project starts during the concept generation stage. If some structure of order is not established at this stage it becomes harder to establish it later without backtracking and starting over. Order implies proper arrangement, something that is determined during the development of the organizational concept. As we will see later, this order also needs to be made legible, a design concern that needs to be addressed and developed throughout the entire design process.

The basic scheme will be most responsible for establishing basic order. In general, if a project has a straightforward scheme, it will likely be perceived as orderly. Nevertheless, a simplistic scheme, although sometimes appropriate, will often be perceived as dull and uninteresting. For this reason, overly simple schemes may need to be balanced with some perceptual interest achieved by other means, including manipulations for enrichment as well as other expressive design inclusions. It is the balance between these three components (order, enrichment, and expression) that will determine how perceptually successful the project will be.

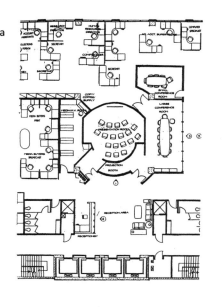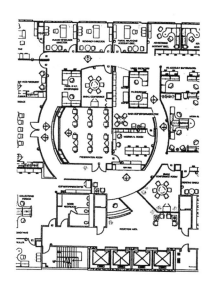

Figure 6.8 The complex central mass of plan (b) provides a better sense of order than the one provided by (a). The circle in (b), although not fully disclosed, remains strongly legible, while in (a) the circle idea is lost because of its lack of continuity.

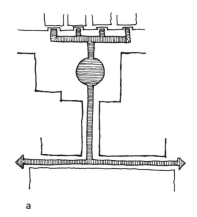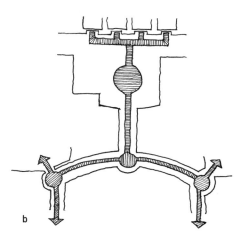

Figure 6.9 Drawing (a) shows the basic idea and drawing (b), the developed one. The curved forms and nodal points added in (b) provide a richer experience.

Order can be attained at various levels of complexity and enrichment can be achieved at various levels of order. Achieving an appropriate level of order in relation to the project's degree of complexity is essential too. Similarly, it is necessary for the designer to balance the need for enrichment and expression against the need for order. We will address the issue of order in detail in Chapter 7. For now, look at the two partial plans for an office shown in Figure 6.8. They both feature a complex mass in the center. Notice how Figure 6.8b exhibits a better sense of order due to the readability of the circular form. One can almost imagine a superimposed concept diagram over Figure 6.8b, showing the concentric circles in the middle.

Establishing First-level Enrichment

Similar to order, enrichment is initiated during the conceptual stage. An experienced designer thinks si-

multaneously about all these issues while generating organizational concepts. Young designers are also encouraged to think simultaneously about order, enrichment, and expression while generating concepts. While many manipulations to provide interest are normally introduced later, it is possible and desirable during the development stage of design to start thinking about experiential events for the project. We will devote an entire chapter to enrichment. For now, look at the simple manipulation for enrichment illustrated in Figure 6.9. Notice how the basic scheme was manipulated to produce a configuration that provides a richer experience.

Establishing First-level Expression

Expression in design can be achieved in many different ways. Many expression-givers in interior design fall outside the scope of spatial design. Expression has more to do with character; the materials chosen and the ways

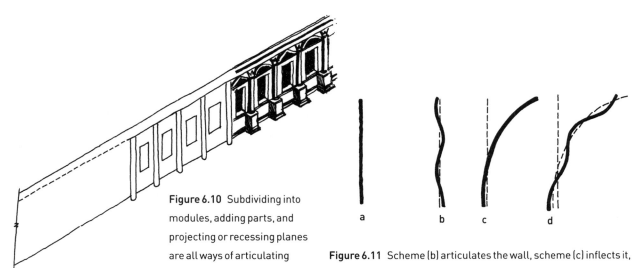

Figure 6.10 Subdividing into modules, adding parts, and projecting or recessing planes are all ways of articulating planes.

Figure 6.11 Scheme (b) articulates the wall, scheme (c) inflects it, and scheme (d) does both.

they are combined, the furnishings used, and the approach to detailing define the character.

However, spatial design can and does provide expression. Different arrangements, for instance, carry different connotations about levels of openness, formality, and progressiveness and different sizes and geometries imply different levels of power and influence.

Not only do the size and proportions of rooms and spaces have expressive qualities but manipulations of the enclosing planes can also be rich in expression. These manipulations fall into two categories: articulation and inflection. **Articulation** refers to the modification of planes or volumes by their skillful subdivision into clearly expressed parts. These facilitate legibility, and, when used skillfully, add interest and afford order at greater degrees of complexity. Some spatial articulation can occur during the ideation stage, but surface articulation usually occurs later in the process. Figure 6.10 shows three levels of surface articulation for the purpose of clarifying its meaning. Refer also to Figure 6.9b, where some basic plan articulation can be seen at the intersection points.

Inflection means deviation from a given course, as when a straight scheme becomes angular or circular. This type of manipulation can, and often does, happen during the generation of the organizational concept. It is important to distinguish between articulation and inflection and know how to use these powerful tools of design manipulation. Figure 6.11 shows three diagrammatic transformations of a straight wall into curved walls. In Figure 6.11b the course of the wall stays the same and the curvature is

added for flair and interest. This is an example of articulation. In Figure 6.11c the wall not only becomes circular but the course of the wall is altered. It is no longer (directionally) a straight wall. This is an example of inflection. Figure 6.11d combines the previous two examples to produce a wall that is both articulated and inflected from its original state. Figure 6.12 shows various straight and crossing path schemes transformed with angular and circular inflections.

Stages of Concept Generation

The process of generating concepts, whether organizational or character types, varies from designer to designer. Each one follows what comes easily and works best for him or her. However, the process of concept generation should encompass a handful of important steps. We will explain them next and recommend a sequence that will help you conquer this important design stage.

At the heart of a concept is an idea, or series of ideas, that establish the basic design approach for the project. There can be subapproaches complementing the main approach but a strong concept has to have one identifiable approach that reads as the main one. The formulation of this approach is the main goal of the concept generation process. There are, however, other tasks that must occur before and after this formulation. The following are recommended stages of concept development:

1. Understanding the Project
2. Identifying Dominant Issues

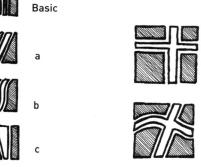

Figure 6.12 A basic plan arrangement can be transformed by using inflection and articulation. In these examples, the straight paths and walls are transformed into angled and curved ones.

Basic

a

b

c

Basic

a

3. Conceiving Workable Approaches
4. Externalizing the Approaches
5. Evaluating the Approaches
6. Consolidating Ideas and Choosing a Direction

As a designer you need to gain an understanding of the project and identify its dominant issues. Next, through analysis and insight you must conceive possible design approaches. These must be externalized and recorded with drawings and/or verbal statements. Once this is done you can evaluate their soundness and appropriateness and eventually consolidate ideas, as necessary, before choosing a desired direction. A more detailed explanation of each of the six stages above follows.

Understanding the Project

Chapter 5 discussed the factors that make up a project's reality. These included the nature of a project's user population, the realities of its context, and the requirements of the program. It also reviewed some of the tools used by designers to consolidate and make sense of information. The understanding of this information is crucial to the development of appropriate concepts and must precede the concept generation stage. Additionally, understanding the project as an example of a particular type, and as a unique example of that type, are useful for the generation of concepts. The level of understanding achieved during the early stages of a project can be considered the initial level of the project's understanding. You will never have the luxury of full understanding at the onset, but you will need a reasonable level of understanding in order to

move forward. The more you become immersed in a project, the greater your level of insight and understanding will become.

Identifying Dominant Issues

At this stage, it is not enough to understand the project's users, context, type, and program. Although useful, this information also represents a collection of vast, often confusing, and sometimes contradictory information. To truly understand the essence of a project the designer needs to be able to identify its **dominant issues**. Every project has dominant issues. They vary from project to project and some are more obvious than others. A particular programmatic requirement, a crucial functional relationship between project parts, a gifted (or problematic) site exposure, a particular feature of the building and/or site, and a desire for a particular historical or symbolic gesture are all examples of potential dominant issues.

Some projects are loaded with dominant issues but in others the designer may struggle to identify a handful. Some of the issues will be self-evident, as in the case of a project across the street from an important historical monument, or explicitly requested by the user, as in the case of a particular relationship between two departments or units. Some important issues can be discerned as the result of reflection, as in the case of the realization that a particular department is more or less important than previously thought. Discerning some issues may even be the result of an accident, such as the realization of the special way in which the sun's rays penetrate one side of the building in the late afternoon. Completing statements like the ones listed

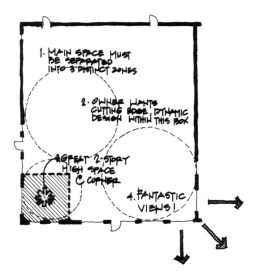

below can help you identify dominant issues for a project.

This project is all about…
Truly significant aspects of the site include…
Unique aspects of this project include…
The functional requirements obviously point to an organizational pattern that…
A few adjectives that fit this project are…

How does a designer choose which dominant issues to use to generate design concepts? When it comes down to generating ideas for concepts, designers have to rely on their ability to think not only analytically but also creatively and to make selections among competing ideas. It is important, once dominant issues are identified, for you to scrutinize them closely and pinpoint their relative importance and potential to influence decisions about organization, form, and aesthetics. Figure 6.13 shows important dominant issues for a hypothetical project.

Conceiving Workable Approaches

How does one go from a short list of dominant issues to concept ideas? There is a myth that concepts have to be unique and different. This is not so. While concepts are often unique and different, they are more frequently straightforward and ordinary. There are times when extraordinary thinking produces ordinary, but fitting, design approaches. While insight and creativity play a role in the generation of concepts, rational systematic thinking is just as important.

A period of reflective, critical thinking follows the generation of dominant issues. This is usually done with pencil in hand and many ideas are sketched loosely in diagram form along the way. The goal is to generate ideas for the main approach, ideas that respond to an important essence of the particular design problem. Some designers believe there is a period of incubation during which the subconscious digests information, eventually leading to inspiration and insight. This inspiration and insight, again, does not necessarily lead to innovation and far-out ideas but to a focused, appropriate response. The ideas are the result of insight, not divine inspiration. We could call it informed and fitting inspiration.

The ideas generated in response to the dominant issues may come up as a logical, sequential development or they may pop up while sketching or doing something else. Ideas usually arise as either thoughts or diagrams/drawings while you sketch. It is imperative to capture ideas when they arise, even before judging them. It is recommended that students generate and record more than one (approximately three) design concept approaches. As a rule of thumb, if it pops up in your mind, record it. This brings us to the next step, formalizing the approach through externalization.

Externalizing the Approaches

There are two principal ways to externalize and, thus, formalize concept approaches: verbal and visual. Verbal approaches are short statements or longer descriptive scenarios; visual approachs include diagrams and sketches. Let's take a closer look at each of these approaches, starting with the verbal ones.

Short statements can be effective in recording ideas. A good short statement should include a description of a physical arrangement or relationship and the effect it produces. For example, the following two statements serve to concisely articulate a specific design intention: "A bi-nuclear arrangement that splits control" or "a long evocative wall that provides a strong, linear, and unified backdrop to activity." Statements don't need to be long provided they express the basic approach clearly.

Descriptive scenarios are longer descriptions that paint a picture of an organization, its features and their effects. Scenarios have a tendency to get more specific and detailed and there is the danger they will become too detailed for the purposes of concept generation. Although scenarios are better suited as tools to articulate experiential intentions later during the development phase, they can be used to describe concepts of large or complex projects as well as projects with concepts involving sequence. They are also helpful to integrate organizational and character concepts because of their highly descriptive nature. The following scenario illustrates such a case for a hypothetical restaurant/bar:

The project consists of a series of aligned chambers, each transversed by a cross-axis leading to related zones at either end, except the last one which includes an additional termination point straight ahead. One enters into a small chamber that serves as a welcoming area. To either side are waiting areas, each one having its own unique character. As one moves forward, one enters the second chamber.

To the right is a bar area, to the left a comfortable lounge. Next is the third chamber leading to two dining areas, one on either side. The one on the left is more private and formal. Ahead are two more chambers. The first one incorporates a bar within it and leads to two different lounge areas; these are more part of the club than the restaurant. Finally, one gets to the last chamber, which also serves as a control point to the club. Straight ahead is a dancing area with a band stage at the very end. To the left is a bar and informal seating area (more for standing and hanging out). To the right is a more comfortable seating area.

Scenarios are wonderful tools to describe qualitative attributes of projects. It would be easy to take the previous scenario to the next level of detail. Notice how the addition of qualifiers and details (shown in italics) paint a more vivid picture of the scene:

The project consists of a series of aligned cylindrical chambers. *They are each distinct in their finishes, progressing from the subtle to the bold* and are transversed by a cross-axis expressed by straight paths from side to side, which lead to related zones at either end. . . . One enters into the first chamber, *the smallest and the only one immediately adjacent to the exterior. During the day it is bathed with natural daylight, the light reflecting off the light-colored fabric on the walls and the polished stainless steel trim.* This chamber serves as a welcoming area, *incorporating a free-form cherry wood and green marble maitre'd station.* To either side are

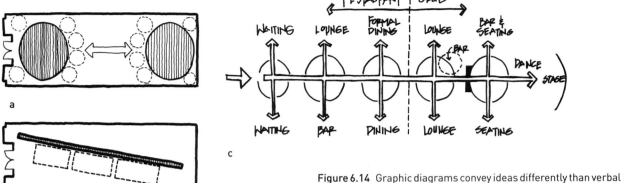

a

b

c

Figure 6.14 Graphic diagrams convey ideas differently than verbal descriptions. The overall organization is grasped almost instantaneously.

waiting areas. *The one on the right is neutral, formal and elegant; the one on the left casual and a bit more colorful, the wood becoming reddish.* As one moves forward one enters the second chamber *after passing a low, dark, and compressed transitional space . . .*

Diagrams are great devices to record organizational concepts. They are excellent tools of abstraction and are our main vehicle to represent concepts. Proper evaluation of concept ideas cannot occur without some form of plan diagram that gives preliminary architectural form to the idea. Concept diagrams will be dealt with in detail later in this chapter. For now, let's look at Figure 6.14. It shows diagram versions for the bi-nuclear arrangement and the long evocative wall mentioned under the short statements above, as well as the multichamber restaurant/bar project just described.

As you can see, diagrams convey organizational and relationship ideas effectively and economically. Also useful are more pictorial sketches. Anytime it is necessary to address qualitative issues or visualize three-dimensional form it is useful to turn to **conceptual sketches** instead of diagrams. The three-dimensional sketches shown in Figure 6.15 for the long wall scheme and the first chamber of the restaurant/club are more effective than the plan diagrams in conveying a loose idea of the spatial qualities of these spaces. Having representative sketches can really help you in the process of visualizing ideas and make their subsequent evaluation easier.

Evaluating the Various Concept Ideas

The evaluation of concept ideas is one of the many instances of reflective judgment during the design process. Each stage of design requires at least one formal evaluation. During the ideation stage, both the quality of the approaches generated (the soundness of the ideas) and their design interpretation (their actual interpretations on paper) should be scrutinized, however vague and abstract at this point. You should ask questions such as: Is this approach appropriate and fitting given the realities of the project? Is it likely to facilitate meeting the project goals? Below are some relevant evaluative questions for the three examples above.

1. Bi-Nuclear Scheme

Does it make sense to divide the project into two nuclei as proposed?
Is the proposed way of doing this in Figure 6.14a appropriate?
Could the idea of separation, if deemed appropriate, be conveyed differently?

2. Long Evocative Wall Scheme

Is the idea of the long wall appropriate?
Does it address one of the main issues?
Could it be executed successfully?
Are there other approaches to achieve the desired simplicity and unity?

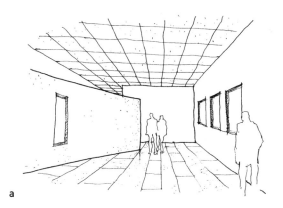

Figure 6.15 Three-dimensional concept sketches force designers to illustrate, and help others to see, a more literal conception of design ideas.

3. Multi-Chamber Scheme

How much does the chamber idea contribute to the desire to subdivide the project into zones?
Is it really necessary to subdivide the project?
How would these spaces be perceived?
Is the resulting fragmentation detrimental?
Are there other ways of implementing such a scheme?

It is critical at this stage to raise these types of questions in order to discard or modify problematic ideas and retain only the best. These are not the questions you want to be asking late in the design process. These are fundamental form-generating issues and once you buy into them you want to commit and stick to them for the duration of the project.

In design, decisions are made hierarchically, moving from the basic and general to the detailed. It is imperative to resolve issues appropriate to any given stage prior to moving on. The next stage will have its own group of challenges requiring attention. Each layer of selected and approved ideas provides the foundation for the next level. It would be wasteful to start second-guessing and changing concept ideas late in the design process, when layers of additional decisions have been made based on the earlier ones.

Consolidating Ideas and Choosing a Direction

Having evaluated the merits of a concept or group of concepts and identified the merits and drawbacks of each, you are in a position to choose the best idea, or possibly, combine aspects of various schemes in order to generate a new hybrid concept. The goal is to select a winning concept for further development. In some cases, if time and other resources permit, you may want to carry more than one concept forward for further development.

Generating Concepts

So far we have talked about the importance of organizational concepts, what they are supposed to accomplish, and the stages involved in their development. Now we will move into the actual process of producing concepts with special emphasis on concept diagrams.

Considerations in Determining a System of Organization

There are four important aspects which, combined, produce the organization system for a project. These are the size and configuration of the given site, the hierarchy of the spaces to be accommodated, how they relate to each other, and the way one moves around the project to get from space to space.

As we discussed in Chapter 5, the existing space you are given for your project often has particular geometries that suggest an approach to organization. In general, a long and narrow space will tend to dictate a linear organization; a large square space will suggest a centralized organization. Since we dealt with site issues in Chapter 5 we will focus on the three other aspects here.

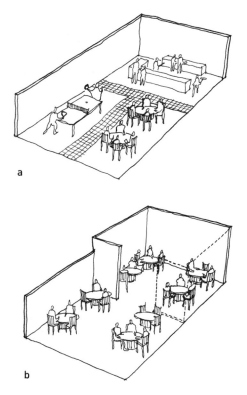

a

b

Figure 6.16 There does not need to be a one-to-one correspondence between function and space. Several functions can occur within the same spatial envelope (a) and, likewise, one function can span more than one spatial envelope (b).

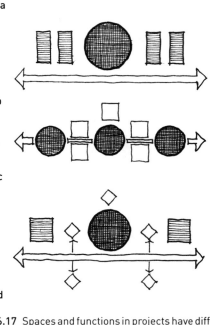

a

b

c

d

Figure 6.17 Spaces and functions in projects have different levels of importance or dominance. Some projects have no dominant space (a), while some have one or more centers (b–d).

Hierarchy

Understanding two distinctions is important before we discuss hierarchy. The first is the distinction between functions and spaces. Functions in the program need to be assigned some space. However, as we explained in Chapter 3, this does not mean that for each function there will be one corresponding space. Two, three, or more functions can occur within the same room or space. Conversely, some functions may be split up so that one part occurs in one space and another part in an adjacent space. Figure 6.16 shows two diagrams illustrating these examples. For purposes of our present discussion, we will be talking about spaces, not functions.

The other distinction is about what we mean by prominence when we talk about hierarchy. Two conditions can make a space prominent: its symbolic importance (a grand dining room) or its functional importance (the sample room in a design firm). Both of the prominent rooms above need special placement consideration. However, note how in the first case the grand dining room may occur at one end of the building with, perhaps, a grand corridor leading

up to it, while, in the second case, the sample room needs to be centralized in relation to the design studios. In other words, prominent rooms and functions do not always translate into central locations. Having made these distinctions, we may now proceed with our discussion about hierarchy.

In terms of hierarchy, you may have one project where all the spaces have approximately equal importance or prominence (all domains), and another project where a single space is prominent and dominant (a center). In between you may have all kinds of possible combinations, such as three major and five minor spaces or one major plus two intermediate and five minor spaces. The particular circumstances will suggest specific arrangements in most cases. Figure 6.17 illustrates these examples in diagram form.

Relationships

The way spaces relate to one another will also determine how spaces are organized as a system. Relationships determine issues of proximity. Some spaces may belong together and form a cluster. Some spaces may

Figure 6.18 The formal path leading to a dominating space at the end is a common arrangement for special destinations.

Figure 6.19 The three nuclei in the tri-nuclear organization (a) are equivalent hierarchically; the central nucleus of the system shown in (b) is clearly dominant.

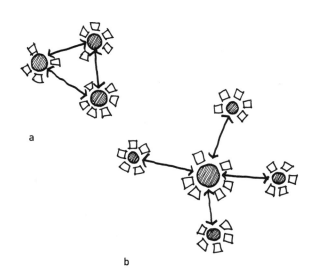

a

b

need to be as far apart as possible. Relationships also determine issues of centrality. Some spaces, like the example of the sample room above, need to be accessible to many other spaces and therefore must be centralized. Relationships also determine sequence. In some projects, like a bank's check-processing facility, there is a sequential flow the checks follow from the moment they arrive, thus dictating a specific sequential organization of functions.

Movement

In Chapter 4 we discussed the important role of movement in the shaping of space. Quite simply, you cannot generate an organizational concept without committing to a circulation system to link your spaces. Whether movement will be free or constrained, dignified or casual, grand or minimal, needs to be reflected in your organizational concept.

Using the Place Elements to Organize Space

Since interior projects consist of numerous spaces of various levels of importance, it is useful to think of a project in terms of the place elements introduced in Chapter 3 in order to arrange its parts. Five of them—arrival places, paths, nodes, domains, and centers—are especially useful for the overall organization of space in interior projects. Other place elements are useful to indicate the nature of separations and/or connections between spaces.

It is imperative to reflect the hierarchy of places in your project. Towards that end, you may think of places (other than circulation routes) as either centers or districts. You may recall that centers are places of

primary importance and that there can be more than one. Their special status is reflected by virtue of their location, size, or treatment. Single dominant spaces, such as the grand dining room in our previous example, may be centralized, placed at the end of a long and dignified path as shown in Figure 6.18, or assigned to some other prominent location, such as an important intersection.

How about projects having more than one nucleus? These can be thought of as either multinuclear or satellite organizations. A multinuclear organization can have several nuclei of equal or unequal importance. Each nucleus becomes a center of its own, receiving the corresponding appropriate placement and treatment. A satellite organization is one having several nuclei but with one that is clearly central and dominant. The dominant nucleus is placed at the center with the others around it, in subordinate fashion. These, in turn, are surrounded by their own subordinate spaces. See Figure 6.19.

Next, it is necessary to define the paths that provide access to centers and domains. These can be highly defined and controlling or loose and unrestricted. While addressing circulation, remember to consider two types of secondary, but important, kinds of spaces related to circulation: nodes and arrival spaces. Nodes, you may recall, are strategic focal points and often occur at important intersections, although this is not a requirement. The arrival space is important early on because it is the point from which everything emanates and its placement has a great impact on the resulting organizational system. You can think of it as a point of distribution.

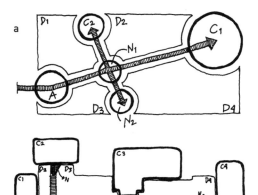

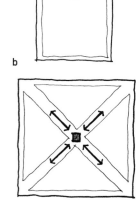

Figure 6.20 These concept diagrams are depicted in terms of our five basic place components: arrival space (A), paths, centers (C), domains (D), and nodes (N).

Figure 6.21 Diagram (a) shows a project with a strong edge separating two sections. Diagram (b) shows a project with a central landmark as generative force.

Reducing a project to these five elements during the ideation stage can greatly facilitate the organization of a project and the appropriate placement of its parts. Figure 6.20 shows a diagram for a retail store as well as one for a shopping center, both reduced to these five elements.

The other place elements should not be underestimated at this stage. They too can become important elements in the organization of a project. Figure 6.21a shows a conceptual diagram for a project in which a strong separating element (edge) is a crucial part of the concept. Figure 6.21b shows the diagram for a project in which a landmark is central to the concept scheme.

Diagrams

Earlier, we described different ways to formalize concept approaches. These fell into two categories: visual and verbal. We talked about sketches and diagrams as the two principal visual approaches used to externalize concept approaches. Sketches work best for visualizing three-dimensional ideas. Diagrams are the choice for visualizing organizations and relationships. We will now turn our attention to plan diagrams and how to use them to generate and record organizational concepts.

Types of Diagrams Used for Organizational Concept Generation

Our previous discussion on establishing a responsive and coherent scheme made an important distinction between two levels of specificity. These can be repre-

sented by two types of schemes. The basic scheme is concerned with the most general organization of the project. It establishes a sound overall approach for the project and gives it structure. The functional scheme adds specific functions and gets more detailed. It establishes the functionality of the approach. Correspondingly, we will learn how to use two kinds of organizational concept diagrams: the parti diagram and the functional diagram.

Parti Diagrams

The **parti diagram** represents the basic scheme, providing organizational structure to the project by expressing the essence of the solution without getting into detail. In order to capture only the basic essence, it distills the approach to its most basic components, nothing less and nothing more. If the approach is rigid, formal, and symmetrical, it captures that symmetry and formalism. If the approach is curvilinear and divides the project into two nuclei, it captures that flair and division. The parti diagram is not concerned with details about specific areas; that's what the functional concept diagram is for.

A good parti diagram helps to establish a sound approach to organization on which the rest of the project can be developed. It should convey the basic subdivision of the project and the principal movement system tying its parts into a specific organizational structure (linear, central, and so on), including the overall geometric approach (straight, curved, angled, and so on). Figure 6.22 shows two parti diagrams for the same office project. Figure 6.22a shows an arrangement consisting of two movement

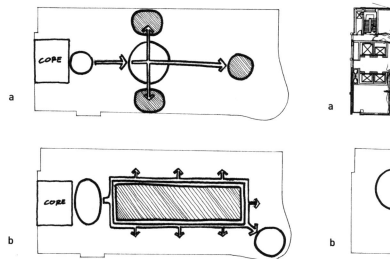

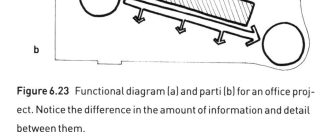

Figure 6.22 Two parti diagrams showing the basic essence of the scheme (arrival point, movement system, basic arrangement, basic geometry, and special destinations).

Figure 6.23 Functional diagram (a) and parti (b) for an office project. Notice the difference in the amount of information and detail between them.

axes (the principal originating at the entry point) intersecting at 90 degrees at a central, important space. From there the axes continue towards three special end destinations. The leftover spaces define four zones or districts within which the project's functions will be organized. Figure 6.22b shows a loop around a central rectangular mass with a special destination at one of the far corners. Three leftover zones are defined, two long and narrow ones along the main sides and one at the far end of the building.

Functional Diagrams

The **functional diagram** corresponds to the functional scheme. It is an outgrowth of the parti diagram but more comprehensive. Functional diagrams utilize bubbles and diagrammatic symbols to represent a more detailed solution to the design problem. They reflect specific decisions made about placement, size, and the relationships of functions based on the requirements of the project and are useful for testing different scenarios to see if they will work. More detailed spaces and functions are plugged in diagrammatically (but to approximate scale) to see how they fit. While the parti diagram establishes the basic approach to the solution, the functional diagram tests its workability in a relatively loose and quick way. If the parti establishes a sound organizational foundation for the project, a good functional diagram adds a sound functional foundation. Oftentimes, while trying to resolve your

functional diagram, you will discover that the scheme doesn't work very well. This is usually due to space problems (either there is too much or not enough) or geometric incompatibilities. In these cases, the workability of the concept may be too impractical and you will have to either revise or abandon the scheme and start again. Figure 6.23 shows both the functional diagram and parti for an office project.

It is likely that you have already used block plans in your design process. Functional diagrams are similar to block plans, yet they differ in two important ways. The first difference is in regard to the approaches they take to fit functions into the given site. Block plans emerge from bubble diagrams. Bubble diagrams are their point of origin. The designer superimposes the bubble diagram into a scheme that works for the given site. Functional diagrams, in contrast, have the parti diagram as their starting point. Detail is added to the parti diagram in order to fit specific functions within the structure and geometry already established. Relationships from the bubble diagrams are respected but the configuration follows the one established by the parti. In these a strong basic idea concerning form provides a structure for organization.

The second difference is in their scope. The purpose of block diagrams is to solve the puzzle of space distribution. The design problem is seen as a need to fit and distribute spaces in the site. Functional diagrams go beyond this requirement and force you to make a con-

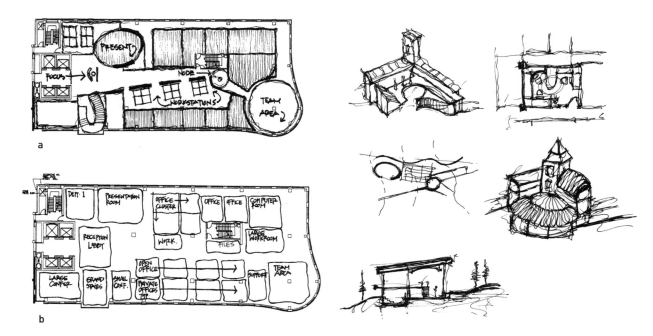

a

b

Figure 6.24 The differences between a block and a functional diagram for a project can be considerable, as shown here. While the block diagram may be helpful in sorting out spaces, the functional diagram incorporates more design thinking, displaying a specific design approach, and incorporating locations of special design events such as focal points, important nodes, and so on.

Figure 6.25 Personal concept sketches are usually done very quick and loose.

scious effort to create meaningful places at different scales to provide a stimulating experience. They force you to incorporate good places into the solution of the design problem. A good functional diagram locates centers, districts, nodes, and the other place elements we have discussed. It also identifies potential locations to provide special design events. A good functional diagram, for instance, not only helps to identify separations between parts but to make initial decisions about the character of such separations. Additionally, early ideas about the experiential character of circulation, the manipulation of daylight and views, and the location of focal points and planes are explored in the functional diagram.

Of course, functional diagrams are also responsible for showing that all the requirements fit and the space adjacencies work. The determination of locations for the different functions, their size, configuration, subdivision, and relationships all need to be addressed and resolved in the functional diagram. The thing to remember is that all this is done within the context of creating a strong sense of place and a stimulating experience. Figure 6.24 shows block (Figure 6.24b) and

functional (Figure 6.24a) diagrams for an office design. Notice the difference.

Despite the need to maintain a general sense of scale when developing functional diagrams they should be generated loosely enough to make them quick. Two important requirements towards this end are to draw them freehand, representing spaces in bubble form, and using other abstract representations (lines, arrows, asterisks, and so on) for circulation and other spatial features. Keeping the process loose and quick allows the designer to explore different alternatives during the ideation stage of design and it encourages spontaneity. Having multiple schemes enriches the process of exploration. Drawing the contents close to scale will provide important information about how the project requirements fit (or don't fit) in the space with your concept idea.

Graphics for Diagrams

Diagrams help us communicate with ourselves and with others. They help us to capture ideas when they arise and to remember and react to them later. They also help others understand our thinking and react to

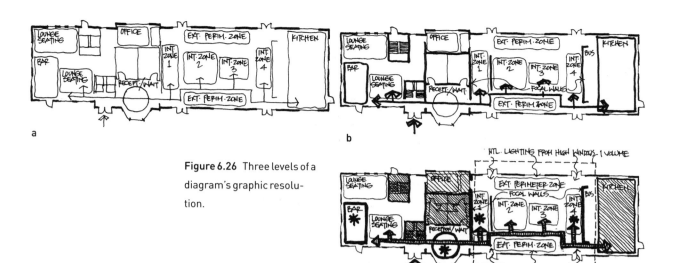

Figure 6.26 Three levels of a diagram's graphic resolution.

it. Concept diagrams that arise while we generate ideas can be quite personal and loose. There is no need to be too careful when sketching personal diagrams for our own use. In fact, looseness and spontaneity are to be encouraged during the creative process. Figure 6.25 shows examples of loose concept diagrams.

It is a different matter when we intend our diagrams to communicate to others. At that point they go from private to public and require an increased level of clarity and resolution. In this section we address the qualities that public diagrams must possess and the graphic techniques to produce them.

Requirements

A good public diagram, whether a parti or functional diagram, possesses three basic virtues: clarity of content, clarity of intention, and economy of means. Clarity of content means that all the pertinent pieces for that diagram need to be shown and delineated clearly. Clarity of intention means that the design intent, at all levels, needs to be clear enough so others can understand it. Economy of means refers to the practice of keeping information simple. For both parti and functional diagrams there are important decisions about what is to be included and excluded. For partis the question is, how can I show the essence of the approach with the fewest possible elements? For functional diagrams the question becomes, how can I be thorough and inclusive without including too much detail?

Of particular importance under clarity of intention is differentiation through hierarchy. We have been emphasizing the importance of hierarchy in design, that

not all places in a project have the same importance, that not all circulation should have equal prominence, and that there are specific spots in projects which have very strong and evocative qualities while others will be hardly noticeable. These differences have to be obvious in your diagrams! This is what makes graphic differentiation so important.

The graphics you use in your diagrams must be hierarchical. The types of symbols you use, the emphasis you give them, and how you use tone and texture are crucial if you want to produce clear, readable, and attractive diagrams. Figure 6.26 shows three levels of graphic resolution. The first diagram (Figure 6.26a) is clean but flat. Even though all the parts are there, it lacks differentiation. The second diagram (Figure 6.26b) incorporates a hierarchy of line weights and different arrow types. It is clearer and makes a stronger impact than the first. The third diagram (Figure 6.26c) adds tone, texture, and special symbols to represent areas of special importance. It is even easier to read than the second diagram and its impact and appeal are also improved.

Diagram Grammar

You only need to use a few symbols and a handful of simple graphic techniques to produce clear and strong diagrams. Only three types of basic symbols are necessary to produce concept diagrams: bubbles to define areas, lines with arrows to indicate circulation, and special symbols to represent special spots or events. Next, you need ways to differentiate among symbols of the same type to convey hierarchy. This is accomplished by varying the size of the symbol, the line

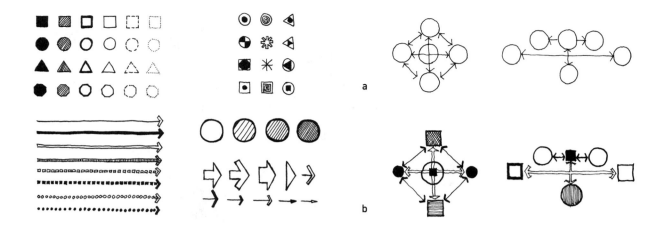

Figure 6.27 The graphic vocabulary for diagramming includes graphic symbols to differentiate bubbles for hierarchy, different lines and arrow styles to indicate movement systems, and special symbols to convey special locations.

Figure 6.28 These simple diagrams show the enhanced readability of diagrams achieved when you use simple graphic devices, such as varied line weights and textures inside the shapes.

weight of its outline, and/or the texture you use inside the symbol. Figure 6.27 shows examples of the three symbols and their variations. Here's your vocabulary! It's that simple. The secret lies in practicing and becoming competent at executing these drawing techniques. Figure 6.28 shows two simple diagrams in both basic (Figure 6.28a) and enhanced (Figure 6.28b) form.

Diagram Development

Depending on your habits and personality, you are likely to prefer one of two basic approaches to develop your concepts. Some designers like to work with only one idea. They stay with it, modifying and transforming it until it is resolved. Other designers prefer to generate multiple ideas with variations and later narrow them down through successive evaluations and selections until they arrive at the winning solution. Except for a few seasoned designers and others who are naturals at the focused approach, the rest of us will generally have a greater chance of arriving at an optimal solution using the multiple idea approach. It is, therefore, recommended that you generate multiple concept ideas and test them to see which one(s) gives you the best solution. The only caveat here is for those who might be inclined to exaggerate and explore too many ideas. If you have such tendencies, be aware of it and put some limits on your horizontal thinking. Figure 6.29 shows, in diagram form, a hy-

pothetical path to a winning solution using the multiple idea approach.

The Next Task of Design

The tangible outcome of the ideation stage is a concept to be developed further. Under certain circumstances you may allow yourself to carry more than one, perhaps two, concepts forward to the next stage. By now you have a sound organizational structure for the project, as expressed in the parti diagram, as well as a sound functional foundation as diagrammed and tested in the functional diagram. Additionally, you are likely to have taken some solid steps towards the goal of providing order, and some initial ones towards providing enrichment and expression.

The next task is development. There is usually some overlap between tasks, evident from the fact that before the end of ideation you have already taken some steps towards establishing ideas that pertain to development. Nevertheless, it is during the development stage that you can really elaborate and refine your design ideas and intentions. This leads to the necessary modifications and manipulations that help transcend mere utility and embody the project with a real sense of place, full of order, enrichment, and expression.

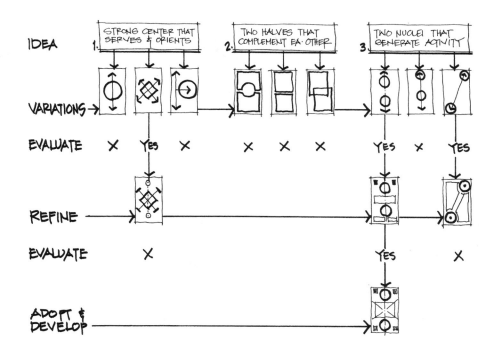

Figure 6.29 Hypothetical path of concept development and selection.

One of the remarkable aspects of design is that, despite the constraints imposed by the requirements of a project, there is ample opportunity for personal interpretation. A good way to illustrate this is to compare library designs by two late, famous architects: Louis Kahn and Alvar Aalto. Kahn's library at the Phillips Exeter Academy and Aalto's at Mount Angel Abbey are projects whose forms, although derived based on similar understandings of the needs of a library, differ substantially.

Exeter Library was conceived both as a place to celebrate knowledge (through books) and a place for community (students coming together). Kahn saw a library "as a place where the librarian can lay out books … and the reader should be able to take the book and go to the light." He felt that reading should occur individually by a window, in a private carrel. In response to this his design solution consisted of two concentric doughnuts, the outer one being the place to read by the light, away from the books. The inner doughnut was the place to store books away from the harmful effect of direct sunlight. The hole in the middle was a great central space, a multi story atrium from which one can enter and see books all around through large circular openings. In this fashion the invitation to books takes place and one can grab a book and go to the light to read (Figure C6.1). The central

hall is the heart of the building as community, both symbolically and functionally, for it is there that you run into and interact with your friends.

The design for Mount Angel Abbey Library, like that of Exeter, was developed in part based on the relationship between a person and a book in light. At Mount Angel Abbey we also find carrels and reading rooms around the perimeter, by the light. The book stacks are towards the center, between the readers and the central area, similar to Kahn's approach at Exeter. That is, however, where the planning similarities between these projects end. While concentric square doughnuts defined Exeter's form, Mount Angel Abbey's form is fan-shaped, as is the case with other Aalto libraries. Although his fascination with this shape is seen in many of his other buildings, the use of the fan shape is especially appropriate in his libraries. One of the basic functional requirements of library buildings is the need for a control point from which the librarian assists patrons and monitors them as they exit. Aalto gave great importance to such points placing them at the narrow end of his fan-shaped buildings, the rest of the library expanding outwards from it (Figures C6.2 and C6.3). The book stacks are arranged radially from the desk such that the librarian has visual control over the entire library space.

Although there is no monumental lobby space at Mount Angel, Aalto provided a space to serve as the heart of the library and, like at Exeter, one from which the library and the books are seen and the invitation to books occurs. This is the mezzanine between the control desk and the rest of the library. It is enhanced with dramatic lighting making it an important focal area. This circular area features counters and chairs and is, itself, an interior place for reading. Although it is not at the perimeter, like Kahn's reading areas were required to be, the abundance of natural light it receives makes it consistent with the idea of reading by the light. See Figure C6.4.

These two libraries, designed by two of the greatest architects of the modern era, are both exceptionally good libraries. While the basic type requirements for a library were understood well by both architects they had enough differences of emphasis and interpretation to produce two radically different designs

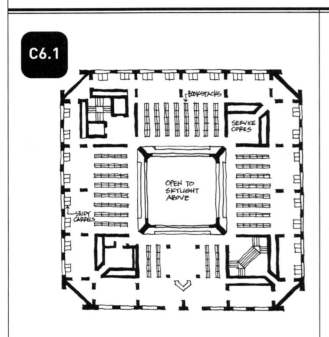

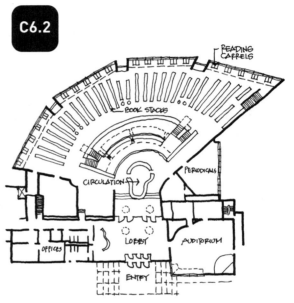

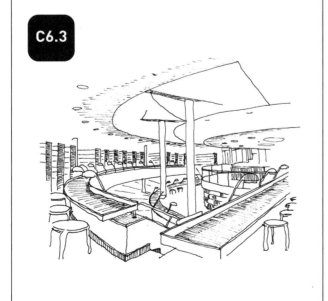

Presented here is a quick approach to organizational concept generation. It consists of five steps:

1. Establish basic distribution of spaces
2. Establish main circulation
3. Articulate general solids, voids, and screens
4. Articulate and/or inflect the scheme
5. Test the idea

The first step consists of laying down on paper, more or less to scale, the basic spaces of the project. By basic we mean the principal areas. To do this, you have to generalize. If there is a requirement for a cluster of offices, for example, you use only one shape for the entire group. By grouping related functions together, you should be able to reduce the entire project into just a few components. Figure C6.5a shows the requirements for a hypothetical project expressed in terms of five areas placed within the project's site. For our purposes we will keep the example generic. Let's assume that the areas have been placed after carefully considering adjacency and exposure requirements.

The next step (often developed in conjunction with the first step) is to clearly establish the main circulation. Every project has a main axis, loop, or network for moving around. Your task is to decide where this main circulation goes and to reflect it in your concept diagram. See Figure C6.5b.

The next step is to consider the project three-dimensionally. Up to now, we have been thinking about our hypothetical project in terms of five general areas. Now we start defining open and closed areas. Some of the areas are likely to be open, others are likely to consist of enclosed spaces, and still others may be a combination of open and closed. Furthermore, the relationships, between the circulation path and open areas, and between adjoining open areas, may be open, closed, or somewhere between.

Figure C6.5c shows the areas of our hypothetical project articulated into closed rooms (shaded), open areas, and screening devices between areas. This is when you start to orchestrate the project massing by making these decisions and reflecting them on your study diagrams. Work loosely on tracing paper, and don't be afraid to change or discard ideas. Crumpling a sheet of tracing paper with a bad solution into a ball and tossing it away can be as pleasurable as keeping a good one.

Once you have the basics of a solution established (which you think will actually work when tested), you may perform some basic articulations and/or you may inflect the scheme by turning it, curving it, and so on. Keep in mind that not all projects need to be turned or curved. Figure C6.6a shows our basic scheme with some form articulation added; Figure C6.6b shows it inflected through a diagonal maneuver. Don't get too detailed. Before you do so, you want to test your idea and see whether it is going to work. Up to now you have been using approximations and working loosely and now is the time to draw the idea up at a larger scale, to draw furniture and other contents (quickly but accurately), and to see whether it really works. If you are lucky, it will work nicely, and all the pieces will fit efficiently and harmoniously. In most cases, though, you will find that you have to manipulate the geometry to make things work. In some cases, you will find that the idea requires so much modification that it loses its integrity. In those cases it is best to abandon the idea and pursue a new scheme.

Figure C6.7 shows six schemes for a hypothetical store project illustrating different ways of inflecting the forms. The space has been conceived as two longitudinal spaces connected side-to-side at various points. One of the long sides is a little wider and incorporates the cashier's station. Figure C6.7a shows the scheme in basic form with some definition starting to emerge at the transition zone. In C6.7b the side walls and the transition zone show a more refined articulation. Figure C6.7c is similar, but in it, an uneven spacing of the center columnlike elements is explored. It results in a wider cross-opening at the center. Figure C6.7d explores a diagonal arrangement of the same basic idea and figures C6.7e and f explore curvilinear solutions. Notice that the idea is basically the same. Despite the wide variations of geometry, the concept scheme remains two elongated spaces with multiple connections between them.

You can see that the same basic idea can be varied through articulation and inflection. Deciding which scheme is the best for the project requires testing them to see which one works best and which one best reflects the personality of the project

C6.5

Figure C6.5 The three basic steps for "quick" organizational concept generation: Disposition of major spaces (a), introduction of main circulation (b), preliminary definition of solids, voids, and screens (c).

a   b   c

C6.6

Figure C6.6 Articulation and Inflection: you can establish some preliminary articulation early on (a), and/or inflection, if appropriate (b).

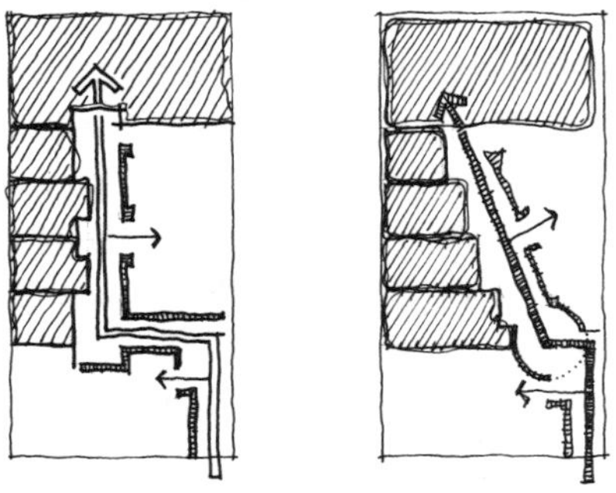

a   b

C6.7

Figure C6.7 The same scheme (a) can be articulated and/or inflected many different ways. Articulation can establish a regular (b) or hierarchical (c) distribution. Inflection can be diagonal (d), undulating (e), or sweeping (f). There are many other possibilities in addition to these.

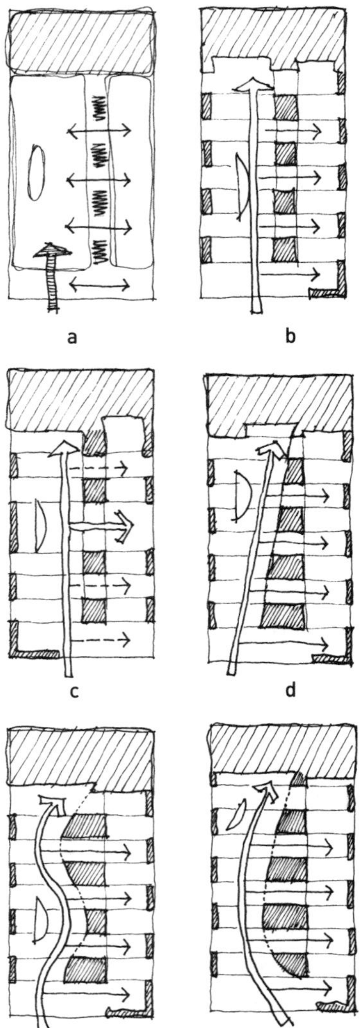

a   b

c   d

e   f

CASE STUDY
Sifting through Programmatic Complexity to Provide Clarity and Convenience: Duchossois Center for Advanced Medicine
Design Firm: HLM Design

Health care projects are among the most complex design projects. The complexity is due in part to the many functions involved and the intricate relationships between them. Solutions often result in complicated arrangements that create wayfinding and general orientation problems. The Duchossois Center for Advanced Medicine provides valuable lessons about the process of shaping a large project based on a sound understanding of its basic parts and units. It also illustrates how conceptual decisions about how an organization wants to conduct its business get translated into physical form. This project is a good example of how, even for a large utilitarian and institutional project, design must transcend function and incorporate visual and experiential qualities that portray its sponsor with pride and offer the visitor pleasant and inspiring experiences.

The center is an enormous health care facility associated with the University of Chicago. Overall, it oc-

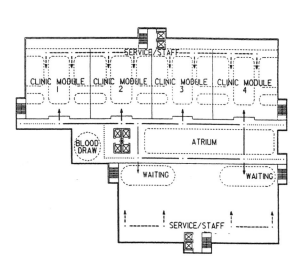

Figure CS6.1 Diagram of prototypical patient-centered organization.

Figure CS6.2 Diagrammatic stacking plans.

Sixth Floor:
A. General & G.I. Surgery / Transplant
B. Gastroenterology
C. Hematology, Oncology, Dermatology
D. Hematology, Oncology, Nephrology
E. Lab Testing / G.I. Offices
F. Gastrointestinal Procedures
G. Infusion Therapy / Cancer Resource

Fifth Floor:
A. Endocrinology
B. Cardiac, Thoracic, Vascular Surgery
C. Cardiology
D. Cardiology / Pulmonary Medicine
E. Lab Testing / Medicine Admin.
F. Donation / Apheresis
G. Heart Procedures
H. Pulmonary Procedures

Fourth Floor:
A. Orthopedic Radiology / Therapy
B. Orthopedic Surgery / Rehab.
C. Rheumatology
D. Neurosurgery / Neurology
E. Lab Testing / Surgery Admin.
F. Neurophysiology Procedures
G. Ear Nose and Throat Surgery

Second Floor:
A. Food Court / Express Registration
B. Urology
C. Pain Therapy / Pre-Surgery Testing
D. Bridge to Parking / Mitchell Hospital
E. Mammography
F. Ambulatory Surgery

First Floor:
A. Registration / Billing Inquiry
B. Eye Center
C. Radiation Oncology Clinic
D. Entrance Lobby / Security
E. Pharmacy / Building Admin.
F. Radiology

Ground Floor:
A. Mechanical Space
B. Radiation Oncology D&T
C. Future Kitchen
D. Tunnel to Mitchell Hospital
E. Instrument Processing
F. Mechanical Space

cupies 525 thousand square feet distributed among six floors. Approximately one thousand patients visit the center daily and more than one thousand physicians and health care professionals staff it. When a project gets to be this size, its complexity can be truly overwhelming. In this example, we briefly examine the way this project was conceptually shaped based on its particular needs and operational goals. Additionally, we show some representative examples of the kinds of design features that helped to humanize this large institutional building.

The predesign process included and was informed by a comprehensive master facilities planning exercise. Existing facilities and conditions were surveyed and trends as well as needs were analyzed and evaluated. A user group of over two hundred faculty and staff members provided programmatic data and assisted in the evaluation of working modules and similar facilities. During the conceptual stage, several stacking options were developed and evaluated. Clinic module prototypes were also developed and scrutinized. Finally, similar facilities using comparable health care delivery models were visited.

The basic programmatic requirement for the center was to provide a one-stop health care system that would house the adult specialty clinics of the University of Chicago hospitals plus outpatient diagnostic and treatment facilities. The center wanted to adopt a health care delivery system based on the principle of patient-centered care, having as its main goal the provision of maximum convenience to the patient. As part of the health care delivery approach, group practices would not be physically grouped by medical or surgical specialty, as is the norm. This facility would have only one group practice, which would diagnose and treat diseases by organ specialty. The operational model adopted was one that brings physicians and equipment to the patient to facilitate multidisciplinary participation and patient convenience. Instead of the patient moving from department to department within the facility, the patient would remain in one place and physicians and equipment would be the ones moving. Figure CS6.1 shows a conceptual diagram of the type of physical organization implied by this model.

In order to consolidate ambulatory care practices, it was necessary to combine space and equipment for multifunctional "centers." Floor plate arrangements had to facilitate the access to and sharing of space and equipment and at the same time remain within accept-

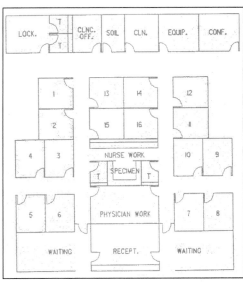

Figure CS6.3 The large open atrium from levels four through six serves to provide relief and orientation.

Figure CS6.4 Diagrammatic plan of a prototypical medical module.

Figure CS6.5 Lobby of the Pediatric Specialties Clinic.

other atrium connects levels four through six. A large linear space with a vaulted skylight above, it divides the facility in the middle, with the clinics on one side and the diagnostic and treatment functions on the other. The large atrium serves as a major internal focus area. The waiting and circulation areas on floors four through six are located adjacent to it (Figure CS6.3).

Once the basic block of clinics for the facility were determined, module prototypes were developed and evaluated. Figure CS6.4 shows a diagrammatic plan of a prototypical medical module. Modules had to be flexible enough to meet the needs of medical and surgical specialists within the allotted square footage and structural grid. Each module contains examination rooms and support functions such as reception areas, clinical coordinator space, work areas, and toilet rooms. Also part of the module is a peripheral zone containing materials management support spaces, and toilet, lounge, and conference rooms for staff use.

An important goal of the project was to increase the perception of quality of ambulatory care practice as well as to promote the convenience and dignity of patients. To this end, a number of physical and service-related amenities were incorporated such as convenient drop-off areas, valet parking, a skybridge connecting to an existing parking structure, convenient and modern scheduling and registration systems, a sophisticated signage system for orientation, comfortable and private changing areas, electronic information systems, a food court, a sundry shop, and a commercial pharmacy.

Beyond providing basic conveniences, the success

able limits of complexity to prevent disorientation and frustration. The concept developed featured two parallel linear halves on each floor, one containing the clinical programs and the other the diagnostics and treatment functions. These were offset in order to make space for a curved vehicular plaza at the street level and create a sense of entrance on one side of the building. The planning that followed was all based on this structural organization as shown on the diagrammatic stacking plans in Figure CS6.2.

To provide visual relief and enhance orientation, two atria were incorporated. One is by the main public access point and connects levels one and two. The

Figure CS6.6 Rhythm, pattern, and color in corridors.

Figure CS6.7 Lobby serving the General Medicine Clinics.

Figure CS6.8 High end waiting and registration area.

of a project relies heavily on the sensitivity of the design treatments and their ability to create a desired and appropriate image. In that respect, the design of the center has much to offer visitors as illustrated here by images taken from the third floor. Figure CS6.5 shows a playful and inviting lobby serving the Pediatric Specialties Clinic. Even the corridors, so often dull and totally utilitarian in institutional projects, are given life and interest through rhythm, pattern, and color (Figure CS6.6). The lobby serving the General Medicine Clinics is, appropriately, more serious and straightforward and features visual qualities once unheard of in health care facilities (Figure CS6.7). In this case, the connotations expressed by the design are of class and elegance. Similarly, the waiting and registration areas shown in Figure CS6.8 convey the above average degree of design care given to these important public functions of the facility.

Review

Summary

The two principal tasks during the ideation stage are to establish both the project's basic fit and its initial organizational structure. During this stage the project's many realities and needs are synthesized into a scheme. Behind all meaningful schemes is a strong concept or overall approach to the project. Since there are many kinds of design concepts, it is useful to divide them into two broad categories: organizational concepts, concerned with the arrangement of the project; and character concepts, concerned with the look of the project.

To begin exploring concepts it is necessary to have a sound overall understanding of both the project's general requirements, and its dominant issues. Concepts are almost always derived in response to one or more of these dominant issues and are externalized as short statements, descriptive scenarios, diagrams, and sketches. Once recorded, they can be evaluated, making it easier to select specific ideas for further development.

Organizational concepts are crucial because they provide the structure used to shape a project's spaces and their relationships. They establish an organization that is responsive to the project's realities and requirements, and, at the same time, provide coherence and order. Additionally, it is possible to include initial manipulations towards the goals of enrichment and expression.

For purposes of establishing the scheme of a project it is useful to think beyond basic organizational patterns and conceive the project in terms of places of various levels of importance (arrival space, centers, and domains), paths, and important junctions along the paths (nodes). Thinking in these terms helps to reveal a project's fundamental parts and to establish a sense of hierarchy in the project

In terms of spatial issues, the required outcome of the ideation stage is an organizational concept that establishes a sound organizational foundation. It should contain the most basic and essential decisions for the project on which future decisions will be based. Two important kinds of diagrams used to depict organizational concepts are the parti diagram and the functional diagram. The parti diagram conveys the structure of the project in its simplest way. The functional diagram adds more detail and accounts for all the major parts of the project, making sure they will fit within the scheme dictated by the parti.

Chapter Questions

1. You have seen that there are many kinds of concepts. Explain, in your own words, what the concept of a project means to you.

2. Refer back to the concept for a design project you have done while in school. How was it expressed (short statement, scenario, diagram, sketch)? How many ideas were involved? Was it predominantly an organizational concept or a character concept?

3. In your opinion, what kind of project understanding is most crucial to develop good concepts?

4. Think of your current design project. Name three to five dominant issues, explicit or implicit.

5. Have you done concept diagrams before? Were they more like the parti diagrams or the functional diagrams described in this chapter?

6. What are the main differences between a block plan and a functional diagram?

7. How do you ensure, during the ideation stage, that every required function is accounted for and fits?

8. Explain two ways you could perform a manipulation for enrichment during the ideation stage.

9. Explain two ways you could perform a manipulation for expression during the ideation stage.

10. Think of examples of centers, nodes, landmarks, and edges for a house, a store, a restaurant, and a dance club.

Exercises

1. Identify the dominant issues for the design project you are currently working on. Which is the most dominant one?

2. Based on your responses to the questions above, list five potential concepts (organizational and character) for your design project.

3. Refer to the space shown in Figure 6-13 of this chapter. Assuming the space is to house a coffee bar, think of at least five concept ideas (organizational and character).

4. Select one organizational concept for Exercises 2 and 3 and develop three variations for each of them.

5. For Exercises 2 and 3 develop one each of the following: a short concept statement, a concept scenario, a quick, loose concept diagram, and a sketch for a particular space or area.

6. For Exercise 4 above, select one concept and draw both a parti diagram and a functional diagram.

Endnotes

1 *The American Heritage Dictionary* (Houghton, Mifflin Company: Boston, 1985) p. 304.

PART 3

DEVELOPING THE DESIGN

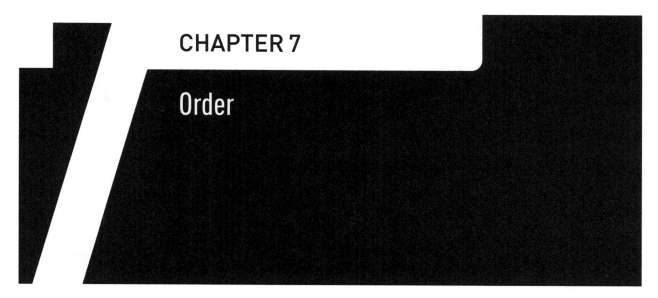

CHAPTER 7

Order

INSTRUCTIONAL OBJECTIVES

Describe different kinds of order related to fit, visual harmony, and orientation.

Explain three basic factors that facilitate spatial understanding.

Explain the role of the ten place elements in facilitating project imageability.

Describe strategies to facilitate the legibility of project parts.

Describe grouping strategies to facilitate orientation.

Explain ways to facilitate the understanding of relationships between parts.

Explain strategies to promote the awareness of motion and sequence.

Explain strategies to promote the understanding of projects as a whole.

Describe the limits and possibilities of enclosed corridors related to orientation.

Show the effects of varying the size, placement, and orientation of single and multiple

masses in space.

Show the effects of different levels of boundary legibility.

Show the effect of partial-height elements related to disclosure and orientation.

Order must be understood as indispensable to the functioning of any organized system, whether its function be physical or mental.[1]

From Vitruvius in antiquity to modern times, writers on the subject of architecture and the environmental design disciplines have spoken about the importance of order in design. Bernard Leupen put it quite simply: "Every design is based on order . . . the need to order is prompted more than anything else by our general desire to arrange the world so as to make it easier to understand."[2]

The design of building interiors requires the disposition and placement of many parts whose proper and systematic arrangement is crucial to the success of the project. Stanley Abercrombie has stated that "the reasoned relationship of parts to parts, of parts to wholes, of buildings to places, the power of repetition and modularity, the perception of complete units, the expression of construction realities, and the signification of inherent meaning—all are born only of order, not of chance."[3] Order is, arguably, one of the most basic goals of any environmental design effort. It helps buildings' users understand their environment and their relationship to it so they may feel oriented and at ease. It also produces a general sense of harmony in the visual environment. Its opposite is disorder and disorientation.

In Chapter 6 we looked at how during the ideation stage you establish the main organizational principles needed for the generation of the project's floor plan and asserted that a project's sense of order originates during that stage. In this chapter we explore the idea of order and its many dimensions manifested in the design of building interiors. We will look at some of the ways order is produced in architectural interiors. Of these, we will focus on spatial order, how to establish it and how to reveal it. Specific design strategies to achieve spatial order, including the use of the place elements introduced in Chapter 3, will be discussed as well as the importance of the composition of a project's enclosed and open areas.

Order in Buildings

Below we explain three basic types of order related to built environments. We also discuss the way interior environments are experienced sequentially and describe three important factors that facilitate the understanding of and sense of orientation in interior projects.

Kinds of Order

Order in design is manifested in many different ways. A large number of design tasks involve the orderly arrangement of parts or elements. Different functions have to be organized into a cohesive scheme that works effectively as a unit, physical elements have to be balanced in harmonious arrangements, and spaces have to be arranged in such a way as to facilitate orientation. Below we discuss these three important manifestations of order in the design of building interiors.

Order related to Proper Fit

When we think of order, we think of organization. Order is certainly concerned with the organization of parts. It is also more than that. A project must be organized in such a way that its parts are recognizable and their sum produce a coherent whole; it must do this in the process of addressing the needs of a particular architectural program in a particular setting. Compositional order that does not respond well to the project's function and/or context is not good order. Response to function and context involves an order of its own that must be addressed and solved properly.

When a project's functions have been arranged in such a way that relationships between parts have been respected and the relationship of the project to its context has been optimized we could say there is a good fit between the problem and its solution. This is one way of thinking about order. This type of order is simply characterized by a proper response to the project's requirements. It requires **functional fit**, the proper response to the functional programmatic requirements of the project as well as **contextual fit**, the proper response to the opportunities and challenges of the surroundings and inherent characteristics of the project.

Functional fit is achieved when the project addresses the essence of the overall design problem and its subproblems at the functional level. It can be judged based on the appropriateness of fit achieved between the program and the resulting project organization. Contextual fit is concerned with establishing meaningful connections and responses between the project and its context. It can be judged by the project's level of response to its internal and external contexts.

In addition the solution to the design problem has to be accomplished economically, and end up with neither missing or unnecessary extra parts. We could

Figure 7.1 Visual harmony is achieved when the parts of a composition evoke a sense of perceptual correctness and balance.

call this an **order of economy**. A project that achieves these types of order gives the sense that the essence of the design problem has been understood and responded to efficiently at all scales.

Order related to Visual Harmony

Interior design, being concerned with the composition of parts to assemble a whole, shares many characteristics with the other visual arts. They require the proper placement of, and equilibrium between, different components to achieve an agreeable aesthetic effect. This represents yet another kind of order in interior environments, **architectonic order**. The aesthetic effect we refer to is not concerned with issues of style but, rather, with the perceptual correctness of the composition of parts in the visual field. Relevant here are such architectural issues as the proper use of scale, the correct handling of proportions, and the proper balancing of project parts to achieve a harmonious state of balance and equilibrium. These concerns have been articulated from ancient times, beginning with the first treatise on architecture by Vitruvius, and remain relevant today. The sense of resolution and correctness that derives from the proper composition of architectural components gives our world a sense of equilibrium and stability (Figure 7.1).

In addition to architectonic order, there is another more mundane kind of order concerned with the orderliness of objects in general. Relevant here are the orderly arrangements of furnishings, equipment, or fixtures in space as well as the orderly arrangement of other smaller and harder to control items such as papers on a desktop or books on a shelf. We have all witnessed, frequently in our own dwellings or workspaces, the disturbing effect of disorganized environments due to what we could call the stuff of daily life. While designers lack control over the tidiness of their clients once the project is occupied, they surely have the opportunity to provide proper storage spaces to facilitate the organization of all these small objects that constantly conspire to clutter our lives.

Order related to Orientation

Christian Norbert-Schulz distills the basic act of dwelling into two basic and crucial psychological functions: identification and orientation. Orientation is the relevant one for our purposes here. It is concerned with "man's need to orientate himself, to know where he is."[4] Romedi Passini has defined spatial orientation as "a person's ability to understand the space around him and to situate himself."[5] We can all relate to this basic human need which, when fulfilled, gives us a sense of security and well-being. Conversely, the effects of its absence can range from mild apprehension to actual terror, depending on the circumstances.

Within order related to orientation we can distinguish among order concerned with the clarity of the spatial organization, order concerned with the proper disclosure of the external context for orientation purposes, and order concerned with the clarity of the circulation system.

In Chapter 5, we stressed the importance of responding appropriately to the functional and contextual realities of a project and offered some suggestions to make that task more effective. The need for order related to proper fit is addressed through the kind of

Figure 7.2 The realities of the physical world demand regularity and repetition in construction. Many designs, in fact, emphasize these properties.

process suggested in that chapter, involving careful analysis and insightful response. Order related to visual harmony requires much effort from the designer, starting from the early stages, but can be resolved later on. Chapter 10, "Resolution," is entirely devoted to this topic.

In this chapter we will focus on order related to orientation. We will examine the role of place elements in facilitating our understanding of the interior environment, strategies to organize space for strong legibility, and the effect of the disposition of open and enclosed spaces on our ability to read the produced spatial organization. First, though, we need to examine some important aspects of order and interior environments.

Levels of Order

The design of environments requires the assembly of multiple parts into a whole that possesses some level of organization. By the mere act of arranging a group of functions or spaces into some logical organization the designer brings some order to potential chaos. The act of building, itself, demands a reasonable use of regularity, and, thus, order. Pierre Von Meiss reminds us of this fact: "To build we must use fairly simple geometry. It is first of all a necessity for design and above all for building. . . . regularity is thus the very essence of building."[6] (Figure 7.2)

The synthesis of programmatic requirements into an orderly arrangement of spaces and the use of regularity, uniformity, and simple geometry in construction, by themselves, have a strong potential to establish a basic order, the kind produced by the proper assembly of parts, and the neatness it produces. How-

ever, a project's sense of order has to go beyond basic order and offer order in other ways. You should attempt to go beyond mere orderly arrangement and seek to produce meaningful wholes, paying attention not only to the neat organization of parts, but also to their assembly into a system based on a clear organizing principle. The organizing principle may be simple or complex but it has to be present and it has to be perceivable. Considerations about the relationship to context, internal hierarchy, relationships of spaces, and the way to move around the project have to not only work well together, but also respond to the organizational principle adopted.

The ideation stage discussed in Chapter 6 gets at the root of the search for an adequate organizational system for a project. Organizational concepts, we saw, not only seek a suitable organizational system, but also endow the project with a sense of hierarchy. Of all the tasks performed during design, the early development of the plan is the key to ensure the provision of structure based on an organizing principle. The plan sets the topological distribution of the project, locating parts and functions according to the organizational principle chosen. Morphological concerns related to its form are also important. They need to be developed insightfully to ensure that the project will be perceived and understood as intended. With this in mind, we look next at the way we perceive interior projects. This will give us some insight into what kinds of spatial arrangements and features are necessary to facilitate such understanding.

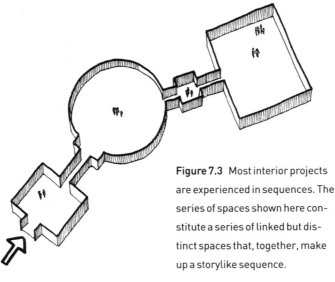

Figure 7.3 Most interior projects are experienced in sequences. The series of spaces shown here constitute a series of linked but distinct spaces that, together, make up a storylike sequence.

Experiencing Interior Spaces

It is important to remember that interior spaces are never experienced in the same way as the plans we draw. Floor plans allow us to see an entire floor at once and quickly grasp its organization. In real life, walls and distance prevent us from having that kind of instantaneous total disclosure of an entire level. Consequently, we usually experience environments one space at a time and form impressions that rely on mental maps we conceive by remembering the spaces we have left behind and adding the space that we occupy and the spaces we see ahead. Figure 7.3 shows a sequence of main and secondary spaces, displaying the fragmentary and sequential ways we experience most building interiors.

Since we don't see entire environments at once, our experience is fragmented and relies on memory and our individual abilities to form accurate cognitive maps based on the information seen. Environmental information and clues are perceived, understood, organized in our minds, and later remembered, helping us compose a collection of individual impressions into a coherent total image. Achieving order related to orientation, is thus more difficult than it appears. Designers not only have to produce responsive spatial arrangements and organize them based on unifying principles, but have to make them readable and understandable as well.

In Chapter 2 we summarized the rituals we perform in buildings starting with the sense of anticipation prior to entering and ending with our departure from the building. The sequence in which we experience a particular environment will affect the ease with which we understand it. Projects that have a predictable and consistent sequence, museums for example, can be planned to reveal themselves in some logical progression with a definite beginning, middle, and end.

Not all projects have predictable, rigid sequences. Furthermore, designers enjoy considerable control over the nature and rate of visual disclosure of a project so they can manipulate how a project is revealed.

From our discussion so far we can state a goal for designers concerning order: projects should be designed to facilitate a sense of spatial understanding for users of varying levels of familiarity. How exactly is this done? Our next topic presents three general factors that facilitate understanding of and orientation within interior environments.

Factors that Facilitate Understanding and Orientation

Except in the simplest of spaces, most environments are understood after repeated exposures. At some point, during the nth visit, the environment starts making sense in our minds, sometimes instinctively, sometimes from the discovery of an important part of the environmental picture, and other times after conscious efforts on our part to try to understand how things go together.

As we move around space, we form mental pictures of the environment around us. Unlike a small object or space, most interior environments cannot be understood by observation from only one vantage point. Because most environments are experienced one space at a time, it is the collection of diverse and fragmented pieces of environmental information gathered from many locations at different times that add up to our total picture of that environment.

Three factors identified by Kevin Lynch as components of environmental images at the city scale give us a useful model to understand environmental images of interior spaces. They are identity, structure, and meaning. Lynch reminds us that while it may be useful to abstract these for analysis, in reality, they are always interrelated.[7]

Identity

Identity is the quality of individuality objects possess that allows us to distinguish them from other objects and recognize them as separate entities. Related to identity is what Lynch called **imageability**, the quality of some physical objects that makes it likely that they'll evoke a strong image in the mind of the observer. Whether due to their shape, color, or arrangement, highly imageable objects are likely to produce "vividly identified, powerfully structured, highly useful mental images of the environment."[8] Projects rich in order will have a strong identity both in their parts and as a whole.

Structure

Structure refers to the spatial or pattern relation of the object to the observer and to other objects. It is concerned with the relationships among the different entities and how these are assembled as a unified whole. As discussed above, the presence of an organizing principle behind the arrangement will make it stronger and easier to comprehend and appreciate. We also said that this organizing principle could vary in its complexity. Depending on the project, it may take a while to decipher this organizing principle. Once it is

discovered though, we can make intelligent assessments of the space without having to figure out all the parts. Understanding this principle is like understanding a pattern. Once you discover it, you can repeat it indefinitely even as it gets more complex. A strong organizing principle, together with a well-orchestrated assembly of parts will endow the project with greater legibility, allowing users to grasp the structure more easily.

Meaning

Meaning refers to the significance the object has to the observer, whether practical or emotional. While meaning often works somewhat independently of the physical characteristics of environments, it is a crucial variable in the mix of how we perceive environments. Some places are remembered not by the singularity of their form or their placement within a structure, but by the significance they have for us. Whether due to the symbolic association, practical function, or degree of familiarity, these places stand out in our mental maps even if lacking in memorable features. As we invest time in projects, they become familiar to us and acquire more significance in our lives. With meaningful places we rely less on mental pictures of spaces having particular features because we see them as places associated with certain functions, people, and events having specific degrees of significance to us.

Of the three factors discussed above, the first two, identity and structure, rely the most on design. Meaning, as explained above, is usually assigned to places for reasons other than their physical attributes. Nevertheless, places that are rich in meaning can be fur-

Figure 7.4 Domains are legible as areas of particular characteristics, uses, and extent. This "neighborhood" in an office setting is one of its domains. Our mental picture of some environments features collections of domains that are related in some fashion.

Figure 7.5 This conference room in an office setting is an example of a center. Sometimes centers are highlights among less meaningful domains, other times they are of such importance they become, literally, central features of the organization.

ther enhanced by how legible and distinct we make them (identity) and where they are placed within the total organization (structure).

Designing for Order

So far we have made a strong case for the importance of order and orientation in design. In short, the order afforded by design can help orient us in space by facilitating our understanding of our environment, its place within the larger context and our position within these environments at any particular time. Now we turn to ways of achieving order in our designs. We will start with the role of the place elements in facilitating order and orientation. Next, we will review ways of facilitating project understanding at various scales. Finally, we will examine the implications of spatial massing and composition.

The Role of the Place Elements in Providing Order

In Chapter 3, we introduced the place elements, a group of perceivable environmental entities useful for the creation of places and for their general understanding. These were derived mostly from the five elements Kevin Lynch used to classify physical forms related to urban environments, and also from Christian Norberg-Schulz's elements of existential space. Other studies worldwide have corroborated Lynch's findings.[9] A study focused on wayfinding in interior environments by Romedi Passini and his collaborators revealed that Lynch's five elements were useful in classifying physical elements people use to describe as-

pects of building interiors.[10] In Chapter 3, we expanded these five elements to ten to better address specific aspects relevant to interiors.

These elements are significant because Lynch's studies show that the spaces or elements people use to describe their images of environments can be synthesized into these categories. Consequently, their role in helping people understand their environment is significant. Below, we look at the ten place elements used in this book and explain their significance related to order and orientation in interior environments.

Domains are the departments in an office or store, or the different dining areas in a large restaurant. Their approximate placement and size are important in developing an accurate mental map of the whole. Understanding the boundaries between circulation spaces and these domains, and, in some cases, those between one domain and the next is important to the formation of accurate mental maps. Figure 7.4 shows an example of a domain in an office environment.

Centers are domains of extraspecial importance. They become memorable because they are significant. Consequently, whether physically distinct or not, we remember these spaces and sometimes even organize our mental picture of environments around them. Knowing their inherent importance, designers can further emphasize their power to evoke a powerful and lasting image by endowing them with distinct physical features. An important conference room (Figure 7.5) may very well be one of the centers of an office facility.

Unlike cities, most interior environments have one principal point of entry. The space it leads to, the ar-

Figure 7.6 Arrival spaces are of great perceptual importance because of their role as gateways to the rest of the project. The example here shows an arrival space of a restaurant, revealing glimpses of what lies ahead.

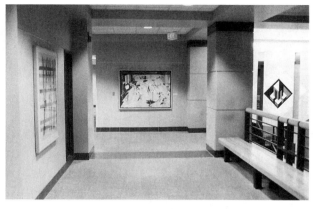

Figure 7.7 We see most parts of projects while walking on their paths. Yet, some revealing more than others as we move along. The path shown allows the user to catch glimpses of other parts of the project.

Figure 7.8 Nodes are important points of reference. Whether small or large, like the one pictured here, they are strategically placed and often have distinctive features that make them memorable.

rival space, is crucial to our understanding of the environment. It is the first point of reference from which the project emanates. As such, it is the kind of reference space around which we tend to organize the other components of an interior environment. The nature of the sequences that follow from this space and how much of the space beyond is visible from the arrival space can have a significant impact on our ability to understand the total environment. Arrival spaces give us the first impression of a project, and represent the first point of reference from which to construct our mental map of the environment. See Figure 7.6.

Paths are crucial to our sense of order and orientation inside buildings. It is while moving through them that projects are revealed. A strong and clear circulation system may be legible and impactive enough to become the structure around which we organize our mental picture of interior environments. This is not coincidental. You may recall that in Chapter 4 we derived our organization systems for entire projects from the circulation systems. These truly have the power to be generative elements that dictate the overall organization of projects. In many projects, if you understand the circulation system, you understand the organization of the project. The corridor shown in Figure 7.7 is the main spine from which the spaces of that project will be seen and accessed.

Nodes tend to be memorable for a number of reasons. First, they are places of intense activity, full of vibrancy, energy, and meaning. Second, they tend to be physically distinct, due to the dynamic qualities of converging paths, expanding space, and so on. Third, due to their strategic placement and often increased

size, they are visible from multiple locations and frequently they offer opportunities for a wide visual scope. Thus, a node is often a central, important space, as the multistoried atrium in Figure 7.8 shows. Nodes enhance our sense of order because we tend to remember them vividly. This makes them important points of reference in our mental maps of interior environments.

Next, we group edges, connectors, and ends together because their significance to orientation is similar. These three elements help determine the extent of domains and clarify distinctions about where one area ends and another begins. Their range of legibility varies but can sometimes be strong, as in a full and massive barrier between a private domain and a public and busy path. Figure 7.9 shows a path in a restaurant with a low, transparent edge separating the path

Figure 7.9 This edge between the corridor and the dining hall of a restaurant provides clear spatial demarcation.

Figure 7.10 Furnishings can be noticed as recognizable groupings that define areas or as single and distinct landmarks. The example here shows a contrasting seating group in the foreground, which stands out as a distinct entity.

Figure 7.11 Landmarks in interiors don't have to be monumental. Important features such as prominent staircases often become the landmarks inside buildings.

from the adjacent dining area. Strong edges can be memorable building elements. As such, they become a tool that can enhance our ability to remember project parts and thus improve our mental pictures of projects.

The significance of furnishings for imageability is that they are recognized as objects with distinct figural qualities. Most often we see them in groups and read them as regions of furnishings. These regions can be read as domains having uniform characteristics. Distinct qualities given to a specific group of furnishings can help make that region memorable and therefore more legible. For instance, a person might recall a specific area of a project where the furnishings were arranged at an angle as opposed to being straight like everything else. Figure 7.10 shows an example of furnishings which can be read as distinct groupings with-

in the same general space, in this case because of their different style and color.

The main trait of landmarks is distinctiveness. These are, perhaps, the most noticeable of all place elements. Landmarks are clearly remembered. Their inclusion in projects and their strategic placement for maximum visibility from multiple locations make them excellent points of reference that can significantly improve our ability to understand and get oriented in interior settings. A common landmark inside buildings is a staircase, especially if it is monumental in nature (Figure 7.11).

The insightful use and manipulation of the above place elements can help increase the legibility of interior environments. When they are orchestrated into a cohesive system they produce especially legible and coherent environments. The organizational decisions made during the ideation stage are crucial in establishing such an appropriate orchestration. These are further refined to make order and structure clearer and easier to read, but it must be emphasized that it all originates during that all-important stage of concept formulation.

Promoting Project Understanding

Having reviewed the role of the individual place elements, we will next examine ways of promoting project understanding at various levels, from the individual part to the totality of the entire project.

Project understanding takes place at many levels. We distinguish five principal ones: individual parts, groupings, relationships between parts or groups, sequences, and the project as a whole. We will look at

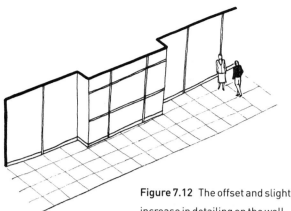

Figure 7.12 The offset and slight increase in detailing on the wall here are enough to highlight this section of the wall and make it distinctive.

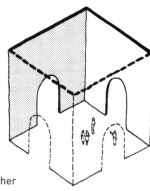

Figure 7.13 Simple form, whether spatial or solid, is easier to remember. Pure shapes, such as the square room shown, are instantly recognizable.

Figure 7.14 Dominance requires accentuated contrast in size, shape, or level of finish. The above example features contrasting size, shape, and surface treatment.

these next and suggest strategies for facilitating project understanding at each of these levels.[11]

Individual Parts

An individual project part may be a space or a mass. While not all parts need to be comprehended as individual entities, many do stand out as single features. We offer four design strategies to increase legibility at this level:

1. **Distinctiveness:** Parts with strong figural qualities read clearly against the background formed by adjacent elements. Ways of achieving distinctiveness usually rely on uniqueness and differentiation from nearby spaces or masses. Also necessary is a clear, uncluttered presentation of the object in question. Figure 7.12 illustrates how a simple offset or slight increase in the level of detail of a wall makes it stand out as a part.

2. **Simple Form:** Gestalt psychology established that our eyes are drawn to simple shapes first, usually focusing on the simplest one and proceeding to more complex ones only after the initial one has been grasped. Consequently, shapes that are simple, clear, and composed of few parts will be easier to perceive. The principle of simple form applies to both the perception of mass and the perception of space itself. Simple volumes, such as the cube in Figure 7.13, help make spaces distinguishable.

3. **Dominance:** Dominance is similar to, yet different from distinctiveness. While in both cases the part in question is differentiated from the rest, in

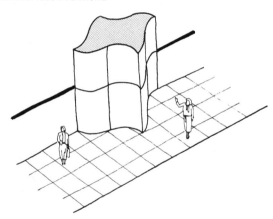

the case of distinctiveness it is merely different, and with dominance it is clearly dominant. Oftentimes, these parts become landmarks around which other parts are organized. Dominance can be established by means of size, intensity, or interest. In Figure 7.14, the protruding part is not only different, but also clearly the dominant feature of the composition.

4. **Contrast:** Contrast is a useful strategy to achieve differentiation among adjacent parts. It helps make entities more readable, especially at the point or edge where parts come together. A common use of contrast is the contrast of scale as shown in Figure 7.15.

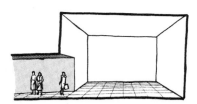

Figure 7.15 Scale and light contrasts are common strategies used to differentiate one area from another, as shown here.

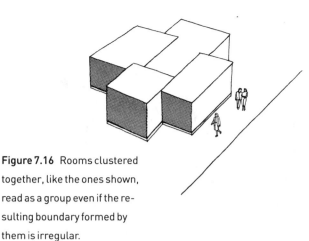

Figure 7.16 Rooms clustered together, like the ones shown, read as a group even if the resulting boundary formed by them is irregular.

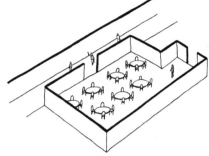

Figure 7.17 When objects, furnishings, or even rooms occur together inside a common boundary they read as a group. In this example the group of tables is held together by their common enclosure.

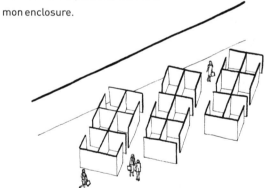

Figure 7.18 Objects sharing the same orientation, such as the angled furniture clusters shown, reinforce their sense of group.

Groupings

Functions or spaces are often clustered together in groups and read more as a group than a collection of parts. Individual parts may or may not be discernible. We present four design strategies useful to achieve legibility of groupings.

1. **Clustering:** Clustering consists of grouped spaces in tightly configured conglomerations (Figure 7.16). Parts may butt against each other or just come close. In any case, there has to be a high degree of proximity between them for the group to read as a cluster. The resulting shape may be simple and regular, or irregular, expressing the individual volumes, protrusions, and indentations of the component parts. The key to their legibility is that the cluster read as a single entity.

2. **Common Enclosure:** In the case of parts sharing a common enclosure, the parts may be grouped tightly, as in a cluster, or loosely. What unifies them and makes them read as a single group is their common boundary, which serves as a collecting device unifying all parts within it. The tables inside the common container shown in Figure 7.17 are grouped by virtue of being inside the same boundary.

3. **Common Orientation:** In the case of parts sharing a common orientation, closely spaced parts are oriented in the same direction and, consequently, read as a group. In these cases, proximity between elements is as important as the common orientation. Figure 7.18 shows an example of similarly oriented furniture clusters.

4. **Datum:** A datum is a powerful unifying device used to group dissimilar parts through a common field or ground. It can be a vertical backdrop against which a number of parts are arranged, a floating ceiling plane grouping several parts underneath, a unique flooring plane or pattern on which a group of parts are arranged (Figure

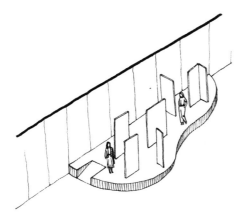

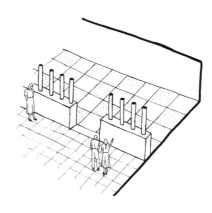

Figure 7.19 A datum group's parts, even if disparate, work together because of the common backdrop. In interiors it is usually a plane below, above, or behind the parts. In the example above, the raised floor platform serves as a datum for the parts sitting on it.

Figure 7.20 The strategy of clear intersection works by disclosing the point or edge where adjacent parts connect. In this example, the solidity of the bottom half of the wall, combined with the transparency of the top half, reinforce the separation between the two areas while simultaneously revealing their relationship.

Figure 7.21 The strategy of visibility works by maximizing the extent of what is seen from a particular space. Openness and strategic placement of tall elements are key components to make it work, as illustrated in the example here.

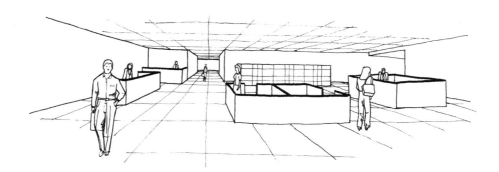

7.19), or, as in the case of common enclosure, a full enclosure helping to group a number of parts inside it. Key to the success of a datum is correspondence of extent between the datum and the parts it groups. It has to read as if the background wall, or the overhead plane, or the distinctive floor had been custom measured to house the parts they group.

Relationships between Parts or Groups

The next aspect requiring legibility is the relationship between parts. Positional relationships between parts as well as the nature of the connection between adjacent ones can be made easier to perceive and understand. Two design strategies are discussed.

1. **Clear Intersection**: Clear intersection occurs when joints or seams between parts are visible and clearly articulated. This usually involves an edge or a connector. Whether they are tall or low,

full- or partial-length, separating barriers that reveal the two sides enhance the readability of the relationship between them. Other than walls, clear intersections can be achieved through intermediary spaces, ceiling or floor treatments, furniture arrangements, and so on. Figure 7.20 shows an example of a separation between two areas clearly revealed by the characteristics of the dividing partition.

2. **Visibility**: Visibility simply refers to the increase of the visible field by means of openness, expanded views, transparencies, or overlaps, such as in the space shown in Figure 7.21. Open environments are generally much easier to figure out because the relationship between parts is clearly seen.

Sequences

Relationships between parts concern the way adjacent parts relate to one another. Sequences are concerned with how a group of more than two spaces link together to

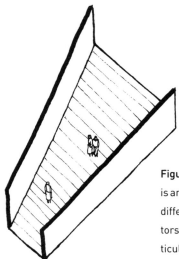

Figure 7.22 The corridor here is an example of gradation. The different widths can help visitors remember whether a particular space is near the narrow or wide end of the corridor.

Figure 7.23 A good strategy to make a sequence memorable is the use of contrast. Whether achieved by the alternation of open and closed spaces in the plan or by the alternation of low and tall spaces, as shown, the contrasting spaces are marked and remembered.

form a pattern and give users clues about where they are or where they are heading. We discuss three design strategies here that facilitate legibility of sequences.

1. **Gradation:** Gradation is achieved through subtle asymmetries, gradients, and any method of differentiation that successfully makes one side gradually become different from the other. The differences can be subtle, but as the observer notices them, he or she understands the progressive differentiation and can, therefore, distinguish among them, especially between the contrasting ends. The widening effect of the corridor in Figure 7.22 makes it easy to distinguish which end of the corridor you are in.

2. **Contrast:** We listed contrast as a design strategy for singling out individual parts. Contrast is also highly effective in creating different experiences as one moves along a sequence. Changes of scale or lighting levels (subtle or abrupt) help to break down sequences into discrete parts with unique characteristics, thus making the sequence more memorable and legible. Once again, contrast of scale is a commonly used and effective way of making sequences readable and memorable (Figure 7.23).

3. **Route Markers:** Route markers are design elements, distinguishable treatments, or objects placed at intervals along a route. Their presence helps to increase the awareness of movement in the observer. By marking spots along the length of a trajectory, you increase awareness of the experience of movement. As one passes and recognizes

another of the objects used as markers, one is reminded that one is in motion. Sequence patterns are a special kind of route marker. Instead of isolated and different markers, here a series of similar elements are linked in some pattern that is revealed gradually but regularly as one moves along the sequence. The elevation sequence shown in Figure 7.24 shows a repeating architectural element marking regular intervals of a route.

The Whole

Understanding the whole is the most difficult level of order to grasp, especially in large or complex projects. The problem is that we never see the entire space at once. Sequences may be long and difficult to remember, and we may never actually move through the entire space. Understanding the whole is not always necessary. Sometimes it is sufficient to understand where you are in relation to where you came in, or where you are in relationship to the exterior. However, the more users have a fairly clear mental picture of the total environment they're in, the more at ease they will be. We suggest four design strategies to facilitate legibility at the overall project scale.

1. **Repetition:** As the name implies, this strategy relies on the repetition of parts or approach. Repetition of parts occurs when perceptible units such as space modules are used repeatedly in some kind of regular pattern. Repetition of approach involves the repetition of sequences or arrangements of multiple parts. In the latter case, the sequence or arrangement acts as a unit, and it is the

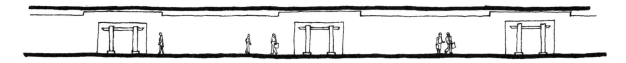

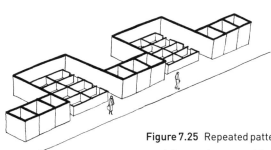

Figure 7.24 This example shows the use of route markers to provide useful regular points of reference along a route, usually along one wall.

Figure 7.25 Repeated patterns help users get acquainted with the modules used to assemble their project. The example here shows a basic arrangement that is repeated throughout the project.

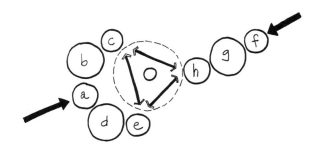

Figure 7.26 A central space connecting spaces (c), (e), and (h) visually would help visitors understand the relationship of the three sequences (a)(b)(c), (a)(d)(e), and (f)(g)(h). Large central spaces from which you can see many areas at once are often used to achieve the strategy of visibility.

unit that gets repeated throughout the space (Figure 7.25). Repetition is helpful because it reinforces patterns and can help us make accurate predictions about spaces we haven't visited based on what we have seen.

2. **Consistency**: Consistency of approach helps us decipher patterns by reinforcing our assumptions as we attempt to figure things out. It is, similar to repetition described above, a strategy that also reinforces the occurrence of a pattern. Consistency, however, does not require repetition of units. All that is required is continuity of intent. An example of this would be a long wall with a gradated use of color, slowly becoming lighter as one moves on. After a minute, one could assume that the wall color will continue to get lighter ahead. Consistency of approach provides us with consistent clues that we can use to make reasonable generalizations.

3. **Visibility**: As we have stated before, it is seldom possible to see entire projects at once. We form our mental idea of the whole by combining perceptions of individual spaces. This usually requires some educated guesswork on our part as we try to figure out relationships between spaces we have not experienced together.

For example, say you visit a certain unfamiliar building one day and visit three spaces. A day later you go back and enter through the same door. This time, however, you visit three different spaces. On day three you go to the building once again, but this time you enter on a different side of the building. From this

information, we can assume that you are familiar with the three spatial sequences experienced. Beyond that, we can speculate that you have some idea of how the spaces adjacent to the entrance used on the first two days relate since both were close to the same entrance and therefore to each other. That's as much as we can claim you know. You are most likely to be clueless about how the sequence of spaces from the third day relates to the previous two, since there are no spaces in common. Now, suppose the last space of each of the three sequences shared the common characteristic of terminating at a balcony overlooking a central atrium space where you can see from one to another (Figure 7.26). All of a sudden, the relationship between them would be clarified and even the relationship of the three sequences might start to make sense.

The principle of visibility works by providing certain spaces or vantage points from which multiple

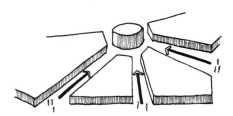

Figure 7.27 With the strategy of points of reference, views from different areas converge on a common space, object, or plane. In this example, the space and object are centrally located, although they are not large.

spaces can be seen. Examples include multistory spaces and other large spaces that allow us to see many spaces and/or features at once, providing instant information about how spaces relate to one another and relate to their position within the whole.

4. **Points of Reference:** The strategy of points of reference works by providing spaces or features that can be seen from multiple parts of a project, thus providing useful markers for orientation. The strategy is somewhat similar to visual scope but instead of relying on a large space from which a lot can be seen, it relies on common spaces or features that can be seen from different vantage points. Although all spaces providing visual scope also serve as points of reference (since they can be seen from various vantage points), not all points of reference are vantage points. Spaces that provide visual scope are large, show a multitude of spaces at once, and thus make spatial relationships readily understood; spaces serving as points of reference, although connected visually to several areas, don't necessarily reveal the relationship between areas. See Figure 7.27.

Points of reference can be isolated efforts supplied by the designer to help users understand the project or important strategic places around which project parts are organized.

Space Composition and Order

One of the most important variables in the perception of space is **legibility**, the extent to which space is read-able. If there is some unifying organization tying a project together, and if we are allowed to see enough of the project parts and how they go together, sooner or later we will be able to understand the whole. Two factors affecting legibility are the clarity of individual parts and the relative complexity of the spatial composition. Projects can be more or less legible depending on how we arrange their open and enclosed areas to allow more or less visibility. Enclosed spaces are seen as masses or objects in space. Open areas are the spaces surrounding the enclosed spaces. We turn our attention now to different effects derived from their composition.

As discussed previously, it is while walking through the corridors and aisles of a project that we truly experience its spaces and sequences. The result is in a storylike spatial experience composed of recalled information, unfolding information, and anticipated information. In projects consisting of mostly enclosed spaces, little information is revealed as we travel through corridors and we have limited visual access to the enclosed rooms we pass by. It may be impossible in some of these projects to get an idea of the whole. At the very least, however, we should feel oriented in relation to the point of entry, the sequence of the path, and the location of our destination. In open projects, we enjoy much greater visual access to a project's parts and features. Because we see more at once, we become better acquainted with the whole and can rely more on accurate real-time impressions and less on our memories.

Below we will look at some examples of how the composition and placement of enclosed spaces affects the resulting spatial patterns and our sense of orientation. Among the variables are the number, size, and

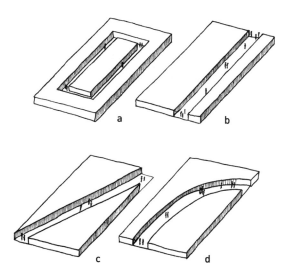

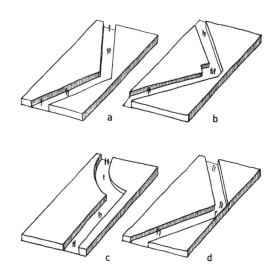

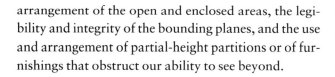

Figure 7.28 It is hard to find points of reference for orientation in totally enclosed corridors. The examples here show a full-loop corridor (a), a straight-run corridor (b), a diagonal corridor (c), and a curved corridor (d). Despite their configurational differences, these corridors share the quality of low imageability.

Figure 7.29 Closed corridors that change directions facilitate orientation by breaking the corridor into segments and providing a specific tangible point of reference at the intersection point. Configuration (a) is a simple example of this. The other three options add features to enhance legibility. Configuration (b) features an expanded intersection point. Configuration (c) features different shapes for the two segments. Configuration (d) brings the intersection point to the exterior perimeter.

arrangement of the open and enclosed areas, the legibility and integrity of the bounding planes, and the use and arrangement of partial-height partitions or of furnishings that obstruct our ability to see beyond.

Enclosed Spaces with Closed Corridors

The spatial experience of projects consisting of enclosed spaces is limited to the experience of enclosed corridors and individual rooms. It is difficult for visitors not familiar with these projects to get a sense of the whole since these projects are partitioned so much. Corridors usually offer no useful clues to help the user know where he or she is. Institutional and office buildings often have these characteristics. Guest room floors in hotels also tend to be this way. Figure 7.28 shows four diagrammatic floor plans as examples. Figure 7.28a shows a circulation loop, a common occurrence in institutional buildings. There is no visual access to rooms on either side of the corridor or to the exterior. The only points of reference serving as orientation cues are the point of entry to the loop, the location of doorways leading to specific rooms, and the signage that identifies the occupants of the suites. Even with those clues, it is easy to lose one's sense of orientation in these corridors. Figures 7.28b–d are variations of the same

type of arrangement. It is also difficult in these examples to get a real sense of orientation. In Figure 7.28c, users don't even know they are moving diagonally because they have no sense of the configuration of the floor's boundaries. Even when they find out about this relationship they can never experience it directly from the corridor. Only when inside a room or suite can they really see both the diagonal orientation of the front wall and the straight exterior wall. In Figure 7.28d, one experiences walking on a curved corridor, but, once again, from the corridor, one has no sense about how it is oriented to the building's perimeter.

Figure 7.29a–d offers a different situation. In these four examples the corridor changes direction near the center, therefore establishing a useful point of reference. Without looking at doors or suite numbers you can conceptualize the corridor into three parts: the first leg, the transition point, and the second leg. In Figure 7.29b the transition point is articulated slightly and given more importance, thus becoming more memorable. In Figure 7.29c each leg of the corridor has a unique configurational character, making it possible to distinguish each leg by its shape: the straight one and the curved one. There is less room for misinterpretation when explaining to someone which leg of

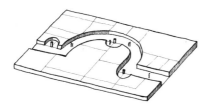

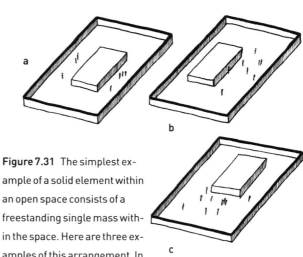

Figure 7.30 In large complex projects it is counterproductive to use too many corridor segments. After a certain point they confuse more than they inform. The corridor system here shows one alternative approach to achieve differentiation. The number of corridor segments is kept to three while nodes are added at intersections and at the midpoint of the circular segment to provide markers that facilitate further differentiation.

Figure 7.31 The simplest example of a solid element within an open space consists of a freestanding single mass within the space. Here are three examples of this arrangement. In example (a) the mass is centered in space; in examples (b) and (c) the mass is pushed slightly to one of the sides. The floating mass is readable in all three examples, although the spaces around the mass in examples (b) and (c) become different from one another, and are thus easier to differentiate.

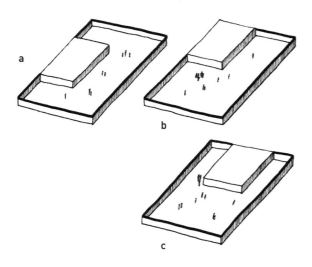

Figure 7.32 In these three examples, a single solid mass is attached to the boundary. Space legibility is simple in all three. The resulting configuration of the open space varies. In examples (a) and (c), the resulting open space is U-shaped but has different proportions. In example (b), the resulting open space is a simple L-shape configuration.

the corridor you were on at a given time. Figure 7.29d is similar to Figure 7.29a except the transition point occurs all the way back at the perimeter window, thus increasing its impact and offering a welcomed sense of orientation in relation to the exterior. In this instance it becomes possible to see where you are in relation to the neighborhood outside.

As with the examples shown in Figure 7.29, it would be possible to design corridor systems with, not two, but three legs. The legs of the corridor and their intersections would become identifiable locations and have the potential to enhance the user's sense of sequence and orientation. The only potential danger with this approach is that too many offsets get to a point where they can confuse more than orient. Therefore, the number of corridor segments should not exceed a reasonable number. For very large and complex projects it is desirable to use other de-

sign strategies such as to create points of reference within each leg instead of adding more corridor segments. Figure 7.30 offers one idea.

Open Spaces with One Enclosed Mass

Visual disclosure is ampler in open spaces. This makes them easier to understand. Figure 7.31a–c show three diagrammatic plans of open spaces with one single freestanding mass of enclosed spaces. In all three, the boundary wall is left untouched, thus making it possible to grasp the totality of the open space when walking around it. Notice that it is necessary to move around to see the whole space. The location of the floating mass in all three cases is such that the entire space is not visible from a single vantage point. The character of the open areas is different from case to case. The fact that the solid masses in Figure 7.31b

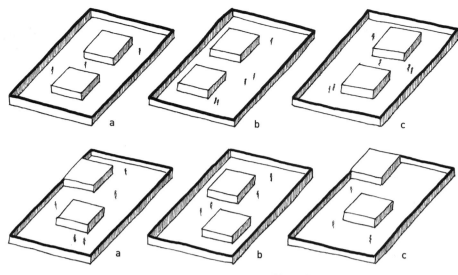

Figure 7.33 The three examples shown feature two freestanding masses each. The masses are centered in both directions (a), pushed to one of the long sides (b), and pushed up towards one of the short sides (c), respectively. Although similar to the examples in Figure 7.31, these configurations are slightly more confusing due to the increased number of parts (one added mass and one added space sandwiched between the two masses).

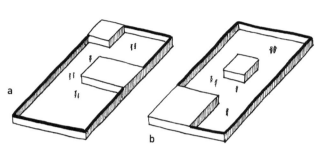

Figure 7.34 Offset masses in space increase complexity and make the space configuration slightly harder to decipher. Despite the clarity that the arial view affords, a person in the space would have to walk around for a while to figure out the configurations.

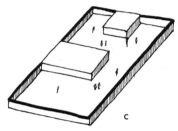

Figure 7.35 Three examples of different size masses offset in space. The perceptual effects of the resulting open spaces around and between the two masses vary from case to case.

and c are closer to one side improves the legibility of the space. Now, it is possible to distinguish between the narrow sides and the wider sides.

Figure 7.32 a–c shows three diagrammatic plans similar to the ones we just saw above except, in these, the solid mass is attached to the perimeter. The effects are similar to the previous ones except the attachment to the perimeter wall system breaks its continuity, thus making the extent of the outer boundary somewhat ambiguous. In these cases, users are forced to make some assumptions, or actually investigate the existing conditions by going into the enclosed spaces to figure out what the perimeter is like beyond the enclosed mass. In terms of overall orientation within the open space, the task is actually simplified since the open areas are easier to read with the mass moved away from the center.

Open Projects with Multiple Enclosed Masses

We now turn to examples having, not one, but multiple solid masses in space. One inevitable result of having more parts is an increase in spatial complexity. Even the simple configurations shown require more investigation than before to get a sense of spatial understanding. Figure 7.33a–c shows three diagrams of plans with two freestanding masses each. The arrangements are similar to the ones in Figure 7.31 above. The same general observations made there apply here, but now the number of subspaces is greater and more walking around is necessary to assess conditions.

In Figure 7.34 we further complicate things by offsetting the pairs of masses. In Figure 7.35 the masses are offset and of unequal sizes. Notice that the shapes we have used in our examples are simple rectangular ones. With compound shapes, spatial complexity is

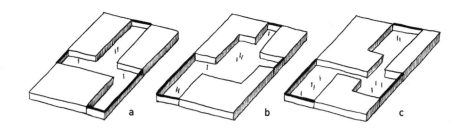

Figure 7.36 These three examples feature masses attached to the perimeter. Configuration (a) features three simple rectangular masses. Configurations (b) and (c) mix rectangular and L-shaped masses, adding complexity. In these cases, due to the obscuring of the boundary, the principal clues used for legibility are the resulting configurations of the internal spaces. The examples with the most visual continuity (a) and (b) tend to be the clearest.

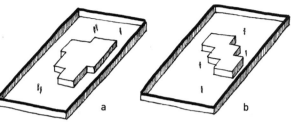

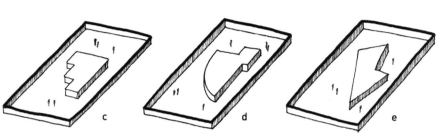

Figure 7.37 Five single but irregular freestanding masses. Despite the complexity of some of the shapes, the fact that they are single masses assures a reasonable degree of clarity. The example featuring two equal sides (b) can be somewhat disorienting as far as distinguishing where you are at any given time. Masses with no equal sides offer greater differentiation among sides.

even greater and the task of understanding the space more challenging.

Spaces with Partial Obscuring of Boundaries

As we saw above, arrangements in which the perimeter boundary has an exposed, simple, and uninterrupted shape tend to be easier to read than those in which the configuration of the boundary is interrupted by attached masses. We will focus here on a few examples where a substantial portion of the perimeter boundary is claimed by masses of enclosed spaces. Figure 7.36a shows an example with three rectangular masses of different sizes claiming three of the four corners. Notice the irregularity of the remaining network of open spaces.

Figure 7.36b and c show examples that utilize L-shaped masses. In these examples, the resulting open space configurations are even more complicated and difficult to read. The central space and the two partial cross axes of the configuration in Figure 7.36b makes it simpler to understand than the configuration shown in Figure 7.36c. This last one results in a network of open spaces producing three spaces with a couple of narrow corridor-type spaces joining them. These conceptualizations are much easier to make when we see the floor plan from above. In real spaces the twists and

turns have a disorienting effect and it takes much longer to figure things out.

Spaces with One Irregular-Shaped Mass

Irregular-shaped masses can enrich or confuse, depending on their legibility and the characteristics of other building components around them. Figure 7.37 shows five diagrammatic examples of plans having one irregularly shaped mass in the middle. Differences include the regularity of the offsets and the treatment of the different sides.

These examples are oversimplified to make a point. We have been using the geometry of the mass alone to differentiate one side from the others. In reality, you have other means to differentiate between sides, such as placing furnishings in the foreground, and using finishes and lighting. In other words, it is possible to have masses with similar sides and use some other design devices to make sides read differently from one another. Nevertheless, the impact of masses in space is quite powerful and makes them a principal variable to use for differentiation.

Let's turn our attention now to examples where the internal mass is rotated at an angle in relation to the bounding planes. The principles at work are the same

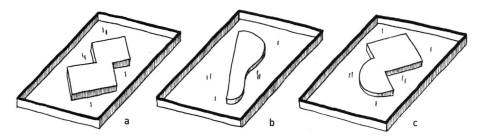

Figure 7.38 These three examples feature single, irregularly shaped, freestanding masses. The spaces created are dynamic and complex. Configuration (a) features an L-shaped mass positioned diagonally. Configuration (b) shows a mass with one straight and one curving side. Configuration (c) features a composite shape composed of a square and a semicircle. Flowing shapes, like in (b), tend to be easier to read as a continuous mass, while masses with offsets require more walking around for verification.

Figure 7.39 The three examples feature simple rectangular masses with asymmetrical superimposed forms protruding from them. Example (a) shows a diagonally oriented rectangle coming off the main straight one. Example (b) shows a fan shaped mass superimposed over the main rectangle. Example (c) shows a curvilinear mass coming off the corner of the main rectangle. All these protruding masses become distinct, if not dominant, parts that stand out and are remembered.

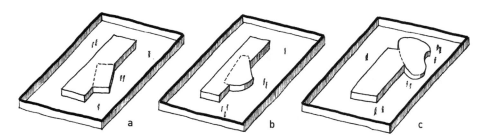

as those discussed above. Namely, the use of uniform or consistent patterns, and the deliberate differentiation among physical characteristics of the sides, will make it easier for users to understand their environment and feel oriented in it.

Figure 7.38a–c illustrates three examples with a single rotated mass floating in the center. In these examples all sides form unique spatial configurations between the mass and the perimeter. Every side becomes unique. This creates the challenge of having to distinguish between, and form mental maps of, unique irregular shapes. As can be seen in the diagrams, the arrangements themselves are rather simple; we are just dealing with one object inside one container. However, the object's shape is irregular, and its relationship to the container is further complicated by the fact that the two are not parallel. Nevertheless, as soon as the observer realizes that the mass is one continuous uninterrupted object the mystery is solved and the observer can enjoy the richness of the composition.

Let's now look at one useful variation of these mass-in-space studies: the ordinary mass with superimposed volume. Many projects don't have the kinds of curved, offset, or angled masses we have been showing as examples. Instead, they have ordinary simple rectangular masses. Sometimes the superimposition of portions having unique form characteristics helps to improve imageability. For one thing, the mass becomes more memorable. Additionally, better distinction between sides is possible, and the unique part becomes a strong element that serves as a point of reference, acting as a landmark.

Figure 7.39a–c shows three examples. These have similar effects, although using different geometries and compositions. Whatever the design vocabulary used (classic or contemporary), and whether the approach is subtle or bold, this technique can effectively increase the imageability of otherwise plain and featureless masses in a project, and identify important destinations (usually where the unusual shape is).

The Shape of the Boundary

Interior projects take place inside given compartments in buildings that have particular geometric characteristics. The actual boundary may be readable as such, as in the case of an office building with glass windows around the entire perimeter. At other times it is only partially revealed. There may be two sides exposed to the outside, for instance, while the other two may be adjacent to interior spaces thus resulting in

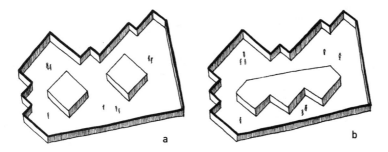

Figure 7.40 The two examples here feature irregularly shaped perimeter configurations. Both examples have the same perimeter. In example (a), the interior consists of two simple staggered masses. In example (b) there is only one mass, offset on the diagonal perimeter side and diagonal on the stepped perimeter side. This avoids the high complexity that would result if the stepping walls on both perimeter and mass were on the same side.

Figure 7.41 This example shows the effect of partitions that block the view ahead but do not go all the way to the ceiling. While they block some of the view ahead, we can always see above them. The resulting sense of the whole is not disrupted as much as with full height partitions because you can see the continuity at the ceiling plane.

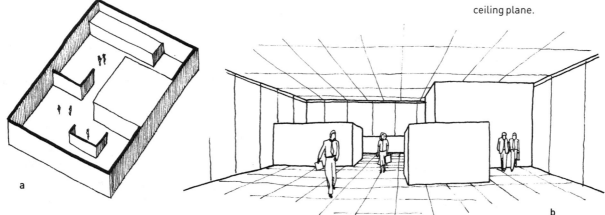

walls that blend in with the rest and are unrecognizable as boundary walls. The legibility of the boundary is important to our sense of orientation. While we may be able to get around based on an understanding of the route system, it will be nearly impossible to get a clear mental picture of the whole if we don't get a reasonable sense of the boundary. Understanding the extent of the container housing the project helps us understand the project from the outside in.

So far we have looked at examples having simple rectangular perimeter boundaries. We have also assumed that the entire outside perimeter is readable as the boundary. Next, we look at more complex boundaries and briefly discuss their effects. Figure 7.40 shows two examples featuring a complexly shaped boundary. The freestanding masses in Figure 7.40a are simple in shape and arrangement. Still, the resulting spaces between them and the perimeter are varied and irregular due to the complex shapes of the boundary. Here we see the reverse of the effects we saw in the

examples of simple boundaries with irregular interior masses. Figure 7.40b shows the same perimeter, but, this time, the internal mass is more complex.

Open Spaces with Partial-Height Elements

So far we have focused on full-height boundaries and internal masses. In other words, we have dealt with masses whose walls go all the way to the ceiling plane, creating a complete visual separation between one side of the wall and another. A very different effect is achieved when tall, yet not full-height walls are used to separate different areas. While a separation is achieved between both sides of the partition, the implications for orientation are different. With partial-height walls, even when they are high enough to obstruct your view straight ahead, you can see the ceiling plane continuing above, an important visual cue. Noticing this, you instantly know that the condition is merely a break within the same container, and not an end of the space. You realize that both sides of the par-

Figure 7.42 Excessive regularity is as disconcerting as disorder. Notice how the floor plan shown lacks any differentiation throughout. Spatially, it is both monotonous and lacks instinctive clues useful for orientation. The only way to know where something is located is by counting modules and workstations.

tial wall are inside the same boundary, an important orientation clue. Figure 7.41a and b show a plan and a perspective view illustrating this phenomenon.

The compositions formed by a project's enclosing boundaries, the masses in it (whether freestanding or attached), and other view-obstructing interior elements, establish what we see when we move around a project. Results will vary in levels of complexity and clarity, depending on the arrangement. A great part of our sense of order or disorder of a project will be determined by how these compositions are handled. Designers need to devote enough attention to the task of composing spaces for order and legibility. This task needs to begin early during design.

Order and Complexity

As you may have gathered from this chapter, it is impossible to separate the issues of order and complexity. They go hand in hand. Order is possible, and necessary, at all levels of environmental complexity. More complex environments require more order; simpler ones can get by with less. This brings up the issue of appropriate levels of order. In this chapter, and throughout this book, we have been advocating the importance and necessity of order in interior environments. Does that mean that all projects need to be crystal clear?

The answer to the above question is no. Total order can result in boring environments. Total order would mean total regularity without differentiation. Imagine a large project laid out with total and unyielding regularity. It would become as disorienting as a project lacking order. See Figure 7.42. The optimal level of order for a given project, thus, will lie somewhere between the two extremes of perfect order and total chaos.

Appropriate levels of order need to be considered in relation to the project's size, program, and users. Large projects of many interrelated units serving the visiting public, for instance, need more order than smaller projects for familiar users. Some projects may have two levels of order: a clearer one for strangers who visit, and a more challenging one for those who spend time in them daily.

Even in projects that cater to the visitor, it is often unnecessary to reveal the entire order right away by providing instant clarity and disclosure. In fact, it could be argued that order that requires some effort to discover is more rewarding than order perceived without effort. This can be accomplished by either utilizing a more complex order or by manipulating the level of disclosure of a simple arrangement to make it harder to decipher.

Are we saying now, after arguing so strongly for order, that some disorder is actually desirable? Not quite. What we are saying is that complex or hard to decipher order is sometimes appropriate. The key is that there has to be a system or principle of organization behind the arrangement, and it should be possible, with more or less effort, to figure it out. As long as these two ingredients are present, the designer has a multitude of possibilities to manipulate order to fit the circumstances.

Order is indeed an important and far-reaching concept in the design of interior environments. The topic thus does not end here. Chapter 8 will continue what we have started to discuss and address ways to manipulate the levels of order and clarity to produce interest and enrichment. Chapter 10 will address the issue of resolution of form to achieve perceptual order.

People demand a certain degree of clarity in the environment. The optimal degree of order for a given environment varies depending on the people involved and the specific circumstances. It is unrealistic to attempt to understand order without considering factors such as variety and complexity. In fact, a great deal of research has focused on complexity and the degree of preference associated with stimuli of different levels of complexity. Here, we briefly discuss a few basic aspects of this research with a special focus on a framework developed by Rachel and Stephen Kaplan involving complexity and other environmental attributes.

Amos Rapoport has summarized some of the findings of complexity-related research as follows:

1. Animals and humans prefer complex patterns in the visual field.
2. There is an optimum preference range, with both simple visual fields and chaotically complex visual fields disliked.
3. Complexity can be achieved through ambiguity (meaning multiplicity of meanings and not uncertainty of meanings), through rich and varied environments, and through environments which unfold and reveal themselves gradually.

Daniel Berlyne was one of the pioneers of complexity research. His area of research was the study of animal behavior, with a special emphasis on curiosity and exploratory behavior. When Berlyne started his investigations, the prevailing view about animal motivation emphasized the fact that animals act to satisfy basic needs, such as food and sexual gratification. But, as Ray Crozier explained, Berlyne observed that much behavior was driven by motivations other than the satisfaction of specific needs. He observed that a great deal of behavior was of a more diversive and exploratory nature and driven by the desire to explore novel situations and events.[1] Based on this insight, Berlyne conducted research and developed theories about exploratory behavior in humans. He suggested that the pleasure derived from works of art could be related to arousal level. He chose to express this in terms of arousal because states of arousal, from sluggishness to high alertness, can be detected and measured objectively.

According to Berlyne, "a work of art is regarded as a stimulus pattern whose collative properties, and possibly other properties as well, give it a positive intrinsic hedonic value.[2] Much of his research focused on his collative variables, named *collative* because they require one to combine the effects produced by them. The variables were ambiguity, complexity, novelty, and surprise. *Hedonic value* is a technical term for pleasure or enjoyment. His findings corroborated some existing notions of aesthetics that posited pleasurable effects are produced when there is a balance between simplicity and complexity, or between order and variety.

In simple terms, Berlyne's findings established, firstly, that increases in ambiguity, complexity, novelty, and surprise increase one's level of arousal. Thus, scenes of, say, high complexity can be said to have a high arousal potential. He proposed, and his research demonstrated, that hedonic value will increase as the arousal potential of the stimuli (for example, the complexity or novelty of the environment) increases. However, the increase in pleasure will not continue indefinitely. It will reach a peak and then start to decline when stimuli produce uncomfortably high levels of arousal. Figure C7.1 shows the result as an inverted-U curve, known to psychologists as the Wundt curve. What this means is that people prefer moderate over either low or high levels of ambiguity, complexity, novelty, and surprise. They want some stimuli, but not too much, with the optimal level varying somewhat from person to person.

In an effort to remove distracting associations with known figures and shapes, Berlyne and his colleagues used randomly generated nonsense images for their experiments, as opposed to images of real art or environments. Another researcher, Joachim Wohlwill, later performed similar studies with works of art and photos of outdoor environments. While the results of his research produced the inverted-U relationship, Stephen Kaplan noted that in the case of the outdoor environment, stimuli were relatively weak and the results failed to reach an acceptable level of significance.[3]

Fueled by, among other things, a conviction that the actual content presented by real environments has an important effect on how much people like them, the Kaplans started conducting research of their own concerning environmental preferences. First, they compared preferences of natural and man-made environments. Natural environments were uniformly preferred over their built-environment counterparts. Due to the high variation in preference from scene to scene and a somewhat inconsistent performance of complexity as a predictor, the Kaplans suspected there had to be other predictors of environmental preference. After some analysis, they came up with three other variables.

They noticed that the most preferred scenes featured either a trail that disappeared around a bend or a brightly lit clearing partially obscured from view by foliage in the foreground. In both types of cases, the scene appeared to promise new information if one moved deeper into it. These characteristics were adopted as a variable and labeled "mystery." Another variable was devised as a result of the realization that scenes varied in the degree that their elements "hung together." Scenes where the elements did not hang together were difficult to grasp and were generally disliked. They named this variable "coherence," referring to "the ease with which the information in the scene can be organized into a relatively small number of chunks."[4] The fourth and final predictor in their framework was concerned with the perception that it was possible to predict and remain oriented in space as one wandered deeper into the scene. It was called "legibility," after Lynch's term with a similar meaning.

What these four variables share is the fact that they all provide information that users can utilize to make sense of the environment. The Kaplans divided the information offered by the variables into two categories: understanding and exploration. The degrees of coherence and legibility afforded by the environment assist in its understanding. Coherence can be determined within a single scene. As the Kaplans explained, "a coherent scene is orderly; it is organized into clear areas. People can readily discern the presence of a few distinct regions or areas, and those make it easier to make sense of, or understand a place."[5] Legibility requires anticipating characteristics of the rest of the space based on a present scene. It requires that some features in the environment be distinct. Featureless environments possess low legibility. However, environments with a strong sense of hierarchy and distinctive features make the reading of their organizing structure easier.

Complexity and mystery, in turn, are related to exploration, although in different ways. The exploration associated with complexity is stationary, visual exploration, as when you visually scan an intricate pattern to explore its contents and relationships. The exploration associated with mystery is more ambulatory. A scene rich in mystery tends to draw you in with the promise of additional information.

It is interesting to note that the Kaplans do not subscribe to the view that too little complexity is boring and too much is overwhelming. They attribute this view to a confusion between coherence and complexity and believe that these two variables act together and influence each other. It is possible, for example, to have acceptably high levels of complexity as long as the organization of the parts is coherent. Conversely, a scene with even moderate complexity can overwhelm if its parts are disorganized or lack coherence.

Unlike other areas of research, this is one where research specifically geared to interior environments has been conducted. Separate studies conducted by Suzanne Scott in relation to interior environments confirmed some of the Kaplans' assertions. In an open-ended study aimed at identifying visual attributes related to preferences in interiors, Scott confirmed preferences for environments that are complex, exhibit strong legibility, and possess some degree of mystery.

A separate study by Scott aimed at testing the effectiveness of complexity and mystery as predictors of interior preferences also found positive correlations between these two variables and preference. As stated by Scott, "the strength of the positive correlations observed between complexity and preference and mystery and preference offer rather convincing evidence supporting the contention that people prefer more involving settings."[6] The study also found a fairly strong correlation between mystery and complexity scores and suggests that "these are not independent qualities and that manipulation of physical design characteristics contributing to perception of one may also contribute to perception of the other. For example, subdividing a larger setting to increase its complexity may simultaneously provide screening devices that introduce mystery."[7]

This study also contributed to a better understanding of the physical characteristics that produce complexity in interiors as well as the influence of the exact nature of the view beyond on perceptions of mystery. In addition to confirming that the number and variety of the elements present in a scene are related to perceived complexity, the study also suggests that composition or pattern of elements in a scene as well as its spatial geometry (volumetric shape and internal articulation) are important contributors to environmental complexity. In terms of mystery, the study provided an insight into the fact that the exact content of the view beyond is likely to influence the degree of preference expressed for the scene. In the study, correlations between mystery and preference were greater when the qualities offered by the view beyond were considered preferable, thus pointing out that the content of an upcoming space is at least as important as the evidence that the space lies beyond and can be accessed if one ventures farther into the scene.

The two quoted studies by Scott demonstrate the frequent correlation of research conducted in different fields. In this case, cognitive models of preference, born of studies of natural and urban landscapes were also found to be useful to explain preferences in interiors. It is important to note, though, that there are slight, sometimes important differences between one discipline and another. Thus, preferences indicated for nonsense random patterns, natural scenes, urban scenes, buildings, and interior spaces, despite their commonalties, will also exhibit nuances specific to the scale and discipline involved.

The application of these findings is not clear cut and presents some challenges. In an office setting, for instance, it may be desirable to have a relatively low level of complexity so that people can concentrate. Yet, a case can be made for a relatively high level of intricacy in such an environment since people spend so much time in it day after day. Higher levels of complexity can enrich such an environment by making it possible for the regular user to discover new things from time to time, as happens when one reads a good book for a second and third time.

---

1 Crozier, Ray. *Manufactured Pleasures: Psychological Responses to Design*, (Manchester University Press: Manchester, 1994) p. 61.

2 Ibid, p. 61.

3 Kaplan, Stephen. "Aesthetics, Affect, and Cognition: Environmental Preference from an Evolutionary Perspective," *Environment and Behavior*, Vol. 19, No. 1, (Sage Publications: 1987) p. 6.

4 Ibid, p. 10.

5 Kaplan, Rachel, Stephen Kaplan, & Robert L. Ryan. *With People in Mind*, (Island Press: Washington, 1998) p. 14.

6 Scott, Suzanne. "Complexity and Mystery as Predictors of Interior Preferences," in *Journal of Interior Design*, 19 (1), (1993) p. 31.

7 Ibid, p. 31.

C7.1

Figure C7.1 Berlyne's inverted-U curve showing the effects of arousal potential on hedonic value.

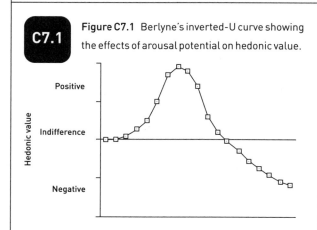

Source: Copyright © 1994 by Ray Crozier. From Manufactured Pleasures *by Ray Crozier, Manchester University Press, Manchester and New York, 1994, p. 63.*

Figure C7.2 Matrix of the Kaplan's model of preference.

C7.2

Preference Matrix

	UNDERSTANDING	EXPLORATION
2-D	Coherence	Complexity
3-D	Legibility	Mystery

Source: From With People in Mind: Design and Management of Everyday Nature *by Rachel Kaplan, Stephen Kaplan, and Robert L. Ryan. Copyright © 1998 by Island Press. Reprinted by permission of Island Press, Washington, D.C. and Covelo, California. All rights reserved.*

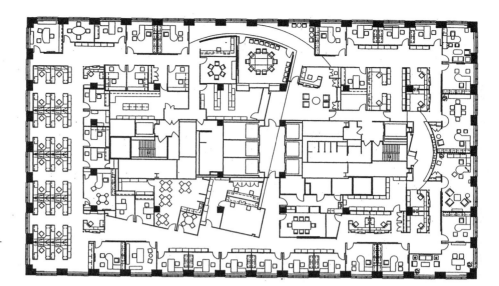

Figure CS7.1 Floor plan showing manipulations of the central zone.

CASE STUDY
One Strong Design Manipulation and a Memorable Route Help Achieve Interest within an Established Order: APCOA/Standard Parking
Design Firm: Mekus Studios

The APCOA/Standard Parking Office is a 37 thousand-square-foot facility housing two parking giants that merged into one. The design provides good examples of the transformation of a simple scheme by the inflection of a single area and the design of a strategic circulation route.

The project consists mostly of enclosed rooms. The only open space of significant size is the open-plan area on the west side of the floor. The totality of the floor is never perceived at once, and a mental image of the project is attained only after one has moved through the entire floor via its corridors. The general circulation scheme is a simple loop around the floor with an additional major cross path through the elevator lobby.

Despite the simplicity and straightforwardness of the basic scheme, we can see how the form manipulations performed around the center radically transformed it (Figure CS7.1). The central portion of the interior mass is rotated approximately ten degrees and extended outwards. The resulting mass is articulated as if it were a separate superimposed part, yet one that is still integrated with the orthogonal interior loop. It becomes the main focal mass of the space, transversing the elevator lobby and extending in both directions to transform an otherwise ordinary office space into a dynamic composition.

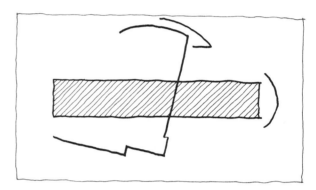

Figure CS7.2 Conceptual parti diagram

The parti diagram (Figure CS7.2) shows an abstract, simple representation of the project's floor plan. The orthogonal basic grid provides an easy-to-understand organization and thus establishes order. The rotated central mass provides diversity and interest. The elevator lobby, reception area, main conference room, two secondary conference rooms, break room, and several support rooms all assume dynamic, irregular shapes.

The shapes and subdivisions produced by the rotated mass and its articulations also create an interesting interplay of obstructed and unobstructed interior vistas. The twists and turns experienced as one moves around the facility make the perception of the simple plan organization a bit more challenging and rewarding. See Figure CS7.3.

Three important aspects of the rotated mass reinforce each other and make this zone the heart of the project: its location at, practically, the geometric center of the plan, its distinct orientation and shape, and the important functions it houses. Because it is at the

Figure CS7.3 The diagonal line and offset at the elevator lobby to reception area route, as well as the curved forms on the north end, add dynamism to the project.

Figure CS7.4 Displays of projects and parking structure directories are prominent features of the reception area, the starting point for the marketing tour.

center of the space and contains the elevator lobby and entry/exit sequence everybody who visits the floor experiences the rotated mass and can always get oriented in relation to it. Its unique axis of orientation, its protrusions into the corridors at both ends, and the distinct shapes it adopts at both ends (circular on the north, angled and stepped on the south) make it a recognizable, prominent, and consequently memorable mass on the floor. This mass is prominent not only as a backdrop to other activities around it, but also as home to some of the key communal functions of the office, and therefore, an important destination that draws people and activity.

The central rotated mass acts as a divider of space, helping to break down the scale of the floor into well-defined and easily recognized neighborhood areas with comfortable proportions. Particularly clear and

successful are the two corner neighborhoods on the east side of the floor. These feature clear and definite entry points, clear edges to separate them from adjacent areas, and short L-shaped corridors to keep the relative distance from end to end manageable and adjacencies strong.

The other interesting aspect we want to point out about this project is the incorporation of a special tour route to conduct "moving marketing presentations." Prospective customers are taken around designated portions of the office in the process of the tour, thus making the marketing experience interactive and locomotive. The success of the marketing tour is due to the skillful integration of strong anchor destinations with memorable events and in-between channels of moving that reinforce the main selling points without "stealing the show."

Propelled by the movement-inducing dynamic qual-

Figure CS7.5 One of the highlights of the marketing tour is the semicircular wood-paneled node on the east side of the floor.

Figure CS7.6 The comfortable and elegant conference rooms provide a fitting destination after the marketing tours.

ities of the rotated central mass, the tour starts in the reception area, where prominent displays of projects and parking structure graphics are featured (Figure CS7.4). After a short walk through corridors that feature samples of parking garage graphics and materials and vivid colors, one arrives at the tour's principal node, a semicircular space that features specialized displays set into a wood-paneled wall (Figure CS7.5). Two turns later, one reaches the main diagonal cross-corridor leading back to the starting point. Along the route the clients can catch a glimpse of the displayed computer room, which serves as the brain for the administration of all the facilities under APCOA/Standard Parking's management. One of two conference rooms becomes the final destination for further talks (Figure CS7.6).

Review

Summary

One of the major contributions a designer makes is endowing the built environment with order. Environmental order manifests itself in different ways: order related to proper fit, order related to visual harmony, and order related to spatial orientation.

Designers should strive to provide more than just neat and functional organization, and provide an overall structure based on sound organizing principles. Interior environments are experienced sequentially, one space at a time. Sometimes, what appears clear on paper while looking at a floor plan is hard to

figure out as we move about in built space. Three factors that help facilitate the understanding of interiors are identity, structure, and meaning. Environments strong in order have easily identifiable main components, a systematic structure derived from an organizing principle, and meaningful destinations.

The ten place elements introduced earlier in the book play important roles in providing environmental legibility and order. Notable are the role of arrival spaces, paths, nodes, and landmarks. To feel oriented inside buildings it is necessary to understand components at various hierarchical levels: parts, groups, relationships between parts, sequences, and, finally, the whole. Many design strategies are available to make these various components stand out clearly so they can be understood and remembered. By making individual parts and groupings recognizable, their points of intersection visible, their sequences memorable, and the structure of the whole comprehensible through the proper provision of environmental information, designers bring order to the projects they design.

A crucial aspect related to legibility and order is the composition of the masses and spaces of a project. Predominantly enclosed projects with closed corridors are the most difficult to understand due to the lack of visual accessibility. Open spaces are easier to decipher. Nevertheless, it is possible to design predominantly open projects of great complexity. The number, size, placement, orientation, and shape of masses and the complexity and level of disclosure of the boundary all combine to produce spaces of different levels of complexity and readability.

Order is possible at all levels of complexity. In

general, the more complex a project is, the greater the need for order to help users feel oriented. Optimal levels of order will vary from project to project depending on their scope and users. The level of order established and the level of difficulty involved in understanding it are factors controlled by the designer. If appropriate design choices are made, the level of order achieved will help orient users in space by facilitating their understanding of the environment, its place within the larger context, and their position within these environments at any particular time.

Chapter Questions

1. Name three examples of order related to fit.
2. What is meant by architectonic order related to visual harmony?
3. What are the main concerns of order related to orientation?
4. Describe how interior environments are experienced.
5. Name and define the three factors that facilitate understanding and orientation in interiors.
6. How can domains and centers contribute to order?
7. Why are arrival spaces so important for orientation?
8. How can paths be used to supply order?
9. How do nodes and landmarks contribute to order?
10. Name and define four design strategies to facilitate understanding of project parts.
11. Name and define four design strategies to facilitate legibility of groupings.
12. Name and explain two design strategies to clarify the relationships between project parts.
13. Name and describe three design strategies to increase awareness of motion and sequence in interior environments.
14. Name and explain four strategies to help users understand a project as a whole.
15. What effect does attaching masses to the perimeter boundary have on legibility and orientation?
16. Why does it sometimes make sense to design freestanding masses with no equal sides?

Exercises

1. Select an important space, a *center*, of a past or present design project and determine three design strategies to make it more memorable inside and outside.
2. Sketch two ways to make an *arrival space* enhance the user's sense of orientation.
3. Sketch three *paths* with different levels of disclosure to the rest of the project.
4. Design two versions of a vibrant *node* for any project type.
5. Design one memorable *landmark* for an interior project.
6. Make a part (mass or space) of one of your projects stand out by using one or more of the strategies discussed in this chapter.
7. Sketch two ways of using a *datum* to group parts of one of your past or present design projects.

8. Select a prominent space from one of your past or present projects and expand its level of *visibility* towards other interior areas. Sketch the result.

9. Sketch two *sequences* of past or present projects using some of the strategies we discussed to make them legible and useful for orientation.

10. Design one idea using the concept of *points of reference* to facilitate orientation in interior projects.

11. Sketch two ideas to increase the imageability of closed corridors in a compartmentalized project.

12. Sketch two ideas (one formal, one casual) to group all the solids of a past or present project within one (freestanding or attached) mass.

13. Sketch two ideas (one formal, one casual) similar to the ones above using, not one, but two masses.

Endnotes

1 Arnheim, Rudolf. *The Dynamics of Architectural Form,* (University of California: Berkeley, 1977)

2 Leupen, Bernard. *Design and Analysis* (Van Nostrand Reinhold: New York, 1997) p. 25.

3 Abercrombie, Stanley. *Architecture as Art: An Esthetic Analysis*, (Van Nostrand Reinhold: New York, 1984) p. 147.

4 Norberg-Schulz, Christian. *Genius Loci*, (Rizzoli International: New York, 1980) p. 19.

5 Passini, Romedi. *Wayfinding in Architecture*, (Van Nostrand Reinhold: New York, 1992).p. 45.

6 Von Meiss, Pierre. *Elements of Architecture*, (Van Nostrand Reinhold International: London, 1990) p. 110.

7 Lynch, Kevin. *The Image of the City*, (MIT Press: Cambridge, 1960) p. 8.

8 Ibid, p. 9.

9 Passini, Romedi , p. 111.

10 Ibid, p. 120.

11 TK.

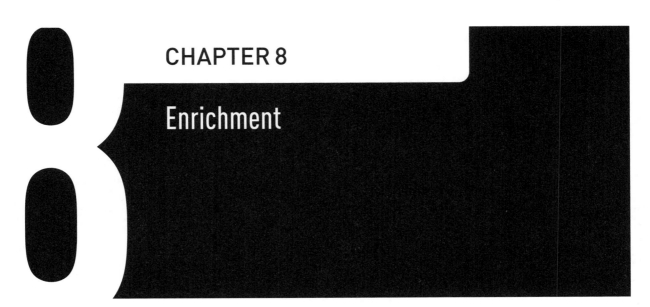

CHAPTER 8

Enrichment

INSTRUCTIONAL OBJECTIVES

Explain the need for both environmental stimulation and environmental stability.

Present general principles to enrich interior spaces.

Show ways to incorporate meaningful events along circulation routes.

Present strategies to enhance the formal qualities of the path itself.

Show ways to design the views within and beyond the path.

Suggest a framework for the enrichment of personal experience while stationary.

My house is practical. I thank you, as I might thank Railway engineers, or the Telephone service. You have not touched my heart.[1]

The introductory quote by Le Corbusier reminds us of the need to address a key, and sometimes forgotten, function of design: to enrich, to touch the human heart. The commitment to find ways to do this is what distinguishes a designed solution from an engineered solution. This chapter addresses ways to make projects more than engineered, functional solutions.

In Chapter 7 we discussed the role of order in design. Regularity and clarity make interior environments easier to understand, satisfying our inherent need for making sense of the world. However, too much order can be monotonous. We also need variety and interest in our environment. One of the challenges for the designer is achieving an adequate balance between these seemingly conflicting needs. In reality, order and enrichment are highly intertwined and form part of a single puzzle. Expression is also a piece in this puzzle, but it will be covered in the next chapter. These different variables are presented in separate chapters to facilitate understanding of their unique contributions. In real projects, they are usually explored at the same time that different design ideas are studied.

In this chapter we first discuss the role of enrichment in the design of interiors. The rest of the chapter presents ways of making projects and our experiences in them, richer. The strategies are broken down into three categories: general enrichment strategies, enrichment while in transit, and enrichment while stationary.

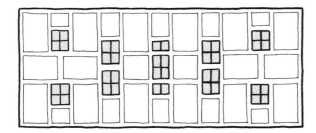

Figure 8.1 The simple act of moving some of the solid masses of the floor plan presented in Figure 7.42 produces a more interesting design.

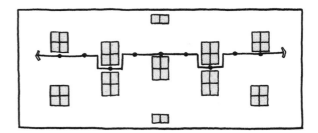

Figure 8.2 This arrangement seeks to enhance the circulation experience. The project's masses have been rearranged to increase variety and interest. Sometimes one is walking between a mass and open space, other times between two masses, and still others between two open spaces.

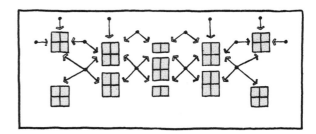

Figure 8.3 Depending on their desk location, workers in this facility have one or more masses close by. These act as anchoring devices and internal focal points.

Order and Enrichment

We concluded our last chapter by saying that too much order can be as undesirable as too little order. The optimal level of order for a project must fall somewhere between those two extremes. Order makes a project visually agreeable and understandable. Order involves repetition and follows rules based on a predetermined principle of organization. It offers constancy and predictability. We quickly become familiar with highly ordered projects.

The human mind values predictability and constancy in the environment, but it also seeks novelty and variety. Opinions about how much and what kind of the above qualities are optimal can be quite personal. They can vary from project to project and from designer to designer. Furthermore, the potential approaches and combinations used to produce order, novelty and variety are limitless. It is possible to achieve a desirable balance of these qualities with alternate design solutions quite different from each other.

Let's start by examining how reducing the degree of regularity can enhance a project. Consider an alternate version of the highly regular project presented in the last chapter in Figure 7.42. Suppose you had the same programmatic needs to fulfill but wanted to add some novelty and interest within a similar design vocabulary of rectilinear forms. Just by manipulating the placement of the solid modules as shown in Figure 8.1, the project acquires enough variety to alleviate its severe sense of repetition. The project is now inherently more interesting and has more differentiation between zones, even though the parts are still highly repetitive.

Let's take it a step further. Suppose you were concerned with the experience of moving through the project and wanted to make it more interesting. Figure 8.2 shows the solid modules of the same project arranged to provide various different experiences as one moves from one end to the other. Although the movement is basically straight throughout most of the length, the two offsets and their placement divide the floor into three zones with two transitional areas between them.

Finally, suppose you wanted to enrich the daily experience of each worker as perceived from his or her desk. You might then arrive at something like what is shown in Figure 8.3. The typical worker, regardless of location, now has an identifiable sense of place that provides a focus for the area and anchors users in space. If the solid masses viewed from there had some special surface articulation or wall treatment that was pleasant to look at, the experience would be further

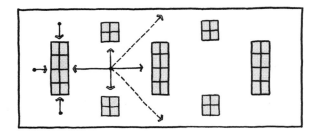

Figure 8.4 This arrangement is similar to the one in Figure 8.3 but it provides an even stronger sense of containment and group territory.

enhanced. Figure 8.4 shows a similar example with an even stronger sense of definition and containment, especially in the interior zones.

Each of the manipulations mentioned in our example above enriched different aspects of the project. The modifications performed in Figure 8.1 gave the project, in general, an increased level of interest, due to the additional variety. Users and visitors could still sense order and harmony throughout, but without the excessive original regularity. The simple modifications increased the level of spatial articulation and complexity, but modifications were done in such a way as to provide relief and engage the mind without confusing it.

The modifications performed in Figure 8.2 made the act of moving through the project more interesting. Now, in the process of traveling from one point to another, users encounter meaningful intermediary events that enrich the journey. The modifications in Figures 8.3 and 8.4 make it possible for users, while working at their desks, to engage a bit more meaningfully with their internal surroundings. Instead of interior masses being just rooms, they now perform the additional duties of anchoring adjacent open areas and providing beneficial focal points on which to rest the eyes.

Are these kinds of interventions necessary? Not really. Projects can be functional without them. Are they desirable? Of course they are. They enhance the experience of the people using the space. Some designers give more consideration to these matters than others. It is important that you develop your awareness and skills to perform these kinds of manipulations to make your projects more enriching.

A Case for Project Enrichment

The success of most interior projects relies more on function than anything else. As we said earlier, the context of the project and the requirements of the program give a project its fundamental form. Response to these alone determines the size and location of the different areas of a project. However, response to function alone will rarely produce the best form. Form has to be dealt with in its own right, respecting the placements and adjacencies dictated by the context and program, but following its own agenda to produce experiential desirable qualities. It takes conscious and intentional effort from you as the designer to provide more than good function and pleasant aesthetics.

It is common for design to be limited to the functional and the artistic. Designers put a lot of effort into resolving the way things work and the way they look. What we are proposing here is that design should be as concerned with the way things are, the way they are arranged, and the effect these design decisions have on those who experience them. You may think of this dimension as the poetic dimension of projects.

Architecture is unique among the arts in that people operate within its structures most of the time. Designers, as part of their craft, have the responsibility to determine buildings' spaces and their sequences. In doing so, they have the power to create experiences that seduce and stimulate, or to downplay physical aspects of the building in order to provide a barely noticeable background to the theater of life. This is a remarkable power. While an attractive appearance is always desirable, we remind you that even visually plain projects can possess poetry in their composition.

Achieving qualities and experiences that engage the user and enrich his or her experience requires designers to adopt a separate agenda concerning these issues. These qualities and experiences rarely occur without a conscious desire to produce them. They require the designer's commitment to seek them out and work on them so they occur seamlessly without neglecting or disturbing the other requirements of the project. It may become necessary for you to negotiate between the various requirements and agendas of the project in order to balance them satisfactorily. This will often require compromise. For example, you may occasionally have to consider moving a room a couple of spaces down from its optimal functional position in order to achieve a more desirable experiential or compositional effect. These types of decisions are sometimes difficult and are not always possible. They need to be considered on a case-by-case basis and require proper insight and input from users and the design team alike.

So, your task is to manipulate the required physical parts of the project in order to achieve more evocative effects and meaningful encounters within it. Is this really possible, you may ask, with the kind of strict and limiting programs designers have to work with? It's seldom simple. It often requires an approach where project parts perform double functions. A wall may be the enclosing plane of a room needing privacy and also the canvas for an experientially rich corridor on the other side. The resulting configuration of the wall, therefore, may be a compromise that works for both of these intentions.

Another approach, used sometimes, is the incorporation of spaces and events not required by the program to enrich the experience of users. The enlargement of an important intersection to create an energetic node, and the addition of small niches for people to gather in are examples. Of course, the addition of space to a program is a sensitive matter requiring proper justification in the eyes of the client. It is often impossible to add additional square footage to a project, and whatever amenities are desired have to be planned skillfully within the physical size constraints of the project.

Intentionality

The effect the interior of a building has on its users is produced by a combination of factors, some having nothing to do with the environment itself. In Chapter 2 we explained how factors such as the nature of the occasion, the people involved, nearby activities, and other similar factors affect our experience. Even when we consider building aspects only, the resultant effect is produced by an interplay between a number of elements we perceive simultaneously, at different levels, many of them unconsciously. The spatial character, the order of spaces, the furnishings, the materials, the colors, the sounds, the lighting, the artwork, the details, and the specific combination of all of the above act in unison and produce an overall effect on us.

It is impossible to separate form from meaning. Most everything in the environment elicits associations that conjure certain connotations and levels of personal response. Certain aspects of design stimulate more symbolic associations than others. Specific design styles, materials, and graphic representations (artwork and photography, for instance) usually have strong associations with specific attitudes and ways of being. Other aspects are more neutral and harder to label. We tend to experience these as they are, for what they offer or present to us, without much symbolic interference. In this chapter we will focus on formal rather than symbolic aspects of form. Symbolic aspects of design are addressed in the next chapter.

We need to consider some important questions in order to formulate a personal philosophy regarding the extent to which we allow ourselves to manipulate design for effect. For instance, how does one go about manipulating space to increase the level of engagement between users and their environment? Is it even right to perform somewhat arbitrary manipulations for the sake of effect? To what extent is well-intentioned artistic license a right or privilege of the designer?

Personal positions related to these questions are likely to vary. Some designers favor straightforwardness over cleverness, some favor simplicity over complexity, some like the realistic and pictorial over the abstract and obscure. Whatever your personal position may be, it is important that you are clear about it and pursue it consistently within each project. Design manipulations for effect may sometimes come across as superficial. It is therefore imperative that all interventions are well thought-out and considered carefully before implementation. Many seemingly good ideas are better left undone if they will lose their impact and seem foolish after their novelty wears off.

Stimulation and Stability

Having issued all the above warnings, we maintain that it is worthwhile to manipulate project forms, spaces, and elements to increase their richness and enhance the users' experience. The rest of this chapter addresses specific attributes and strategies for your consideration. We will start by introducing two opposing human needs that you need to understand before embarking on the task of manipulating projects for enrichment. They are stimulation and stability.

Stimulation

We have said that optimal qualities of the visual field lie somewhere between total regularity and total disorder; the exact levels depend on the particular realities of each project. Despite our need to perceive order and the sense of orientation and satisfaction that comes with it, we also have a desire to experience environmental stimulation. An efficient, functional, and orderly environment that does not stimulate will rarely satisfy. People need some level of stimulation.

Optimal levels and kinds of stimulation are relative. A nightclub, for instance, demands much more stimulation than a hotel guest room. In the nightclub, the combination of design features, colors, lights, loud music, and interesting people produce a very high-load environment. This, we recognize, is appropriate for the project type. The hotel guest room, in contrast, other than being cheerful and welcoming, needs to be a good place to unwind and relax. Therefore, bright blinking lights, extravivid colors, and loud music are not likely to be appreciated.

Stability

Although we make the point that some level of stimulation is healthy for all projects, some projects, or parts of projects, benefit from less environmental stimulation. Spaces where repose, peacefulness, and concentration are desirable don't need to be highly stimulating. Hospital rooms, for example, need to be pleasant in a quiet, nonagitating way. Stable places can be evocative and powerful in some ways, but should not be visually loud. Areas of mental activity requiring high concentration, such as private offices in some work facilities, should be conducive to concentration without much distraction. Areas meant for relaxation, such as the hotel guest room mentioned above, usually need to be more subdued than stimulating. Keep in mind, however, that the desire for subtle and subdued qualities doesn't necessarily mean the elimination of all stimulating features.

Part of the challenge of design is determining the appropriate level of stimulation and the means of achieving it. Understanding the effects of these two fundamental, and opposite, forces will help you make judgments about the correct balance of the stimulation/stability spectrum for a specific project. In the rest of this chapter we discuss attributes and strategies that help make projects engaging. They can all be handled in ways that provide more or less stimulation and can therefore be utilized in both high-load and low-load environments.

Enrichment in Building Interiors

In Chapter 2 we analyzed the basic events of the building experience. Starting from the approach to the building, we described the process of arriving, waiting, proceeding to, and arriving at the target destination within the facility. In Chapter 3, we presented a related set of project parts labeled the place elements. Some of these, such as arrival spaces and destination spaces, relate directly to the various rituals of the building experience. By thinking of the basic events of the building experience and the places where they occur, we can gain awareness of opportunities to enrich the experience of users. Below, we address a few of the place elements especially apt for enriching design manipulations and point out some instances in which to use them.

The arrival space gives visitors their first impression of a project. Whatever message that is to be communicated to the user begins here. Additionally, this space represents an important transition from the space immediately outside, and between itself and the rest of the facility. Among the main design variables available for manipulation in order to provide opportunities for engagement are the overall impact of the space, the level of visual disclosure to other spaces in the facility, and the freedom of movement from the space.

Waiting involves anticipation. It sometimes induces a state of heightened awareness as we anxiously wait for someone to rescue us and take us to our real destination. Other times, the act of waiting supplies a few minutes between tasks during which we can have a chance to unwind. For some, the close proximity to other people can be uncomfortable. Waiting areas offer opportunities to provide engaging graphic or verbal information about the entity housed in the facility (whether a corporation, a doctor, or a restaurant). They are also good places to add elements of visual relief.

As we will see, the circulation spaces of a project present great opportunities to engage the user with building elements as well as with the rest of the facility. The design of the main corridors is one of the most important design factors of many projects. Unfortunately, corridors are often not given the attention they deserve. If properly orchestrated and articulated, the circulation experience can delight, entice, and provide engaging sequences.

Destination spaces, you may recall, are the spaces where we usually do what we came to do in the facility, be it work, eat, study, socialize, or shop. When we engage in our target activity, the building, its interiors and elements take a secondary, supporting role. The actions in these spaces focus on paperwork, food, books, people, or merchandise, among many possibilities. Even in these spaces, where the facility, like a butler, should be unobtrusive except to provide utilitarian assistance when needed, there are opportunities for enrichment. Design manipulations can enhance users' abilities to focus on the task at hand, connect with adjacent surroundings, and find momentary relief in well-conceived and well-placed views and vistas.

Below we present a number of enrichment strategies. For convenience, we have grouped them into three categories: general enrichment strategies, enrichment strategies for users while in transit, and enrichment strategies for users while stationary. The first group can be exercised anywhere within the project, either throughout or in select areas. The second group is specific to circulation areas. The third group is closely associated with areas where we spend time doing something while stationary, such as destination spaces and waiting areas.

General Enrichment Strategies

Variety

The relatively simple manipulations performed in Figures 8.1 through 8.4 at the beginning of this chapter show the profound effect of variety in projects. Although the organization of the project in the various schemes remained relatively formal and regular, the modifications provided relief and interest. In projects where parts are not repetitive, there is a natural occurrence of variety. In projects that feature repeated parts it is up to the designer to provide enough variety to avoid monotony and make the project more challenging perceptually. Sometimes all it takes is a few basic shifts as seen in the examples mentioned above. Other times a greater degree of variety and differentiation may be desirable. In those cases, variety becomes complexity.

Complexity

Environmental complexity has been a well-researched topic in studies of environmental preference (see Capsule #7: "Complexity, Order, and Other Environmental Attributes"). Research indicates that people tend to prefer more environmental complexity up to a certain point at which any further increase produces discomfort. That critical point varies from individual to

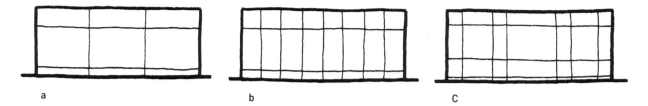

Figure 8.5 The three elevations shown are examples of modulation using lines. The level of intricacy can be minimal (a), moderate and regular (b), or moderate and irregular (c).

individual. Design features to add complexity can be anything from lines on a wall to the heavy articulation of surfaces, ornamental features, or multiple and varied objects in space.

The relationship between complexity and order has also been studied. Environments high in order have been found to tolerate higher levels of complexity than those with less order. Therefore, the number and kind of elements in a space and their specific arrangement go hand in hand and work together. Complexity is rewarding because it stimulates the brain. Complex orchestration of parts requiring some mental effort to decipher is stimulating as long as the effort required is not overly taxing. There is a sense of accomplishment in understanding arrangements that challenge our mental faculties.

Environmental complexity occurs at many levels and can be produced a number of ways. The surfaces of enclosing planes and other elements (such as columns) can be articulated in increasingly complex ways. The number and arrangement of masses and objects in space can be manipulated to achieve increasing levels of complexity. Also, the treatment and orientation of project components (floors, walls, furnishings, and so on) can be treated as different layers and arranged in contrasting ways to achieve complexity. We examine them in more detail below.

Surface Articulation

One important way you can provide environmental complexity is through the articulation of the enclosing planes. The degree of complexity can be minimal, just enough to provide some interest, or it can be substan-

tial, enough to challenge our senses and even overwhelm us. One simple way to provide subtle articulation is by **modulation**. Modulation is the subdivision of any element, such as a surface, into smaller components or modules. These modules, in turn, add up to the whole. Modulation on surfaces usually relies on the use of regulating lines. Thus, a simple and featureless wall can acquire a sense of texture by the addition of lines produced by either molding strips or reveals.

Figure 8.5a shows a simple wall subdivided by the use of lines. Although the level of complexity achieved is minimal, the modulation of the wall is enough to give it some interest. The lines have to be placed so that a good sense of scale and proportion is achieved. Otherwise, the attempt to enrich will do more harm than good. Figure 8.5b shows the wall modulated into an increased number of equal parts. Although the result produces a degree of richness, the composition is not very interesting. The modules of the wall in Figure 8.5c feature an irregular rhythm, thus resulting in a more varied and complex arrangement incorporating a sense of hierarchy.

The example in Figure 8.6 shows modulation on both the floor and ceiling. Here the modules are smaller in size and larger in number than in the previous wall example. There is some complexity. The floor tiles are arranged in a repetitive pattern and this makes the composition easy to understand despite the variety of tiles. In fact, it is possible to keep adding layers of complexity to a composition such as this and keep it within acceptable perceptual levels if the parts are arranged in some perceivable pattern. The ceiling composition shown here is nonhierarchical and repet-

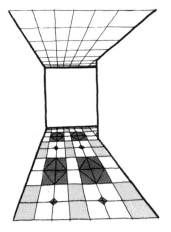

Figure 8.6 Patterns and lines applied to floors and ceilings also increase relative complexity and supply richness. The orderly arrangement of the floor pattern makes it rich without seeming overly complex, despite the intricate pattern.

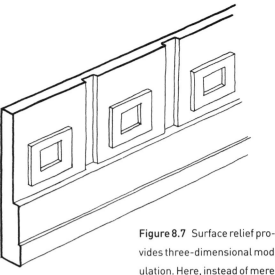

Figure 8.7 Surface relief provides three-dimensional modulation. Here, instead of mere lines or reveals, the effect is accentuated by deeper recesses and protrusions between the different parts.

Figure 8.8 Spatial complexity can be controlled by the manipulation of how much one can see at a given time. In this example the intensity of the view (a) is reduced by the addition of screens blocking part of the view (b).

itive. The end result is increased textural richness at the ceiling plane.

Modulation can also be accomplished by **surface relief**. With this technique, alternating parts of a surface advance or recede to create differentiation. The result is similar to the one created by lines, but, in the case of relief, the sense of depth is manipulated to create more pronounced effects. Notice how the composition shown in Figure 8.7 uses depth to provide a sense of articulation to the wall unattainable with just lines.

Spatial Composition

Complexity can also be attained by the composition of elements in space. By manipulating the disposition of architectural and interior elements in the visual field you can produce interesting and rich compositions. Factors that play a part and can be manipulated

are the number of parts, their size, shape, and arrangement. While the number of parts is often dictated by the program, such as the number of tables in a restaurant's dining area or the number of display fixtures in a retail store, it is possible to manipulate the amount of architectural articulation around them to increase or decrease the overall level of complexity. It is possible, for instance, to have a complex foreground of objects with a simple background or a simple foreground with a complex background and overhead plane. It is also possible to control the way groupings are created and the separations between them to dictate how much is seen at once. Figure 8.8 shows two views of a dining area in a restaurant. Figure 8.8b includes a separating element subdividing the overall space and reducing the perceived overall complexity by decreasing how much is seen at once.

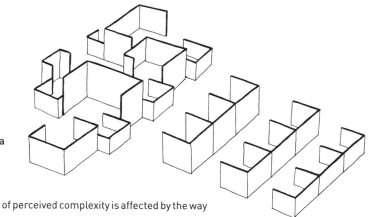

a

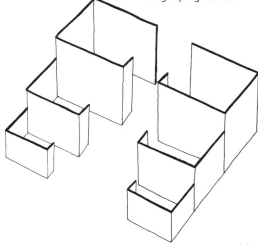

b

Figure 8.9 The level of perceived complexity is affected by the way in which different pieces are arranged. Groupings that mix unequal elements (a) tend to be more complex than those where similar parts are grouped together (b).

Figure 8.10 Where unequal elements are grouped together, simplicity and harmony can be achieved if they are grouped to form a pattern as shown in this simple example of a smaller to larger progression.

The size and shape of the various objects in the visual field also enters the complexity equation. Groups of similarly sized and shaped objects will be fairly uniform and perceived as simpler than the same number of objects of a different size and shape. Grouping objects by similarity of size or shape will produce a greater sense of order and thus allow more variation. Figure 8.9 shows a simple example illustrating this principle. Two groups of workstations are arranged somewhat randomly in Figure 8.9a, and grouped according to similarity in Figure 8.9b.

A way of providing ordered complexity when dealing with parts of different sizes or shapes is by using pattern. If a harmonious pattern is established and it is easy to see, then the arrangement can be successful despite the variety among the objects. Figure 8.10 shows an example of this using a variety of furniture workstations. They are arranged in a simple pattern (by size), producing a simple composition despite the use of parts of different sizes.

Arrangement is important in manipulating complexity. You can make a simple group of a few components more interesting by using an irregular spatial composition. Conversely, you can control the complexity produced by a collection of many disparate parts by utilizing more regular arrangements. Even projects that have immense inherent density and variety of parts can be controlled by the use of pattern and regularity.

System Overlapping

One unique way to produce complexity in the interior environment is to think of different spatial components as layers that can be manipulated independently of each other. You can think of a project as consisting of the following systems: the enclosing boundary, the floor plane, the interior walls, the ceiling plane, the furnishings, the building structure, and other miscellaneous objects in space, such as suspended elements and fixtures, and details. All these systems overlap with each other to produce the final composition. A perfectly ordered arrangement would have all these systems aligned neatly in parallel or perpendicular relationships to one another. See Figure 8.11. Notice, however, what happens when some of these systems are rotated laterally in relation to the others as shown in Figure 8.12. An interesting, more complex, effect is produced while maintaining a sense of order by the consistent treatment of each system and the clarity with which each of them reads.

This technique can be used in subtle ways by per-

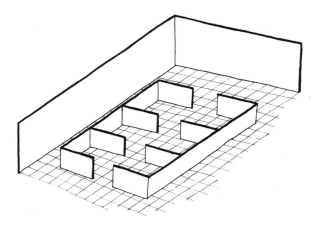

Figure 8.11 Floors, walls, furnishings, and ceilings can be thought of as different systems that can operate as different layers. In this example, all the systems are oriented uniformly.

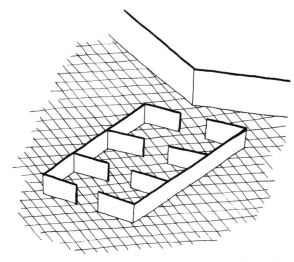

Figure 8.12 In this example, the floors, enclosing walls, and furnishings are treated independently from each other and given different orientations to produce a more complex arrangement.

Figure 8.14 Masses of an unconventional shape are novel and can increase the interest of a space.

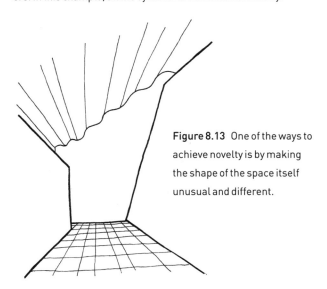

Figure 8.13 One of the ways to achieve novelty is by making the shape of the space itself unusual and different.

forming slight rotations (or other kinds of variations) and by the alteration of a few systems. It can also be used in ways that produce extreme complexity by rotating all systems so they each have different orientations.

Novelty

Another enriching factor in the environment is novelty. Novel shapes and arrangements attract our attention and engage our minds. Novelty goes beyond mere variety. The novelty can be due to the uniqueness or the unconventionality of the approach taken. In any case, the approach taken is different from the norm. As with any of the other variables, the degree of application can vary from subtle to extreme. A space can be slightly unique or highly unusual.

Spatial novelty can be produced by the nature of individual masses and elements in space and their shapes, and also by their combination into specific arrangements having novel effects. In general, regular shapes, usually rectangular, and uniform rectilinear arrangements are considered the norm, the conventional default approach we customarily see. Almost any design deviating from these approaches has the potential for being novel and attracting our attention, if done skillfully.

Examples of novelty include unusual shapes of spaces (Figure 8.13), or masses (Figure 8.14), unusual treatment of specific visual elements, such as openings and elevations (Figure 8.15), and unusual arrangements in space, such as the effect produced by taking otherwise normal arrangements to an extreme, as in the case of extreme geometry and rhythm (Figure 8.16).

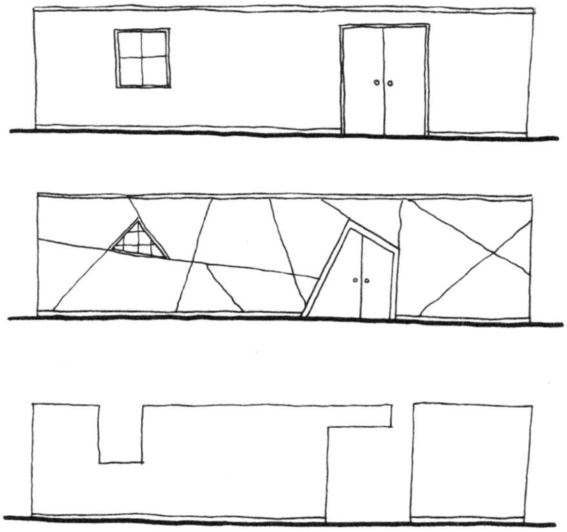

Figure 8.15 Surfaces such as elevation compositions can be treated in unusual ways. A simple elevation requiring a door and a window (a) can be composed in different, even highly unusual ways as shown in (b) and (c).

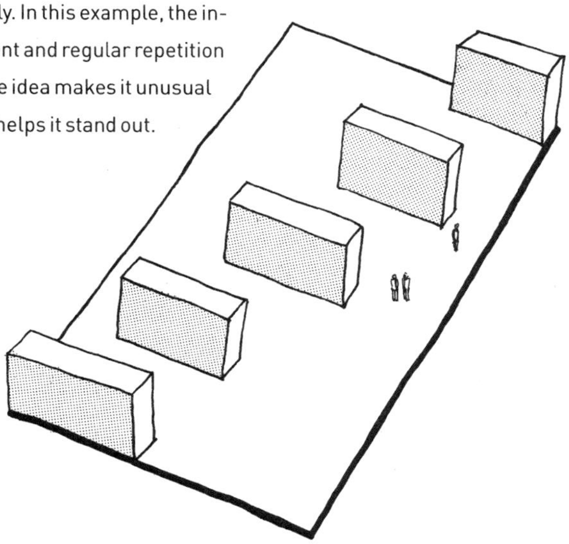

Figure 8.16 A simple arrangement such as the staggering of masses, can stand out as different and novel, if handled severely. In this example, the insistent and regular repetition of the idea makes it unusual and helps it stand out.

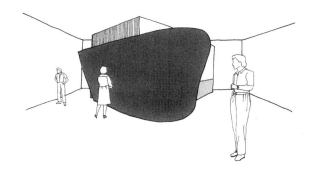

Figure 8.17 The novel mass introduced in **Figure 8.14** is intensified here and made bolder.

Boldness

Boldness, a specific kind of novelty, requires its own category. It relies on exaggeration to make something stand out in the environment. Often associated with boldness of treatment, such as surface treatment, it can also be expressed spatially. Accomplishable in interiors by exaggerated applications of anything from color, to light, to texture, when related to space it usually involves the exaggeration of shape or scale, making them much more intense than normal.

An example of boldness of shape would be the exaggeration of an unusual shape to an extreme, such as the conversion of the shape shown initially in Figure 8.14 to the more extreme version shown in Figure 8.17. Clearly, the shape has transcended the quality of novelty and become much bolder, almost threatening.

Boldness of scale involves the exaggeration of size. While large spaces can be associated with grandiosity, large masses are more effective at achieving boldness because of their heaviness and their figural character. They become almost defiant. It helps if they have some degree of verticality and detachment from surrounding walls. Being able to see the entire mass as a free-standing object in space helps to accentuate its massiveness.

Tension

A strategy that is sure to engage the mind, and the emotions, is the use of deliberate tension in the environment. The goal is to create a situation of temporary discomfort in order to heighten the user's alertness. Long-term exposure to environmentally tense spaces can be detrimental and should be avoided. Short-term exposures of appropriate intensities can be enhancing, especially when part of a sequence that eventually provides welcomed relief.

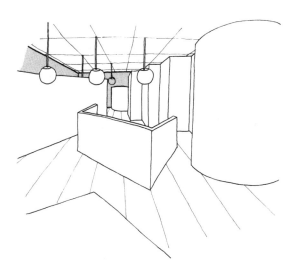

Figure 8.18 Excessive complexity or incongruity of parts often produces tension. The number and random placement of parts shown here make this environment somewhat tense.

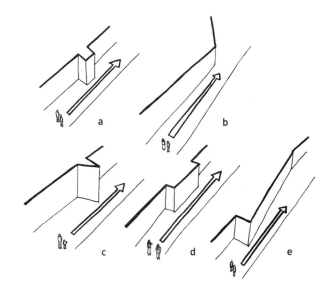

Figure 8.19 A common way to produce tension is through the compression of space. The five examples shown compress space along a route to achieve different levels and durations of tension.

Tension can be produced by overtaxing the senses with extreme levels of the already discussed conditions of complexity, novelty, and boldness. High levels of these conditions can actually be appropriate in high-load environments like nightclubs, some retail applications, especially those targeted for the youth, and short-term high-load settings, such as some restaurants. On the other hand, environments such as workplace and institutional settings do not normally tolerate these conditions.

Two additional strategies to provide enrichment through tension are the use of intentional visual discord and intentional compression. Visual discord is equivalent to dissonance in music. It requires intentional incongruity. Its intensity and extent have to be carefully considered in order to avoid highly negative reactions. The technique is inherently risky, as many people will not appreciate any deliberate attempts to produce disharmony. Additionally, intentional discord can easily be confused with lack of design skill. An example of visual discord to produce tension is a chaotic or overly complex spatial arrangement as shown in Figure 8.18.

Tension through compression can be successfully applied in selected points along a route or sequence by the deliberate compression of space to produce a tightening effect. The tightening can be sudden (Figure 8.19a) or gradual (Figure 8.19b). Its duration can be just an instant (Figure 8.19c) or longer (Figure 8.19d). Finally, relief can come suddenly or gradually (Figure 8.19e).

Ambiguity

The use of ambiguity to engage users relies on the presentation of mixed messages in order to confuse and/or challenge the mind. Instead of a crystal clear and consistent message, a muddled one is presented. This is another tricky strategy requiring good judgment and skill for success. The American architect, Robert Venturi, argued for the value of ambiguity in design in his classic 1966 book, *Complexity and Contradiction in Architecture*. He noted: "An architectural element is perceived as form *and* structure, texture *and* material. These oscillating relationships, complex and contradictory, are the source of the ambiguity and tension characteristic to the medium of architecture. The conjunction 'or' with a question mark can usually describe ambiguous relationships. Is it a square plan or not? Are they near or far? Big or small?"[2]

Examples of ambiguity in interiors include an almost perfectly symmetrical elevation with enough inconsistencies to provoke the question: Is it symmetrical or not? (Figure 8.20); a juncture placed along the path leading to a reception area with a focal point at one end and a geometry that opens up and invites at the opposite end, making one wonder: Is the reception area to the right or to the left? (Figure 8.21); and a corridor utilizing a forced perspective to make it seem longer than it actually is, provoking the question: Is it a short or long corridor? (Figure 8.22).

All these instances of ambiguity may or may not be

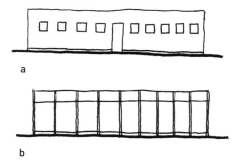

a

b

Figure 8.20 Ambiguity can be used playfully, such as in the elevations shown here. They appear to be perfectly symmetrical, when in fact they are not. The number of windows in (a) and the width of the modules in (b) are not consistent from side to side.

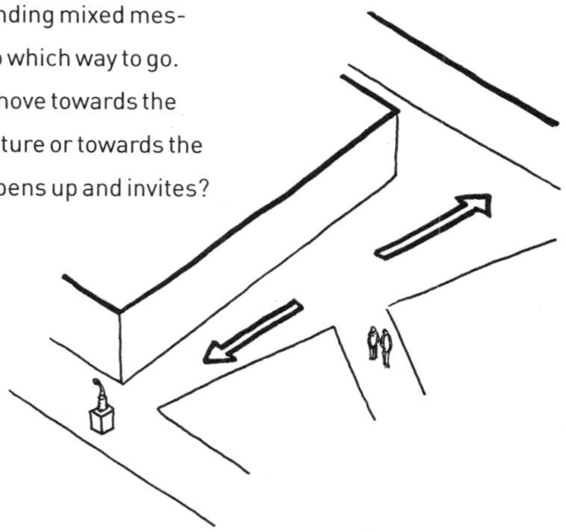

Figure 8.21 A subtle example of ambiguity is an entry sequence sending mixed messages as to which way to go. Does one move towards the focal sculpture or towards the side that opens up and invites?

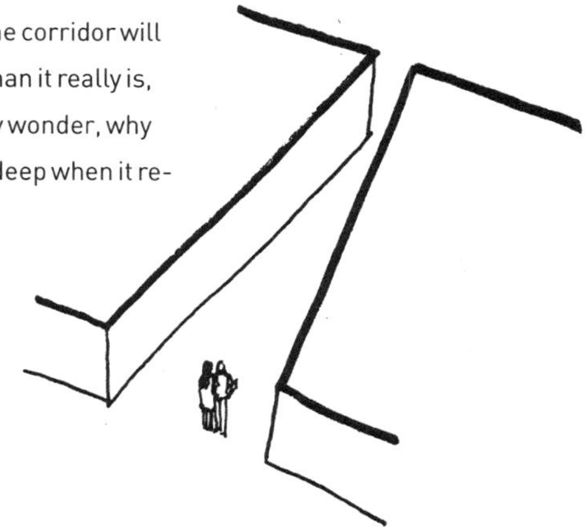

Figure 8.22 Illusions, such as the use of a forced (exaggerated) perspective here are also ambiguous. The corridor will seem longer than it really is, and a user may wonder, why does it feel so deep when it really isn't?

justifiable. In general, they are more justifiable when they are a result of the inherent complexities and contradictions of a project. They can be questionable when they are arbitrary, although there are times when they may serve a worthwhile purpose. In some cases, it may be useful to make users aware of the location of the sculpture in the corridor shown in Figure 8.21, even though the intended direction towards the reception area is to the other side. People may need to eventually make a stop on the side with the sculpture. If, for instance, a nurse tells visitors that the X-ray lab is by the sculpture, they will know exactly where it is because they will remember seeing it when they came in. Similarly, there may be some usefulness in making a corridor seem longer than it is to exaggerate and enhance the sense of transition between two areas involving different experiences.

Pictorialness

As our society has evolved, we have grown accustomed to environments that are complex and more abstract than in the past. There is greater tolerance and demand for the less literal and the more cerebral. The pictorialness, symmetry, and straightforwardness of the past are no longer dominant. Nevertheless, well-composed pictorial project parts still continue to engage and delight many of us. Not everything has to be complex, novel, or ambiguous to be enriching. In fact, many people still prefer the straightforward to the overproduced or ambiguous. Although pictorial compositions lost favor with the emergence of the more abstract modern movement during the twentieth century, they did not disappear. Well-composed picto-

rial elevations, often formal and symmetrical, are still a joy to look at. They engage our minds and make us appreciate them. The same is true for the well-composed detail, be it a column or a railing. Whether simple and serene or more active through articulation, it is still a source of delight. See Figure 8.23.

Activity Manipulation

One final general strategy for enrichment involves, not the kind of manipulation of building elements for effect presented in the examples above, but the strategic placement of certain functional areas that become instruments of enrichment by attracting people. Examples include spaces whose vitality results from a concentration of human activity and spaces that foster in us a sense of special meaning because some specific opportunity has been thoughtfully provided.

A specific example of the first case above is a space,

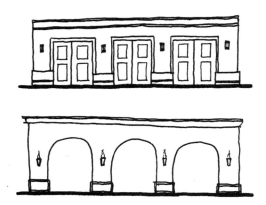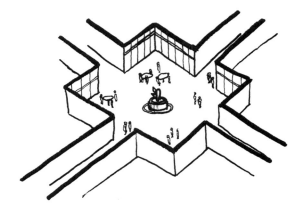

Figure 8.23 Well-composed pictorial spaces and elevations have delighted for centuries and are still appropriate today. Shown here are two straightforward, formal and symmetrical elevations.

Figure 8.24 Intensifying use to create vital areas of high energy produces enrichment by use. The activity, sounds, and movement themselves become the agents of variety and complexity.

such as a node, located strategically in such a way that it is impossible to get around the building without going through it. Because of its centrality, it is likely to have constant traffic and activity. Furthermore, if some strategic function can be located within or adjacent to that area, acting as a magnet, then not only would people be passing by, but others would stay. This may elicit images of the urban plaza with cafes around it. It is not that different, although the scale and specific functions are likely to vary in interiors. In these cases, the vitality and energy of the people themselves that enriches and attracts others to join in. It has nothing to do with the composition of elements for effect and everything to do with the strategic placement of functions to maximize the impact of human presence.

These kinds of spaces can be most successful in public or semipublic areas not requiring high degrees of privacy or tasks requiring concentration. Applications are possible in restaurants, stores, hotels, some areas of office projects, and within the major circulation routes of most projects. See Figure 8.24.

An example of spaces that foster in us a sense of special meaning because of the kind of opportunity they present for a given use is a well-placed, small-scaled space off a main route or major space, where one or two persons can sit to talk, work, or just rest. We are talking, of course, about the art of designing the small human niche, cultivated by some designers but unknown to many. These spaces are seldom included in the program of requirements supplied to the designer at the onset of a project. They are provided by thoughtful designers who understand the nature of people and their desire for small intimate spaces in certain settings that provide a comfortable place to step into without losing connection to the greater totality beyond. Figure 8.25 shows an example of one of these spaces.

Enrichment When in Transit

There are many opportunities to create enrichment in a project's circulation spaces. People are usually between tasks when in transit. During those times people can be highly receptive to environmental stimulus. It is while moving that we truly experience what has been called the fourth dimension of architecture, seeing the physical environment changing and emerging as we move through space. All projects have circulation spaces, some more formal or explicit than others. The design of corridors and other circulation spaces requires thoughtful consideration. Enriching projects have engaging circulation routes.

Below we consider the path or corridor as a vehicle for enrichment. We'll look at the effect of sequences, the qualities of their components, and their capacity to engage us in them and the rest of the project.

Sequence

A good part of our experience inside buildings takes place as we move through space. Our perception of space while moving is especially important because the physicality of movement and the goal oriented nature of most walking episodes produce a state of alertness that help us absorb more of the surroundings.

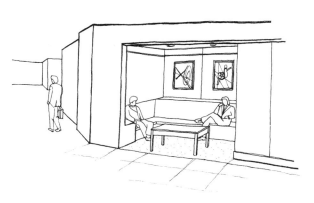

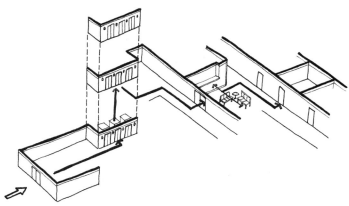

Figure 8.25 Small off-the-path spaces where one can step off and feel grounded, yet still be in the middle of things, provide enrichment.

Figure 8.26 A typical trip to many destinations, like to the clinic shown here, involves a sequence featuring distinct experiences.

Moving through space offers the potential for exploration. Human beings seek variety and distraction. Whether through a trip to the coffee room at the office, a trip to the restroom in the restaurant, or a side trip while shopping, we welcome opportunities to take a break and look around. Sometimes these trips are meant as a break; other times they are necessary. In any case, they provide the benefit of providing an opportunity to explore the environment around us.

Regardless of the degree of urgency and our level of familiarity with the environment, just about every trip we take within a given environment offers an exploratory experience. This can occur at different levels. We can discover the spaces of a new environment as we move through it, and we can also notice qualities and details we hadn't noticed before in familiar territories. Additionally, the unfolding human drama often seen from the path is like an ever-changing theater stage, full of interest and surprises.

Exploration can be actual exploration of unfamiliar territory but it also refers to the kind of exploration we do when we visually scan, say, a wall with intricate pattern and detail. In the latter case, the brain is engaged in the exploration of a complex composition and is challenged to make sense of it. Therefore, it spends a few seconds taking it all in and trying to understand it. Assuming there is some engaging complexity and a well-composed arrangement, we are likely to be not only momentarily entertained but also delighted. If we think of the path as a vehicle for enrichment, we can consciously plan it in ways that increase the perceptual richness it offers. This section will give you some ideas.

To design the circulation system of a project you have to take into account the kind of movement different segments are required to facilitate. Movement in buildings is not always leisurely or recreational. In fact, it is rarely so. Most movement we do in buildings has a specific purpose and destination. We move with resolve to reach our destinations, often so preoccupied that we barely notice the environment around us. In cases of emergency or extreme rush, we actually run, and anything we encounter on our path is an obstacle. In those cases, the only image we welcome is that of the door or passage leading to our destination, be it a space inside or the door leading to the exterior.

Environments require efficient movement. Most movement inside projects will have a fair amount of resoluteness. Therefore, while we want to still provide experiences along the way, these should not be so distracting or indirect as to be annoying, or worse yet, dangerous. Any attempt to enhance the experience of users while moving should not slow people down too much. Emergency egress paths, especially, need to be clear and direct for obvious reasons. But even clear, efficient paths can provide opportunities to slow down and step aside.

People's main concern while moving along a route (with some exceptions) tends to be their final goal or destination. If the journey is long, it may include several subgoals or intermediate arrival places. When visiting a clinic on an upper floor of a multistory building, for instance, we arrive first at the front door, then in the building lobby, the elevator lobby, the elevator, the elevator lobby of the target floor, the entrance outside the destination clinic, the reception area of the

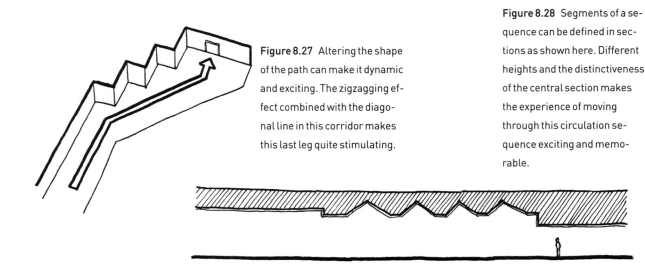

Figure 8.27 Altering the shape of the path can make it dynamic and exciting. The zigzagging effect combined with the diagonal line in this corridor makes this last leg quite stimulating.

Figure 8.28 Segments of a sequence can be defined in sections as shown here. Different heights and the distinctiveness of the central section makes the experience of moving through this circulation sequence exciting and memorable.

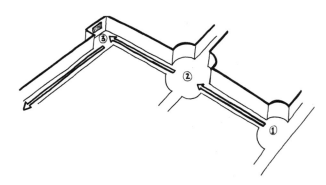

Figure 8.29 The use of some of the place elements we have discussed in the book, most notably, nodes and landmarks, along circulation routes is an effective way to accentuate certain points. In this example, three nodes establish distinct, recognizable points along the path.

clinic, and, finally, the examination room. See Figure 8.26.

If unfamiliar with the above environment, we may, at any given time, not be able to think beyond the next intermediate destination, moving in chunks from one to the next until we arrive at our real target destination. All the transition points become the salient locations that will be mentally recorded and remembered during subsequent visits. Those locations may very well have special design features that, when traveling more leisurely, users will notice and appreciate. After all, all those transitions force the user to slow down or stop, setting up, potentially, a moment of enough conscious awareness for an aesthetic experience.

Many routes will lack the natural transitions presented in our clinic example above. In those cases, it is up to you as a designer to find ways to break up the route and provide meaningful events along the way, especially for long routes. Here is where you can put on your movie director hat and plan the route in ways that produce enriching experiences.

Events along the Route

Think of the route's sequence as a story line, with plots, subplots, and one or more climaxes. To do this, keep in mind that we tend to move from goal to goal until we reach our destination. It is those goals that often stay in our minds. That's where your planning of the nodes, centers, and landmarks of your project can become a factor, and make a positive contribution, turning ordinary circulation systems into experiences full of events.

A sequence can be made engaging by transitions along the trajectory, and by the presence of distinct events along the way. Transitions can be changes in direction or transitions in the physical character of the path. Figure 8.27 shows an example of a route featuring some changes in the path's direction and configuration. Figure 8.28 illustrates how changes in the physical spatial character of the path provide a story line in itself.

The transition points in Figures 8.27 and 8.28 above have good potential for becoming recognizable and memorable events. Other potential distinct events are the centers, nodes, and landmarks along the route. Figure 8.29 shows a fairly linear and potentially uneventful route sequence enhanced by the incorporation of strategically located nodes

Other possible events along the route are surprises (or rewards), whether anticipated or not. These are

Figure 8.30 A view from a typical corridor is long and narrow, features some defining side boundaries, a view straight ahead, and perhaps views of adjacent spaces.

often in the form of enriching encounters with meaningful objects, details, and views. These may come as total surprises or be anticipated destinations hinted at prior to reaching them.

Qualities of the Path Itself

In addition to having an engaging sequence, the circulation route can be enriching by virtue of its inherent physical qualities. Despite their typological similarities, paths can have distinctive characters. Let's examine the components of a prototypical path. Most paths' segments are, basically, similar. They tend to be long, narrow spaces. We normally travel along them in linear fashion. As we move, we see the sides of the path obliquely, from the near parallel relation of our line of vision to them. There is some view, planned or unplanned, at the end of the corridor which we see straight ahead and some distance away. As we move along we may, depending on the specific situation, see adjoining spaces beyond the corridor. See Figure 8.30.

Our job is to make the path special. Once we have a basic path outlined on our preliminary floor plan we may ask the questions: Are the visible components of the path engaging in and of themselves? Should they be? To what extent? Answers to those questions will inform the direction we take. Aspects that can be controlled and enhanced include the shape of the path and the qualities of its enclosing surfaces.

The Shape of the Path

Despite the recurring configuration inherent in the typology of the path, as described above, there are a few variables that give paths different characters.

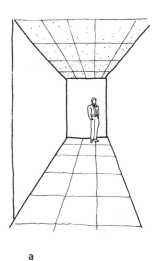

Figure 8.31 The level of openness or enclosure of a corridor greatly affects its character and perceived length. Enclosed corridors that are self-contained can get uncomfortably long (a). Corridors with openings provide visual relief to adjacent features and activities, and don't seem as long and tedious (b).

a

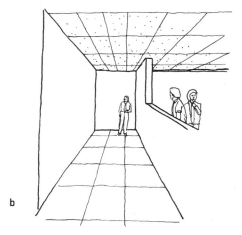

b

These are their length, their degree of enclosure, their height-to-width proportions, and their configuration in both plan and section.

Paths come in different lengths. Many of these are perceptually comfortable but others get to be too long. Acceptable lengths vary depending on the height-to-width proportion of the path, as well as the degree of lateral enclosure and the articulation of the side walls. In general, enclosed corridors with solid side walls on both sides will seem longer than those connected visually to adjacent spaces, especially if the side walls are flat and plain. See Figure 8.31.

One way of keeping long paths within acceptable length limits is to break them up into smaller segments by the addition of intermittent spaces, such as cross corridors (Figure 8.32), or by offsets in the path or enclosing walls (Figure 8.33).

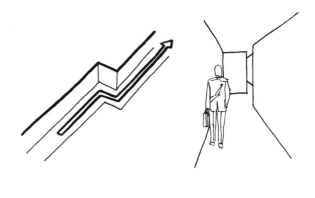

Figure 8.32 Intersections and intermittent spaces help relieve the perceived length of corridors by breaking up their linearity.

Figure 8.33 A strategy to alleviate long corridors is to offset the path at some point before it starts feeling too long. This breaks the path into subsegments.

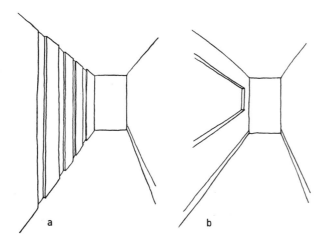

Figure 8.34 Modulation on the side walls enrich the formal visual qualities of the space by the addition of rhythm, pattern, and texture. Vertical (a) and horizontal (b) lines will have very different perceptual effects horizontal lines accentuate the depth dimension of the corridor.

At a more subtle level, vertical and horizontal articulations on the side walls, ceilings, and floors affect the perceived length of a path. Figure 8.34 shows the effect of side wall articulation on two corridors of equal length. Articulation or pattern on the ceiling and floor planes can also have an impact on the perceived depth. In general, lines along the length of the corridor will make it appear longer than lines perpendicular to it (Figure 8.35).

Although the level of enclosure around a corridor is somewhat dictated by the privacy and enclosure needs of the spaces adjacent to the path, there is some room for manipulation. In terms of enclosure, paths can be fully enclosed, partially enclosed, or fully open. They can also be a combination of these pure conditions. The principle of variety is a handy one to use when designing paths. To the extent that the program will allow flexibility, it is a good idea for you to design paths that offer variety through contrast. This can be achieved by contrast between the two sides of the path or by contrast between successive segments of the path (Figure 8.36).

Another important contribution of the enclosing planes is their role in determining the relative autonomy of the path. A path with no barrier on one side has the potential of blending with it. It can read as an extension of the adjacent space, or it can read as a distinct path if some differentiation is provided by the ceiling and floor planes. Whether through level changes or through a change of finish, the treatment of the two important horizontal planes can change the feeling the path has in relation to the adjacent spaces. This is one case where the design can result in

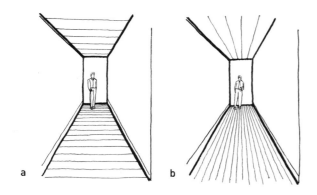

Figure 8.35 Lines and pattern on the floor and ceiling planes also add texture. Similar to the case of side walls, lines along the length of the corridor (a) will make it seem longer. Lines across the corridor (b) will have a shortening effect.

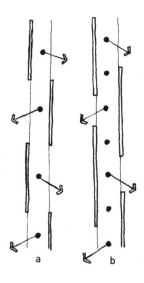

Figure 8.36 The experience of moving through corridors can be enhanced by the use of variety and contrast. These examples show a corridor with alternating open and closed sides (a), and a similar one with overlapping walls resulting in smaller openings (b).

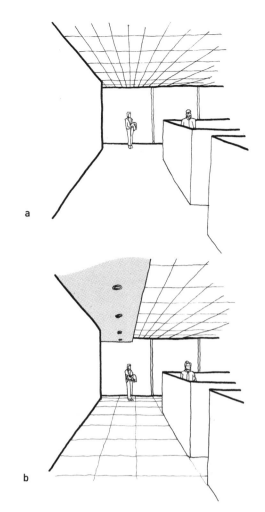

Figure 8.37 The ceiling and floor planes are important elements in determining the perceived autonomy of a path. Example (a) reads as one space where the edge defined by the furniture establishes an aisle. In example (b) the path reads as a distinct, well-defined corridor due to the ceiling and floor treatments.

clear autonomy, clear affiliation, or an ambiguous condition where one may question whether it is a corridor or a continuation of the adjacent space. Figure 8.37 shows examples of both a path with little architectural differentiation (Figure 8.37a) and one where the ceiling and floor help to accentuate the distinction between the path and its adjoining space (Figure 8.37b).

Height-to-width proportions of paths, like their length, impact the way we perceive and experience them. Some proportions feel better than others. Different combinations will produce paths that can be categorized as tall, balanced, and low-height paths. Each of these are illustrated in Figure 8.38. All three have their appropriate applications. The one to be careful with is the low-height path. Despite the nice intimate scale it can provide, it can also be quite uncomfortable if it gets to be too long.

Despite the predominance of the path with parallel sides, due in part to its inherent economy, there are other possible plan configurations. While these normally require more space, they add dynamic qualities and produce path segments of great interest. Figure 8.39 provides just two of many possible examples. You should master these and other similar ones and try to use them where sensual or dynamic qualities are needed.

Similar manipulations are possible in section. While most corridors consist of parallel, plumb sidewalls, and a flat ceiling plane above, this is by no means the only configuration possible. While some of the possibilities can violate the sense of what is considered normal, some of them will be appropriate at times. Your

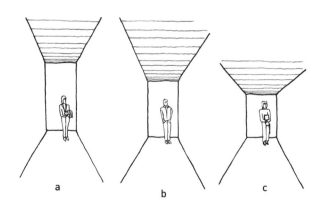

Figure 8.38 Corridors come in different heights: tall (a), normal (b), and low (c).

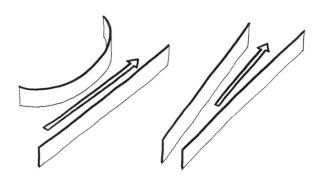

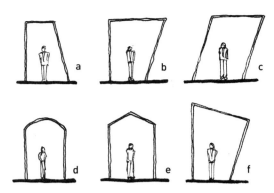

Figure 8.39 Corridors do not have to always consist of parallel walls. There are times when it is possible and desirable to make corridors dynamic by the modification of one or both sides. The two examples shown modify only one side to achieve dynamic results.

Figure 8.40 Most corridors tend to be boxy in section. There are times when the geometry can be changed for effect. This can be done by changing one side wall (a) and (b), changing both side walls (c), changing the shape of the ceiling (d) and (e), or a combination (f).

repertoire of corridor sectional configurations should include a wide range of possibilities. These can range from the articulated to the unconventional. See Figure 8.40 for some examples.

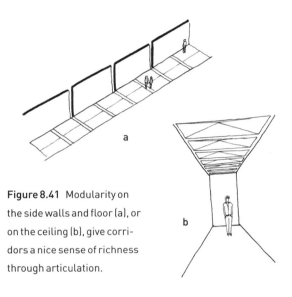

Figure 8.41 Modularity on the side walls and floor (a), or on the ceiling (b), give corridors a nice sense of richness through articulation.

Qualities of Enclosing Surfaces

The treatment of enclosing surfaces affects the level of interest of a path and should be carefully considered. Included are the side walls or screens, the floor plane, and the ceiling plane. Design variables to consider include modulation, spatial texture, and pattern. Modulation can be used on any of the enclosing planes alone or in combination. A rhythm of vertical elements on one or both of the side walls, a subdivision of the ceiling plane into units through articulation, and the use of pattern via modular flooring materials can all be used to modulate surfaces. See Figure 8.41. The subdivision of paths through modulation endows it with a sense of strong rhythm that can be rather attractive if well executed.

The articulation of paths does not need to always result in distinct modules. In some cases a reduced approach will provide a pleasant rhythm without a feeling of strong subdivision. Rhythm along one of the dominant surfaces can be quite engaging and afford the path a nice sense of spatial texture (Figure 8.42).

In addition to the kind of articulation shown in the previous examples, simple elements such as openings on the side walls, and cross corridors form part of the overall path composition and contribute to its sense of variety, rhythm, and texture.

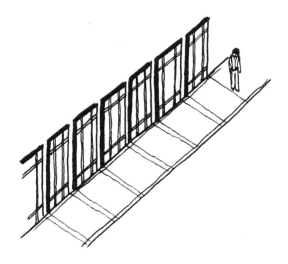

Figure 8.42 When the modules used are smaller and feature additional line work or pattern, the result is a greater sense of spatial texture.

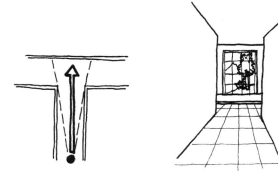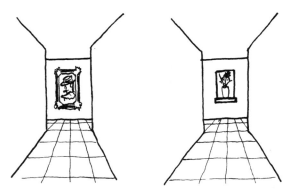

Figure 8.43 The framed view at the end is an important strategy used in many corridors (a). Variations include the framed exterior view (b), the framed piece of artwork on the wall (c), and the niche with object inside (d).

Manipulation of Disclosure

So far, we have talked about the role of events along the path sequence and the inherent qualities of the path in providing experiential richness. A third way paths engage us is by manipulating the kind, degree, and rate of disclosure of spaces and features within and beyond them. Equally important is how the path affects the overall spatial composition when seen from adjacent spaces, that is, when looking into the path while being outside of it.

The View at the End

One of the most noticeable aspects of any path is the view straight ahead. Depending on the arrangement, it may or may not be possible to see the final view at the end of the path from a given point in it. In paths that zigzag or meander, the end is often blocked from view until one arrives at the last leg of the path. In straight paths we see the view at the end. Except for the portion of a side wall immediately next to us at any given time in our trajectory along the path, nothing is likely to be as strong as the view at the end, whether we are conscious of it or not. Even if we are still at a distance, we are looking at it head on. It is unmistakably there and it has great power to make an impression on us.

What is revealed at the end is important and requires proper attention. Possible strategies for you to consider include the strategic use of focal points, prospect, and enticement.

Focal Points

The use of focal points can be an effective strategy to enrich our experience in circulation areas. These usually occur at the end of the view ahead. These views are carefully framed. Possibilities include a view to the exterior or space beyond, a piece of artwork, or some well-placed evocative object, such as a vase with flowers sitting on a shelf, perhaps set into a well-proportioned niche on the wall (Figure 8.43d).

While the side walls of a corridor are usually seen obliquely and not straight ahead, there are conditions when we may see a side wall or a portion of it straight ahead. This occurs in cases where one of the two sides is open to the adjacent space, allowing a straight ahead view from these spaces towards the wall. In these cases it becomes necessary to consider the view of the wall seen from the adjacent space. The wall needs to work as both a side wall of the corridor and a wall segment seen as a vista from the adjacent space.

Prospect

Prospect is the framed view we see at the end or beyond the turn. It serves as somewhat of a focal point except its composition is not necessarily a picturesque termination. In the case of prospect, we see what lies beyond, say a wall of an adjacent mass in the distance, with its own set of needs and requirements. You could think of prospect as a carefully composed partial view of something beyond. Because whatever is going to be seen beyond will have a degree of visual prominence, it requires careful attention to make the resulting view at least adequate. Unfortunately, the view at the end of many interior corridors is the default result of whatever happens to be beyond, with no regard for its merits or drawbacks. While not every view at the end of a

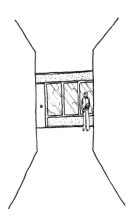 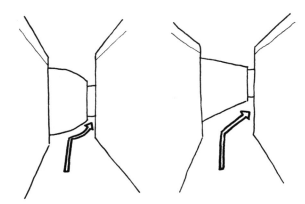

Figure 8.44 Prospect is the view seen beyond the corridor. Consideration needs to be given to the placement of elements seen in order to produce an acceptable, and hopefully pleasing, view.

Figure 8.45 Compositions beyond the corridor can be arranged in ways to entice and attract. Curved walls and angled walls allow partial views beyond that arouse our sense of curiosity and make us want to move forward to explore further.

path needs to be treated with special accent pieces, every ending view should be designed to produce agreeable, if not engaging, results. Figure 8.44 shows an example of a prospect view that is not quite a focal point but has been carefully considered to produce pleasing results.

Enticement

In addition to careful, pictorial compositions of the views at the end of the path, and sensitively composed views of what lies beyond, it is also possible to design arrangements that lead the moving person in a desired direction. This is usually achieved through the use of arrangements with directional properties, the use of arrangements that disclose what lies ahead only partially, and the use of powerful elements that attract at the ends. Diagonal arrangements and circular configurations favoring one direction are effective in this regard. See Figure 8.45. It is possible to increase the level of attraction of the view at the end by arousing people's sense of curiosity. Circular shapes and compelling distant views (because of their composition, boldness, brightness, and so on), arouse our curiosity and draw us towards them. See Capsule #7: "Complexity, Order and Other Environmental Attributes."

The View Beyond the Path

While in many cases, the view at the end of the path may be dominant, lateral views to adjacent spaces also form an important part of the circulation experience. Views to adjacent spaces reveal other spaces of a facility and provide orientation, distraction, and, some-

times, entertainment. How much is revealed depends on the required level of connection or separation needed and the intentions of the route designer. In areas not requiring total separation there is room for interpretation and manipulation. The variables of disclosure and access discussed in Chapter 4 come into play here.

The process of designing corridor walls and points of entry from the circulation into the spaces is somewhat automatic and driven by functional needs. However, there are opportunities for you to perform manipulations for effect. Two important design strategies to create engaging routes are the manipulation of points of visual connection to adjacent areas, and the manipulation of the correspondence between visual and physical access.

Points of Visual Connection

Most circulation spaces in individual interior projects afford some degree of visual connection to adjacent spaces. Sometimes the extent of the view continues to the outdoors in the form of external views. Visual connection from the circulation area to adjacent areas is desirable. However, caution must be exercised because total continuous connection can be as monotonous as total separation. The optimal level lies somewhere in the middle. Partial visual connection is gratifying since it provides relief from the enclosure of the corridor. It is possible to create a playful pattern of "now you see it, now you don't" between the corridor and adjoining spaces to stimulate users' minds and enrich their experience.

While a balanced mix of visual separation and visu-

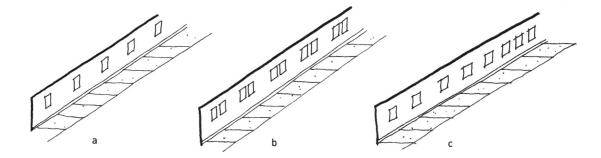

Figure 8.46 Openings along side walls of corridors connect us visually to adjacent spaces. Their arrangement can be straightforward and rhythmical (a), rhythmical in pairs (b), or gradated (c), among other configurations.

al disclosure, in itself, is likely to result in generally agreeable arrangements, it is possible to have an even greater impact through the strategic placement of the openings providing the visual connection. If a certain opening between a corridor and an adjacent space coincides with a point along the route where visual relief would be desirable, the overall impact is likely to be greater. If openings between the corridor and adjacent spaces are rhythmic or gradated, the result will have an increased level of playfulness and engagement. See Figure 8.46. If the visual connection is framed strategically to reveal a particularly special angle of the adjacent space, then the impact is going to be stronger. In short, it is not enough to only provide connections. The actual arrangement of the openings requires careful thought and consideration if the effect is to be truly enriching and poetic.

We have seen how the placement of the points of visual connection between areas is crucial to the overall orchestration of the corridor. Also important is the degree of connection afforded. Any given connection can range from a narrow glimpse through a small opening to a full view of the adjacent space. It is possible to use uneven rhythms such as the glimpse, glimpse, wide-view sequence shown in Figure 8.47a. The opposite is possible in predominantly open corridors. Instead of locating openings, you deal with solids, such as column, column, wall (Figure 8.47b).

The placement, size, and arrangement of openings from a corridor requires careful consideration if you want to provide enriching experiences. Every situation needs to be looked at individually and analyzed carefully to arrive at optimal balances between sepa-

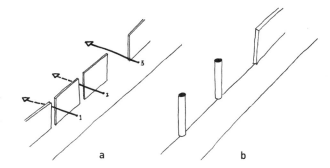

Figure 8.47 It is possible to perform playful orchestrations between open and solid portions of side walls. Example (a) shows the play of openings in a mostly solid wall. Example (b) shows the play with solids in a mostly open boundary.

rations and connections, and to heighten and enrich the experiences of those moving in them.

In addition to internal views, views from the corridor to the exterior are enriching when they occur. These can be lateral views at a distance, immediate lateral views, or views at the end of the corridor. These views can be panoramic or carefully framed views that look in a particular direction with something beyond as a focal point (a vista). Exterior views have the effect of extending the perceived space horizontally. They can provide a great amount of relief, not to mention a sense of connection to the external context. In some cases, circulation routes can be located along the perimeter of a building to provide external views all along the way.

As important as the view from the path to an adjacent space is the view from that adjacent space back to the path. The composition of the framed view back towards the path is to be given proper consideration and not left up to chance. Figure 8.48 shows three of many possible arrangements. Figure 8.48a and b create

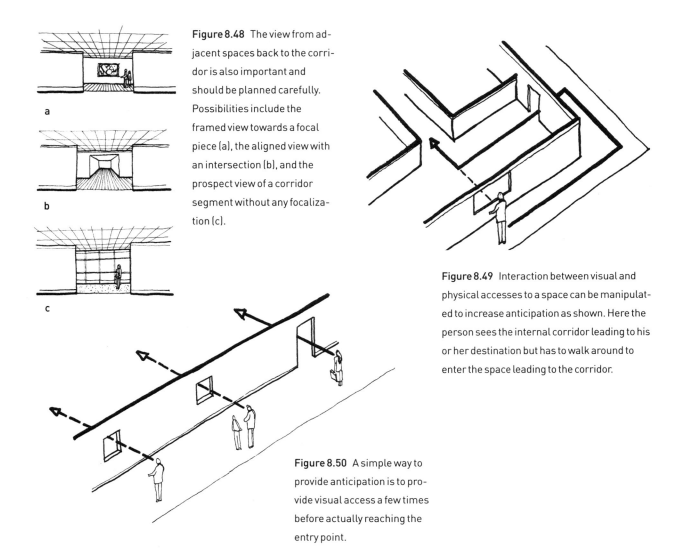

Figure 8.48 The view from adjacent spaces back to the corridor is also important and should be planned carefully. Possibilities include the framed view towards a focal piece (a), the aligned view with an intersection (b), and the prospect view of a corridor segment without any focalization (c).

a

b

c

Figure 8.49 Interaction between visual and physical accesses to a space can be manipulated to increase anticipation as shown. Here the person sees the internal corridor leading to his or her destination but has to walk around to enter the space leading to the corridor.

Figure 8.50 A simple way to provide anticipation is to provide visual access a few times before actually reaching the entry point.

focal points, one terminating the view in a piece of artwork on the wall and the other extending it into the gateway to a corridor centered on the framed view. Figure 8.48c shows a view without a dominant focal point, but one that has been thoughtfully composed to make the framed view rewarding.

Correspondence of Visual and Physical Access

The design of visual access points in relation to the actual point of entry to an area presents some interesting opportunities to provide enriching experiences. In projects where a clear and efficient path is necessary, either because of a project's particular use or the population for whom it is being designed, correspondence between visual access and physical access will be important and, generally, will be the norm. In such cases, ambiguity and tension are not likely to be appreciated. Even in some of those cases, however, it may be sometimes useful to see a view of the destination before

having to make a decision about heading towards it or not.

In cases where more playfulness can be tolerated, it is possible to add some interest to the experience of entering an area by manipulating the relationship between visual disclosure and physical access to an area to create either a sense of anticipation or intentional tension. Figure 8.49 shows an arrangement featuring a view on axis with the circulation of an area, yet requiring the person to go around the corner to enter the space and connect to its path. Figure 8.50 shows an example where several views of the area are presented to build anticipation before arriving at the eventual entry point. Needless to say, these types of manipulations are not appropriate in all cases. If attempted in the wrong project or if arranged such that the entry point is too remote, they can be annoying. They are to be used only in areas of projects where they will be appropriate and even then, only in moderation.

One of the main themes of human behavior, and consequently of the design of places for people, is the duality of exposure and withdrawal. British geographer Jay Appleton devised a theory that provides much insight into these fundamental human necessities. It is called prospect-refuge theory and was conceived to help understand human appreciation of the exterior landscape. The theory is a specific application of habitat theory, which Appleton explains as follows:

> All this leads to the proposition that aesthetic satisfaction, experienced in the contemplation of the landscape, stems from the spontaneous perception of landscape features, which in their shapes, colours, spatial arrangements and other visible attributes, act as sign stimuli indicative of environmental conditions favourable to survival . . . 'Habitat theory' thus asserts that the relationship between the human observer and the perceived environment is basically the same as the relationship of a creature and its habitat. It asserts further that the satisfaction which we derive from the contemplation of this environment, and which we call 'aesthetic,' arises from a spontaneous reaction to that environment as a habitat, that is to say as a place which affords the opportunity for achieving our simple biological needs.[1]

Prospect-refuge theory can be generally exemplified by Konrad Lorenz's account of the advantage afforded by the point between enclosure and openness found while taking a walk in the forest. He states: "before we break through the last bushes and out of cover on to the free expanse of the meadow . . . we reconnoitre, seeking, before we leave our cover, to gain from it the advantage which it can offer alike to hunter and hunted—namely to see without being seen."[2] Both the hunter and the hunted need strategies to fulfill their goals and protect their best interests. The hunter's strategy involves putting himself in a position to maximize opportunity. He must approach his prey as close as possible without getting noticed.

The strategy of the hunted involves assuring safety. It requires having a place inaccessible to the pursuer and putting himself in a position to, if needed, reach that place before being prevented by the hunter. To accomplish this, the hunted will have to be in a position where the hunter will not see him, or if visible to the hunter, one that will give him enough time to react and reach safety. In both cases, as Appleton points out, "it is in the creature's interest to ensure that he can see his quarry or predator, as the case may be, without being seen, and the achievement of these conditions becomes a first objective which renders more likely the achievement of the second, to catch or to escape."[3] Obviously, familiarity with the environment would give either hunter or hunted an advantage, as it would potentially increase the number of routes for attack or escape.

According to the theory, environments whose characteristics are perceived to offer the ability to see without being seen tend to be aesthetically more satisfying. During primitive times, more than now, the ability to see and the ability to hide were both necessary for survival. Appleton suggests that humans carry those evolutionary tendencies within them even though they have long evolved from a primitive existence when hunting and protection against hostile tribes were prevalent. He calls the unimpeded opportunity to see "prospect" and the opportunity to hide, "refuge."

One may question the magnitude with which these programmed tendencies really influence our aesthetic judgments and preferences for places. After all, life in most of the civilized world is relatively safe from antagonistic hunters. We also have to acknowledge that in certain types of situations people want to see and to be seen, such as at the type of bar or café where people go to socialize. Nevertheless, and excluding the obvious application to settings high in crime or terrorism, prospect-refuge theory still offers wonderful insights into some fundamental traits of human behavior. People's tendencies to approach or avoid a place, after all, depend at least as much, if not more, on who is present, than on the issue of environmental load discussed in a previous chapter.

At an even more fundamental level, the issue of prospect and refuge brings us back to the topic of existential space discussed previously in Capsule 3, "A Phenomenological View of Space and Dwelling." There, we described the notion of center at the heart of human dwelling in contrast to the beyond, conceptualized as paths and domains away from the center. Just these three existential space-elements serve to articulate the basic and most fundamental duality of existential space, between the "here" (what is familiar and safe) and the "there" (what lies outside and involves exposure and risk). These correspond to all kinds of dualities frequently found in design, such as open-closed, sheltered-exposed, and private-public.

With prospect-refuge theory we start addressing the important role of the environment in influencing interactions between people by the positioning of places and the visibility between those places. Not only is it important for a person to be at his or her safe and familiar center, but also to be in a strategic position to see who is coming and have a chance to react by welcoming or hiding, as well as to know who is outside and have a chance to decide whether to use the front or back door. Likewise, someone on a path approaching a place can strategically scope a scene and make decisions about whether or not to enter, and which way to go, depending on the potential opportunities or threats presented by it.

Potential application of prospect-refuge thinking is found in many types of settings, some more than others. Public settings where people spend time, such as restaurants, cafés, and clubs, present some of the best opportunities to use prospect-refuge thinking. At a café, a preference for prospect is likely to dominate. People will want exposure to see and be seen, although it would be wise to have a few tables in the back for those seeking less exposure. At a restaurant, people may prefer a table that affords some anchoring; in other words, a refuge. Depending on circumstances, they may opt for one visually accessible from the rest of the space (reducing the sense of refuge but increasing prospect) or one tucked away allowing them to see without being seen, thus providing both prospect and refuge. A good practice is to provide a variety of tables with different degrees of privacy and exposure so people can choose one that fits their particular needs at the moment.

For a quiet, intimate dining experience the emphasis is definitely on refuge. In fact, the desire for prospect may be limited. Through careful zoning of areas, positioning of tables, and use of local lighting (e.g., individual candles at tables), it may be possible to create an atmosphere in which each table feels like an oasis, even though it may be just a couple of feet from an adjacent table.

Prospects and refuges occur at different scales. A town on a hill may be a refuge (familiar and secure) from which you may enjoy views of the prospects beyond. Within the town, the house represents another level of refuge having views from the windows that connect with prospects beyond. Within the house, the personal bedroom represents yet another scale of refuge and the chair tucked away in the corner still another. We can see how the concept of refuge has many similarities to that of center in existential space.

Frank Lloyd Wright was a master of the art of providing a good balance between prospect and refuge. In *The Wright Space*, Grant Hildebrandt applies prospect-refuge theory to analyze Wright's residential designs. In relation to the preferred landscape dispositions of prospect and refuge advocated by Appleton, Hildebrandt writes, "the houses Wright designed after 1902 almost all held an extraordinarily rich array of these analogies, at several hierarchical levels—and did so through a complex and repetitive composition of elements unique to him in his time."[4] The overall structure of Wright's houses was based on a principle involving a strong and protective center from which the house grew outwards towards infinity. Many of his houses emanated from a central hearth space that anchored them in space and symbolized the center of centers. While the houses obviously had bounding walls, they provided open vistas that extended the actual perceived space infinitely. See Figure C8.1.

The organizational structure was just the beginning. As Hildebrandt pointed out, the occurrences happened at several hierarchical levels, providing opportunity and choice. He explained: "the degree of refuge or of prospect is subject to infinite variety and can be manipulated by the occupant at will simply by moving to the condition he wishes to enjoy at any moment. We move around, we take our pick, we suit our mood. And when our mood changes we know there are other spaces in the house that can suit the new mood too. That Wright was able to provide not only a rich array of these conditions, but also a range of choice with regard to them, is an extraordinarily important legacy of his work."[5]

Suggested Exercise

List a few places you have been to that afforded both good prospect and refuge. Discuss them in one or several groups. What were the circumstances? What design features contributed to the perceptions of refuge? To what extent was one able to see without being seen?

[1] Appleton, Jay. *The Experience of Landscape*, (Wiley: New York, 1996) p. 62.

[2] Ibid, p. 52.

[3] Ibid, p. 64.

[4] Ibid, quoting Hildebrandt, Grant. *The Wright Space*, (University of Washington Press: Seattle, 1991) p. 250.

[5] Ibid, p. 253.

C8.1

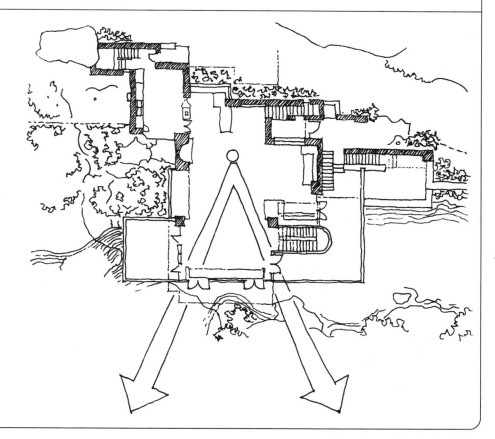

Figure C8.1 Wright's Fallingwater is one of many houses designed by him that exemplify the concept of prospect (openness, view, opportunity), and refuge (enclosure, protection, safety) in built environments.

Enrichment While Stationary

Although it is true that we see more of a given interior environment while we walk around, it is also true that we spend most of our time stationed in the destinations of the facility, be they important ones or ordinary ones. It is in these spaces that people do what they came to the building to do, be it work, shop, cook, or eat. The tasks performed there become the main thing and the environment assumes the secondary role of quiet facilitator. Given an adequate amount of space and acceptable ambient conditions people manage to do what they need to do. Conditions, however, can be taken to higher levels of function and perceptual enrichment.

Many of the general strategies discussed earlier in this chapter come into play here. There are several enrichment strategies specifically applicable to places where people are stationary while performing a task. In general, we would like to suggest that a complete task experience consists of the task at hand in a grounded setting that provides opportunities to connect with nearby surroundings and allows episodes of relief on demand. A way of illustrating this with an everyday example is the experience of food preparation in a residential kitchen. An enriching experience would include a spatially well-defined kitchen whose layout facilitates the various tasks of food preparation while providing visual access to other parts of the house (to connect with ad-

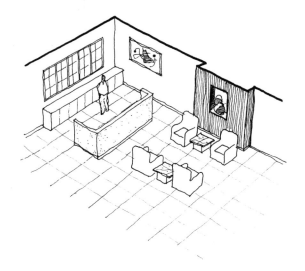

jacent activities and the comings and goings of family members) and to the outside through a well-placed window (to enjoy the view but also to monitor a young child playing outside). If, in addition to all this, it also had a couple of nice views on which to focus the eyes occasionally (one internal and the other external) the kitchen would offer quite a few enriching features beyond mere functionality and good looks. See Figure 8.51.

Facilitating the Task

Facilitating a task requires providing appropriate conditions. Spatially, these include appropriate levels of space, privacy, and connection to related functions. Once these basic needs are met, the next level of facilitation occurs at the proxemic scale of the furnishings and objects in the space (the table in the restaurant or conference room, the individual desk at the office, and so on). When it gets to the task itself, the selection, composition, and arrangement of these objects in space becomes dominant. Other relevant factors, such as complementary lighting and pleasant materials and finishes, are also important. Many of these go beyond the possible contributions of spatial design.

There are, however, contributions to be made at the spatial scale. The location, size, and arrangement of the spaces housing these functions will have an impact on the overall experience. An intimate scale may enhance the experience at the restaurant table, a well-proportioned room of comfortable volume will enhance the experience at the conference room table, and a quiet space of adequate size may facilitate the work done at the desk in the office. Additionally, users

are more likely to be satisfied if they have a physical connection to the greater whole of which their space is a part, and if opportunities are offered to take occasional brief breaks by focusing momentarily on well-planned views and focal points. We discuss these various types of contributions under the headings of grounding, connection, and relief below.

Grounding

The tasks people perform in buildings involve interactions with things and other people, at the material level, and data and ideas at the nonmaterial level. In our restaurant example the main focus is on the table, with the plates, glasses, silverware, and of course, the meal itself taking center stage. If we have company, they are also likely to be a primary focus of the experience. Behind all this is a certain mood that will vary from restaurant to restaurant. The décor and lighting will provide much of that mood. How each table is grounded will affect the individual experience from each table.

Grounding refers to the manner in which a space, or part of a space, is defined in the total environment in ways that make one feel anchored in space, as opposed to drifting in space. People like to feel grounded. An example of this in a restaurant environment is the reassuring experience of being next to a column or side wall rather than feeling like you are floating in the middle of a large room. The concept of containment introduced in Chapter 4 comes into play here. Also important is our relative location in relation to the vertical elements, corners, and edges of the space. Sitting along a defined edge, next to a column, or in a

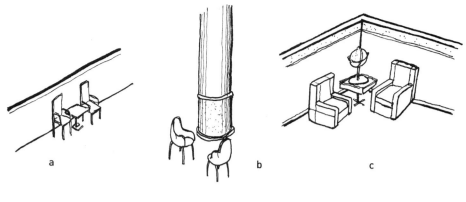

Figure 8.52 Good grounding has been achieved here by placing chairs against an edge (a), in proximity to a column (b), and in a corner (c).

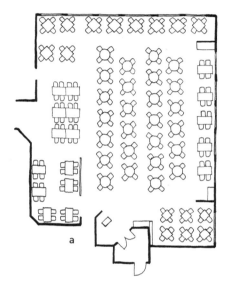
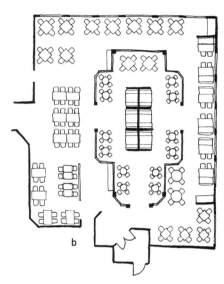

Figure 8.53 Designers often create internal edges and corners to create grounded, well-defined spaces. In this example, the floating tables in (a), find better-grounded locations in (b), where edges and corners have been added.

corner generally offers good grounding experiences. See Figure 8.52.

In large rooms, even though the external envelope may provide only four corners and four edges, it is possible to subdivide space internally to create more corners and edges. Compare the two plans shown for a restaurant in Figure 8.53. The one in Figure 8.53a has a large internal zone with floating tables that don't feel grounded. The one in Figure 8.53b shows the same space subdivided to create more edges and corners inside, thus adding opportunities for feeling grounded. Grounding is important in all types of projects. Other than restaurants, projects such as office spaces (especially those with large areas of open workstations), stores, and hotel lobbies will benefit from having spaces that are well-grounded.

Connection

Even if we sometimes appreciate isolation when we need privacy to concentrate and perform certain tasks, we also value the ability to stay connected with our surroundings, not only because of our inherent interest in human activity, but to know what's happening around us, who is coming and going, and when we need to be on alert. For that reason, it is often desirable to have some degree of connection between areas. That way, people in a restaurant can see other tables and areas beyond, people in an office can see adjacent workers, and people in a hotel lounge can see people in the adjacent lobby. Even though these types of connections are often desirable, deciding when to provide connections and how much to provide are tricky design issues, since the optimal degree of connection to adjacent areas will vary from project to project, from department to department, and from individual to individual. Having too much connection can be a real annoyance to anyone not desiring it.

People love to watch other people. In some settings such as cafés, tea-houses, and even the theater, the social aspect of seeing and being seen is an integral com-

Figure 8.54 Visual connection to adjacent spaces provides stimulation and useful information. It is especially satisfying when we find protected spaces from which to look out or down into space.

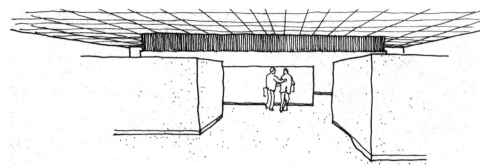

Figure 8.55 Internal relief is a neglected art. Yet, people need things to look at for momentary distraction. In many interior settings features need to be high enough to be visible above the furniture and other view-obstructing elements.

ponent of the overall experience. Exchanges of stares can be open and candid or they can be discreet. Sometimes we feel especially at ease when located in strategic spots that allow us to look at people around us without being noticed, such as when we look down from a strategic location higher up. See Figure 8.54.

Another type of desirable connection is to the outdoors. In addition to providing relief, visual connections to the outside give people valuable information about the approximate time of day, weather conditions, and other external contextual conditions.

Relief

In addition to providing valuable information, the kinds of connections described above also provide relief. The visual openness to the adjacent areas allows for expansion of vision and mind, providing beneficial mental breaks. In this section we discuss another means of providing relief: the use of relief features seen from stationary points.

Views to adjacent areas and the exterior allow the eyes and the mind to expand outward and experience relief. Also useful are focal points where views to framed features are provided. These can be both ex-

ternal and internal. With external foci, the strategy consists of framing specific views that may have special meaning due to their significance, beauty, or other associational qualities. Examples include framed vistas of important monuments, natural or landscaped features, or areas of special vitality based on their use. Well-placed furnishings in relation to existing windows can sometimes make an ordinary view extraordinary because of the power of the framed vista.

While many designers provide focal points in circulation areas, others neglect the art of providing internal features for people to focus on from their stationary locations. People in places such as waiting areas, office cubicles, and lobbies need spots they can focus their attention on from time to time to give their eyes and minds a rest. Examples include artwork (both flat and sculptural), intricate detailing of architectural and decorative elements, and all types of accessories. They generally need to be mounted high up on a wall or on the ceiling so people can see them from their stations without having to stand up. Figure 8.55 shows an example of the upper portion of a wall being provided with a special treatment to act as a plane of internal relief.

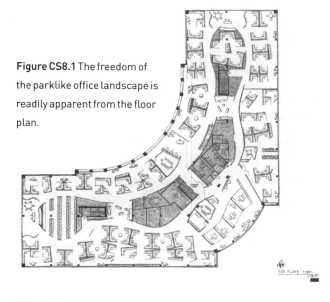

Figure CS8.1 The freedom of the parklike office landscape is readily apparent from the floor plan.

Figure CS8.2 Much of the circulation occurs along meandering, curving paths.

Figure CS8.3 A fencelike serpentine dividing screen behind the receptionist and wood fins at the reception desk add texture to the project.

Figure CS8.4 Additionally, the elliptical shallow soffits display subtle articulation and a sense of playfulness.

CASE STUDY
A Case of Unconventionality: The Doane Pet Care Company Headquarters
Design Firm: VOA

The Doane Pet Care Company Headquarters was an unconventional corporate office project full of freedom and wit. The program consisted of the consolidation of multiple groups into a single facility in Brentwood, Tennessee. The principal goal of the client was to improve communication and interaction between teams. In terms of a general approach, the client wanted a free-form parklike concept. That's exactly what they got from VOA, the selected design firm.

Looking at the floor plan (Figure CS8.1), one imme-diately gets a sense of looseness and freedom. The paths defined by the curvilinear central cores meander in flowing, naturalistic fashion (Figure CS8.2). The office areas are predominantly wide open, just like an open field in a park. For the most part, enclosed rooms are assembled in one of the four free-form core masses that divide the project into two, mostly open, sides. Only one department in the space is walled off from the rest of the project and this was due to the confidential nature of its work. Other than that, the few enclosed spaces are placed strategically to subdivide open areas into units of perceptually comfortable proportions.

Characteristic of the space is the absence of orthogonal planning. Architecturally, there are very few instances in which partitions meet at 90 degrees. Even

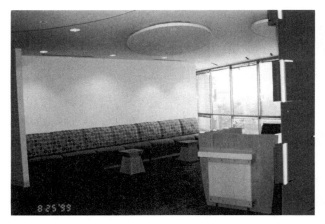

Figure CS8.5 The waiting area seating and reception desk display innovation and a casual approach.

Figure CS8.6 The joint of the two segments of wall coming together is another example of the playful approach to detailing employed throughout this project.

adjacent systems furniture clusters are rotated in relation to each other, thus creating unique and unusual spaces between them. This is clearly not your textbook design project. The irregular nature of some of the leftover spaces and skewed relationships between adjacent pieces would surely upset many design instructors intent on stressing the "proper way" of doing design. Yet here we have a real corporate project designed by a top firm pushing the limits of conventionality. This project serves to illustrate that, while most clients might still prefer conventional designs, others need more environmental interest and demand designs that go beyond the ordinary to produce stimulating and interesting environments.

In addition to the unconventional geometry of the floor plan, the design provides enrichment through its innovative and nonpretentious approach to detailing and furniture selection. The fencelike serpentine screens behind the reception area (Figure CS8.3) and break/work table (Figure CS8.4), and the elliptical shallow floating ceiling planes are examples of innovative and playful detailing. Similarly, the furniture creation and selection approach exemplified in those two illustrations and Figure CS8.5 for the reception desk, the waiting area banquette, and the casual work/break table and stools further convey an innovative and rather humble approach, considering it is a design for a corporate headquarters project. A final illustration of the project's playful detail is the way the two walls are joined above the opening (Figure CS8.6).

Review

Summary

While projects need regularity and order to be perceptually clear and satisfying, they also need to be rich and stimulating. Humans need both stability and stimulation. It is necessary, thus, to achieve a balance between these two seemingly opposing forces. Providing a sense of enrichment in projects requires the commitment of the designer. Enrichment is possible and desirable in any space of a project, particularly in arrival spaces, waiting areas, circulation spaces, and destination spaces.

General enrichment strategies are applicable anywhere in a project. These include the use of variety and complexity. Project complexity can be achieved via complex surface articulation, complex spatial compositions, and by complex system overlapping. Other enrichment strategies include the use of novelty, boldness, and tension.

Two somewhat opposite general enrichment strategies are ambiguity and pictorialness. Ambiguity is produced when an arrangement has more than one possible interpretation. Pictorialness relies on the careful composition, articulation, and framing of harmonious, straightforward spaces and surfaces. General enrichment can also be produced by manipulating the use of space in ways that concentrate human activity in certain areas.

Some of the most enriching experiences in interior spaces occur while people move around along the circulation route. Sequences can be like stories, with plots, subplots, and climaxes. The shape of the path, itself, can be a source of enrichment. The length of the path, its configuration, proportions, and degree of connection all play a major role in the character of the path. Also crucial is the articulation and modulation of the side walls, floor, and ceiling.

What we see from the path becomes part of the total experience. The view at the end of a path and the view along a path to adjacent spaces are important considerations. Opening size and placement can be orchestrated in stimulating ways. The level of correspondence between visual access and physical access can also be manipulated to delay gratification and produce tension, followed by relief.

In addition to facilitating the tasks people perform in buildings, designers have an obligation to provide enriching environments in a project's destinations. Enrichment strategies in these cases include providing proper grounding, connection, and relief.

Exercises
1. Think about past or current design projects you have been involved with. What attempts to enrich experience have you tried to use? Has there been a pattern to your use of enrichment strategies? What?
2. Name three specific design strategies you would use to enrich
   - an arrival space
   - a waiting area
   - a corridor segment
   - a design studio space
3. Draw a plan or axonometric of a highly regular and modular space (see, for example, Figure 7.42 in Chapter 7), and perform at least one variation to make it more varied and interesting.
4. Think of one of your projects. Name three ways you could increase its level of complexity.
5. Take a single important elevation from one of your projects. Draw three complex variations of it.
6. Draw one space and one mass using the principle of novelty.
7. Draw a mass and an elevation using the principle of boldness.
8. Draw three corridor segments using compression to create tension followed by relief.
9. Draw one spatial arrangement featuring intentional ambiguity.
10. Draw a pictorial version of the elevation used in Exercise 5 above.
11. Take a circulation sequence from a previous project. Modify it as necessary to incorporate some meaningful events along it.
12. Take a circulation segment from one of your projects and explore different treatments for the side walls, floor, and ceiling to achieve different effects.
13. Pick one of your projects with several corridors. Draw a focal point at the end of one of the corridors.
14. Pick one of your projects with several corridors. Draw an enticing composition at the end of one of the corridors to attract people by making them curious about what lies ahead.

15. Draw a corridor sequence incorporating various views of the destination space prior to getting to it in order to build anticipation.

16. Pick a past or current project. Design an internal focal plane or mass on which to occasionally rest the eyes in order to take a break from the task at hand.

Endnotes

1 Le Corbusier, *Towards a New Architecture*, (Dover: New York, 1986) p. 179.

2 Venturi, Robert. *Complexity and Contradiction in Architecture*, (Museum of Modern Art: New York, 1977) p. 20.

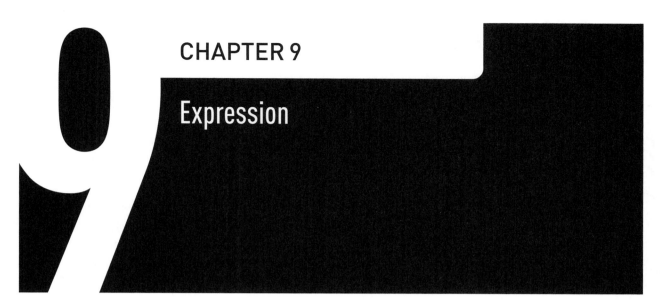

CHAPTER 9

Expression

INSTRUCTIONAL OBJECTIVES

Introduce the concept of expression as an integral part of design.

Explain some of the factors affecting design expression and interpretation.

Present two different kinds of architectural meanings and how they work.

Explain how design features can express fundamental aspects of humanity.

Explain how contextual factors can be expressed in design.

Discuss ways in which design properties and assemblies can be expressive.

Discuss the expression of two basic aspects of design related to programmatic

necessities.

Explain how identity is expressed in design.

Describe the many variables that affect identity.

Explain how the mode of self-presentation affects the way expression is manifested.

Explain the roles of the designer's personal style, attitudes, and preferences on

expression.

"Architectural expression" is a wide term covering not only the outward manifestation of the inner purpose of the building, i.e. the characteristics of the building programme, but also questions of manners, of the personal equation of the 'ego' of both client and architect, and of the claims of materials and structure to be expressed for their own sake, either directly or by implication.[1]

So far we have elaborated on important design tasks such as conceiving appropriate organizational structures, establishing order, and providing enrichment in design projects. Our next topic, expression, is particularly important because it permeates and colors all of these tasks. In the process of determining which kind of structure, what kind of order, and which enrichment strategies to use for a particular project, the designer has to decide what type of expression the project should have. Idea, order, and enrichment need to be customized into a unified response to the particular realities of the project. The qualities thus embodied will give the project particular meanings appropriate to its unique realities. The project will then attain a presence similar to that of a living organism, with a distinct personality and all.

Should a given project be a self-conscious, elegant, subtle, and self-disclosing one, perhaps even with a few metaphoric allusions thrown in for the enjoyment of the connoisseur? Or, should it be self-conscious, extremely elegant, even pompous, with straightforward boldness and no intellectual games? The possible qualities attainable through design expression and their combinations are countless. The possibilities appropriate for a particular project are narrowed down by the specifics of the project but still leave ample room for interpretation. What are the possibilities and how does one decide among them?

Mastering the art of determining appropriate expressions for projects and then executing designs that

Figure 9.1 The particular characteristics of interior spaces communicate the attitudes and beliefs of the people who own them. The treatments in this room give us clues about the character of its owner.

Source: From Here of All Places *by Osbert Lancaster, John Murray (Publishers) Ltd., 1958.*

incorporate those expressions successfully is one of the goals of design. Some aspects of expression are straightforward and objective, although much of expression in design is highly personal and subjective. This chapter will expose you to some of the ways design expression can be manifested in your projects. It is difficult to give precise rules about how to incorporate specific expressions in design, much less about which one is appropriate for a particular project, because project details vary widely from case to case and what's appropriate in one case is not in others. However, we will expose you to some of the possibilities and, hopefully, provide some insight about the factors to consider when making decisions about project expression.

Expression in Design

Expression

Every design expresses something, whether intentionally or not. It tells us something about the character (real or desired) of those who use the space, the attitude towards the context in which the project occurs, and about some of the preferences and design tendencies of both the designer and the user group. Designs, like people and their belongings, embody ways of being and acting. Particular expressions are chosen and approved by clients because they help convey, materially, who they are or aspire to be. The interior design of a place can embody the particular essence of the group using the project.

The particular expression adopted for a project is usually pervasive and, thus, seen throughout the project. However, specific expressions can also be localized, occurring only in certain parts of a project. A project or portion of it may express desired emotional qualities (joy or somberness), attitudes of the client (conservatism or innovativeness), specific intentions (a desire for a heightened sense of entry and arrival), and the status of the owner (powerful and successful, or emerging and upcoming). The room in Figure 9.1, for instance, communicates information about the character of its owner.

The particular project being designed, its context, its owners, its programmatic needs, and its designers all contribute to the final expression. The self-image and personal intentions of both the owner and the designer are particularly important, as we will see.

Interpretation

Communication in design, in many ways, operates the same way as other types of communication. It involves the sending of a message by the sender and the reception and interpretation of the message by a recipient. The built environment, due to its physicality, is always present in very tangible ways and, therefore, is always up for interpretation. Every aspect of a design is open to interpretation, whether intended or unintended. A design message may even be accidental. An example of an intentional message is a project designed with a formal layout, classic forms, overpowering volumes, and rich materials to convey a sense of dignified power. An example of an unintentional message is the inaccessibility of an important public area of a building (due to careless design or legitimate de-

Figure 9.2 These two restaurants would appeal differently to people with different backgrounds.

sign constraints) resulting in the perception (erroneous but understandable) that you are intentionally being discouraged from going there. An example of an accidental message is the unplanned effect caused by direct sunlight penetrating a project in some magnificent way at certain times of the day. The designer may be praised for orchestrating such a powerful and inspiring combination of forces when he or she was really not consciously trying to produce it.

Design as a language communicates through **formal properties** and **symbolic content**. Particular arrangements created by the specific forms used constitute the formal properties of the project. The meanings conveyed by these properties, as well as the materials, finishes, furnishings, and accessories used, constitute the symbolic content. Whatever associations are derived from them are likely to vary from culture to culture, from group to group within a culture, and from person to person within a group. Despite the variety of interpretations, however, there tend to be similarities of interpretation among people from the same group. In general, people from a particular culture or group share certain attitudes, values, and physical vocabularies, such as building forms, physical symbols, and so on. This may make it easier to communicate through design with a group of users from a homogeneous group that shares similar views. In such a case, it is more likely that specific forms and symbols employed are interpreted similarly by the users.

Another highly influential factor affecting how people interpret the built environment is the background of the person or group doing the interpretation. People grow up in and become accustomed to specific physical backgrounds with particular qualities. Given average conditions, people tend to develop visual affinities with certain environments they encounter during their formative years. Their conception of what a particular building type normally looks like is influenced by the visual qualities encountered repeatedly in those settings while growing up. For example, a typical restaurant in a rural area may be simple and rustic, and one in downtown New York City artsy and pretentious. Someone from a rural area may feel more at home entering the restaurant shown in Figure 9.2a while an urbanite may prefer the one in Figure 9.2b.

A person's education in subjects related to art and design also has a significant influence on how they interpret the physical environment. We can expect different interpretations from a person with minimal design literacy and a person that makes a living as a designer. A client trained in the arts is more likely, for example, to appreciate nuance and subtlety, abstract gestures, and historic allusions. Someone else may not care much for any of these qualities.

Even among people of similar design literacy levels, interpretations can be quite personal, often colored by the lens through which they look at a design. The historian, the art critic, the designer, and the technical person will all tend to assign greater value to different aspects of a design depending on their particular areas of knowledge and interest. To complicate matters further, it is not uncommon for people from similar backgrounds and areas of knowledge, such as, say, two design critics to have opposing views about a particular design and to defend their respective points of view passionately.

Figure 9.3 Some very basic architectural expressions carry profound existential connotations. Stairs, those utilitarian devices that transport us from one level to another, embody the act of ascending, a powerful symbolic act.

Figure 9.4 Interpretations of design works vary according to the point of view of the person doing the interpretation. The pure volume that provides so much pleasure to the modernist designer can be seen as a lifeless file cabinet by the general public.

Furthermore, as design philosophies, fashions, and trends change over time, interpretations and meanings will change too. What is valued today may not be appreciated tomorrow, and vice versa. Expression and interpretation in design are, indeed, very subjective and unstable matters.

Interpretation and Meaning

In order to understand the dynamics of expressing meaning through design and the way those meanings are perceived and interpreted, it is useful to distinguish between two types of meanings: those that are understood spontaneously and those that are learned through convention. **Spontaneous meaning** can be conveyed through literal iconic signs or through inherent expression. These are understood directly, without training. Iconic signs utilize literal representations of the desired meaning as when a building for an automobile corporation is shaped like a car.

Inherent expression relies on the spontaneous symbolism associated with the formal qualities of objects or compositions and what these represent. Spontaneous symbolism, Rudolf Arnheim explains, "derives from the expression inherent in perceived objects. To be seen as expressive, the shape of an object must be seen as dynamic. There is nothing expressive, and therefore nothing symbolic, in a set of stairs or a staircase as long as it is seen as a mere geometrical configuration. Only when one perceives the gradual rising of the steps from the ground as a dynamic crescendo does the configuration exhibit an expressive quality, which carries a self-evident symbolism."[2] Arnheim is referring to the symbolic meaning of ascending and the deep connotations it carries. (Figure 9.3).

Most associations we make in our efforts to interpret the environment are not spontaneous and natural, but learned associations, acquired by convention. We have said that **learned associations** between symbols and meanings can vary widely from one culture to another. This fact helps to explain the different interpretations made by groups from different cultures of the same symbols. The same phenomenon occurs between different groups and subgroups of the same culture who learn to perceive and give meaning to certain aspects of the physical world (symbols) in particular and consistent ways. Charles Jencks speaks about differences in **visual codes**. People from different backgrounds, upon looking at the same design, will use different codes (based on learning and culture) for its interpretation. Buildings that incorporate various codes can be seen as having opposing meanings: "the 'harmonious, well-proportioned pure volume' of the modern architect becomes the 'shoe-box' or 'filing cabinet' to the public."[3] See Figure 9.4.

How is a designer to proceed, you may wonder, if there is no certainty about whether the meanings and values you intend to communicate through the expressions of your design will be understood and interpreted correctly? What kind of expression is best? How concrete do our expressive messages need to be? There are no right or wrong answers to these questions. Opinions vary among designers and critics. Of the two critics mentioned above, for example, Arnheim advocates going beyond arbitrary convention, allying design intentions "with features of more basic,

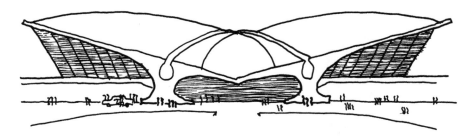

Figure 9.5 Whether one likes the birdlike qualities of Eero Saarinen's TWA terminal in New York is a matter of opinion. The particular forms he used carry meaning beyond their sculptural articulation. In this case, it is not too difficult to associate the flowing forms with birds and flying.

spontaneous expression."[4] He adds that "the most powerful symbols derive from the most elementary perceptual sensations because they refer to the basic human experiences on which all others depend."[5] Arnheim warns that, "the use of identifiable subject matter (such as, literal, pictorial, iconic signs) as a component of architectural shape may interfere with a building's spontaneous symbolism because of the concessions its dynamics must make to the shape of that subject matter." He notes that "Eero Saarinen's TWA air terminal might soar more purely if it looked less like a bird."[6] Arnheim, thus, prefers elementary symbols that are perceived naturally and are associated with basic human experiences.

Jencks is in favor of iconic signs, which "speak with exactitude and humour about their function. The literalism, however infantile, articulates factual truths … and there is a certain pleasure (which doesn't escape children) in perceiving a sequence of them."[7] Unlike Arnheim, he praises the literalism of Saarinen's TWA terminal (Figure 9.5): "The TWA terminal in New York is an icon of a bird, and by extension, of aeroplane flight … Here the imaginative meanings add up in an appropriate and calculated way, pointing towards a common metaphor of flight—the mutual interaction of these meanings produces a multivalent work of architecture."[8] Looking at architectural components as words, and these in turn as signs, Jencks points out the predominance of conventional symbolic signs over natural ones: "Most architectural words are symbolic signs; certainly those that are most potent and pervasive are the ones which are learned and conventional, not 'natural.'"[9] For Jencks, the symbol-

ic sign learned by convention is clearly the dominant one.

Spectrum of Expression

The rest of this chapter will present some of the types of expression that can be manifested in a design project. Selecting which ones are embraced and given preference and which ones are ignored is a matter of personal preference and will vary from designer to designer. Beyond personal preferences, the requirements and context of a project will also suggest pertinent expressions for the specific project. The best way for you, as the designer, to be prepared is to have an awareness of the possibilities, become familiar with different ways to execute expression, and develop the ability to diagnose a project to discover what particular type of expression is most fitting. Keep in mind that it is often possible and desirable to communicate with different groups at different levels on any given project. In fact, projects with multiple meanings acquire multiple levels of validity and have the power to delight many audiences.

When it comes to architectural expression, the entire spectrum of the physical environment comes into play. Successful designs have a sense of coherence among all their layers and, as a result, communicate clearly. In these cases, all (or most of) the elements reinforce each other to produce a consistent and powerful expression. In other cases, to contrast, there can be multiple meanings operating simultaneously and even sending different messages. This may work as long as there is a recognizable sense of hierarchy and balance. The basic components of the expression spectrum are layout, space, surface, detail, fur-

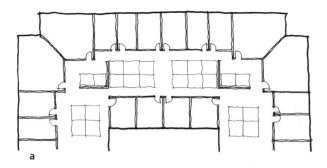

a

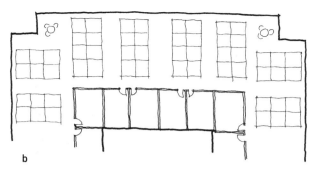

b

Figure 9.6 The size and placement of functions project attitudes about, among other things, the hierarchy of an organization. These two plans reflect two different organizations, the one in (a) much more hierarchical than the one shown in plan (b). Plan (a) shows four hierarchical levels: corner offices, other perimeter offices, interior offices, and general workstations.

nishings, and accessories. These are elements that can be manipulated by you.

Layouts require many decisions about the placement of functions in relation to the context and to each other. They establish who goes where and who is next to, or far from, whom. They communicate messages about status, hierarchy, relationships between different groups, the degree of constraint or freedom throughout the project, and so on. The two simple office plans shown in Figure 9.6 show different attitudes about hierarchy. Figure 9.6a shows a strong hierarchy with large corner offices, medium-sized perimeter offices, and small interior offices. The plan in Figure 9.6b is much more democratic with same-sized offices located away from the perimeter, and open office areas given exposure to the outside.

Space and its articulation communicate stylistic approach, hierarchy level, and degree of conventionality. Surfaces communicate stylistic approaches and preferences. Through the use of composition, pattern, texture, material, and color, designers can create combinations that communicate an infinite number of expressions. Figure 9.7 shows a view of a prominent civic building interior with generous volumes, strong architectural shapes, and well-articulated surfaces. The next layer of expression is the detail. Details can be shaped in many ways and can incorporate materials and colors that convey a myriad of different expressions. Compare, for example, the two railing systems shown in Figure 9.8. Each different expression has its own unique character.

Furnishings, whether chairs, desks, tables, or display cases, can also have variations in shape, materials,

Figure 9.7 Spaces, their shapes, and the character of their surfaces establish the architectural expression of a space as shown prominently in this civic building.

a

b

Figure 9.8 Particular expressions are manifested through the detailing of architectural features. In the examples shown, the railing systems shown in (a) and (b) manifest different characters.

Figure 9.9 Furnishings and accessories contribute greatly to the overall expression of a space. These highly functional and decorative interior design elements come in many styles to suit the particular expressions desired by the designer. Notice the influence of the chairs, tables, plants, planters, decorative railings, and light fixtures in this room.

colors, and trim, conveying widely different styles and meanings. The many stylistic and material choices make it possible to achieve almost any desired look. Beyond furnishings, accessories are usually specified by the designer. These include items like desk accessories for work settings and the tablecloths, china, candleholders, and silverware in restaurants. Accessories, like most furnishings, are manufactured products that come as they are, and are generally not changed by the designer. Nevertheless, as with furnishings, there is a wide range of styles available, which makes it possible for designers to specify accessories congruent with the desired design expression of the project. The lounge space shown in Figure 9.9 illustrates the important contribution of furnishings and accessories to the character of a space.

In addition to the above, there are also elements of expression not controlled by designers. These are also part of the total picture and contribute considerably to the visible expression of a project. They include the people in the setting, their attire, and the type of language used. Although the designer usually has no control over these elements, it is important to have an awareness of them as part of the total picture and realize the fact that designers do not control every single element of expression.

Types of Expression

There are many types of expression. You have great latitude in determining what types of expression you want to emphasize consciously for a given project.

These are not just personal whims but represent your responses to the specific qualities of the project and the client. Once these intentions are clear, it is up to you as the designer to decide how to best achieve the desired expression. Below we discuss different types of expression grouped into six classifications: expression of universal human experiences, expression of contextual factors, expression of formal design properties and assemblies, expression of programmatic necessities, expression of identity, and personal designer expression.

Expression of Universal Human Experiences

Certain expressions found in the built environment operate at a very basic level by revealing to us simple fundamental aspects of our own humanity. Arnheim talks about "the symbolic overtones of practical life"[10] and explains that works of architecture make symbolic statements that convey relevant human qualities and situations. "We speak of 'high' hopes and 'deep' thoughts, and it is only by analogy to such elementary qualities of the perceivable world that we can understand and describe non-physical properties."[11] Thus, elements such as verticality, depth, and the like can be utilized to evoke some of these human associations. Whether attempts to evoke some of these abstract qualities will be perceived consciously by users is questionable. Some users, because of their training or sense of intuition, will be more conscious of them. Others may sense these qualities subconsciously. Yet others will not perceive them in any way. Expressions in this category are most effective when the function expressed is asserted strongly for empha-

Figure 9.10 Similar to the act of ascending, the act of descending carries powerful symbolic connotations. These may vary depending on the particular occasion and arrangement. In this example, the descending path leads to a somewhat mysterious, cavelike environment.

sis. Among the possible expressions in this category are the following three dualities.

Ascending/Descending

Ascending symbolizes improvement, moving towards better things, even towards the sublime. Heaven is always up, as are the offices of the top-ranking officials of a corporation. The act of ascending, thus, can be a very symbolic act. One climbs a few steps up to get to a special location, such as a king's throne. Descending can carry connotations of moving deeper into the earth, where one can find security and protection, or perhaps the intriguing, obscure, and unknown. Figure 9.10 shows a downward view towards a mysterious-looking lower area.

Other than with the main staircases in some buildings, gestures of ascending and descending are not widely used these days because of increased sensitivity to the needs of the physically disabled. Nevertheless, many old buildings still possess great examples of subtle, and not so subtle, level changes that express the functions of ascending and descending in ways that emphasize their metaphoric overtones.

Constraint/Freedom

Another aspect with strong symbolic connotations is the relative degree of constraint or freedom allowed by a given space or project. These are usually related to programmatic requirements but the way they are treated can carry deep symbolic connotations. People form perceptions in response to the level of overall space available around them and also the degree to which the space permits them to move about at will.

We have talked before about how the use of contrast can be a powerful tool to heighten the awareness of specific qualities. In this case, moving from a tight space to a generous one can emphasize the sense of freedom the larger space affords, and vice versa. Similarly, progressing from a confining and inflexible system of corridors to an area that offers many travel choices and the freedom to pursue them can surely heighten the sense of freedom given by the latter space.

Admittance/Rejection

As in the previous example, the duality of admittance/rejection is usually dictated by programmatic requirements. Here, too, you can find opportunities to emphasize either the admittance or rejection aspect of the equation. Admittance refers to the degree of welcoming offered by a particular arrangement. Admittance presupposes connection and openness between spaces while rejection prevents admittance, either by mere discouragement or by absolute denial.

Rejection usually involves some kind of barrier to prevent passage. The solidity of the wall, the number and character of points of connection between the two sides, and the level of control at those points, can send clear messages about how welcome one is to come in. Even more fascinating is the handling of admittance. Admittance has many levels. It ranges from reluctant tolerance, as when a manager reluctantly admits a street person to a fast-food establishment, to eager invitation, as in the case of a store desperate for cus-

Figure 9.11 Of the many ways of expressing admittance, the gateway or portal is one of the most powerful. The three variations shown for stores in the same complex are representative of the variations of expression possible within the portal idiom.

Figure 9.12 Respectful rehabilitations retain elements that convey the historic expression of a place without subjecting the vocabulary of the new design to the same stylistic constraints, as seen in this former warehouse type space.

Figure 9.13 Historic recreations manifest historic expression in new constructions. In these cases a new environment is inspired by an older design style, as shown in this old-world setting in the lounge of a new hotel.

tomers, looking for ways to entice and attract them. When it comes to admittance, it can be allowed (reluctantly or indifferently), encouraged (enthusiastically), or demanded (aggressively). The three storefronts shown in Figure 9.11 feature portal-like gateways that highlight the point of entry into the respective stores, thus encouraging admittance. Notice the different expressions of the same basic idea.

Expression of Contextual Factors

Oftentimes, the contextual forces related to a project not only influence some of the design decisions but actually acquire a dominant form of expression. These forces can be historic, cultural, regional, or current.

Historic Expression

Many interior projects occur in older buildings or neighborhoods having distinct design features typical of the time when they were built. In many cases the style adopted for a project is congruent with the style of the building. Examples include literal, carefully researched restorations, where every aspect is reproduced as it was originally; renovations, where the basic character of the original style is preserved without getting overly literal; respectful rehabilitations, where new functions going into old buildings respect the character of the original style without feeling an obligation to mimic what was done originally (Figure 9.12); and historic recreations, where new projects are designed in an older, traditional style (Figure 9.13).

In these cases, stylistic approaches from the historic period in question are either incorporated into the project or taken as points of departure for the development of new designs. Depending on the project, these may be applied in pure form or expressed abstractly to retain their original essence. **Historic ex-**

Figure 9.14 Forms based on ethnic traditions, such as the pointed and ornate arches in this restaurant, contribute to the expression of culture.

pression can be pursued at all, or just some, levels of the design spectrum (from layout to the selection of accessories). Historic expression requires knowledge of the design aspects particular to the project's history. Lacking this, the designer is in danger of conceiving and executing the historic expression inaccurately.

Cultural Expression

Whenever a project has a strong and specific cultural component based on its location or the nature of its users, the project may need to reflect design expressions from the culture in question. Most cultures have recurring design characteristics one can draw from literally, such as arches and sombreros traditional in Mexican architecture and culture. Even more challenging is when the designer is attempting to interpret aspects of a culture in a nonliteral way, like designing a Mexican restaurant without cacti, sombreros on the wall, or the colors of the Mexican flag.

As in the case of historic expression, **cultural expression** can incorporate the entire spectrum of design elements or just select ones. Figure 9.14 shows ethnic forms used in a restaurant setting.

Regional Expression

Regional expression can vary due to regional cultural differences or to regional topographical differences. In the United States, for instance, certain regions possess strong subcultures with unique characteristics and particular visual affinities. One such region is the Southwest, where the strong presence of Mexican and Native American people and culture has created a unique visual style associated with it.

Figure 9.15 Some regions, such as the Southwest, possess strong regional character due to topography, ethnicity, and other factors. The view shown here is unmistakably typical of the region.

Topography and location also affect the visual character of a region as well as the materials used for construction. In the example above, the arid topography of the Southwest makes the visual uniqueness of the area even more pronounced. Projects done in this region are likely to reflect this expression and incorporate adobe construction and unique regional shapes, as the exterior and surroundings of the church shown in Figure 9.15 illustrate.

Current Norms and Conventions

Every project occurs within a certain set of norms and conventions prevalent at the time, including the particular dominating design tendencies of the period. Some periods in history have enjoyed consistent and widely accepted rules while others have been characterized by disagreement and change. Whether you, as a designer, adopt the prevailing design tendencies of the time or take a different view becomes your prerogative. Individual designer positions will be dealt with a little later. For now, it is sufficient to say that some projects, especially during times of stylistic transition and progress, can become conscious efforts to express

a

b

Figure 9.17 Certain physical characteristics of the environment can be accentuated and highlighted for their own sake, like the emphasis on texture on this wall.

Figure 9.16 Every period in history has its own prevailing stylistic norms and conventions. Modernism was characterized by a simple austere machine aesthetic (a). Some designers operated within the new conventions but gave them a more organic feel (b).

Source: From Here of All Places *by Osbert Lancaster, John Murray (Publishers) Ltd., 1958.*

personal philosophy or the realities of the project and its context.

Expression of Formal Design Properties and Assemblies

Designers have much control over the treatment of design elements. Shapes, textures, thicknesses, colors, and lights can be emphasized or de-emphasized at will to create particular forms of expression. These design properties are objective and tangible. They can be manipulated as part of a greater design strategy of expression or for their own sake. For example, the texture of a wall could be accentuated to create a rich and evocative surface (Figure 9.17). It can become expressive and possess a strong character without having to symbolize any meaning beyond the desire to be rich and textural. This type of expression is akin to the idea of enrichment discussed in Chapter 8; the treatment doesn't carry any conscious symbolic meaning beyond the richness produced by the special treatment. Conversely, you may choose textured surfaces on a project in order to symbolize a cave or fortress.

In addition to manipulating specific design properties for effect, you can also manipulate composite design assemblies. These assemblies, as a whole, produce

the new tendencies of the time. During the reign of modernism, for instance, the desire was to incorporate the machine aesthetic, using it as a metaphor of the times. Designs became streamlined and devoid of decoration. Although many designs started looking alike, there were still various ways of interpreting these prevailing tendencies. For instance, Figure 9.16 shows cartoonish versions of two different interpretations of modernism. This points to the fact that, even during times of specific prescriptive design norms, there is room for individual interpretation based on

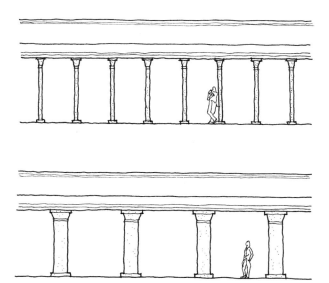

Figure 9.18 The function of support can be expressed in many ways. One of them is through the treatment of supporting columns. A normal-looking arcade, for instance, can be transformed through the use of more slender columns spaced close together (a), or the use of fewer, but heavier, columns (b).

Figure 9.19 The floating overhead canopy reduces the scale of the defined area below and, thus, gives it a greater sense of shelter.

Figure 9.20 The function of connection can be highlighted by emphasizing the threshold between the parts being connected. Highlighting a connecting path by differentiating the floor material is one way to emphasize the bridging element.

parts of the design that fulfill and express specific functions. Examples include the functions of support, shelter, and connection. These basic functions can, if desired and deemed appropriate, be emphasized or de-emphasized to produce specific effects. A greater number of columns spaced closely together would exaggerate the function of support. Fewer but oversized columns would accomplish the same effect with a different feel (Figure 9.18). A floating ceiling canopy over a space in a high area tends to accentuate the function of shelter (Figure 9.19). Emphasizing a connecting path through the treatment of the floor reinforces the idea of connection between two points (Figure 9.20).

Programmatic Necessities

The programmatic requirements of a project dictate the basic configuration a project takes. Here we discuss two basic aspects of the programmatic realities of a project that help to shape its basic spatial expression and give it overall character. These are the degree of openness of the spaces and the degree of connection between them.

Openness/Closedness

In Chapter 4 we elaborated on issues of spatial definition, containment, encapsulation, and so on. Choices made regarding layout and spatial definition, large-ly in response to the program, give spaces distinct characters in terms of degree of openness, spatial definition, and encapsulation. In the past, there was not much choice. Due to structural limitations, projects were mostly subdivided into compartments connected via doors and corridors. Luckily, nowadays we have more choices. A project's degree of openness is one type of expression easily apprehensible on most projects. The openness, or compartmentalization, of a project will quickly tell us information about the level of privacy users require and whether people operate individually or in groups. These visual cues immediately tell us something about the nature of the project and how it is structured and organized. It may be composed of a few large spaces, of one large space and a few small ones, or of many small spaces. Openness, of course, can refer to the overall feeling of openness in a

Figure 9.21 Openness can be manifested through the freedom produced by generous and/or uncluttered spaces, as well as by the perceptual freedom produced by taller spaces. The two restaurant spaces shown are approximately equivalent in size. Yet the one in (a) expresses more openness than the one in (b) due to its more generous height and less dense arrangement of tables.

space, which is the result of spatial volume, light levels, and density of components, among other factors. Compare, for example, the different degrees of openness in the two restaurant spaces shown in Figure 9.21.

Connected/Segregated

The way in which different spaces are connected reveals much about the nature of an entity and the way it operates. Connections between main parts, as well as between subparts, tell us about their level of autonomy, as well as about the levels of flow and admittance desired between parts of the project. Are the spaces relatively open to one another or are they encapsulated by full walls on all sides with small punched holes providing restricted access? Not only is the level of physical access involved here but also the degree of visual disclosure between separate areas. This aspect is related to openness/closedness just discussed above. The two work hand in hand, the first one referring more to the general character of spaces and the second one to the nature of separations between them.

Identity

Perhaps the most exciting and vital design expression of a project is the visual expression of its identity. **Identity** refers to the embodiment, in tangible ways, of the qualities that distinguish a particular client. You can think of it as the physical manifestation of the entity's personality, with an important distinction. A client's identity is often a combination of who the client is, thinks it is, and wants to be. There are some important differences to note. Who an entity is, its true personality, is innate. Who an entity thinks it is relies on self-perception. This self-perception may or may not accurately reflect reality. Who an entity aspires to be is not a reality yet, if ever, so it too, may or may not be accurate and realistic. Depending on the correspondence of the three, it may be easier or harder for you as the designer to determine the appropriate identity to express in a project. A simple example to understand the interaction of the three identities would be the case of a person shopping for a car. Let's suppose this person is a conservative, middle-class man, but thinks he is hip and likes to project an image of wealth. If this person were to select a car that expresses his perceived self-identity, he would most likely select an expensive sports car. This would express his self-concept of being hip and his aspirations for wealth. If someone else were to select the car on his behalf, relying on objective perceptions, that other person would probably select a less expensive, conservative car. Which selection would you make if this person were your client and relied on your judgment?

In determining what identity to reflect, there is sometimes a fine line between reality and fiction, between what some entity really is and what it wants others to think it is. As a rule of thumb, designers are more like public relations professionals trying to show their clients in the best possible light than journalists trying to disclose them objectively.

There are many qualities that contribute to personality and, therefore, many considerations that have to be made to decide how to externalize identity. These qualities represent predispositions and preferences

Figure 9.22 Particular treatments and images can project qualities that are congruent with the affinities of specific age groups. This is particularly evident in the world of retail where some stores cater to the younger crowd (a) while others cater to a more mature crowd (b).

that result in particular ways of being. In our example of the man shopping for a car, the person is predisposed by nature to be conservative and not fancy or innovative. This is a specific predisposition related to his degree of progressiveness. For purposes of discussing identity and its expression in design, we have divided all those predispositions into six classifications: membership, progressiveness, attitude, sophistication, preference, and self-presentation. Although these relate and overlap, discussing them separately will enhance your understanding of some of the subtleties involved in each.

Membership

Membership is a measure of inclusiveness and exclusivity. Individuals often identify themselves with particular ways of being. Those having similar characteristics see themselves as members of the same group and see those with different characteristics as not belonging. Important variables contributing to this view are the ages of the people, their status, and their background. Retail corporations are particularly conscious of these differences. Through careful market research they determine specific market segments and develop specialized strategies (including design qualities) to cater to very different clienteles. Projecting an image consistent with the characteristics of the group will validate and reinforce the self-concept of the group members and send messages to outsiders in an effort to invite and attract compatible types.

Age Groups ❖ The importance of catering to specific **age groups** is also apparent in the world of retail where marketing efforts are directed towards special age groups for whom certain merchandise is intended. Shops, accordingly, will project very intentional images sensitive to the affinities of the target group. This is specially pronounced when it comes to fashion where every store will project, in no uncertain terms, an image that will attract the intended audience by catering, among other things, to their age. So, there are stores catering to children, to teens, to young adults, to adults, and to the mature adult. The visual symbols used throughout the architecture, signage, graphics, and the merchandise, project an image that caters to a specific age group. Looking at the two stores shown in Figure 9.22 one gets an immediate sense that the one shown in Figure 9.22a caters to a younger crowd than the one in Figure 9.22b.

Status ❖ **Status** is as important a consideration as age group. The status we refer to is status related to wealth and buying power. It is no secret that economic status is often related to social status, but it is the buying power component that interests us here. Many

Figure 9.23 Projection of status is an important component of group-membership. Restaurants range from inexpensive and unpretentious, to expensive and exclusive. Low levels of lighting, the use of tablecloths and cloth napkins, and the use of fine plates and silverware are usual indications of exclusive, status-conscious restaurants.

Figure 9.24 Restaurants and stores often import design elements from foreign backgrounds to go with their desired theme. The storefront shown, in an exclusive urban shopping center, clearly communicates the origin and nature of the merchandise it sells.

people of high status value environments that reflect their status. They shop and dine in places where the status expressed by design is consistent with their own. Distinctions between real status, self-perceived status, and aspired-to status can get blurred and confused. While many people have notions, some more realistic than others, of where they stand on the status ladder, and live and consume based on those notions, many pay less attention to these matters. Designing an office for a rich client who likes fancy restaurants and expensive gift shops is a different matter from designing for a rich client with few pretensions who prefers to shop and dine with the masses. The former will probably want an office that looks and feels exclusive. The latter may ask you to downplay his or her success and communicate a sense of restraint.

While admittance to the prestigious private clubs of the privileged may be reserved to those that meet certain status qualifications, admittance to prestigious restaurants and stores is more public, and most of us can usually enter these places if we dress and behave in fitting ways. Many of us enjoy going to expensive shops and restaurants for the occasional splurge. Additionally, it is possible to make an economically priced restaurant or store appear classy and exclusive. The thing to remember is that every project will have a range of acceptable expressions when it comes to projecting status. Which level to express becomes a delicate decision made by you and the client on a case-by-case basis.

Exclusivity due to status is expressed by the use of expensive materials, furnishings, accessories, and merchandise. In a store, it is likely to be expressed by less density of merchandise, sophisticated-looking fin-

ishes, upscale graphics, and expensive merchandise. In a restaurant, low level intimate lighting, tablecloths, and fancy dinnerware are the usual symbols of more exclusive establishments. See Figure 9.23.

Background ❖ Other than status, people are bound together as groups based on the **contextual background** within which they operate or from which they come. Whether due to shared culture, subculture, or geographic location, these commonalties establish bonds, mutual understandings, and affinities that find expression in the built environment. One can generalize that people of the same nationality will feel at home in environments reflecting traits from their culture, that people from coastal areas will enjoy the presence of water, and that people from the woods will enjoy dense vegetation. These are, of course, generalizations, and although they are often accurate, designers have to check and confirm them.

Whether designing for a clientele that shares a common contextual background or trying to project an image of a certain contextual background for, say, a theme restaurant, you will be relying on the typical visual symbols of the context being targeted. We have already discussed cultural and regional common contexts in a previous section. Other common backgrounds affecting membership are those established by occupation, neighborhood, membership in special-interest organizations, and so on.

In addition to the expression of the contextual realities of the user group, we also encounter the projection of exported contextual traits. This is the case when someone designs a seafood restaurant with a nautical

Figure 9.25 Some environments project innovativeness while others project conservatism. This applies to all building types, regardless of age group, status, or background. The two stores shown convey different degrees of progressiveness.

theme in a landlocked area, or an ethnic gift shop far removed from the country of origin. See Figure 9.24. In these cases, the native, inherent characteristics of the environments are imported into the project, something that must be done with sensitivity and skill.

Age group, status, and background establish commonalties that can be expressed through design. In some cases these expressions cater to the members of a particular group, while sending messages to others that the place is not for them. In other cases, as with shops and restaurants, they allow people to have a temporary experience associated with a particular group, or way of being. It is also possible to design places where everyone can feel at home. Some types of projects, such as clinics and some public buildings, even demand it. If done with sensitivity and skill, these can be attractive, genuine, and successful. If not, they can be as bland as food that tries to cater to everyone's taste.

Progressiveness

Progressiveness is a measure of how conservative or innovative individuals and groups are. In general, younger people will tend to be more progressive than older people. Youngsters tend to have a taste for the new, different, and, sometimes, radical. Adults, on the other hand, generally pay less attention to the latest fads.

There is, however, a range of progressiveness within every age group. This is due to personality. Every age has innovative people that defy conventions and conservative ones that stick to traditions. According to the level of progressiveness desired, some projects express new and innovative approaches while others express traditionalism and conservatism. In general,

conservative types tend to stick with conventions. Innovative types tend to break away from them.

An important question arises when the progressiveness level of the client differs from that of the visitor. The correct level depends on both the client and the targeted market. In some cases the person who owns the space may be highly creative and innovative but the prevailing audience that supports the establishment may be varied, or even conservative. In this case, the owner may choose to cater to the tastes of the patrons and not his or her own. In other cases the owner decides whom to attract and tailors the level of progressiveness of the facility to cater to that specific segment.

In general, conservative projects rely on proven, conventional, and straightforward forms and compositions. Progressive projects defy convention and utilize novel forms, finishes, and compositions. The storefronts shown in Figure 9.25 portray two different levels of progressiveness, the one in Figure 9.25a being more traditional and conservative, and the one in Figure 9.25b being more unconventional and progressive.

Attitude

Regardless of age group and degree of progressiveness, people and organizations have unique attitudes they value and like to project. These **attitudes** are related to the way these people or groups interact with others. Among the factors that are expressed in this category are pride, friendliness, humor, and formality.

Pride ❖ Some people and organizations have and like to project a sense of importance and **pride**

Figure 9.26 Displaying the sense of pride of owners and users can be accomplished in different ways. One of the ways of expressing pride is through display of treasured possessions, accomplishments, and hunting trophies.

Source: From Here of All Places *by Osbert Lancaster, John Murray (Publishers) Ltd., 1958.*

through the design of their built environment. The level of pride can range from mere self-confidence to blatant arrogance. Their level of pride will affect the character their spaces take on, be it assertive, upright, and distinguished, or pompous and pretentious. Other people and organizations give less importance to matters of pride, even if they possess self-pride. In these cases, the environment is likely to express a sense of restrained success or even tasteful humbleness. All these combinations are likely to produce slightly different design expressions. The ability to capture the exact level of nuance comes with practice and is a trait of the accomplished designer.

Pride can be exhibited through designs of elegance and sophistication that project success, or through details and accessories that speak of the success, sophistication or status of the client. To some, the display of

Figure 9.27 Friendly environments are welcoming. Friendliness can be expressed by bright, cheerful environments with comfortable and accessible furniture that invites and comforts.

treasured possessions and accomplishments are ways of expressing pride, as portrayed in Figure 9.26.

Friendliness ❖ Some people and organizations, whether by personality or by conscious intent, project feelings of warmth and **friendliness**. Others project a sense of coldness, sobriety, and impersonality. In either case, their built environments are likely to reflect these tendencies. In some cases, it may be necessary to compensate to make the prevailing tendency more fitting with the requirements of the enterprise. For example, an overly friendly client may choose to tone down the friendly aspects of his built environment in order to project a more professional image. Similarly, a cold, impersonal organization may choose to have a cheerful and friendly environment in order to compensate for its lack of grace. In general, public projects such as clinics and service centers should be welcoming and friendly; private and exclusive projects, such as a private and confidential government entity, may need to convey reserve and distance, at least up front, to discourage intrusion by outsiders. Friendliness is often expressed by openness, cheerful colors, and a general sense of admittance. Many designers and clients make conscious efforts to produce reception areas that are friendly and inviting, such as the one shown for an office in Figure 9.27.

Humor ❖ This variable is concerned with the level of seriousness a client wants to project. Although related to friendliness, it does not always have to be consistent with it. A warm, friendly enterprise may also have a serious tone, while a cold, impersonal one may exhibit a bit of **humor**, even if dry. Depending on the desired intentions, the environment can be straight-

Figure 9.28 Humor has useful applications in the design of some environments. The children's clinic shown in (a) uses stuffed animals to liven things up and reduce the fear of its patients. The store in (b) incorporates a car mixed with the merchandise to produce a humorous surprise.

Figure 9.29 Arrangement, materials, shapes, and content, all contribute to formality. The store in (a) is relaxed and casual; the store in (b), serious and formal.

forward and serious or may tolerate humor through the use of unlikely objects, funny artwork, and so on. In general, humor is produced by incorporating unexpected content, be it through space and form or furnishings and accessories. Figure 9.28a shows the clever use of props, in this case stuffed animals, to give a children's clinic a humorous as well as a friendly tone. Figure 9.28b features a retail space with a Volkswagen vehicle in the display area. This unconventional approach contributes to the playful and humorous character of the store.

Formality ❖ Related to both friendliness and humor is **formality**. Despite the general notion that warm, friendly people have a sense of humor and are less formal, it is entirely possible to have other combinations. It is not uncommon to project warmth and friendliness in a formal environment or to have humor and formality, or seriousness and casualness coexist harmoniously. Formality in the environment is produced by straight, symmetrical, rigid, and static arrangements. Informality, or casualness, is associated more with asymmetrical, irregular, dynamic arrangements. Formality is also characterized by uprightness, seriousness, and stiffness, while casualness is relaxed and pliable. Compare the levels of formality of the two storefronts shown in Figure 9.29.

Hierarchy ❖ Related to the issue of status is **hierarchy**. This specially applies to the workplace environment where people of different status levels come together. How those in power decide to position themselves and everybody else becomes an important factor. Are groups mixed or are they arranged by status level? Are the arrangements democratic or hierarchi-

cal? Who gets the perimeter offices with windows and the corner offices? Are there certain places accessible only by the powerful few or is every corner of the facility accessible to all? Are some areas fancier than others or is the level of finish and detail consistent throughout the facility?

Hierarchy is expressed mostly by the size and location of spaces in a project. The choices made indicate attitudes about the relationships between people of different status and rank.

Figure 9.30 Sophisticated expression can occur in any kind of project, regardless of style, as shown in these two scenes from very different projects.

Sophistication

Predispositions of membership, progressiveness, and attitude start to form a basic identity profile for a given user. The next factor, **sophistication**, will affect the look these other preferences take. Sophistication refers to the client's taste. It is a measure of how discerning one's taste is.

Characteristics of aesthetically discerning people are their ability to intuitively sense good composition (proportion and balance), to appreciate nuance and subtlety, to understand and appreciate abstraction, and to distinguish and appreciate special artistic content. In general, discerning clients will be more in tune with the sensibilities of the designer and appreciate, sometimes demand, sophisticated design efforts. The not-so-discerning client is likely to prefer more mundane solutions. Note that good taste is not indicative of preference for a particular style or design approach. In fact, different levels of aesthetic sophistication are possible within any style. Thus, one can find sophisticated expressions for any style from traditional to contemporary. The two spaces shown in Figure 9.30 are examples of tasteful designs done in two radically different styles.

Expressions of sophistication often carry a degree of pretentiousness. A barbershop, for instance, usually does not need to look sophisticated. It is quite enough for it to be ordinary and straightforward. An exclusive hair salon, on the other hand, often makes a conscious effort to look sophisticated, classy, and even pretentious.

Preference

Under the heading of **preference** we group a number of miscellaneous stylistic preferences people and groups have. These preferences may be based on personality or may be learned over time. They can carry great importance and people often feel strongly about them. Specific preferences have an effect on the types of designs clients will like and sometimes demand. Below we list some important design aspects for which people develop stylistic preferences.

Figural Character of Spaces, Masses, and Objects ❖ The ways in which **space** and its elements are shaped and assembled will result in different characters. Some compositions are flowing, while others are choppy. Depending on the character of the client and the desired expression some design arrangements will be more suitable than others. Important factors include the shapes used, the perceptual weight of elements, and the character of the compositions.

Shapes ❖ The **shape** of interior space can take many configurations. These are most apparent in the shape of walls, the configurations of lines and patterns on two-dimensional surfaces (walls, ceilings, and floors) and the shape of furnishings and their components. People have preferences concerning the overall character of the shapes in their environment. Some may prefer straight lines, others diagonal lines; some tight curves, and others smooth, sweeping curves. Curves often carry connotations of flair and sensuality; straight lines, of straightforwardness and formality. Figure 9.31 shows three different applications of the use of curvilinear shapes. These occur on the ceiling, wall, and floor planes, respectively.

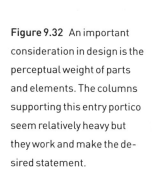

Figure 9.31 Client and designers prefer some shapes to others. Additionally, some shapes are more appropriate in certain projects than others. Curvilinear shapes always make an impression. Three applications of curves are shown: on an entry canopy (a), on a glass wall (b), and on a floor pattern (c).

Weight ❖ Perceptual **weight** is another factor of stylistic preference. It refers to the **light-handedness** or **heavy-handedness** of design elements. These can range from the size of vertical supports to the proportions of trim, column bases, and other elements. Some people enjoy a light feel, while others prefer a meatier look. A good example is a column and its proportions. Notice the relative heaviness of the columns shown in Figure 9.32. Consider now the trim of the three storefronts shown in Figure 9.33 ranging from the heaviest to lightest.

Figure 9.32 An important consideration in design is the perceptual weight of parts and elements. The columns supporting this entry portico seem relatively heavy but they work and make the desired statement.

Figure 9.33 Weight is also an important consideration in the proportions chosen for trim. The three storefronts shown display various degrees of trim heaviness, ranging from very heavy (a), to moderate (b), to light (c).

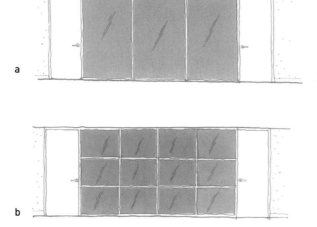

Figure 9.34 Different compositions convey different expressions. The wall composition in (a) features few full-height parts and produces a subtle, uncluttered elevation. The composition in (b) features greater modulation and produces a richer, more complex effect.

Figure 9.36 Objects, masses, and planes can look like assemblies achieved by the careful combination of many parts. This is the way the column shown in (a) is put together. They can also look like plastic-type objects that are shaped from a single piece, such as the column in (b).

Composition ❖ In addition to shapes and weight, **composition** plays a significant role in determining the figural character of spaces, masses, and objects. The size, number of parts, and arrangement of subcomponents impacts the final appearance of a given composition. Is the composition broken down into few large

Figure 9.35 Compositions can look like an overall piece that has been subdivided, such as the two elevations shown in Figure 9.34, or they can look like individual parts that have been brought close together to form a group. This elevation is equivalent to the elevations in Figure 9.34, but this time it is fragmented into distinct individual parts and has a very different feel.

pieces or many smaller pieces? Are parts assembled in seamless fashion, or do they read as many individual pieces on the same background?

Figure 9.34 shows the composition of two elevations. The elevation in Figure 9.34a features just a few large pieces while the elevation in Figure 9.34b shows the same wall divided into a greater number of smaller pieces. Notice the difference. Now look at Figure 9.35. It shows the same elevation shown in Figure 9.34b fragmented into separate individual sections. Notice the specific look it takes.

Another related composition issue refers to the method of construction. Does a mass look like it was carved from a single piece or built by assembling many pieces together? This question brings up the distinction between inflection and articulation introduced in Chapter 6. Compare the two columns shown in Figure 9.36. The column in Figure 9.36b is made up of one piece that has been shaped. It is pure as it is and consists of only one part. It can only be changed by carving it further. The character of the column in Figure 9.36a is quite different. It is clearly composed of parts that have been assembled. Each part contributes to the whole but also reads as a distinct part that can be changed independently.

Load Level ❖ The issues of order, complexity, and **environmental load** have already been introduced. Any project has an appropriate range of adequate load level depending on the nature of the project and its users. These range from environments that are highly stimulating to ones that are calming. See Capsule: "People and the Environment" in Chapter 2. In some cases, such as a nightclub (high load) or a relaxation spa (low load), the adequate levels will be self-

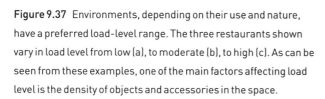

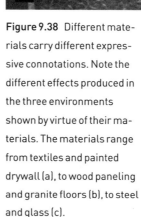

Figure 9.38 Different materials carry different expressive connotations. Note the different effects produced in the three environments shown by virtue of their materials. The materials range from textiles and painted drywall (a), to wood paneling and granite floors (b), to steel and glass (c).

Figure 9.37 Environments, depending on their use and nature, have a preferred load-level range. The three restaurants shown vary in load level from low (a), to moderate (b), to high (c). As can be seen from these examples, one of the main factors affecting load level is the density of objects and accessories in the space.

evident. In other cases, the designer has to probe further to get a reading about the client and his or her preference for complex, energetic environments, or simple, calm ones. Since we have already discussed this variable, we will just re-emphasize that clients will have preferences regarding load levels, and designers need to understand and respond to those preferences in projects reflecting the client's personality. Notice the different load levels of the three eating establishments shown in Figure 9.37.

Materials ❖ A highly influential aspect of projects is the choice of the **material palette**. Materials have an

immense impact on the expression of a project. Possibilities and variations are countless. We will focus here on one particular distinction of material palettes (among many possible) to illustrate differences among preferences: the distinction between natural material palettes and manufactured ones. Natural material palettes use woods, stones, and natural textiles and give a more organic feel. Manufactured palettes use materials such as metals, plastics, and glass and give a more industrial look. Some designers favor one approach or the other, while others combine the two successfully. The choice between these two fundamentally different palettes will produce radically different looks and project very different expressions. These material expressions can be found mostly on walls, frames, doors, trim, and furnishings. Notice the different feel of the three scenes in Figure 9.38 based on their material palettes.

Figure 9.39 Compositions can vary widely in their degree of abstraction. Some can be pictorial and literal (a), and others more abstract (b).

Figure 9.40 Ornamentation, although still used, has been replaced by detailing. Ornamentation implies applied embellishment, while detailing implies intrinsic articulation. The approach used carries specific connotations and stylistic inclinations. The modern detailing approach used for the coffee bar design in (a) is quite different from the ornamental drinking fountain in (b).

Abstraction ❖ Another important aspect is the client's attitude towards the use of **abstraction**. We have said already that not everyone appreciates abstraction. Some people prefer more straightforward, literal, and pictorial compositions that look like something they can recognize. Projects with highly abstract compositions will not please everybody. Neither will projects with highly pictorial compositions. You, as the designer need to understand the preferences of your clients in this regard and design accordingly.

Similarly, some people enjoy pictorial artwork and patterns on the walls and floors, while others prefer abstract representations. While the more traditional client will demand flowery carpet borders and artwork containing landscape scenes, the more modern one will frown at such choices. Figure 9.39 shows views of two storefronts, one (Figure 9.39a) more symmetrical and pictorial and the other (Figure 9.39b) more abstract.

Ornamentation ❖ One final important category under preference is whether or not to incorporate **ornamentation**. Ornamentation was used extensively in architecture and interiors until the modern movement all but banished its use. Remnants of those sentiments persist and many designers still see applied decoration as fake and unnecessary. Nevertheless, many clients and designers do enjoy and demand decoration. Knowing the client's position related to the use of applied ornamentation will allow you to make appropriate choices and compromises to fit the project.

These days many designers utilize inherent detailing and carefully selected accessories, artwork, and finishes to give projects the richness once supplied by applied ornamentation. Figure 9.40 shows examples of a carefully detailed contemporary coffee bar (Figure 9.40a) and a more ornamental, yet restrained, drinking water fountain in a niche (Figure 9.40b).

Self-Presentation

The last classification related to identity is **self-presentation**. While the other variables establish certain kinds of expressions, this one acts more as a modifier. Self-presentation refers to the intensity with which

Figure 9.41 Expression can be loud and bold. The gigantic wristwatch suspended from the ceiling of this clock store is an example of a rather bold statement.

clients choose to express their identity. It is a potency measure and is related to levels of extroversion and intensity. Like the factors discussed above, the type of presentation used will depend on the personality of the client and the requirements of the project being done. This variable is related to and affects all the other ones discussed previously. A client's unique combination of membership, progressiveness, attitude, sophistication, and preferences will be colored by the intensity with which those tendencies are expressed. The client may like to show off his or her success in a big way or may keep a low profile despite the success. Extroverted clients may wish to be true to their personality and paint their office with bright, bold colors. On the other hand, a mellow manager of a high-energy restaurant that caters to a young crowd may have to go counter to his or her mellow personality and ask for a more appropriate high-load environment.

The two extremes of this measure could be labeled boldness and subtlety. A brief discussion of each follows.

Boldness ❖ **Boldness** is all about high intensity. Visually bold environments are intense and extroverted. They don't hold anything back. Expressions of membership, progressiveness, attitude, sophistication, and other preferences are presented forcefully with little restraint. If part of the environment is off-limits to certain people, the barrier will be of such proportions that there will be no confusion about the matter. If the company is successful, you may expect to see exuberance. A progressive client will express innovation in no uncertain terms. If the users have a

sense of humor, the place will surely make you laugh. If a group has preferences for, say, sensual form and complexity, expect to see unabashed curves and a very intense, complex environment. Of course, the designer is likely to help a bold client tone down a few items to achieve a healthy balance, but left untamed, this group would go all out and express its predispositions loudly.

Boldness can be achieved many different ways, including the incorporation of high complexity, bright lighting, accented contrasts, strong colors, bold graphics, and unusual forms and furnishings. The gigantic wristwatch suspended from the ceiling in Figure 9.41 is an example of the bold use of props for expression.

Subtlety ❖ **Subtlety** relies on restraint. Visually subtle environments express themselves in quiet ways. By subtlety we don't mean lack of expression. In these cases preferences and predispositions are communicated without boasting. Success may be expressed without being ostentatious, traditionalism may be shown without becoming too literal and stuffy, and warmth may be shown without excessive use of warm colors.

A project may have a subtle expression due to the personality of its users, or it may be a conscious choice made rationally to fit the project. It can often be influenced by you, as the designer. Taken to an extreme, subtlety can become minimalism, although subtlety implies intricacy handled delicately rather than simplicity and absence of expression. Subtlety is characterized by slimness, the use of soft colors, soft lighting, low contrast, and overall restraint. Obviously, there is

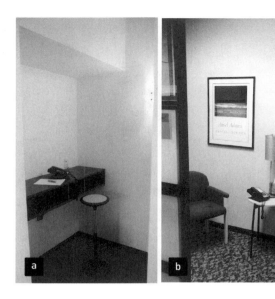

a lot of ground in between exaggerated boldness and pure subtlety and many projects find their comfort zone somewhere in the middle.

Figure 9.42 shows two small telephone rooms within an office setting. They are subtle in approach. Yet, notice the difference between the two. The room in Figure 9.42a is bare and minimal, while the one in Figure 9.42b is subtle and restrained but with more richness than its counterpart.

Designer's Personal Expression

Every project's expression, however indicative of the realities of the program, context, and client's identity, is also an expression of the attitudes and beliefs of its designer. All the kinds of expression discussed up to this point, after all, get filtered through your own judgment and you ultimately decide what gets expressed and how strongly. Additionally, as the designer you carry a responsibility to the profession, and your decisions must take into account the current norms of the design profession. There are timeless principles and current trends that affect the design climate in which you operate. There are also personal tendencies and beliefs held dear by individual designers. All these affect the ultimate expression of a project.

Below we look at three major factors that affect the kind of expression designers choose for a project: the designer's stylistic tendencies, attitudes about reigning design norms, and use of sophisticated ways of expression.

The Designer's Personal Style

All designers have particular design tendencies and a certain design range within which they like to operate. For some the range is broad, encompassing diverse ways of designing, while for others it is quite narrow. Many designers develop distinct styles that become their signature style. If it has some appeal people who share affinities with that style will seek them out to be their designers. Some designers operate within strict modernistic principles of simplicity and austerity, while others are more flamboyant and decorative.

Designers, like clients, have specific preferences and predispositions for all the variables discussed above under image and preferences. They will, consciously or not, try to influence the project to arrive at an expression within their own range of preferences. The final expression the project takes is usually a combination of the expressions agreeable to both client and designer. When clients seek designers whose style is compatible with their own tendencies, the bargaining process becomes a much smoother one. Many clients either don't feel comfortable making or don't have time to make choices about expression and look to their designers to take charge and get the job done.

Other than style, per se, designers can endow projects with particular expressions based on their personal attitudes about composition, materials, and construction approach. Designers may have stylistic inclinations towards either compositions that are seamless and flowing, or ones that are assembled by combining many parts together. They can also express their own convictions about materials and their use.

Some will prefer natural materials, while others will choose manufactured ones. Some will strive for a highly crafted look and others for a very artsy look.

When it comes to craftsmanship, some designers believe that it is important to reveal the way design elements are put together for all to see and understand. American architect Louis Kahn, for example, was known for designs that revealed the structure of a building in its many details. This approach, of course, represents an additional burden of resolving every detail clearly so all of them can be displayed, understood, and appreciated by the visitor. Many designs express exquisite detailing and craftsmanship. These attest to the great skill of the designer who conceived and worked out the details, and in many cases, to the skill of the craftsman who built them.

Another important aspect of design for which designers develop personal convictions is the issue of honesty of expression. This involves questions, as Robertson put it, "of architectural 'deceit' or 'honesty,' and of the borderline between legitimate make-believe and trickery."[12] This is especially relevant in highly thematic projects, like the ones often done for specialty shops and theme restaurants.

The Designer's Attitude about Current Design Norms

As we have stated previously, all design occurs within a given artistic climate of the time. At any time, certain tendencies and trends will be in vogue and designers often feel compelled to go with the flow and design of the current trends. This is not always the case. The design profession, not unlike music and the other arts,

Figure 9.43 Sometimes the shapes, proportions, and materials used can reinforce the character of the products associated with a place. Compare the heavier approach of the fur store shown in (a) to the lighter feel of the lingerie store shown in (b). In this case, both approaches seem to fit with the character of their respective merchandise.

is full of rebels who enjoy going against the tide, either for the sake of noncompliance or because they genuinely disagree with the trend. So, instead of adopting the current style, they ignore it or even mock it.

It is easier for high-profile designers than for newcomers or unknown designers to make references, whether supportive or not, about the design inclinations of others, especially when the whole design community and the press are watching and commenting on their every move. Generally speaking, it is advisable to stay away from design games that use a client's project to send messages to other designers or the professional community at large. If you don't agree with a current design trend, it is more productive to cultivate and practice whatever you do believe in.

The Designer's Use of Sophisticated Expression

Many architectural and interior designers like to communicate beyond the basic expressions of a project. They do so through the use of symbolism, metaphoric expressions, and similar devices. All these

Figure 9.44 The functions or products associated with a given enterprise can be manifested in many ways. One effective approach is the use of straightforward displays that feature the function or product in question.

Figure 9.45 Forms and materials can be expressive of the products and functions associated with a given enterprise. This example shows the clever use of fluid forms and glass to capture the feel of water, the name and theme of the store.

Figure 9.46 Props are often effective in reinforcing the products and functions associated with a given entity. In this example, the forms, logos, and signs of the store are reinforced by the presence of a well-known and charming Warner Brothers character.

are legitimate in design but must be used with skill, restraint, and caution because often these types of design expressions go unnoticed. If the level of symbolism or abstraction is too high, most people will fail to make the desired associations between symbol and meaning. Nevertheless, these techniques can be useful and meaningful in projects whose users or public share common meanings, due to convention, tradition, or history. In these cases, allusions to common symbols, historic events, or important people can be understood and appreciated by all the insiders familiar with them. Possible gestures include the placement of a given function of particular symbolic importance in the center of the project, or the orientation of the main circulation spine of a project on axis with the original location of the company three blocks away.

Another way designers try to endow projects with meaning is by responding and giving expression to the essence of the product or service associated with a given entity. The expressive characters of the two storefronts in Figure 9.43 fit the nature of the merchandise sold in them. The graphics, geometry, and massing of the fur store are appropriately heavy while the same elements in the lingerie store are much lighter and delicate. Figure 9.44 shows an example of a straightforward shoe display in a corporate environment directly communicating the product associated with the company. In Figure 9.45 the designer expresses the essence of the company's name by emulating the fluidity of water through the forms used. Finally, Figure 9.46 shows the humorous literal expression of one of the main characters associated with a company, in this case Daffy Duck.

Any long-lasting intellectual or artistic pursuit requires an ideology, a framework of principles and ideas that explains and justifies our actions and gives them direction. An artist today needs a personal ideology in order to accomplish original work. We build our ideology using pieces we gather throughout our lives from parents, teachers, books, friends, other artists, and most important, from our own thoughts and experiences.[1]

Designers usually start their careers with a vague and loose ideological framework consisting largely of borrowed ideas. That is fine. As they gain experience, though, they start to develop more precise personal beliefs that they express in their designs. As Cesar Pelli points out, "In order to do significant work, however, we need to reinterpret and modify shared ideas and make them part of a personal body of thoughts. The more we develop our individual position, the more we move away from that of our peers."[2]

In this piece, we expose you to beliefs expressed by four influential design thinkers. They are excerpted from proclamations committed to writing by them at particular points in time. To become a great designer, you will need clarity and consistency of approach. This requires having, at any one time, a set of personal convictions that help you decide, for each project, which is the right path to take from among all the possible design approaches possible for that project. The intent of this piece is as much to present four different ways of thinking about design approaches, as it is to encourage you to initiate your own personal ideology.

Venturi on Complexity and Contradiction

In 1966, the Museum of Modern Art published Robert Venturi's *Complexity and Contradiction in Architecture*, a highly influential manifesto that critiqued the shortcomings of modern architecture. In it, Venturi attacks the reductive tendencies of modern architecture and the pure, but boring, designs it produced. He thought architecture had to get up to par with science, poetry, and visual art and acknowledge complexity and contradiction.

"I like complexity and contradiction in architecture," starts Venturi's manifesto. "I do not like the incoherence or arbitrariness of incompetent architecture nor the precious intricacies of picturesqueness or expressionism. Instead, I speak of complex and contradictory architecture based on the richness and ambiguity of modern experience, including experience which is inherent in art."[3] He points out not only the inherent complexity of life but also the increasing complexity of buildings and their programs. How could anyone try to simplify, he wonders, that which is inherently complex?

"The doctrine of 'less is more' bemoans complexity and justifies exclusion for expressive purposes."[4] Here Venturi condemns the practice of selectivity in determining which problems to solve. One can be selective in how one approaches problems, but shouldn't select which problems to approach. Isn't one supposed to tackle them all? "Mies's exquisite pavilions have indeed had valuable implications for architecture, but is not their selectiveness of content and language their limitation as well as their strength? . . . Such forced simplicity is oversimplification . . . Where simplicity cannot work, simpleness results. Blatant simplification means bland architecture. Less is a bore."[5] This doesn't mean that one cannot strive for simplicity. But, according to Venturi, "aesthetic simplicity . . . derives from inner complexity,"[6] and he goes on to demonstrate how the Doric temple achieves apparent simplicity, through real complexity. He is obviously referring to resolved complexity.

Venturi also favors contradiction in his aim for vitality as well as validity. He explains: "I like elements which are hybrid rather than 'pure,' compromising rather than 'clean,' distorted rather than 'straightforward,' ambiguous rather than articulated, perverse as well as 'impersonal,' boring as well as 'interesting,' conventional rather than 'designed,' accommodating rather than excluding, redundant rather than simple, vestigial as well as innovating, inconsistent and equivocal rather than direct and clear. I am for messy vitality over obvious unity."[7] He strives to produce an architecture that "evokes many levels of meaning and combinations of focus: its space and its elements become readable and workable in several ways at once."[8]

Contradictory levels of meaning involve paradoxical contrast, and the level of ambiguity varies. Something can be closed, yet open. Venturi prefers "both-and" to "either-or" and the finer distinctions it permits. He also advocates the "double-functioning" element, which performs multiple functions related to use and structure, as opposed to "both-and," which emphasizes double meaning.

"An architecture of complexity and contradiction," he stresses, "does not mean picturesqueness or willfull expressionism. If I am against purity, I am also against picturesqueness. False complexity currently counters false simplicity..."[9] Complexity must arise out of the program and the structure of the whole and not from just the desire to be expressive. In the end, he assures, "an architecture of complexity and contradiction has a special obligation towards the whole: its truth must be in its totality or its implications of totality. It must embody the difficult unity of inclusion rather than the easy unity of exclusion. More is not less."[10]

Graves on Figurative Architecture

Michael Graves, another critic of modernism, rejects the lack of character of modernism. His humanistic architecture is representational and suggestive, relying on articulation, color, and historical references. He distinguishes between building (the practical aspects of architecture) and architecture (the symbolic representation of culture and its myths).

"The poetic form of architecture," he explains, "is responsive to issues external to the building, and incorporates the three-dimensional expression of the myths and rituals of society. Poetic forms in architecture are sensitive to the figurative, associative, and anthropomorphic attitudes of a culture."[11] Graves strongly believes in architecture's duty to register society's patterns of ritual and condemns the nonfigural abstract geometries of the modern movement.

While acknowledging the practical physical side of architecture, he reminds us "that the components of architecture have not only derived from pragmatic necessity, but also evolved from symbolic sources." A defender of the integrity of an element's anthropomorphic and figurative meanings, Graves expresses dismay at modern architecture's audacity to transform the window from an element that helps "us make sense not only of the landscape beyond but also of our own position relative to the geometry of the window and to the building as a whole,"[12] to disorienting window walls. He advocates the use of thematic and figural aspects of de-sign. Associations can be made with natural phenomena (ground as floor), and anthropomorphic allusions (column as man).

Figurative architecture assumes "that the thematic character of a work is grounded in nature and is simultaneously read in a totemic or anthropomorphic manner."[13] Thus, a wall, similar to the window which helps us understand our size and presence in the room, fulfills both pragmatic and symbolic functions. Its tripartite division (wainscot, body, soffit), while not intended to imitate man, helps to stabilize the wall relative to the room, an important secondary function.

Modern architecture lost its sense for figural void, the form of space. Amorphic, continuous space, such as in Mies's Barcelona Pavilion (once again) "dissolves any reference to our understanding of figural void or space." Such space is "oblivious to bodily or totemic reference, and we therefore always find ourselves unable to feel centered in such a space. This lack of figural reference ultimately contributes to a feeling of alienation in buildings based on such singular propositions." It is crucial, concludes Graves, "that we re-establish the thematic associations invented by our culture in order to fully allow the culture of architecture to represent the mythic and ritual aspirations of society."[14]

Porphyrios on Classical Architecture

Another critic of modernism, Demetri Porphyrios also attacks the scenographic and eclectic tendencies of postmodernists and instead advocates authentic classicism. "The aim of modern eclecticism," he points out, "has been to look at historical styles merely as communicative devices, as labels and clothing. Style itself was seen as having no natural relationship to the tectonics of building." He criticizes "the pluralism that sprung out of an age of conciliatory culture, widespread visiting of the beliefs of all countries and all ages, accepting everything without fixing any part, since truth is everywhere in bits and nowhere in its entirety."[15]

While modernism showed, and not concealed, the elements used to construct a work of art, "postmodernist works show themselves for the contrivance they are, but in doing so they also state that everything else in life is a contrivance and that simply there is no escape from this. Hence the self-referential circularity of the postmodern quotation and the extreme fascination with parody and metalinguistic commentary."[16]

Porphyrios believes the metalinguistic attempts of the high-tech branch of postmodernism resulted in buildings that are "only make-believe simulations of high-tech imagery."[17] Meanwhile, the postmodern classicists rely on parody. "They favour playful distortion, citation, deliberate anachronism, diminution, oxymoron, and so on. Ultimately, this is yet another make-believe cardboard architecture."[18] The third group of postmodernists criticized by Porphyrios are the deconstructionists who "loudly reject such ideas as order, intelligibility, and tradition. Architecture is supposed to become an experience of failure and crisis. And if crisis is not there, well then, it must be created."[19] While these three versions of postmodernism are different, they all share a similar scenographic view of architecture.

His view is that of a classicist. Classicists, he explains, "adopt the theory of imitation. Art, it is argued, imitates the real world by turning selected significant aspects of it into mythical representations . . . Similarly, a Classicist would argue architecture is the imitative celebration of construction and shelter qualified by the myths and ideas of a given culture."[20] Contrary to the mute realism of modernism, "what makes classical architecture possible is the dialogic relationship it establishes between the craft of building and the art of architecture. Our imagination traverses this dialogic space between, say, a pergola and a colonnade, and establishes hierarchies, levels of propriety, and communicable systems of evaluation."[21]

While many designers tend to value what is new and different, Porphyrios suggests that the contribution of an architect "lies in what he/she chooses to borrow."[22] He sums up his view: "Architecture has nothing to do with 'novelty-mania' and intellectual sophistries. Architecture has nothing to do with transgression, boredom, or parody. It has nothing to do with parasitic life, excremental culture or the cynical fascination with the bad luck of others. Architecture has to do with decisions that concern the good, the decent, the proper . . . Surely, what constitutes a proper life varies from one historical period to another. But it is our responsibility to define it anew all the time."[23]

An Architecture of Reality

The final view presented is by Michael Benedikt. He, like Porphyrios, condemns postmodernism's insistence on communicating superficially through architecture. Instead of the return to classicism, though, Benedikt advocates an architecture that relies on "the real" for effect. He speaks of moments when reality produces an "unreasoned joy" due to the "simple correspondence of appearance and reality" and "the evident rightness of things as they are." During those moments "the world becomes singularly meaningful, yet without being 'symbolical.' Objects and colors do not point to other realms, signs say what they have to and fall silent. Conventional associations fall away . . . we are not conscious of reference, allusion, or instruction."[24]

Benedikt calls those privileged moments "direct aesthetic experiences of the real," and suggests that, "in our media-saturated times it falls to architecture to have the direct aesthetic experience of the real at the center of its concerns."[25] He questions the view that for something to be meaningful it has to "say" something, that reality has to be "read like a book or deciphered like a code for its messages."[26]

He compares the allusion, reference, and symbolism in postmodern architecture to "the much-discussed process in postmodern literature where the . . . dizzying self-reflection on and in the literary act are typical,"[27] and poses the question of whether a building's meaning should be "fabricated with building-parts by the architect . . . by any process analogous to the way writers construct worlds and meanings with words in literary fiction." Of course not, he says. "We count on buildings to form the stable matrix of our lives, to protect us, to stand up to us, to give us addresses, and not to be made of mirrors."[28]

"Real architecture is architecture especially ready—so to speak—for its direct esthetic experience, an architecture that does not disappoint us by turning out in the light of that experience to be little more than a vehicle contrived to bear meanings . . . Real architecture is, then, architecture in which the quality of realness is paramount. And here, with realness, is how the idea of reality can best enter the realm of architectural discourse. Like 'proportion' or 'scale,' like any number of qualities ascribable to architecture good and bad, 'realness' becomes an attribute of buildings that can be pointed out and discussed, can be found lacking here, present in greater degree there . . . and so on: in short, realness becomes an observable quality amenable to some level of conceptual formulation."[29]

Benedikt concludes his argument by saying: "While it may be argued that ironic poses and movie-set history, allegories and recondite allusions, reflect most accurately and properly our information- and entertainment-oriented culture, they can also be seen as a defeat: a sliding of architecture into the world of television. For it can be argued equally well that an architecture that stands against, or in contrast to, the culture-wide trend to ephemeralization and relativism—as a kind of last bastion of dumb reality and foil to it all—constitutes the more appropriate, timely, and potentially esthetic response."[30]

These four views are personal, sincere, and different. Whether we agree with them or not, they affirm a position, an ideology, a strong belief. A personal ideology gives direction to our work. In developing a personal set of core beliefs, and in facing the many design decisions that require judgment and reflection, it is good to bear in mind two questions proposed by Cesar Pelli: The first one, is it correct? seeks to find out whether the solution satisfies external expectations. The second question, is it right? seeks to find out if the solution is helping or harming people and surroundings. As Pelli explains, it is relatively easy to find out what are the correct options. These are constantly being defined for us. "But we have to seek the 'right' direction for ourselves, using our own internal compass."[31]

---

1 Pelli, Cesar. *Observations for Young Architects*, (The Monacelli Press: New York, 1999) p. 196.

2 Ibid, p. 196.

3 Venturi, Robert. *Complexity and Contradiction in Architecture*, (The Museum of Modern Art: New York, 1977) p. 16.

4 Ibid, p. 17.

5 Ibid, p. 17.

6 Ibid, p. 17.

7 Ibid, p. 16.

8 Ibid, p. 16.

9 Ibid, p. 18.

10 Ibid, p. 16.

11 Graves, Michael. *Theorizing a New Agenda for Architecture*, edited by Kate Nesbitt (Princeton Architectural Press: New York, 1996) p. 86.

12 Ibid, p. 87.

13 Ibid, p. 88.

14 Ibid, pp. 89–90.

15 Porphyrios, Demetri. *Theorizing a New Agenda for Architecture*, edited by Kate Nesbitt (Princeton Architectural Press: New York, 1996) p. 93.

16 Ibid, p. 93.

17 Ibid, p. 94.

18 Ibid, p. 94.

19 Ibid, p. 94.

20 Ibid, p. 95.

21 Ibid, p. 95.

22 Ibid, p. 96.

23 Ibid, p. 96.

24 Benedikt, Michael. *For an Architecture of Reality*, (Lumen Press: New York, 1988) p. 4.

25 Ibid, p. 4.

26 Ibid, p. 8.

27 Ibid, p. 12.

28 Ibid, p. 14.

29 Ibid, p. 30.

30 Ibid, p. 64.

31 Pelli, p. 194.

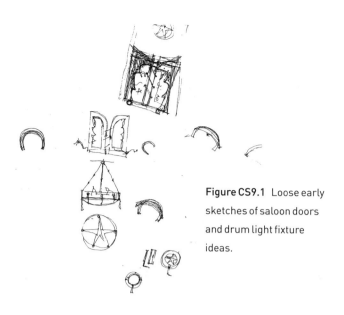

Figure CS9.1 Loose early sketches of saloon doors and drum light fixture ideas.

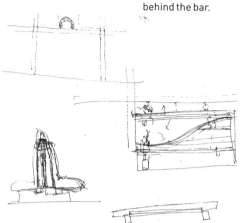

Figure CS9.2 Early sketches of banquette and feature wall behind the bar.

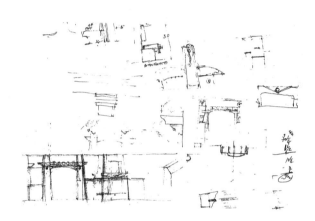

Figure CS9.3 Loose sketches of banquette designs and miscellaneous details.

CASE STUDY
Western Detailing at El Dorado Grill
Design Firm: Linville Architects

The El Dorado Grill provides a good example of the role of detailing in interior projects. It is a high-end, southwestern-themed restaurant. At El Dorado, it is the details, both of the existing building space, and of the added interior components, that give the place its character. Our focus here, hence, is on the development and resolution of the details.

The restaurant is housed in a charming old warehouse with exposed brick walls, wood floors, and rustic ceiling rafters. After seeing the project site early on, Ed Linville, the project designer, recognized its inherent character and, as he put it "surrendered to it," thus leaving it pretty much intact except for some necessary cleaning. The existing natural wood in the space had the kind of golden glow that Linville wanted to incorporate in the project. This also allowed him to use contrasting, deeper colors to achieve the required level of richness, articulation, and formality.

El Dorado features a detailing approach that reinforces the southwestern theme in a refined, subtle way. Among other things, it includes a backdrop wall behind the bar with a western scene etched in glass, a host station featuring cowboy imagery, a mesa-inspired wall mass housing the fireplace, banquettes with saddle-inspired leather upholstery, and a custom-designed light fixture inspired by a Native American drum.

All these detail ideas started as rough doodles on paper. Figure CS9.1 shows rough preliminary sketches of saloon doors and the Native American drum fixture. Figures CS9.2 and CS9.3 show early conceptions of the banquette and fireplace, and of the background wall behind the bar, respectively. These ideas were next subjected to a process of further evaluation and refinement.

Finer levels of detail were addressed with each subsequent step. These started as freehand drawings done to scale, as shown in Figure CS9.4 depicting the back-

Figure CS9.4 Development drawing of host station and background wall.

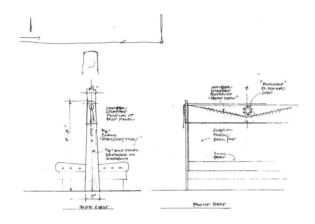

Figure CS9.5 Development drawing of banquette design.

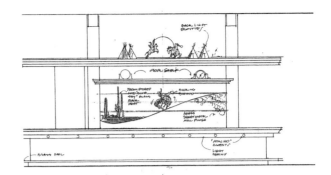

Figure CS9.6 Development drawing of feature wall behind bar.

drop wall behind the host station. You can see how definite treatments, materials, and motifs started to emerge. However, once Linville started to consider a detail idea seriously, he liked to begin drafting it hardline. This forced him to make precise decisions about dimensions and proportions and helped to accelerate the process of resolution.

Proportions, materials, motifs, and small details were resolved during this stage of detailing. Figure CS9.5 shows the development of the banquette, with brass tacks, Mexican concho medallions, a leather headrest, and the El Dorado logo incorporated into the design. Similarly, the imagery, shapes, and proportions for the bar and its backdrop wall were carefully laid out, as shown in Figure CS9.6.

The details went through one more stage of refinement and resolution. This happened when they were drafted in final form for incorporation in the con-

struction documents. These are documents the contractor will prepare his own shop drawings from, so all the information for each part of the project, including the details, needs to be accurate, precise, and resolved. It may be that they were fully resolved in the preceding stage and are only drafted in final form during this one, but quite often, last minute matters are decided or changed at this time. In other words, if something has not been previously resolved because it either was overlooked or left for later, this is when to address it. Figures CS9.7 through CS9.10 show some of the final details for the host station, fireplace, booths, and drum fixture. Notice the precision and level of detail. These drawings, and other similar ones not shown, tell the full story about these creations. The designer considered these walls and objects from every angle and made decisions about form, shape, proportion, articulation, materials, colors, accents, and so on, as if he were designing the products themselves.

Details are sometimes subjected to some tweaking during the pricing and construction stages. Then they get built. Although you as the designer would have a pretty good idea of what they are going to look like, it is really after they are built that you can enjoy seeing the fruit of your creation. Hopefully, the effect is the one intended. Figures CS9.11 through CS9.14 show photos of the details discussed above after the project was completed and occupied for some time. It's amazing that these features and objects, now part of the tangible and real world, all started as rough doodles on a piece of paper. Yet, here they are for all the restaurant's visitors to experience and enjoy.

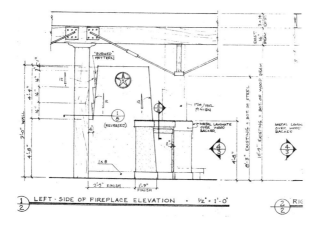

Figure CS9.7 Finished detail of host station and background wall.

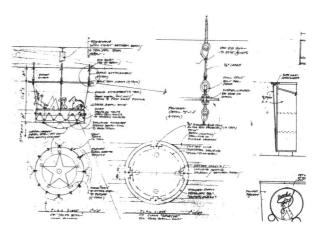

Figure CS9.10 Finished details of drum light fixture.

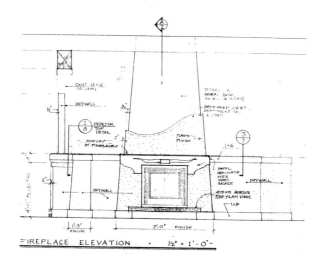

Figure CS9.8 Finished detail elevation of fireplace front.

Figure CS9.11 View of host station area.

Figure CS9.12 View of fireplace front.

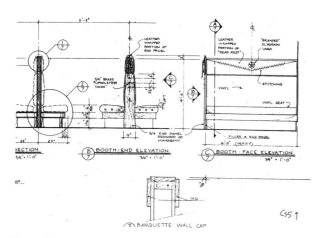

Figure CS9.9 Finished details of banquette.

Figure CS9.13 View of banquettes.

Figure CS9.14 View of drum light fixture.

Review

Summary

Designed environments embody the qualities of the people and organizations that inhabit them. Previously discussed design aspects such as order and enrichment with expression are treated in particular ways in order to customize the project, and give it a personality. These expressions communicate messages, some intentional, others not. The meanings associated with these messages vary widely from culture to culture, from group to group within a culture, and from person to person within a group, making the job of choosing among alternatives a challenge to you as the designer. These meanings are based on associations, some spontaneous and others learned by convention.

Designers can give expression to all aspects of design. They control most of the elements that go into a project, such as layout, space, surface, detail, furnishings, and accessories. There are, however, other factors contributing to expression that are beyond the control of designers, such as the people who use the space, their attire, language, and so on.

Expression works at many levels and there are many types of design expression. Among them are expression of universal human experiences, expression of contextual factors, expression of formal design properties and assemblies, and expression of programmatic necessities.

The expression of identity is one of the most important and challenging. Identity is like the personality of a project. Identity, like personality, is determined by predispositions and preferences. These can be divided into a handful of classifications. These are membership, progressiveness, attitude, sophistication, preference, and self-presentation.

Designers' own personal attitudes, convictions, and preferences are also expressed in projects. Three factors that affect the kind of designer expression manifested are the designer's own personal style, his or her attitude towards current design norms, and the designer's use of sophisticated means of communication.

Chapter Questions

1. Which two types of meaning were introduced in this chapter? How are they different?
2. Within the spectrum of the physical environment and its parts, which components can the designer affect and use to give expression?
3. Which three dualities did this chapter introduce as expressions of universal human experiences?
4. What are four types of contextual factors affecting expression?
5. Which two dualities did this chapter present as basic determinants of the project's programmatic necessities?
6. Could you explain the concept of identity as presented in this chapter?
7. Which four variables influence one's sense of membership?
8. Why is status important when it comes to membership?
9. What aspect of design does progressiveness influence?

10. What five aspects of attitude were presented in this chapter?

11. What are three variables presented in this chapter under preference?

12. What is self-presentation and why is it important?

13. Which aspects of designers' personal expressions were presented in this chapter?

14. Name two examples of spontaneous associations.

15. Name two examples of associations learned by convention.

16. Name one example of constraint/freedom as it relates to the expression of universal human experiences.

17. Name one example of admittance/rejection as it relates to the expression of universal human experiences.

18. Name a situation that would be appropriate for the manifestation of historic expression.

19. Name a situation that would be appropriate for the manifestation of cultural or regional expression.

20. Discuss with your classmates the dominant design norms and conventions of our times. What are they and how are they changing?

21. Name four types of groups distinguishable by the concept of membership introduced in this chapter. Be specific. What sets them apart?

22. Name two kinds of projects for which high-load environments would be appropriate.

23. Name two kinds of projects for which low-load environments would be appropriate.

24. What is your own preference about the use of ornamentation?

25. What is your preferred self-presentation approach (bold, subtle)?

26. What are your current design tendencies? Which others would you like to develop?

27. How would you use symbolism in a retail application?

28. How would you use symbolism in a restaurant application?

Endnotes

[1] Robertson, Howard. *Modern Architectural Design*, (The Architectural Press: Westminster, 1932) p. 99.

[2] Arnheim, Rudolf. *The Dynamics of Architectural Form*, (University of California Press: Berkeley, 1977) p. 210.

[3] Jencks, Charles. *The Language of Post-Modern Architecture*, (Rizzoli: New York, 1984) p. 42.

[4] Arnheim, p. 208.

[5] Ibid., p. 209.

[6] Ibid., p. 211.

[7] Jencks, p. 46.

[8] Ibid., p. 46.

[9] Ibid., p. 4.

[10] Arnheim, p. 209.

[11] Ibid., p. 208.

[12] Robertson, p. 99.

PART4

COMPLETING THE DESIGN

CHAPTER 10

Resolution

INSTRUCTIONAL OBJECTIVES

Emphasize the importance of achieving resolution in design.

Show various stages of the resolution of floor plans.

Discuss the process of refining the design of surfaces and details.

Show several ways to manipulate scale for effect.

Explain important peculiarities about the use of symmetrical compositions.

Discuss ways of achieving balance with asymmetrical compositions.

Explain how to use continuity to achieve unity.

Explain how to use repetition to achieve unity.

Explain how to use gradation and dispersion as vehicles for unity.

In any worthwhile activity we see what we do with two different set of eyes. In the midst of doing we give all of ourselves to our labors in constructive sympathy. We are one with our work. A moment later, we look again at what we have done and judge it as if from outside ourselves, with as critical and detached manner as we can muster. We redesign again and again, trying to satisfy our inner demands, though in architecture time is limited and we can rarely please ourselves fully.[1]

Order, enrichment, and expression are seldom pursued individually, one at a time. We have isolated them in order to be able to talk about them individually and facilitate their understanding. The three relate to, and affect, each other. Efforts to address the issues related to these three variables start early in the design process. They are subsequently developed and refined. These efforts take place, as we have said, within the context of producing a fitting and functional design.

Design exploration usually starts with rough ideas early on. These are converted into design drawings in order to be visualized, analyzed, and judged. This is done with the understanding that, if adopted, these preliminary, rough ideas will be adjusted and refined later. Before the design of a project is finalized, the many ideas, and corresponding physical elements, need to be developed and resolved. Parts need to be adjusted, relationships fine-tuned, and details given final form. Additionally, the designer needs to step back, look at the entire project as a whole, and make necessary adjustments to ensure proper cohesiveness.

This chapter is about the process of working out and completing design ideas to solve the many design problems associated with a project, achieve visual harmony, and produce a unified creation. The first part of the chapter will address some peculiar aspects of the design process and discuss what it takes to produce synthesis. Next, we will discuss the process of resolving the project from plan to the more detailed compositional aspects of form. Last, we will address

Figure 10.1 Within each stage, the design process should incorporate complete cycles that achieve synthesis on a level appropriate to the stage. Every stage should produce a tangible outcome derived from the understanding of the project at that stage, culminating in the thorough and complete project solution at the end of the resolution phase.

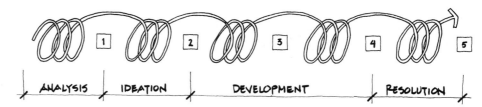

the designer's responsibility to produce environments that are perceptually harmonious and unified.

Design Synthesis

The design process seldom occurs in linear fashion. Except for the smallest and simplest of projects it is uncommon to arrive at an optimal and fitting solution from a single attempt, refine it in linear fashion, and then send it to the contractor ready to build. Most real-life projects are much more difficult to solve than that. They require an ongoing cyclical process of commitment and testing followed by evaluation and adjustment. With every cycle of response and feedback the designer commits to some aspects of the solution, modifies some, and discards others. With every step the designer aims at a higher level of resolution concerning function and the other aspects of design we have been discussing. Figure 10.1 shows a diagram of the process. It is like a spiraling helix, moving cyclically from one stage to the next and incorporating successful ideas developed and additional insights gained during previous stages.

Starting from the ideation stage, it is necessary to commit to and test comprehensive design ideas based on your current understanding of the design problem. These comprehensive ideas, as William Kleinsasser explains, act "like rehearsals before a game, serve as hypotheses or probes out there . . . they will preview the whole and generate better proposals."[2] Each such cycle should include a design scheme developed to a level appropriate to the stage of the project, and de-

vote some time to analyze and evaluate the scheme in order to assess its merits and get a greater understanding of the project. These cyclical evaluations need to generally address three things: the appropriateness of the overall design approach being taken, the way particular aspects of the approach are working, and the way the design problem definition is evolving.

During the early part of the design process, as we saw in Chapter 6, the majority of the effort goes into developing an organizational structure that will give the project unity and direction. Alternatives have to be closely scrutinized and run through one of the review cycles. Once an organizational structure has been determined appropriate, it has to be tested to see if it works with the particular requirements of the program, the geometry of the space, and other such realities of the project. After determining that the concept will work, the attention can shift to particular, more detailed, aspects of the design solution and to efforts to maintain the integrity of this organizational structure as the design goes through modifications. At every step of design it is important to examine the current understanding of the problem for accuracy and breadth since it will tend to shift and come into clearer focus as one gets more information, which invariably leads to a better understanding of the project and its potential solutions.

The problem definition stage is itself cyclical. It starts with a rudimentary understanding of a complex design problem. The problem is redefined into subissues or components, which in turn produce a better understanding of components and relationships. While addressing these, new subissues continue to surface. The more you keep working on the design solution, the

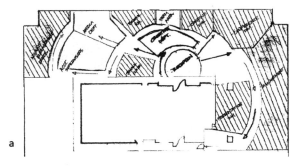

a

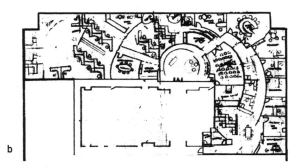

b

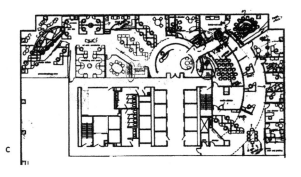

c

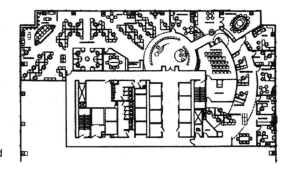

d

Figure 10.2 This series of floor plans for an office project shows different stages of resolution starting with the original organizational concept. This plan was particularly challenging to solve because of the geometry imposed by the concept. It was deemed workable and the designer succeeded in planning it out. Example (a) shows the organizational diagram, (b) an early transposition of the program's specific requirements to the plan, and (c) shows a developed but not totally refined plan. Example (d) shows the final version of the plan.

have to be resolved in order to satisfy two basic goals at two different levels of design: maximizing the quality of the overall design approach, and resolving the many pragmatic and practical issues throughout the plan. Throughout the design process you have to constantly question your current design direction to ensure that the solution is basically a good one and that the many parts of the plan work well. Figure 10.2 shows the development of a student's floor plan for an office project from conception through design development. Figure 10.2a shows the initial organizational concept diagram. Figures 10.2b and c show the plan at two intermediary stages. Figure 10.2d shows the final solution with the plan fully resolved. After spending time with the design idea, the student was convinced that the challenging geometry being attempted would work. It took, however, many adjustments and some compromises to make it all work in the end.

Once the organizational concept has been successfully translated into a floor plan, you can focus on fitting all the requirements of the program more exactly, eliminating wasted space, and, in general, adjusting the plan with greater precision. Even after you have fit in all the requirements, there are often troublesome parts that require ongoing efforts to resolve. Especially tricky are those areas that seem to have a domino effect such that upon fixing one area, you manage to ruin the previously successful adjacent area!

Refinement beyond the Plan

In addition to the plan, the three-dimensional and other detailed aspects of the project also need to be developed and refined. Their resolution should occur in hierarchi-

more layers of information and nuance rise to the surface, changing and refining your definition of the problem and the way you think about the project.

Resolution of the Plan

Resolution starts with the floor plan. Plans go through a number of revisions, starting with the first attempt to translate the organizational concept idea into a floor plan and culminating in the final plan. Plans

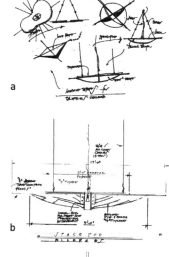

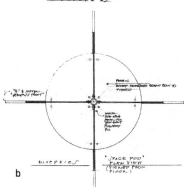

Figure 10.3 Original details are resolved in stages. The sequence shown for a pendant light fixture started with loose conceptual ideas (a) and was transformed into full construction drawings (b) and (c).

Figure 10.4 Special articulations, such as the ones shown for these two ceilings assemblies, require proper study and resolution.

cal fashion. As basic levels of design are determined and committed to, new and higher levels of detail can be addressed. That way, less time is wasted resolving details of preliminary ideas that may be discarded later. Surfaces and details are among the aspects to be addressed after the plan is in place. Surface refinement includes such tasks as developing the composition of elevations by adjusting, adding detail, and articulating.

In addition to elevations, details also need development and refinement. Basic ideas are studied and developed to produce well-executed final details. Figure 10.3a–c shows the development for a custom-designed pendant light fixture in a restaurant. Figure 10.3a shows the original conceptual ideas. Figures 10.3b and c show the details resolved and drawn with great precision.

Many designers give much importance to the articulation of the ceiling plane, an aspect that also requires resolution. The ceiling provides important contributions to the definition of space, the determination of scale, and the provision of expression. In the past, ceilings were often treated with elaborate decorations that made them extremely rich and expressive. Nowadays, ceilings tend to be much simpler. However, it is possible to position and articulate the ceiling planes overhead in ways that

make them both effective in defining space, as well as a vehicle to add texture and relief to projects. Figure 10.4 shows two views of articulated ceiling details.

Sizing and Balancing Project Parts

In Chapter 7 we introduced the different kinds of order needed in a design project. One of these had to do with matters of perceptual correctness. It is what we call architectonic order and involves tasks such as the placement of elements in a composition, their size related to other elements, and the spacing between them. We are talking now, of course, about composition. Proper composition is an obligation of design. The craft of design involves the creation and disposition of so many physical parts that it makes a significant visual impact on the environment. Designed spaces are presented to the world at full scale. The look they take is the look of our physical environment. When you design, you determine the look of the environment. That is no small responsibility.

Aesthetic and stylistic approaches vary from designer to designer and from project to project. The result

Figure 10.5 Resolution requires the proper disposition of parts, subwholes, and wholes. In this example the single column is a complete element in itself. Paired with another column, and with the addition of a pedestal below and entablature above, another whole unit is formed. The addition of a symmetrical entryway, flanked by two of the previous units, forms yet another whole unit. Finally, two of these latter units, with the addition of a central grand entrance, form the lower portion of a complete façade. All these subparts need to be resolved individually and also as components of the entire totality.

may have more or less aesthetic merit. It may or may not be high art. Nevertheless, regardless of the stylistic direction you choose for a project and the amount of art you inject into it, you have an obligation to produce good compositions. This is where the basic principles of design that you have studied in your design fundamentals classes come in handy.

It is assumed that you have been exposed to the basic elements and principles of design in previous courses. Here we will elaborate on the principles that are the most crucial to the resolution and refinement of designs. Three aspects deserve special attention. These are scale, proportion, and balance. They are essential to achieve harmony. If these three design attributes are conceived and executed correctly, the product is more likely to be a harmonious-looking environment, one where the elements will be in accord with each other. They will fit together, look right, and form a cohesive unit. This, of course, is usually easier said than done.

So basic are these concerns to design that they have been featured prominently in all the treatises on architecture and design, starting with Vitruvius' *The Ten Books of Architecture*. In addressing the fundamental principles of architecture he refers to the "order which gives due measure to the members of a work considered separately, and symmetrical agreement to the proportions of the whole."[3] He goes on to discuss three essential concepts to good composition: arrangement, eurythmy, and symmetry.

Arrangement includes "the putting together of things in their proper places and the elegance of effect which is due to adjustments appropriate to the character of the work."[4] It is concerned with the project's agreeable composition at the overall scale. He notes that it requires both reflection and invention.

Reflection is careful and laborious thought, and watchful attention directed to the agreeable effect of one's plan. Invention, on the other hand, is the solving of intricate problems and the discovery of new principles by means of brilliancy and versatility. . .

Eurythmy [emphasis added] is beauty and fitness in the adjustment of the members. This is found when the members of a work are of a height suited to their breadth, of a breadth suited to their length, and in a word, when they all correspond symmetrically.[5]

This refers to the agreeable scale and proportion of units in and of themselves.

Symmetry is a proper agreement between the members of the work itself, and relation between the different parts and the whole general scheme, in accordance with a certain part selected as standard.[6]

Vitruvius's concept of symmetry refers to the agreeable relationships among the units or parts that form a composition.

These three aspects of design are related and part of a logical continuum that works at different scales, starting with one part and its relation to itself and the human body, then the combination of that part with others to create a group or subassembly, followed by the combination of subassemblies to produce, say, one level of an elevation, then the combination of levels to produce the entire elevation (Figure 10.5). All the ele-

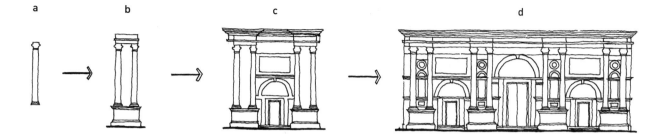

vations, when combined, comprise all the vertical planes of the project. Add to these the horizontal planes (floor and ceiling) and the whole assembly starts to add up to the architectural totality of the project.

Translating Vitruvius's concerns into more familiar terms, we can then discuss three highly interrelated design aspects that help produce harmony in design. They are scale, proportion, and balance.

Scale and proportion are two of the basic design fundamentals students learn about early in their design education. Although the concepts are fairly straightforward, their correct application can take some time to achieve consistently, and even more time to master. Intermediate, and even advanced level students, often struggle with these aspects of design at a basic level. While some designers have an innate, intuitive sense for them, many have to learn them from experience, over time. Needless to say, scale and proportion need to be resolved for a project to be successful. Furthermore, beyond their basic and competent application there are opportunities to manipulate them for specific effects.

Scale

Scale in design refers to the relative size of a space, object, or element in relation to some other part. That other part can be adjacent spaces, the immediate space where the element is housed, the human person, or other objects and elements in the space. The kind of scale we are talking about, although related to size, does not refer to the actual size of things, such as when we talk about a large-scaled complex, meaning a large project.

Scale is influenced by use and custom. Thus, its appropriateness is also judged relative to the kind of space being evaluated and the type of activities that occur in it, as well as to the preconceived ideas we have of similar elements based on what we have experienced in the past. If we are talking about a church, because of its use and symbolic importance, the scale is likely to be grand. If you ask a group of people from diverse backgrounds just how grand the church should be, their answers will tend to vary, depending on whether they are used to grand cathedrals or small parish churches. Which one is more appropriate for the occasion will require the judgment of the designer and the users associated with the project.

In order to master the use of interior architectural scale, you need to understand how scale varies depending on the reference we use for comparison. Additionally, you must master the use of scale at two different levels. First, you need to learn to design straightforward projects that handle scale in a customary and agreeable way. In this kind of project, things are sized in a responsive and fitting manner. There are no other intentions other than providing good, appropriate scale. Beyond this, to truly master scale, you need to learn how to manipulate it for effect. We discussed some of this in relation to spatial level in the section on spatial size in Chapter 4. In this chapter we expand on the topic and present different ways of manipulating scale for effect, taking into account the role of other factors in the space. We will start, however, with a presentation of the basic relationships affecting scale in interior environments.

The Size of Things in Relation to Humans

Of all the relationships concerning scale in interiors, none is more important than the relationship of

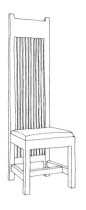

Figure 10.7 This lounge chair is quite different from the previous one. It is meant to embrace and comfort. The actual shape looks like arching arms ready to embrace whoever sits on it.

Figure 10.6 This chair, designed by Frank Lloyd Wright, is intentionally much taller than is needed.

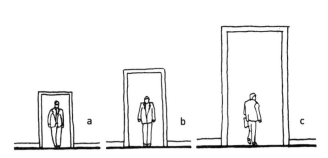

Figure 10.8 The three openings here show three distinct scales: minimal (a), comfortable (b), and grand (c). They each relate to the size of the human figure differently. Opening (a) is oppressive and uncomfortable, while (c) is generous to the point of excess. Opening (b) falls in between.

space and its components to the human figure. This is especially true for the profession of interior design, a profession that specializes in the interaction of humans and environment at the proxemic scale. Height and depth dimensions of interior components, for instance, are governed by the size and reach of the persons using them. Acceptable ranges fall somewhere between some ideal dimension for the application and the outer acceptable limits. Scale decisions in relation to the human body affect the design of wall openings, privacy panels, cabinetry, furnishings, control devices, and so on. Proper dimensions for many different applications are usually well documented in reference books. However, we issue a word of caution. While sizes and dimensions given in standard reference books are usually adequate, it is important to take into account the kind of population being designed for and make adjustments accordingly. Special groups, such as young children, the elderly, and the physically disabled, have unique needs that the standards may not specifically address.

The sizes of objects do not always have to be the customary sizes people are used to. In some cases they can be manipulated in relation to the human body for effect. The size of a chair, for instance, can be exaggerated to increase definition as the extratall chair in Figure 10.6 shows, or to create a feeling of comfort, as shown in Figure 10.7. Door hardware can be oversized to accentuate the physicality of turning the handle to open the door and gain access. It can also be minimized, to create a more delicate and refined experience. Do keep in mind that, in spite of the desired effect, the increase, reduction, or other scale manipula-

tion has to satisfy the basic function it addresses, be it seating or opening, as in the examples above.

In addition to these types of functional items, there are other kinds of design elements involving scale that have a less immediate, yet insistent effect on the human beings using a space. A door, for example, as long as its height is adequate to provide proper clearance for normal individuals, can be relatively short. It can also be much taller than it needs to be. When it comes to doors, we can use a door that barely provides clearance (as long as it meets code), one that provides comfortable clearance with some room to spare, or one so tall that it is either a mistake or its height is trying to tell us something (Figure 10.8).

Everything we physically use in a space, from doors to furnishings to objects, relates very closely to the human body. Although they all have optimal sizes, dimensions can be somewhat adjusted for effect as long as the resulting size falls within an acceptable functional range.

Relation to Application

Related to the above discussion is the size of things in relation to their application, as mentioned above with our reference to different possible interpretations about the appropriate scale for a church. Depending on the type of activity a space is designed for, its scale will need to be grandiose, normal, or intimate. While the scale of palaces, churches, and prominent civic buildings will tend to be monumental, the scale for certain areas in exclusive candlelit restaurants or the seating areas off a main corridor (Figure 10.9) will often need to be small and intimate.

Figure 10.9 The scale of this seating area off a main circulation space has been intentionally reduced to make it more intimate and inviting.

Figure 10.10 In addition to judging interior elements, in relation to the size of the human body, we also make judgments in relation to the customary size of the components. This door is tall compared to most other doors we encounter.

Relation to Element Type

Objects, such as building components, furnishings, and accessories belong to their respective typological families. Windows, doors, tables, chairs, artwork, and plants are familiar objects for which we have preconceived mental images based on our previous encounters with them. Although the exact stylistic image that comes to mind when we think of any of these items will vary slightly from person to person based on background, the essence of the mental picture will be quite similar. Part of that image is the relative size of the object, and its usual overall dimensions as well as the usual dimensions of its parts. These establish a mental point of reference. Variations towards a larger or smaller version will constitute a change of scale.

Most design-related items are available in a range of sizes. Commercial grade doors, for instance, although they tend to be of relatively uniform width, come in many heights. The relatively low 6-foot-8-inch doors used in residential construction are rarely used in commercial projects, where taller doors are usually preferred. Thus, one can choose very tall doors like the one shown in Figure 10.10. Tables, although their height does not change much, come in a variety of widths, lengths, and shapes. Other items, such as pieces of artwork and plants, come in many sizes and designers can choose among them to suit the scale needs of the project. Although these are related to the scale of the object in relation to the human body as previously discussed, here the distinction is that a judgment is made using the customary size of the object as a reference, such as when one says, "That chair seems odd; it's too small!"

Relation of Space to Entire Project

As we saw in Chapter 4, the spaces of a project can vary much from project to project in their shape, size, and character. Within a single project, the predominant spaces may set an overall scale for it. In projects consisting of many spaces, the scale produced by these spaces constitutes a point of reference. Consequently, after seeing a number of spaces, if their scale is generally consistent, subsequent rooms or spaces will be judged in relation to them. Any major scale deviations will be noticeable. "Aha," someone might say, "the scale of this room is more generous than the rest, something important must happen in this space."

Relation of Contents to Space

Once inside a specific space, the objects in it will have an important relationship to the overall space and its architectural features (doors, windows, columns, and so on). Among the important components are the furnishings, equipment, and accessories of the space. The correspondence between these objects and the space can be complementary or discordant, to emphasize specific qualities. In the first case you may use oversized furnishings, fixtures, plants, and artwork to fill the volume of a large space (Figure 10.11). Conversely, you may use small furniture, fixtures, and artwork in a small space to make it feel comfortable (Figure 10.12). These cases can be seen as examples of balanced and appropriate correspondence between objects and space.

The opposite approach would be to accentuate the largeness of the first space by using normal-sized, or even small, objects in it. This usually requires a good

Figure 10.11 There is an important scale correspondence between a room and the objects in it. Rooms with a large volume often require large-scaled furnishings and accessories (as shown) to look right.

Figure 10.12 In contrast to large rooms, small ones almost demand small-scaled furniture and accessories. Otherwise the largeness of these objects can dwarf the room and make it perceptually uncomfortable.

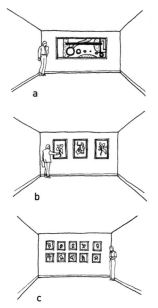

Figure 10.13 The scale of a space or surface is affected more by the size of the objects in them than the amount of space filled. In this example, the artwork in all three scenarios covers approximately the same amount of wall. Yet, the scales provided are very different.

eye and judgment in order to avoid making the disproportion seem like a mistake.

One final example of the relationship of the scale of objects to that of the space can be illustrated by the various effects produced by different arrangements of artwork on a wall. A wall can be equally filled (proportionately) with different possible combinations of artwork by varying the number of pieces and their size. Different combinations can have approximately equal proportions of artwork-to-wall ratios, but produce very different effects. Figure 10.13 shows three different approaches. Figure 10.13a shows one large painting filling the wall. This establishes a large scale. Figure 10.13b uses three smaller pieces covering approximately as much wall space as the large painting

before. The scale established is smaller. Figure 10.13c takes it a step further and covers approximately as much area using a lot of small pieces. The effect is quite different, establishing a smaller scale on the wall. The feel of the three scenes is remarkably different, all due to the size and number of pieces used.

Relation of Contents to Other Contents

The last scale relationship we will discuss is that of the objects in a space to one another. Among the objects are the ones we referred to above (furnishings, plants, and artwork) as well as others such as fixtures, doors, cabinetry, and hardware. In general, the relative size of all these elements needs to be complementary so that everything works together. If the tendency is toward largeness, then everything should be oversized and vice versa. It is possible, though, to purposefully work with more than one scale for effect. Everything may take a normal scale except for, say, the artwork on the walls, or some special details, or some architectural elements, which may be oversized for effect.

One important characteristic of space worth noting here is the way the natural scales of things (some small, some medium, some large) complement each other and the richness that this multiplicity of scales produces. In Figure 10.14 we can distinguish among a variety of scales ranging from the largest (the spatial volume) to the smallest (the silverware on the table).

Approaches to Scale

Resolving scale is a part of all interior projects. As we said previously, there are essentially two possible

Figure 10.14 Real environments, especially complex ones, are often comprised of many scales working together and complementing each other. A good space will normally progress harmoniously from the largeness of the overall space to the in-between scale of objects in it, and the smallness of accessories and utensils throughout, as shown in this view.

Figure 10.15 Not all objects of the same type need to maintain the same scale. In this dining table example, one of the end chairs is intentionally made larger to dominate and give a message about the hierarchy at the table.

Figure 10.16 In this dining table example by Frank Lloyd Wright, not one but all of the chairs are tall. Additionally, there are four light fixtures of similar height integrated into the corners of the table. The purpose here is to produce a sense of enclosure around the table to make it feel contained and intimate.

attitudes towards the use of scale. One consists of the straightforward goal of using normal scale appropriately to achieve harmony. The other involves what we could call manipulation for effect. The criteria for judging the success of any attempt consists of two basic questions: was the approach used appropriate? And, was its execution well done?

The first approach, the straightforward scale, is simple in intent. Its execution, of course, requires good aesthetic sense. The goal is quite simple: to size everything in the space to look in scale. With this approach, all layers of space and objects are treated in a complementary fashion and the approach kept consistent throughout.

The second approach has many possible applications, as we have hinted at with our examples above. It can be harder to produce successfully. However, scale manipulations are an important device at the designer's disposal and it is important that you learn how to perform them. In general, you manipulate scale to create a focus, establish dominance, define space, or produce tension. You establish a focus by making the size of the desired element different (usually larger) so it stands out by contrast, like the chair at the far end of the table in Figure 10.15. Similarly, you can increase the size of any one type of item, be it the furniture or the artwork, in order to establish dominance or help define space. Figure 10.16 shows a design by Frank Lloyd Wright for a dining table setup. He often used to increase the height of the chairs surrounding the table to contain the area and make it more intimate. In this case he also used four special light fixtures at the corners to help establish the area

further. Other effects can be accomplished by the manipulation of scale such as the creation of tension by the intentional and balanced juxtaposition of elements and objects of various sizes. This is hard to achieve and carries a great risk of looking wrong. Nevertheless, a skilled designer can accomplish it without adverse effect.

Proportion

Proportion is also concerned with the size of elements, as well as with the size of the leftover spaces between them. With proportion we look at elements in relation to the composition of which they are a part. Pertinent issues are whether the dimensions of the individual

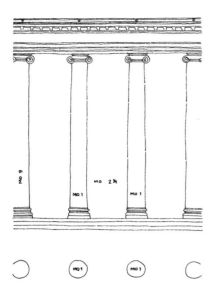

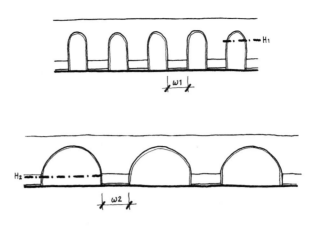

Figure 10.17 During the Renaissance, architects such as Palladio developed rules of correct proportioning for the different classical orders. Palladio's proportioning for Ionic colonnades is shown here. The basic dimension used was the diameter of the column. All other dimensions were developed using this basic dimension as a reference.

Figure 10.18 The concern for proportion is closely related to scale. Each type of scale has its own set of agreeable proportions. In the two arcades shown, the types of arches used establish very distinct scales. In each case, the height of the arches and the amount of solid wall above them are similar. They seem to work well in both cases. In order for them to work, though, notice how both the cutting point of the arch on the sides and the width of the solid portion of the wall between the arches are different in each.

Figure 10.19 Any two-dimensional surface with multiple features in it needs to be studied proportionally. This example shows three proportional studies for openings on a wall. The size of the openings, the space between them, and the remaining space above and below are all considered. In these examples, the openings in (a) have too much space between them and the ones in (b) seem a bit oversized. The openings in (c), as well as their placement and spacing, are the most successful of the three.

the spaces between them for the composition of an Ionic colonnade. Similarly, there were prescribed optimal proportions for the other orders of columns, as well as for room proportions.

A more pertinent example to interior work today, and also related to the interplay of solids and voids, are the proportions of openings on a solid wall. Figure 10.18 shows two arcades, one with many smaller arches and the other with fewer, larger ones. As you can tell, the issue of scale is also involved here. Notice the proportions of the arched openings in relation to each other, the spaces in between, and the space above them.

Figure 10.19 shows a similar example. This time we have a wall with punched penetrations. Notice the progression of adjustments from the elevations shown in Figure 10.19a–c. They get progressively more refined, and the one shown in Figure 10.19c looks the most appropriate. The heights of the openings seem to work well in relation to their width and the height of the overall wall. The widths of the spaces in between also seem to have a good relation to the size of the openings.

Although proportion is associated mostly with two-dimensional compositions, it is also relevant in the third dimension. Let's look at two examples. If we look at two variations of the depth dimension of pi-

pieces, and the spaces in between, are appropriate given the dimensions of the overall composition. This was an issue of great concern during the Classical and Renaissance eras, when the size and spacing of columns were considered at length in order to produce agreeable compositions for temples, palazzos, churches, villas, and so on. Figure 10.17 shows the correct proportions, according to Palladio, of columns and

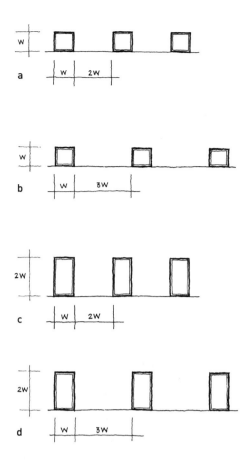

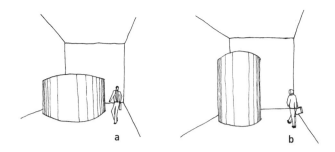

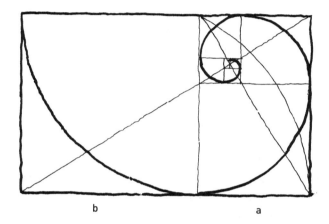

Figure 10.21 The size, shape, and placement of objects in space need to work proportionally. In this example, the proportions of the freestanding mass in (a) don't work well. It makes the passageway tight and leaves a lot of empty space above it. The tall and slender floating mass in (b) has better correspondence to the proportions of the space.

Figure 10.20 The proportions created by the depth of elements needs to be considered carefully. This example shows the relation of the spacing of pilasters to their depth dimension. The height, of course, is also critical to the study. However, for the sake of this example we exclude its consideration. In general, shallower pilasters will tolerate tighter spacings (compare (a) to (c)) and deeper ones will demand wider spacings (compare (b) to (d)).

Figure 10.22 This basic drawing shows the proportioning system prescribed by the golden mean. The proportions are such that the ratio of segment a to segment b is the same as that of segment b to the entire length of a + b.

lasters we notice that there is an important relationship between the depth of the pilasters and the widths of the in-between spaces. Depending on the width of the in-between spaces, some column depths will work better than others. See Figure 10.20.

Now, let's examine a freestanding mass in an open space. Depending on the height of the space and the amount of the space around the mass, different dimensions of the mass will look more correct than others. Figure 10.21 shows two variations of this situation. The mass in Figure 10.21a seems too wide and short, while the one in Figure 10.21b is slender and taller. It's slenderness and extra height seem more appropriate for this space given its height and tight dimensions.

What is the formula? you may ask. The truth is you don't need one. You can develop an eye for propor-

tion. However, if you must rely on formulas there are some formulas you can use. You have probably already heard about the golden mean, the Fibonacci Series, and the Modulor. These can be used to devise well-proportioned rectangles and other shapes. They have been used extensively to compose architectural plans and elevations throughout the years.

The golden mean is a mathematical system of proportion devised by the Greeks. They applied it not only to buildings but also to sculpture and the design of small objects and details. The basic ratio of the golden mean is that produced when a line is divided into two unequal segments such that the ratio of the smaller segment to the larger one is the same as the ratio of the larger one to the entire line (Figure 10.22). The proportions of the golden mean are uni-

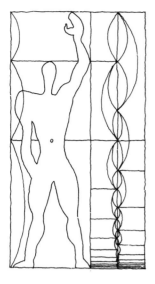

Figure 10.23 Le Corbusier's Le Modulor system was derived from the proportions of the golden mean and the proportions of the human body. It addressed all kinds of proportions, from those of small objects to those used at the town-planning scale on the other.

versal and can be found in flowers, vegetables, and other examples from nature. They have also been adopted by architects and designers, from Palladio to Le Corbusier.

The Fibonacci Series is named after a famous Italian mathematician of the thirteenth century, Leonardo Fibonacci. The proportions of the series are very similar to those of the golden mean. The series consists of the addition of consecutive whole numbers in a series such that the sum of any two sequential numbers equals the next number in the sequence. This produces a series of whole numbers as follows: 1,1,2,3,5,8,13,21,34 and so on. Similar to the golden mean, with this series, if you have a line of, say, eight units of length, and divide it into two unequal sections, of three and five units, respectively, the ratio of the short segment (three) to the long one (five) is equivalent (approximately) to the one between the long one (five) and the total length (eight).

The Modulor was a proportional system devised in the twentieth century by Le Corbusier based on the golden mean and the dimensions of the human body (Figure 10.23). It is derived from the division of an average human height into segments of ratios based on the golden mean. He found the derived proportions useful in determining heights of spaces and fixtures and other anthropomorphic relationships.

Although proportional systems such as the three just reviewed are helpful in providing some basic guidelines to go by, it is wise to avoid the obsessive use of mathematical formulas for two reasons. First, it will make your design process stiff and mechanical. Second, it will not always produce satisfactory results. Not even these three well-known proportional

systems will work satisfactorily all the time. The golden mean, despite its wisdom, was considered to produce monotony if applied strictly. For that reason, it became necessary to perform intuitive corrections in order to produce more satisfying proportional results. Similarly, some critics believe Le Corbusier's best work was produced when he relied less on mechanical means and more on artistic intuition. In matters of proportion, thus, it is helpful for you to develop a good intuitive sense through practice and criticism.

In addition to the examples presented above, issues of proportion arise in cases where you have two-dimensional patterns on surfaces. Whether the variety is achieved by different materials or different colors, the same principles apply. You stand back and look at the proposed composition and start telling yourself: the red strip needs to be wider and moved to the center; the blue squares are too small, and so on. This kind of analysis, though, gets into the issue of balance, our next topic, so we will elaborate there.

Balance

The resolution of scale and proportion in a project involves the achievement of proper balance. These three factors, scale, proportion, and balance are closely intertwined. **Balance** in design refers to the visual equilibrium of elements in a composition. It is affected by the size, shape, and placement of the parts of the composition. The goal is to produce an assembly of parts that looks right, a composition that is harmonious. The principle of balance applies to both two- and three-dimensional compositions. Two-dimensional compositions are seen as planes composed of parts such as in an elevation or patterned floor. These are called pictorial compositions because, especially when seen in elevation, they are experienced as pictures before our eyes.

Three-dimensional compositions are perceived differently. Here the element of depth comes into play, so not only do we see things to the left, center, and right, but objects and elements are also in the foreground, middle ground, or background. These form a more complex kind of composition that incorporates, among other things, the changing apparent size and location of things as one moves about the space.

A project's two- and three-dimensional compositions need to be balanced if they are to appear harmonious. In talking about balance it is customary to divide compositions into two broad categories: symmetrical compositions and asymmetrical compositions. We will use these two widely recognized distinctions to organize our discussion.

Symmetrical Compositions

Symmetrical compositions employ equivalent, usually identical, elements mirrored on either side of a central vertical axis. We are all familiar with symmetry. For many centuries, the only acceptable way to compose was using symmetry. Symmetry is pervasive in our world. Not only are humans composed symmetrically but so are many of our creations, like the cars and many of the other machines and pieces of equipment we make. There seems to be a natural tendency towards symmetry in design. Many novice designers cannot seem to get away from it. This may be

due to the fact that it is easy to use symmetry and it achieves a good level of success in relation to the effort exerted.

There is nothing wrong with using symmetry. Symmetry is a well-tested approach to composition with many successful examples from various epochs and places. It is when the designer starts to impose symmetry on every aspect of every design, whether it is called for or not, that the tendency becomes problematic. The goal of a designer is to determine when symmetry is appropriate and to learn how to execute it properly.

Symmetrical organizations carry connotations of logic, formality, and conservatism. Combined with the proper materials and details they can also express elegance and dignity. Ideal applications include formal, traditional, and dignified projects, such as government buildings, churches, courthouses, and some conservative law firms. On the other hand, symmetrical organizations are stable and static, and therefore, can be dull. The obvious way in which the elements of the built environment are presented through symmetry provides limited perceptual challenge to the observer, and therefore, has limited interest. Symmetrical compositions, however, offer an instantly perceived equilibrium, and a strong figural whole seen against the background of everything else around them. As such they are easy to read as a unit, drawing our attention, and, if framed properly, can acquire magnetic qualities that attract the eye.

There are several important considerations when composing symmetrical arrangements. Four particularly relevant ones are the location of the focus ahead, the relationship between the central axis and the ap-

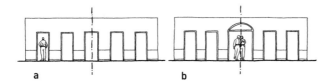

Figure 10.24 Strong symmetrical compositions rely on a strong center and two flanking sides. Of the two elevations shown, elevation (a), while symmetrical, reads more as a series than a static symmetrical composition. Elevation (b) is anchored by the emphasis of the central archway.

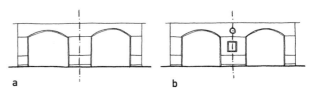

Figure 10.25 Symmetrical compositions with a featureless center are not very strong (a). Even if the flanking sides are intended to be dominant, there has to be something at the center. The small, non-dominant accent pieces shown in elevation (b) give a better sense of balance and resolution.

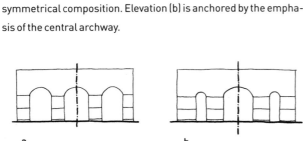

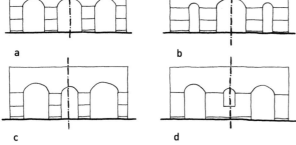

Figure 10.26 The center of symmetrical elevations tends to act like a magnet. The center of elevation in (a), despite not being emphasized by size or treatment, works here because there are only three parts to the composition. By mere placement at the center it achieves dominance. The center in elevation (b) is even more magnetic. In addition to its central position, the central archway is emphasized further through size dominance. Elevation (c) does not work. While symmetry will work adequately with an equal element at the center it will not work well with a same-type element that is weak. It looks like a mistake. Strangely enough, if the element, while maintaining its basic character, gets reduced to a detail or nonequal accent, it works fine (d).

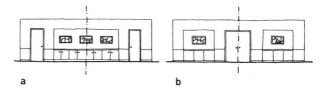

Figure 10.27 Both these possible elevations in a corporate conference room work well. Elevation (a) features a dominant central niche with local symmetry and two flanking sides with the entry doors. Elevation (b) features a pair of dominant doors at the center with two smaller niches at the sides.

proach, the level of intricacy of the composition, and the purity of the symmetry.

The focal point of symmetrical compositions is usually along the central axis. The center of a composition is normally differentiated, often emphasized (Figure 10.24). Whether a framed view to the outside, a piece of artwork, or a formal arrival space, central foci tend to make symmetrical compositions particularly powerful. They frequently give the ceremonial feeling of walking straight towards a meaningful destination. Another approach possible is the placement of two strong, symmetrical elements on either side of the center. If nothing is provided at the center, the composi-

tion may sometimes seem incomplete. Even when the center is not dominant, good symmetry relies on having something, even if only a detail, featured at the center (Figure 10.25). The composition goes from having two parts to having three (tripartite) by the addition of something in the middle. In fact, tripartite compositions are among the most used and most successful kinds of symmetrical compositions.

In scenarios where the center is equal to the sides, its power isn't as strong, because there is no clear sense of hierarchy, except for the one established by position. In cases of only three equal elements (Figure 10.26a) the composition can work. Magnetism will be strongest when there is a dominant center, as shown in Figure 10.26b. The one approach that always tends to look wrong is the placement of a weak element at the center as shown in Figure 10.26c. A smaller element at the center, however, can work if it's read as a detail, like the small central window in Figure 10.26d. Figure 10.27 shows two tripartite symmetrical elevations of a wall that might be found in a corporate conference room. The one in Figure 10.27a features two lateral entrances, while the one in Figure 10.27b has a central entrance. They both feature niches with casework and

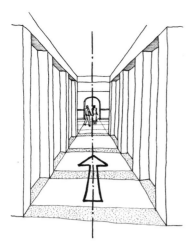

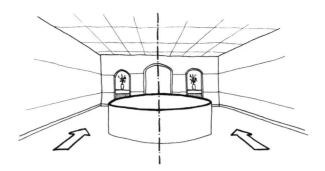

Figure 10.28 Whenever a symmetrical composition, such as a wall, is approached via a central, symmetrical path, the overall effect of the composition is strengthened. This adds formality and a literal sense of walking toward the center.

Figure 10.29 Whenever a symmetrical composition, such as the one here, is approached laterally, and not centrally, the effect is different. The composition shown, while allowing visual access from the center, forces people to approach the end wall from one of the two sides.

artwork. Notice their different effects and the local symmetries in each of their three sections.

A factor of considerable importance is the correspondence between the central axis of the composition and the approach towards, or along, it. In cases where one moves towards a symmetrical composition, the effect is heightened by having a path, symmetrical itself, centered along the central axis of the composition. This achieves a strong formal, stately, and ceremonial effect. If used in the right circumstance, it can be quite powerful (Figure 10.28). Up to the twentieth century, symmetrical compositions of walls and symmetrical approaches to them were carefully orchestrated to achieve centrality and maximize the effect of the composition as seen from a one-point perspective. A different approach would be to have symmetrically arranged paths flanking the central space of the approach, thus creating two lateral approaches towards the end wall (Figure 10.29). In this case, while the mind recognizes the arrangement as perfectly symmetrical, one is unable to experience it perfectly as one starts to move to one of the two sides around the central circle in order to approach the wall.

A whole different effect results when one does not walk towards the symmetrical composition, but rather, along it in parallel fashion. In this case the view of the composition is oblique and one only experiences the full effect if one happens to stop when reaching the center and turns 90 degrees to face it. Where there is not enough distance to stand back and perceive the symmetrical composition, the compositional effort is wasted, as it will not be seen as intended. Sym-

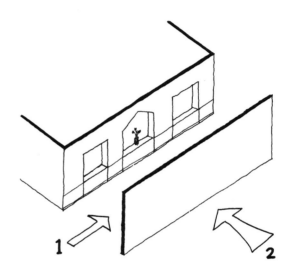

Figure 10.30 Symmetrical compositions are meant to be seen straight on. Using a symmetrical composition for a wall along a narrow corridor as shown here would be counterproductive since the symmetry would never be well-perceived. In a case like this, a composition that addresses sequence and progression would be more appropriate.

metry is meant to be seen from the front. In cases where spaces are narrow, as in corridors, it is best to rely on other compositional techniques dealing with sequence, such as the use of rhythm, instead of symmetry (Figure 10.30).

While simple symmetrical compositions may lack interest, complex ones can be quite engaging. Complex symmetrical compositions that have secondary symmetries and different lateral and vertical relationships provide richness and variety and can be quite stimulating despite their static nature. The elevation

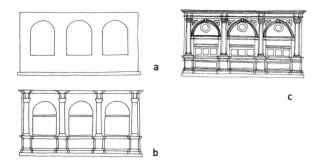

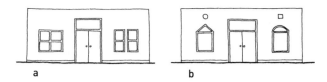

Figure 10.31 Symmetrical compositions can be dull and static. Although they are never dynamic due to their careful equilibrium, they can certainly be stimulating. This example shows the transformation of a simple symmetrical composition into a highly articulated creation. The simple idea of the arched openings in (a) is enriched by the modulation of the arches, and the addition of columns with capitals and pedestals between them (b). The composition is elaborated further in (c) where more detail is added and surfaces are enriched by the addition of relief.

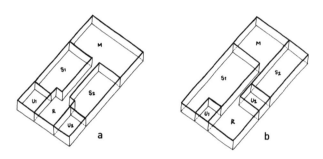

Figure 10.33 Similar to the composition of elevations and other two-dimensional planes, the overall layout of spaces can also follow symmetrical or asymmetrical approaches. These two space layouts show a symmetrical (a) and an asymmetrical (b) composition in a suite consisting of a reception area, two small utility rooms, two main general spaces, and one meeting room. Note the different effects produced by the two approaches.

Figure 10.32 Symmetry does not always have to be perfect. These two elevations show symmetrical compositions that, despite their apparent symmetry, are not quite the same from side to side. In elevation (a), the side window is broken into two units on the right side even though it still looks close enough to its counterpart on the other side. In elevation (b), the pediments over the two side windows, and the ornamental motifs over these, are shaped differently.

Asymmetrical Compositions

The use of asymmetrical compositions is a product of the twentieth century. Its beginnings coincided with the advent of modern architecture and the free-flowing plans introduced by the likes of Frank Lloyd Wright and Mies van der Rohe. Wright rejected the formality and rigidity of classical architecture and favored more natural and organic approaches to planning. He described the emerging composition attitude as follows:

> Modern architecture rejects the major axis and the minor axis of classical architecture. It rejects all grandomania, every building that would stand in military fashion heels together, eyes front, something on the right hand, and something on the left hand. Architecture already favors the reflex, the natural easy attitude, the occult symmetry of grace and rhythm affirming the ease, grace, and naturalness of natural life.[7]

Asymmetry, like symmetry, applies to both spatial organizations and pictorial compositions. Figure 10.33 shows two equivalent spatial compositions, one symmetrical and the other asymmetrical. They both feature one reception area, two small utility rooms, two main spaces, and one meeting room in the back. Notice the difference between the two approaches, the symmetrical one being rigid, formal, and ceremonial, and the asymmetrical one being freer and more dynamic.

Asymmetrical compositions achieve balance through the careful placement of different elements of

composition shown in Figure 10.31 progresses from a simple idea to an elaborate composition. The addition of layers of articulation shown in Figures 10.31b and c make the elevation come to life, endowing it with sufficient intricacy to attract, engage, and delight the eye.

Symmetry does not always have to be perfect. While most symmetrical compositions tend to be pure, with both sides mirroring each other identically, it is possible to have imperfect symmetry by having inequalities between the sides in such a way that symmetry is apparent, but, upon further scrutiny, what is on the right is not exactly what is on the left. See Figure 10.32.

Figure 10.34 Today's design is full of examples of asymmetrical compositions. Two office reception areas are shown here. They are both well balanced. The horizontality of the sofa on one side and the verticality of the display on the other balance each other out in (a). The central chair in the foreground and the flower arrangement in the background serve to produce some secondary interest and act as a pivot point. In (b), the reception desk on one side is balanced against the prominent painting on the other. The sharp vertical line just to the right of the center of the composition serves as a visual break point on this composition. The flowers, once again, serve as a secondary point of interest.

varying sizes and proportional weights. They avoid the kind of side-to-side repetition employed in symmetrical planning. For instance, a mass on one side may be balanced by a group of carefully placed elements of a different size and shape on the other side. Asymmetrical balance relies more on a painterly eye than on specific rules. It requires greater skill and control by the designer but can produce very satisfying results. Figure 10.34 shows two successful office reception area scenes composed asymmetrically.

One of the characteristic effects of asymmetrical compositions is their tendency to be more casual and informal than symmetrical ones. They work best in compositions having no symmetrical components. Figure 10.35 illustrates the difficulty of imposing asymmetry on elevations with strong symmetrical components. The doors in Figures 10.35a and b establish fairly strong symmetrical traits that are hard to counteract without moving them. The results are ambiguous compositions with a mix of symmetry and asymmetry.

Asymmetrical compositions work best when there is nothing located at the center or equally spaced on either side. They tend to also be more dynamic and engaging if executed properly. Figure 10.36 shows two

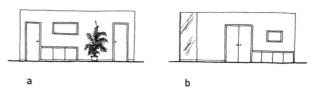

Figure 10.35 It is difficult to impose asymmetry on arrangements containing strong symmetrical properties. Of the two examples shown with given locations for the doors, elevation (a) is particularly difficult to resolve due to the powerful symmetry imposed by the two lateral doors. The resulting elevation is ambiguous and weak. In elevation (b), despite the power of the centrally located pair of doors, the fact that it is just one element makes it easier to incorporate into the asymmetrical composition. Even so, there is something strange about an asymmetrical composition with a principal component perfectly centered.

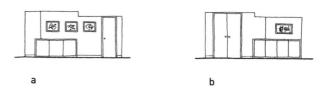

Figure 10.36 Asymmetrical compositions work best with nothing centered. These two elevations are equivalent to the two shown in Figure 10.27, except they are not symmetrical. Compare the two approaches and notice the different effects produced.

elevations equivalent to the two symmetrical ones shown in Figure 10.27. Notice how different these are, much less formal and static. Asymmetrical compositions can also have some level of formality as shown in Figure 10.37. While the path shown has a formal side of uniformly placed rhythmic elements, the opposite side supplies contrast with its planar, nonrhythmic treatment. There is a level of formality produced by the composition of the left side, while the contrasting right side counterbalances and softens, the rigidity of the overall effect.

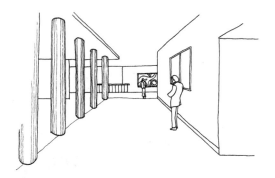

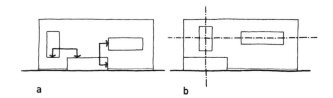

Figure 10.37 Despite their relative informality, asymmetrical compositions can still be arranged in ways that elicit formality. The asymmetrical path shown here has unequal elements on either side. The presence of a regular colonnade on the left side gives it a sense of decorum and formality, even if a casual one.

Figure 10.38 Components of asymmetrical compositions can have strong geometrical relationships among them. This can be achieved by the use of alignments. These can be edge alignments, as shown in elevation (a), or centerline alignments, as shown in (b). These alignments add regularity to the composition.

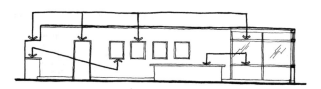

Figure 10.39 A strategy often used to create strong relationships in compositions, either symmetrical or asymmetrical, is the alignment of regulating horizontal lines. These are often derived from existent components in the shell space. In this example, horizontal lines established by an existing window wall are used to establish the heights of the door, the bench, and the artwork. Additionally, the heights of the cabinetry and the underside of the artwork are also coordinated. These relationships help create a consistent unified overall effect.

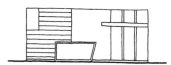

Figure 10.40 Free asymmetrical compositions can work without repeated elements or alignments of any kind, as shown here. They rely on a painterly eye and, if done properly, can have very satisfying results.

Another way of having some degree of formality in an asymmetrical composition is by the alignment of regulating lines (Figure 10.38). While there is no identical repetition from side to side, the regularity produced by the alignments helps to give a somewhat formal sense of order. Alignments can be at the edges of elements (Figure 10.38a) or through their center lines

(Figure 10.38b). Height alignments are particularly useful devices to achieve balanced compositions. The regularity produced in Figure 10.39 by the consistent alignment of elements in relation to the window wall's horizontal lines gives this elevation a sense of resolved equilibrium.

In contrast to orderly asymmetry are totally free compositions having no repeated parts and no alignments of any kind. The result of such an approach is increased informality and dynamism. Needless to say, this approach requires a very refined eye and some patience to achieve an appropriate level of balance. The elevation shown in Figure 10.40 uses this approach and still achieves a sense of equilibrium and harmony.

Resolved scale, proportion, and balance are essential ingredients of a well-executed project. Providing them is one of the taken-for-granted responsibilities that come with the profession of design. While simplistic approaches will make the task easier, they will not likely produce the desired degree of richness and expressiveness. It is therefore necessary to know how to produce well-balanced and harmonious complex arrangements. You should keep in mind that these principles also apply to the balance of colors, patterns, furnishings, and any other element that forms a composition in the project.

Unifying the Whole

An architecture of complexity and accommodation does not forsake the whole. In fact, I have referred to a special obligation toward the whole because the whole is difficult to achieve. And I have empha-sized the goal of unity rather than of simplification in an art "whose ... truth [is] in its totality. It is the difficult unity through inclusion rather than the easy unity of exclusion.[8]

Unity

The word "unity" means oneness. Of course, no actual oneness exists, unless you get down to the single cell organism or the atom. . . . When we speak of unity we do not mean this kind of oneness. We are referring to the putting-together of things, the composing of things, the combining of things into a group to which we can then attribute the quality of oneness.[9]

As the quote above suggests, **unity** in design is ac-complished by composing elements in such a way that they appear to be one entity. In order to achieve unity all the components of the interior must relate to each other and the overall approach of the project. The re-sult of a unified project is a sense of connectedness, re-latedness, and coherence. With unity the project be-comes one and reads as a whole.

Unity occurs at different levels. Within a project, unity needs to be addressed at the level of individual scenes, such as rooms, and at the level of the entire project. Any given part of a project, when seen indi-vidually, should look visually unified in itself. It does-n't necessarily need to be complete within its bound-aries, yet frequently it will be. We will explain the distinction later in the section on how to produce unity and wholeness. Beyond the individual scene or room, the project as a whole needs to achieve a quality of oneness. As one moves from space to space, one should get the feeling that all the spaces and parts are components of the same entity.

How the project relates to the building in which it is housed is often an important consideration. Many times there is no relationship and as soon as one enters a space from the building's public corridor, it appears as though one has entered a totally different world. Such is the nature of a great number of interior projects.

There are times, however, when because of the nature of the building or the project, the designer tries to pro-duce some unity between the qualities of the building and those of the project. The attempts can be subtle, as when using regulating height lines originating in the building spaces outside the project or when repeating motifs of the building within the project. The unification can sometimes be stronger, such as a project that adopts the general feel and detailing of the building, as in some historical buildings, or in cases where the building and the interiors are designed concurrently by the same de-signer.

There are specific strategies used to achieve unity. The two key aims are similarity and continuity. Any composition, whether contained and static or free and sequential, needs both these qualities to achieve unity. We will first discuss unity in single spaces and later talk about achieving unity from one space to the next so as to unify the entire project. For the study of unity within a single scene, we rely here on some use-ful concepts articulated previously by Pierre von Meiss.

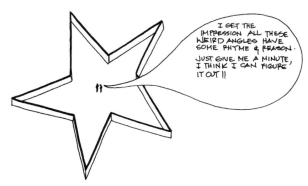

Figure 10.41 The unity of an overall project begins with a cohesive scheme. This oversimplified example illustrates how, if there is some underlying structure, even one not readily apparent initially, it will contribute to a sense of overall unity that sooner or later will be understood.

Unity within a single scene relies on similarity, proximity, common enclosure, consistency of approach, or complementary composition. **Similarity** can be due to the repeated use of elements sharing similar characteristics such as form, size, material, color, and detailing. **Proximity** fosters unity by clustering elements close enough to produce distinct groups that read as unified clusters. **Common enclosure,** whether by surrounding walls, overhead planes, floor platforms, or background datum walls, also serves to unify a scene. **Consistency of approach** is also paramount. Whatever the approach taken, it has to be consistent throughout to make it clear that the scene was created by the same hand. If it's a scheme relying on high contrasts, then look for the use of high contrast throughout; if it's a scheme emphasizing horizontality, then look for the consistent use of horizontal elements.

Unity within a space can also be achieved through good **complementary composition.** By this we mean the skillful integration of complementary, not similar, elements to form a unified whole. This approach can be harder to achieve as it requires a painterly eye and good aesthetic sense. With this approach it's the complementary nature of the components that gives it unity. There is no repetition. Colors can be combined with their complementary opposites, horizontals can mix with verticals, rough can mix with smooth, and light can mix with dark.

When it comes to the unity of the project as a whole, the task takes on new challenges. Now the task becomes to achieve unity from one space to the next, and the next, and so on. The ultimate goal is for the entire project to read as one. For this to happen there has to

be, first and foremost, clarity of concept. Eugene Raskin has stated it very clearly: "clarity of concept is the inescapable basis of unity."[11] At this point we refer you back to Chapter 6 where we discussed concepts. You may recall our distinction between organizational concepts and character concepts. Both of them come into play here. Organizational concepts give the project physical structure. The project becomes a cohesive system based on some logic appropriate to its needs. Although the structure is seldom apparent all at once, especially in larger projects, eventually, as one navigates the project and becomes acquainted with it, the structure, if well conceived, begins to make sense (Figure 10.41). This gives the project spatial and structural unity. While the organizational concept supplies structural unity, the character concept gives it visual unity. Whatever design approach is taken, stylistic and otherwise, has to be continued throughout.

Unity of the overall project is complicated by the fact that one cannot see the various spaces of projects all at once. Most projects, except the very small, are comprised of multiple spaces that one experiences as one moves through them. In some cases, especially in open, flowing plans, you can see clearly from one space to the next and see whatever continuity links the designer has provided. In other cases, where passage from one space to the next is not open, allowing for visual connection, you have to rely on memory to tie the spaces together and perceive whatever unity there is. A good example of this is the case where you are transported from one space to another space via an elevator ride. When you arrive in the second space your only

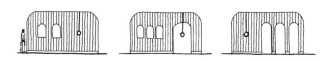

Figure 10.42 Consistency is paramount to achieve a sense of unity. In this example the consistent use of forms, wall finishes, shapes, and fixtures all contribute to unity.

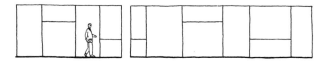

Figure 10.43 The extension of a pattern from one space to another helps to bridge spaces and contribute to a feeling of unity between spaces. There is more than consistency of approach here. The pattern is continued, by extension, from one room to the next.

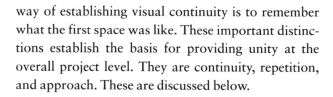

Figure 10.44 Not only can horizontal lines be used to regulate the heights of elements in a space as shown in Figure 10.39, they can also be expressed literally, either through the use of reveals, moldings, or surface relief. When used, they become an element that can be extended from space to space to help foster a sense of unity.

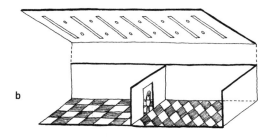

Figure 10.45 The ceiling and floor planes can contribute much to unity between adjacent spaces. This applies to adjacent spaces seen simultaneously. Example (a) shows a consistent, extended floor pattern unifying two contiguous spaces that are broken up by a change of ceiling height. In this case the floor is the unifying element. Example (b) shows the opposite. Here, the ceiling is the unifying element, while there is a break of continuity between the two spaces defined by a dividing wall and a change of floor pattern.

way of establishing visual continuity is to remember what the first space was like. These important distinctions establish the basis for providing unity at the overall project level. They are continuity, repetition, and approach. These are discussed below.

Continuity.

Continuity in a project means that there is a continuation of treatments from one space to another, thus linking different parts of the project visually. This can be accomplished through consistency or extension. **Consistency** simply requires treating elements, approaches, and finishes consistently from space to space. An example is the consistent use of forms and wall finishes from one space to the next (Figure 10.42). Another example is the consistent employment of a thematic idea throughout the project. Themes can create strong links between spaces by acting as a thread that weaves through the entire project, thus holding it together. Themes can be abstract constructs, held together by consistency of meaning, such as an ethnic restaurant utilizing symbols of the appropriate culture, or more direct architectural themes relying on consistent form or approach.

Extension refers to the practice of extending elements from one space to another. Examples include the continuation of a pattern from one room to the next (Figure 10.43) and the extension of horizontal lines from space to space providing a common thread throughout the project (Figure 10.44). Another example of extension, this one using spatial features, would be extending either the floor or the ceiling plane to serve as the unifying element between two adjacent spaces, while the other plane (either ceiling or floor, whichever is not the unifying element) varies from space to space (Figure 10.45).

There is a distinction to be made between consistency and extension. Consistency means the repeated and sustained application of an overall treatment (often

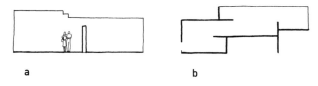

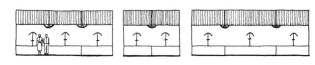

a   b

Figure 10.46 Another approach to unity is to link spaces by the use of overlapping elements. Example (a) shows an overlap at the ceiling plane. Notice that it is not continuous like the one shown in Figure 10.45(b), but partial. Example (b) shows the use of overlapping walls extending from one space to the next, producing a similar bridging effect between spaces.

Figure 10.47 Repetition is a powerful unifying strategy. This example shows the repeated use of intermittent decorative wall motifs and suspended lighting fixtures to produce a consistent look among the three spaces shown.

materials and finishes) with or without interruptions. The key factor is that the treatment is consistent and sustained throughout. Extension means the continuation of certain elements from one space to another, even if the approach is not sustained throughout the project. A variation of extension is **overlapping**, where a certain element (wall, floor, or ceiling) is extended from the space in which it originates to overlap with the adjacent space, thus creating a strong link. In this case, two spaces share a common area defined by the extended, overlapping element. However, it is a limited extension. It does not continue but achieves enough overlap to tie the two spaces together. Figure 10.46 shows examples of overlaps produced by ceiling extensions (Figure 10.46a) and wall extensions (Figure 10.46b).

Most projects rely on consistent treatments among their spaces for unity. Other than using the same finishes throughout the project, possibilities include consistent shapes, colors, details, scales, patterns, and textures. Consistency does not require identical treatments from space to space, just consistency of approach. If, for example, color is being used to unify various spaces, the actual shade of the color may vary from space to space as long as there is some consistency of the hue. Or, if there is a mix of colors in some geometric pattern on the wall, the next space can have a different mix of the same colors and a slightly different geometrical pattern as long as the basic characteristics are retained.

Repetition.

Repetition is different from consistency and extension. It happens when some element occurs over and over again. The recurrence may or may not be consistent throughout. In some cases it may occur throughout, although in others it will occur only selectively. In instances of selective recurrence it is important that it recurs often enough to be recognized as a pattern. Repetition is different from extension because extension implies uninterrupted continuity. With repetition the repeated element appears and reappears from place to place, more like a stamp that gets stamped in one room and then another, than a line that extends between spaces. Figure 10.47 shows three rooms unified by the repetition of the anchorlike wall details and the suspended light fixtures. The repeated element may be identical from one place to the next or just similar, as long as the similarity is recognizable. It may also be either literal or thematic. In the case of a thematic repetition, the one element only needs to tie in with the rest through its theme, not its visual appearance. Thus, in a seafood restaurant, an anchor in one room, a hanging marlin in another room, and a sail in a third room would provide thematic repetition without being visually similar.

Repeated elements can be details, accessories, motifs, plants, artwork, furnishings, and so on. Repetition can be especially effective in instances where there is not much visual connection between the spaces of a project. In these cases, as we have said, the observer relies on recall to make linkages between spaces. The repeated appearance and reappearance of similar elements stimulates recall in the perceiver's mind and serves to increase the sense of unity among the spaces.

Special approaches to the use of repetition include

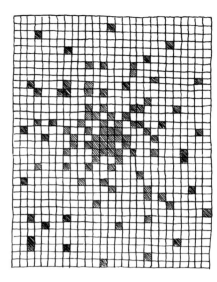

Figure 10.48 The floor pattern shown illustrates the use of dispersion. The pattern is more concentrated at its center. From there it moves outward in random fashion and becomes less dense to the point where it becomes faint, eventually disappearing.

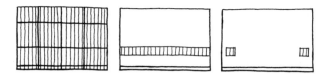

Figure 10.49 This longitudinal section through a space shows the strategy of dispersion used with wall applications, in this case wood. The first space is the most prominent and features wood paneling throughout. As you move into the space the paneling is reduced to a wood band. As you move even further into the space, the wood band becomes a wood medallion that occurs selectively from that point on. The presence of wood, though reduced, never disappears, thus contributing to the sense of unity of the project.

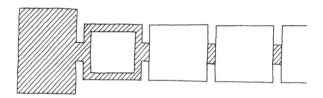

Figure 10.50 In this example the strategy of dispersion is applied to a floor. Like in the wood paneling example before, the first room is a prominent space and features a marble floor throughout. The marble floor gets reduced to marble borders in the next room. Eventually it is used only at the thresholds between major spaces. Here again, even though the amount of the high-end finish is reduced as one moves further into the space, it never goes away, thus contributing to the unity of the project.

gradation and dispersion. With these approaches equal elements are not repeated over and over but are transformed as they move from one space to another. **Gradation** involves the gradual transformation of an element or characteristic. To apply gradation to color, for instance, its hue, value, or chroma would gradually be changed as the color progresses through the space, becoming more or less pure, light, or saturated. An application of gradation involving rhythm would be the gradual increase or decrease of the spacing between elements such as columns. Other examples include the gradual modifications of lighting level and spatial or furniture density. Key to the application of these techniques is the use of a consistent stylistic approach to anchor the variety produced by the gradation. This plus the recognition of a pattern that continues from one space to the next generally provides the necessary level of consistency to achieve unity between the different areas involved.

Dispersion is a special application of gradation where the transformation of an element is less regular. It involves the increase or decrease of density in a planned but somewhat random fashion. It can be especially effective when applied to floor patterns or as a technique of repetition with motifs or materials. To understand the principle of dispersion we are talking about, try to visualize what would happen if you dropped a large container of pebbles on a hard floor.

They would bounce around and be dispersed throughout the floor. After the bouncing ceases you would find that a large number of pebbles end up concentrated close to the point of origin, a moderate number end up some distance away, and a few take such bounces that they actually end up quite far from the point of origin. Although the general pattern of this result is predictable, the exact way the pebbles choose to go is not. You can repeat the procedure several times and the result is always different.

You can use this technique to design patterns that vary in regularity and density, creating areas of high concentration of a pattern, followed by areas where the pattern is dispersed, becoming quite faint and infrequent in some places. Although the presence of the pattern is reduced as you move away from the area of high concentration, it never disappears, thus serving as a unifying motif (Figure 10.48). Similarly, you can use this technique to maintain some continuity of special finishes in a project. You could, for instance, have one or two areas with a high concentration of upgraded finishes and fixtures followed by areas of less concentration of the same finishes. Instead of completely eliminating the use of the special treatments, they are just reduced. Thus, the wood paneling becomes a wood band and, later, a recurring small wood motif (Figure 10.49). Similarly, the marble floor becomes marble borders, and, later, marble thresholds at key junctures (Figure 10.50).

Avoiding Dullness

Unity, similar to order as discussed in Chapter 7, relies on regularity and repetition. A similar concern to the one brought up related to order emerges. It is the danger that too much uniformity will produce dullness and monotony. The same is true of too much balance. It appears that none of these desirable qualities can be taken to the extreme without having undesirable consequences. True, it can be argued that monotony is better than lack of unity, or order, or balance. However, if you want to become a strong designer you must strive to address both of these dualities and seek both unity and interest, order and stimulation, balance and dynamism. Amidst the consistency and regularity there has to be variety, contrast, and a sense of hierarchy. These need to be achieved while maintaining unity and order, and certainly, have to find equilibrium.

While interest is produced by incorporating elements that provide variety, contrast, and hierarchy, a warning is given here that interest doesn't justify the excesses often produced by designers in the name of enrichment. Though complexity is desirable in design, its opposite, simplicity, is also a valuable quality. True competence requires learning how to design with an economy of means so you can produce the richest expression with the fewest strokes and elements. While this may appear simple due to the reduction of the number of parts, it is not so. Remember the quote from Venturi where he refers to "the difficult unity through inclusion rather than the easy unity of exclusion." We are not advocating minimalism, just the elimination, or at least reduction, of nonessentials. Even with a simple approach you still have an obligation to engage the mind and stimulate the human spirit.

These are some of the challenges that make design difficult. They are the same ones that make it fascinating and make us appreciate true competence when we see it, or better yet, when we achieve it ourselves.

The issue of visual harmony is central to the goal of resolution. Not many people have attempted to study the issue of architectural form in depth. One of them is Ralf Weber, who, in *On the Aesthetics of Architecture*,[1] concentrates on the role of form in the experience and judgment of architecture. This valuable book offers many insights about architectural form. Here we summarize Weber's contributions to the issue of visual harmony related to, not space, but the solid elements in space. These are highly relevant to the art of composing interior environments. We separate this brief summary into the topics of centers, perceptual weight, vertical elements, hierarchy, and figure/ground articulation.

Centers

The perception of order depends, among other things, on the impact of the various perceptual centers in a composition. These can be dominant or subordinate. In all cases, they act as some kind of visual focus. The dominant visual area of any display is the visual center of gravity, which is determined by the distribution of the principal centers and their perceptual masses. Additionally, areas of high contrast, areas along symmetry axes, areas along the vertical axes of shapes and larger composite patterns, patterns with strong figural characters, concave and enclosed shapes, heterogeneous elements within homogeneous arrangements, and areas of high contrast attract the eye and establish perceptual centers exerting more or less influence.

Centers are also induced by the contours of a configuration and it is possible to make some generalizations about the location of fulcrums in simple shapes. The single perceptual center of a square or a circle, for instance, is at the geometric center. Vertically elongated shapes pull the perceptual center upward. Not all shapes, however, enjoy a strong perceptual center. It is hard, for instance, to establish a precise perceptual center in elongated shapes, whether vertical or horizontal, exceeding a ratio of 1:2.

Consciously planning the centers of a composition is important. Their location and interaction play a crucial role in establishing order and determining its dynamic character.

Perceptual Weight

The dynamic character of a pattern is also affected by the perceived heaviness of the various parts of the configuration. Perceptual weight is affected by size, tone, levels of articulation and regularity, location, and direction. Larger, darker, articulated, or regular shapes generally carry more perceptual weight than their opposites. Likewise, shapes that are isolated, placed somewhere in the periphery (instead of in the center or along a major axis), or vertically oriented assume greater visual weight.

Vertical Elements

To perceive space, the body favors orthogonal localization. The horizontal and the vertical, thus, provide the framework for stability as well as for the apparent dynamic properties of a composition. The vertical dimension, however, is more significant for figural segregation than the horizontal. Particularly important is the role of the vertical axis of symmetry in the perceived stability of a figure. The highest degree of perceived stability is attained when figures are symmetrical, both horizontally and vertically, and the main direction extends horizontally. The perceptual stability can be increased further by interlocking such a configuration with vertical shapes placed at the axis of vertical symmetry. Configurations, where the orientation of the shape's main dimension and its axis of symmetry coincide, are perceived as dynamic, such as in the case of a vertically symmetrical, tall and slender building, which appears to move upward. This is further reinforced by the natural tendency of the eyes to move upwards faster than they move downwards.

Perceptual dynamics in a composition are produced by the interplay between vertical and horizontal elements. Elevations with main centers aligned horizontally appear static. Perceptual stability will increase when the main perceptual center is located above the actual center of balance. Vertical elements stop horizontal visual scanning and help to anchor vision. Horizontal arrangements can be enhanced, for example, by a strong vertical accent at the position of the main focus. It is also useful to utilize vertical elements to demarcate the axes along which the individual centers of a pattern are aligned.

Hierarchy

Hierarchical arrangements that create subordinate groups and subgroups allow sustained perceptual arousal without overtaxing perceptual capacity. They permit a high absolute complexity while maintaining a moderate level of perceptual complexity. The hierarchical arrangement of perceptual centers in a composition is, thus, generally desirable. Weber points out two crucial factors: the first one is the need for both a distinct overall fulcrum and distinct centers for each of the subordinate component groups. The second one is the need for an organization of a subordinate type at the highest levels where small parts form larger patterns, which in turn are grouped to form a larger group and so on.

Perceptual hierarchy demands that each of the groups and subgroups of shapes of a composition should be identifiable as discrete perceptual wholes. A clear compositional center in each group helps in this regard. Ideally, the point of the shape's equilibrium coincides with the perceptual focus (visually strongest) of the configuration. Distinct foci can be created by the use of heterogeneous shapes, contrasting sizes, rhythms or symmetries, and contrasting tones, colors, or textures, among other devices.

When a composition, say, an elevation, is subdivided, nonhierarchically, into equal parts and these exceed the maximum number of elements that can be perceived at once (between five and seven) the result is monotonous. This condition can be improved by using a rhythmic alternation of different elements and by the incorporation of foci, such as an overall central vertical symmetrical axis. In a composition of similar elements, a strong focus can also be produced by articulating one of the shapes using tone, texture, or color. Yet, the simplest way of creating a strong overall focus is by using a shape that is either different or scaled differently. The effect of a single heterogeneous element is normally so strong that it can easily center an otherwise homogeneous arrangement, catalyzing an otherwise monotonous appearance.

There are several advantages to organizing the various centers of attraction in a composition hierarchically:

- A subordinate arrangement of parts allows the visual segregation of a distinct fulcrum, whereas a coordinate (nonhierarchical) arrangement results in similar and competing perceptual dominance.

- Hierarchical arrangements permit greater absolute complexity without leading to an equally high degree of perceptual complexity. The organization of parts into groups complies more readily with the demands of wholeness in a complex configuration, thus allowing a more complicated arrangement of shapes to emerge.

- In a hierarchical organization, there is a clear difference between various levels of scale, that is, between the sizes of the individual entities in relation to the whole. Consequently, there can be a greater number of levels without resulting in visual chaos.

- Hierarchical organization allows similar elements to be grouped into larger shapes instead of simply fusing with the overall pattern.

- Hierarchical organizations make it easier to achieve equilibrium of areas of interest when exploring perceptual centers.

- Hierarchical organizations allow a gradual decrease of scales in a composition, thus avoiding abrupt jumps from large scales to minute ones, which often result in low levels of stimulation.

- Compositions that are hierarchical but lack detail and articulation at the smaller subordinate levels also can result in low stimulus. The lack of microstructure leads to poverty of information.

Figure/Ground Articulation

An important factor in the analysis of the perceptual impact of corporeal form is the internal articulation of the spatial boundaries. Two of the most predominant properties of a composition's articulation are its textural appearance and the organization of component elements into figures and ground. The completeness of figure-ground organization largely determines the perceived orderliness of the composition. The distribution of contrast endows the shape with heterogeneous structure.

The parts of an elevation possess different visual dominance, and thus appear to advance or recede, resulting in multiple levels of perceived depth. The effect is due to the perceptual organization of stimulus patterns into figure and ground. Depending on the arrangement, some features will attain perceptual dominance or subordinance. The process of perception involves selecting stimuli and unifying them into perceptual figures that segregate themselves from a surrounding ground. Important to the formation of perceptual units is the function of the contour. Contours function as a boundary for enclosed areas, thus defining figures. The ground appears to continue behind the figure.

Other things being equal, Weber gives the following laws as determinants of figure-ground segregation.

- Orientation: Shapes whose orientation follow the cardinal axes form figures more easily.
- Proximity: Small areas dominate. Larger areas tend to become grounds.
- Closure: Fully closed shapes segregate more easily.
- Articulation: Areas with greater internal articulation will form figures more easily.
- Concavity: The concave side of a boundary will induce shapes more easily than the convex side.
- Brightness and Color: Brighter tones and hard colors segregate into figures more easily.
- Symmetry: The more symmetrical shapes will tend to form figures.

Figure-ground organizations vary. The possibilities can be summarized into five basic categories.

1. Unified ground—intervening spaces do not form figures: The negative spaces between or surrounding the primary shapes possess no, or only a weak, figural character of their own.
2. Unified ground—intervening spaces form figures: The negative spaces between the principal shapes assume their own figural character.

3. Nonunified ground—duo-formation of shapes: As in a façade of a curtain-walled building subdivided into endless squares, distinction between figure and ground is impossible, and all shapes assume equal dominance.
4. Nonunified ground—intervening spaces form figures: Negative spaces form figures in their own right but do not result in duo-formations. The figural character of the negative spaces is weaker than that of the main components.
5. Nonunified ground—intervening spaces do not form figures: Intervening spaces do not assume a figural character. The negative spaces cannot group themselves, and the overall pattern appears unstable.

Although it is easy to relegate negative spaces to unimportant subordinate status it is obvious that they impact the overall composition significantly and therefore deserve attention. When there is no clear distinction between figure and ground, or when the permeating order of the organization is locally violated, the result is perceptual ambiguity.

It is possible for both positive and negative spaces to assume a figural character. Grounds can take on a figural character by reducing it to narrow, regular shapes as when a group of windows is spaced tightly producing a pattern of strips between them that takes on the role of figure, thus creating a reversal effect between figure and ground.

---

[1] Weber, Ralf. *On the Aesthetics of Architecture*, (Avebury: Aldershot, England, 1995).

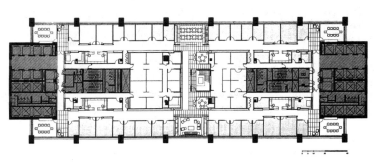

Figure CS10.1 The central interconnecting stairway and surrounding area is one of the principal nodes of the entire project.

Figure CS10.2 This unusual floor plan has the service cores at the two ends. The meeting rooms are at the four corners and the principal aperture is at the center.

Figure CS10.3 Offsets, visual anchors, and material variations break up the long corridors perceptually.

Figure CS10.4 Much consideration was given to the effects of lighting. The use of uplighting and vertical offsets with incorporated lighting behind translucent screens create dramatic effects and leave the ceiling plane uncluttered.

CASE STUDY
Enriching a Project with a Straightforward Floor Plan: A Professional Services Firm
Design Firm: Gary Lee Partners

This design for the offices of a professional services firm is a good example of how a project does not need to have an elaborate floor plan to be stimulating and provide an enriching experience. The client occupies six and a half floors in downtown Chicago. The office personnel consist predominantly of highly educated business consultants and the nature of their work requires that they have private enclosed offices. As a result, private executive offices along the perimeter characterize the typical layout. The floor plate of the building is somewhat unique in that the major core el-

ements are located at the two extremes, thus freeing up the center of the long rectangular floors.

The basic layout of the typical floor is efficient, orderly, and straightforward. Important strategic planning decisions include the location of team rooms at the four corners of the floor and the creation of a dominant communal zone at the center. This central zone features major break areas, conference rooms, informal meeting areas, and the internal stairs that connect all the floors (Figure CS10.1). The result is a floor plate with three magnet areas, a main one in the center and one at each end (Figure CS10.2). An inexperienced designer may look at the floor plan and consider it static and old-fashioned. However, when one understands the three dimensional realities of the project its richness is revealed.

The surface articulation, thoughtful detailing, and carefully selected and placed artwork give this project

Figure CS10.5 Artwork placement was carefully planned at all levels of hierarchy, from commanding pieces at the ends of long vistas (a), to smaller pieces in series (b).

Figure CS10.6 One is frequently pleasantly surprised by framed vistas anchored by impressive artwork (a). Additionally, areas rich in comfort, such as the "club" shown in figure (b), provide employees with welcoming common areas away from their desks.

abundant richness within its clean and crisp modernistic design vocabulary. Being a project of mostly enclosed spaces, it is experienced mainly through its corridors and individual rooms. The use of offsets, strong visual anchors at the ends via artwork, and a major break in the middle give the long east-west corridors plenty of variety and interest (Figure CS10.3). Variety in the type and level of lighting also help to articulate and differentiate the various elements and zones along these corridors (Figure CS10.4). Despite the predominance of perimeter offices, natural light and views are provided through planned apertures at the four corners, as seen in the background in Figure CS10.4, and the two ends of the central public area. The use of reflective stone flooring and translucent glass panels allow natural light to penetrate deeper into the interior space.

The materials palette is simple but rich, consisting of light-colored walls, French white ash millwork with a light natural finish, translucent glass panels, dark carpet, and black granite flooring in select areas. The dominant ends and central area are easily noticed from a distance due to the change in flooring material from carpet to polished stone. Artwork is featured as an integral part of design and plays an important role in the project, providing focal points of different sizes and intensity (Figure CS10.5).

Beyond the richly articulated corridors, the project also features exquisitely comfortable and pleasing gathering places. Figure CS10.6a shows a comfortable lounge area outside a conference room anchored by a great big painting on the wall. Figure CS10.6b shows the principal lounge space, known as "the club," whose furnishings, tactful lighting scheme, rich materials, and artwork help to make it special.

Review

Summary

Successful design requires a cyclical design process involving successive, ever more refined solutions to the design problem. The ultimate goal in the end is total resolution of the project or full synthesis.

Resolution starts with the floor plan, which must evolve from the original organizational concept to a fully functional composition. In addition to making the concept work, the floor plan needs to be refined and resolved.

Proper resolution requires the achievement of harmony. Three crucial aspects of harmony are the appropriate use of scale, the skillful use of proportion, and the achievement of balanced compositions. Scale can be considered in relation to the size and proportions of human beings, in relation to the particular design application being executed, and in relation to learned expectation of size concerning the elements in a space. Scale can also be measured in relation to the size of the entire project, in the relation of specific contents to the space in which they are housed, and in the relation of certain contents to other contents in the space.

Proportion is concerned with the relationship of elements to the composition they are a part of. Balance is the third requirement for harmony. A composition is said to be balanced if all the components are in perceptual equilibrium. Symmetrical compositions have been used since antiquity. They feature two equal sides, mirrored on either side of a central vertical axis. Asymmetrical compositions are a more recent phenomenon. They are more difficult to balance than symmetrical ones. They can rely on some repetition and alignments to give them coherence or they can be totally free of repetition and alignment.

In addition to harmony, the other essential for proper resolution is unity. Unity occurs at many levels. It is useful to distinguish between unity within a scene, and unity within an entire project. Unity within a scene relies on similarity, proximity, enclosure, consistency of approach, and complementary composition. Unity within an entire project requires a strong and cohesive organizational concept to provide a unified structure. Beyond structural unity a project needs to look consistent. This is done through the employment of continuity and repetition. Repetition strategies include consistent repetition, sporadic repetition, gradation, and dispersion.

To a great extent, harmony and unity rely on similarity and repetition. However, it is important to remember that harmonious and unified projects are not good if they are also dull and boring. It is necessary to provide enough variety to achieve a reasonable level of interest, according to the type of project being designed. This calls for a calculated departure from the easy and predictable design tendencies towards regularity.

Chapter Questions

1. Name the two basic goals that need to be considered during the process of resolving the floor plan of a project.

2. Related to design, what is the difference between the terms size and scale.

3. As a designer, you need to be able to use scale in two different ways. What are the two ways presented in this chapter?

4. Give an example of scale manipulation related to the human figure (other than the ones presented in this chapter).

5. Name an example of appropriate scale as related to design application.

6. Give an example of scale manipulation related to element type (other than the ones presented in this chapter).

7. Give one example of scale of content in relation to the space in which it is housed.

8. Name an example of scale of an element in relation to other similar elements in the space.

9. State some of the reasons presented in this chapter for the manipulation of scale.

10. Explain how proportion differs from scale.

11. Name the three well-known systems of proportion discussed in this chapter.

12. Does proper scale and balance ensure good balance? Why or why not?

13. Explain why the focus ahead is important in the composition of symmetrical two-dimensional compositions of vertical surfaces.

14. What is the ideal placement of the approach path towards symmetrically composed elevations?

15. In what ways can complexity and intricacy be added to symmetrical compositions?

16. What would be a feasible way to produce an imperfect but acceptable symmetrical elevation?

17. In what kind of instance is symmetrical composition of elevations not advisable?

18. Describe a way to produce formality in asymmetrical composition.

19. What compositional device would you use to increase regularity in an asymmetrical elevation?

20. Is achieving unity between a project and the building in which it is housed necessary?

21. What strategies can you use to achieve unity within a single scene?

22. In what ways can continuity be utilized to produce unity between different spaces of a project?

23. In what ways can repetition be used to produce unity between different spaces of a project?

24. Give some examples of how you might use the techniques of gradation and dispersion to foster unity in a project.

25. Why is excessive regularity problematic? What can you do about it?

Endnotes

1 Pelli, Cesar. *Observations for Young Architects*, (Monacelli Press: New York, 1999) p. 193.

2 Kleinssaser, William. "Synthesis 9: A Comprehensive Theory Base for Architecture," (1995) p. 255.

3 Vitruvius, *The Ten Books on Architecture*, (Dover Publications: New York, 1960) p. 13.

4 Ibid., p. 13.

5 Ibid., p. 13–14.

6 Ibid., p. 14.

7 Wright, Frank Lloyd. *In the Realm of Ideas*, (Southern Illinois University Press: Carbondale, 1988) p. 20.

8 Venturi, Robert. *Complexity and Contradiction in Architecture*, (Museum of Modern Art: New York, 1977) p. 88.

9 Raskin, Eugene. *Architecturally Speaking*, (Reinhold Publishing, 1954) p. 25.

10 Von Miess, Pierre. *Elements of Architecture: From Form to Place*, (Van Nostrand Reinhold International: London, 1990) pp. 31–54.

11 Raskin, Eugene p. 32.

12 Venturi, Robert p. 88.

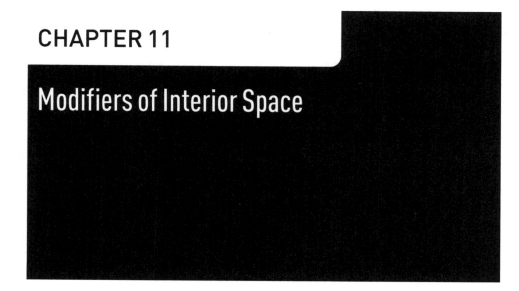

CHAPTER 11

Modifiers of Interior Space

INSTRUCTIONAL OBJECTIVES

Explain the role of lighting in creating mood.

Explain the role of lighting in enhancing three-dimensionality.

Describe ways in which lighting helps to create focal areas.

Explain how lighting can help to animate sequences.

Present how designers can respond to daylighting.

Explain how designers can manipulate acoustical properties for effect.

Suggest strategies to manipulate the thermal and olfactory environments.

Explain the important role of furniture arrangements in dictating use patterns.

Present the role of finishes in providing character and tactile experiences.

Comment on the symbolic and associative powers of color.

Explain the important role of detailing in providing specific expressions.

Explain the effects of people and goods in the interior mix.

S pace and its enclosing surfaces are incomplete without other important factors that help modify them. The task of design involves not only the creation of space but requires that space be properly revealed and enhanced through light, texture, pattern, and color. Referring to architecture in general, Simon Unwin makes a useful distinction between its **basic elements**, those that establish place, and what he calls **modifying elements**. "In their physical realization and our actual experience of them," he explains, "basic elements and the places they identify are modified: by light, by colour, by sounds, by temperature, by air movement, by smells (and even possibly by tastes), by the qualities and textures of the materials used, by use, by scale, by the effects and experience of time."[1] The focus of this chapter is on these modifying elements of space.

Light not only allows us to clearly see form and shape, but it can also be used to accentuate forms, textures, and colors. Materials are chosen not only for their durability or economy. Beyond their basic properties they also possess unique personalities and characteristics that carry strong connotations and give space unique qualities. The meaning of materials is seldom neutral. Colors have immense powers of their own and their qualities influence the totality of space. They are like a hypersensitive musical instrument whose effect is dependent on the skill of the performer. Results can be quiet and gentle or loud and aggressive, and they can also be painful.

It is not the intent of this chapter to cover any of these modifying elements in great depth. These are

Figure 11.1 This restaurant scene, while relatively dark, gives a sense of theatrical drama because of the lighting effects produced by the spotlights.

complicated subjects having their own extensive body of literature. The aim here is to review some of the contributions they make within the context of spatial design to the goals of providing order, enrichment, and expression in projects.

Ambient Elements

Ambient elements are environmental elements, such as lighting conditions, acoustics, thermal properties, and even odors, inherent in any work of architecture. Whether meticulously controlled or left to chance, they are always present and influence the way interior environments are experienced. They particularly affect the level of comfort of a space. While you may be aware of the importance of lighting in interiors, you may not have thought much about how the acoustic and thermal environments can be manipulated to enhance the experience of space users. In this section we look at lighting, acoustics, the thermal environment, and odors.

Lighting

You are surely aware of the importance of lighting in interiors and know some of the basic strategies for lighting interior space. Important considerations include having sufficient light levels for the needs of a space, avoiding glare, and selecting the correct light coloring. We will not focus on these practical matters that you already know. Instead, we would like to focus on aspects of lighting we consider important in the production of rich and expressive projects. Through thoughtful response to project needs and the

manipulation of light, it is possible to heighten sensory experience and enhance the spatial experience.

We would like you to start thinking beyond supplying adequate light levels and an agreeable pattern of fixtures on the ceiling. Lighting, if used correctly, will help you to produce spatial crispness, create evocative surfaces, make objects more expressive, and achieve engaging sequences. Lighting can also be used to create drama and particular moods.

Light, Mood, and Use

The influence of lighting on the mood of a place is well known to most of us. The lighting in a place can make its mood intimate, solemn, cheerful, or festive. One obvious variable is the brightness level of the light in a space. In general, brightly lit spaces will tend to be perceived as more cheerful and dimly lit spaces will be perceived as solemn or gloomy. However, dimly lit spaces, if accented with pools of light, can also be dramatic, despite the overall low level of illumination (Figure 11.1). Our perception of the appropriateness of a particular brightness level depends on the case. A dimly lit office space is likely to be annoying, but so is a brightly lit nightclub. The difference between light levels that promote a feeling of solemnity and one of gloom, for example, is a delicate one. Typically, if a place does not seem illuminated enough for the type of activity that occurs in it, our perception is that someone made a mistake. If, on the other hand, a dimly lit space, despite the low level of light, seems bright enough to conduct the intended activities, and if the low level of light appears to correspond to a desirable mood, the perception will be one of proper fit (Figure 11.2).

Figure 11.2 The relatively low light level in this restaurant is intentional, resulting in an intimate and relaxed ambiance.

Figure 11.3 Rooms, even if not brightly lit, will appear livelier if their enclosing surfaces are well illuminated.

In the case of the nightclub it is slightly different. There, one expects a low level of light. While lighting in, say, the dance floor can be busy and colorful with laser beams crossing in all directions, the general ambient light of the space has to be low or the application will seem wrong for the space. Interestingly, though, the same requirements would not apply to a dance hall for afternoon ballroom dancing. There, one would most likely expect a relatively high level of illumination.

Other factors contributing to the mood created by lighting conditions include the brightness of the light at the source, the size of the source, the number of sources, and whether it appears that the lighting scheme is complete. If a restaurant dining room features candles at the tables, we automatically perceive the intent for an intimate environment. We notice that lighting has been considered and addressed at every table, and accept the low level of light. Furthermore, the bright and cheerful sparkle of the individual candles, however small, adds a certain life to the scene. By contrast, if the same restaurant featured only one large central ceiling fixture intended to light the entire room, and if the level of light produced by that fixture was low to simulate the dimness of a candlelit space, the feeling produced would likely be one of gloom and inadequate lighting. It would seem like more fixtures were necessary, or that the wattage on the one fixture was too low.

One of the main factors used to judge the success of a lighting scheme is the function of the space and the relationship between the lighting scheme and the intended use. In addition to the issue of mood, lighting levels and quality of light are also important to the performance of the activities in the space. While a painter or a jeweler may need a bright studio of diffuse, evenly distributed light, a group having dinner may prefer an overall low level of light, with perhaps, a dedicated, narrow beam accent light over the table (for function and intimacy) and another accent light illuminating a piece of art on an adjacent wall (for drama).

Light-Enhancing Form

It's no secret that light helps reveal form. To reveal form it is more important to light surfaces than to light the air space. A room with moderate ambient lighting and well-lit surrounding surfaces (walls and/or ceiling) will appear to be brighter and better illuminated than one with higher ambient lighting but poorly lit enclosing surfaces. The illumination of the walls in the conference room shown in Figure 11.3 helps this interior room appear well illuminated despite the generally low level of light over the table.

Beyond just revealing form, light can enhance form. When you have a mass in space, say a rectangular room, its shape is perceived mostly by the lines that outline its shape, and the different light values on the different planes. Compare Figure 11.4a and b. Even though the receding perspective lines are identical in both cases, the level of value contrast between the different planes expresses their three-dimensionality differently. The corner shown in Figure 11.4b is enhanced as a three dimensional shape, due to the sharper value contrast at the corner and the stronger shadows. This effect can even be emphasized, intentionally, by purposefully increasing the lighting level on one side to produce a greater value contrast.

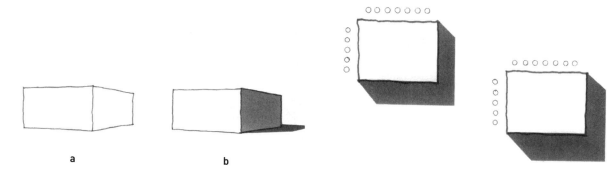

a   b

Figure 11.4 Lighting helps to enhance the three-dimensionality of objects and masses in space. The featureless room corner shown in (a) comes to life in (b) with the addition of sharper value contrast and shadows created by lighting.

Figure 11.5 By the consistent placement of light fixtures in relation to these two interior masses it is possible to simulate the uniform patterns of shade and shadow produced by daylight outdoors.

Another similar strategy is the use of strong light coming from a consistent angle to produce strong shadows. We see the effect of such a scheme regularly outdoors where the angle of the sun high above remains consistent in relation to the masses below. Consequently, the pattern of brightness, shade, and shadow remains consistent through the scene. Although the light sources inside are never high up enough to achieve this effect from a single source, the placement of a row of sources in relation to masses in space can achieve this effect as shown in Figure 11.5.

Light has the capacity to accentuate textures. Surfaces and objects, whether a small sculpture, a detail, or a rough vertical surface, have particular characteristics based on the turns, twists, protrusions, and recesses in them. When these qualities are emphasized through lighting their three-dimensionality becomes richer. It is the presence of highlight, shade, and shadow that make three-dimensional objects and surfaces come to life. Sidelighting usually works best to illuminate surfaces with texture or relief as well as sculptural pieces and details. It accentuates the light and shaded spots created by the particular shapes and textures. In some applications it is necessary to add secondary (softer) lighting on the shaded side so it doesn't become too dark, unless a high contrast is intentionally desired. This rule of thumb, however, does not always work. In cases where the articulations or relief of a surface have a definite orientation, say a horizontal one, lighting from above (grazing) may be more successful in accentuating light, shade, and shadow.

One type of lighting approach that takes away from the three-dimensionality of objects and surfaces is straight-on lighting. Straight-on lighting tends to illuminate the object or surface too uniformly because of the lack of shade and shadow. This produces a washed-out, flat effect. For the same reasons, when illuminating an entire room or space, it is best to avoid uniform lighting from above if you are seeking textural richness. Uniform lighting from above produces almost no shade and shadow, thus creating scenes that are well lit but not very interesting. Common examples of this phenomenon can be seen regularly outdoors where the direct light from midday produces far less interesting results than the angular light from the early morning or late afternoon.

Light-Creating Foci

One common application of light is its use to establish or accentuate focal elements. It can achieve this by highlighting an existing focal object or by creating effects with enough magnetism of their own to become foci. Typical examples of the first application include the use of accent lighting on artwork or merchandise. In these cases, the focal object already exists. It has been located and framed perfectly and all it needs is local accent lighting to make it stand out even more. Figure 11.6 shows two examples. In Figure 11.6a the accent lighting on the central graphic increases its effectiveness as a focus. The two jewelry display cases shown in Figure 11.6b feature internal lighting which makes the contents shine brightly in contrast to the darker surroundings.

Brightness, in itself, can create a sense of focus. It is possible to light an entire plane (such as a wall or ceiling) to highlight it. In this case, the entire surface be-

Figure 11.7 Sometimes entire surfaces, such as the ceiling shown here, become focal points because of the bright light purposefully directed at them.

Figure 11.6 Lighting helps to accentuate focal features. The central graphic in (a) and the display cases in (b) come to life as a result of the focused light falling on them.

Figure 11.9 Space can be defined by light alone as is done regularly in the theater. This space is created by the area defined by bright lighting seen against a contrasting dark surrounding.

Figure 11.8 Focused brightness, especially when seen in relation to darker surroundings, always attracts the eye. In this example, the dark bottles placed against the bright background create a strong effect.

Figure 11.10 The effect produced by the concealed uplighting in this example is cleaner and more dramatic than it would be if the light source were visible.

Figure 11.11 The numerous suspended light fixtures in the store in (a) are a prominent feature of this space. They have an assertive presence. Yet, their relatively high placement and their delicate proportions result in a balanced and pleasant composition. Similarly, the five suspended pendants in the bookstore shown in (b), despite their strong presence, are balanced and do not take over the space. Notice the different effects produced by the various sizes and number of fixtures in these two examples.

comes a prominent feature of the space, such as the ceiling in Figure 11.7. Similarly, it is possible to illuminate a smaller surface brightly and thus convert it into a magnetic focal feature. This focal effect can be produced by the brightness itself without the use of any other complementary features such as artwork. Whereas in the case of a single piece of art the lighting frames it closely, in the case of illuminating a surface, the lighting needs to cover the entire featured section evenly. A dramatic example of a brightly lit segment of wall is the bar display shown in Figure 11.8. The brightness of the backlighting, the contrast created by the darker bottles seen as silhouettes, and the brightness of the TV monitors above make this the focal point of the entire space.

It is possible to create not just a light surface but a **light space**. The resulting effect is somewhat more theatrical. In fact, it is commonly used in the theater. A light space is a volume of space defined by light, not by walls or solid elements. It is achieved by the use of bright lights with sharp cut-off angles within a very dark background. The result is a light shape defined by the pattern of light visible in the contrast between the light and the dark background (Figure 11.9).

Another important consideration about lighting, aside from the light itself, is the source. Light sources of various types are used in projects. These range from the totally concealed, which reveal only the light they produce (Figure 11.10), to fixtures that are seen and whose appearance makes a design statement either as a single object or a composition of several ones (Figure 11.11). Combinations of different sources are also common. One application seen regularly is the use of

Figure 11.12 The fully recessed lights in these examples have a nonobtrusive presence. Their size, spacing, and flush mounting contribute to the balanced composition and help them blend in.

fixtures that are visible, but, because of their simple shape, moderate size, well-planned placement, and type of mounting (usually fully recessed), blend in and contribute positively to the space. Figure 11.12 shows two examples. Light fixtures, as objects, then become

Figure 11.13 The design of lighting patterns on the ceiling requires that we revisit the basics of two-dimensional composition. Possibilities vary widely, depending on whether we use many small point sources (a), a group of a few large point sources (b), or rows of linear sources (c).

part of the overall visual composition we see, together with ceilings, walls, spaces, and other objects. Depending on whether you use small bright units in the ceiling, groups of larger units, or directional strips (Figure 11.13), the two-dimensional composition created at the ceiling plane will take on a different character.

Light Animating Sequences and Projects

We have talked about the desirability of having engaging sequences in projects. We talked about these sequences in spatial terms, with space becoming progres-

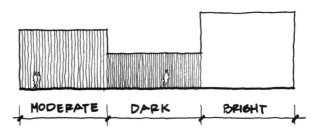

Figure 11.14 The addition of lighting effects to engaging spatial sequences can add drama to the experience. One of many scenarios is to highlight large volumes by brightness and make small passages darker, like caves.

sively (or suddenly) narrower, wider, lower, or taller. Another way of achieving or reinforcing such variations is through lighting. A low corridor opening to a large volume may be dark, in addition to being low. The space it opens up to may be bright, in addition to being ample (Figure 11.14). When the light level changes, the eye requires a period of adaptation to adjust to the new lighting condition. Once adjusted, the vision is stabilized. With this in mind, you can plan your variations to be sudden and radical for high drama or gradual for a mellower effect. The potential uses of lighting for special effects and engaging sequences should not be underestimated. As with other manipulative aspects of design, these attempts can be risky and, therefore, require proper execution for success. It is advisable to take courses in lighting and/or to collaborate with experienced and trusted lighting consultants until you learn to manipulate light for effect on your own.

Before we leave the subject of artificial light, we will suggest that the lighting in a project, because of its significance and extent, requires some planning as an entity of its own. Once the floor plan is decided, at least preliminarily, you can start formulating a lighting concept for the space. You can start defining the areas that require general light, the walls that need emphasizing, the focal points that require reinforcement, and the areas deserving special effects or detailing. In general, you should avoid uniform lighting schemes throughout large areas of the project, much less an entire project, unless a specific circumstance calls for it. Although possibly well suited as a solution from an engineering point of a view, such a scheme would seldom produce the most interesting visual scene.

Figure 11.15 The brightness of natural light is cheerful and inspiring. The glowing quality of this waiting area is due mostly to the brightness produced by the natural lighting that gets in through the skylight above.

Figure 11.16 In this scene at an airport we can see the effects of early morning natural light penetrating a space. On the left side, we see the dramatic effects produced by the long shadows from the columns. On the right side, close to the windows, we see the intensity of the light coming in.

Daylighting

You may wonder why someone who designs interior spaces needs to be concerned with a light source over which he or she has no control. While it is true that you cannot control natural light, and while it is also true that the space in which you are to design a project is likely to be existing (including the windows that let the light in), there are a few things you can do. The key is how you respond to given factors such as site exposure and the natural lighting characteristics of the site. Proper response will help you avoid potential problems on the one hand, and take advantage of opportunities, on the other.

You cannot control nature and the orientation of the existing building where your project is housed. However, you can control where particular rooms and functions of the project go. Exposure to exterior natural light becomes one of the many criteria that affect where you place particular areas of the project (together with hierarchy, ease of access, heat, and so on). In a project with multiple exposures you have to decide who gets the morning light, who gets the afternoon light, who gets the side with the large windows, and who gets indirect, northern light. In some cases you can even add light coming from above. The cheerful mood of the waiting area shown in Figure 11.15 is due to the natural light it gets throughout the day via a large skylight above.

The rooms on the east and west sides of a project get direct, outside light in the morning and afternoon, respectively. If unblocked, light will penetrate deep into the space creating dramatic effects, and/or intolerable glare, depending on the nature of the spaces inside,

Figure 11.17 The type of window coverings used affects not only the quantity and characteristics of the light coming in, but also the nature of the exterior view allowed. The translucent screens in (a) let light in but block views to the exterior. The drapes in (b) filter light coming in but also allow filtered views to the exterior.

their functions and the arrangement (Figure 11.16). Rooms facing south will also get some direct light coming in, although the angle of the sun will be higher and the light won't penetrate as deeply. This light is bright and warm and is likely to be welcomed less in summer than in winter. Northern light, in contrast, is diffuse, never direct and, therefore, softer. Since some of it is reflected from the atmosphere, it is also bluish.

Figure 11.18 The rhythmic effects produced by the interplay of penetrating daylight and regularly spaced vertical elements often produce dramatic effects.

Figure 11.19 Designers have to control the relationship of incoming brightness and interior ambient brightness to produce acceptable conditions. The general darkness of the room above intensifies the brightness of the light penetrating the room through the large window in the background, producing a glaring effect when you first enter.

This kind of light is good for rooms involving tasks requiring uniform, shadowless, and glareless lighting, such as art studios. In addition to decisions about the placement of rooms in relation to orientation, the placement of objects in the room in relation to incoming natural light is also important. Depending on the situation and specific conditions, the proper response may be putting a comfortable chair next to a window, or a desk looking away from it.

Other than the placement of spaces in relation to exposure, designers often have control over how light is blocked or filtered into the space by internal shades, screens, and other devices. Not only do screens and blinds satisfy practical needs such as keeping unwanted harsh light out, they also present opportunities to create special effects with light, ranging from the sensual effect of soft light screened through screens or drapes (Figure 11.17), to the creation of rhythmic effects with streaks and shadows through the use of intermittent columns or other vertical elements placed rhythmically (Figure 11.18). Related to this idea is the strategy of employing objects of particular shapes, sometimes in some sort of pattern, close to windows receiving direct light so that they will cast interesting shadows in the space.

In projects with bright spaces resulting from the presence of openings receiving natural daylight, designers have to make important decisions about how to treat the surfaces of the room and how to complement the natural daylight with artificial light. In rooms with dark surfaces and relatively small windows exposed to daylight, for instance, the light will not bounce around. When the sun is shining, the window areas will appear very bright and the dark wall surfaces, in contrast, will tend to appear quite dark (Figure 11.19). A fair amount of supplementary artificial lighting will be needed inside the room to produce an adequate and balanced level of lighting.

By contrast, if a room with a generous area of glass windows receiving natural light is finished with light surfaces, the incoming light will tend to bounce around and get distributed throughout the space, up to a certain depth. In this case, the entire zone close to the windows will be brightly illuminated naturally with the drop-off occurring gradually as you get deeper into the space. Here, fewer artificial light fixtures will be necessary to supplement the lighting deep in the room, at least during the daytime hours.

Acoustics

Acoustics are an important component of our sensory environment. However, the use of acoustics for effect in interiors remains relatively unexplored. In design schools, students are typically exposed to practical acoustical concerns, such as how to control the transmission of unwanted sounds (i.e., noise) from one space to another, how to prevent unwanted echoes, and so on. All these are important considerations of design that you should be familiar with and know how to apply. What we would like to address here is slightly different.

We want you to increase your awareness of the sounds that make places unique and to learn about ways in which the acoustical properties of the places you design can enrich the experiences in these places. There are not too many types of sounds we hear in interior environments. Among these are the voices of people talking around us (far or near), the sounds of footsteps (loud or muffled), background music, ringing telephones, intercom systems, honking horns and sirens outside, the clicking sounds of glasses and plates at the table, the sounds of paper shuffling, and so on. These are the sounds of our daily lives. Some of them are more pleasant than others, and some of them can be controlled better than others. Although the categories are few, the variations and combinations are infinite.

Every type of place has its own recurring and expected sounds. In the office we hear phones ringing, people talking, receptionists answering incoming calls, and papers shuffling. In the restaurant we hear the sound of silverware, glasses, plates, human voices and, often, background music. At the movies, the sounds of the screen dominate. At the library, we may hear the whispered conversations of people nearby. At the nightclub, there better be loud music! The job of the designer is to decide what is desirable and may need to be reinforced and what is bothersome and may need to be suppressed.

As a designer, you have control over the zoning of functions, the way you place and construct barriers between spaces, and the way you use materials having distinct acoustical properties. Using zoning, barriers, and materials you can locate loud areas away from quiet ones, incorporate sound barriers between areas adjacent to one another, and control the acoustical liveliness within any one given space. The zoning of functions and the construction of separating walls are fairly simple and straightforward design tasks. Trickier, and more exciting, is manipulating the acoustical properties of individual spaces.

Sound Properties of Individual Spaces

When it comes to the acoustics of individual spaces, the common tendency is to respond to concerns about loudness by adding absorptive materials to dampen the sounds. While there is nothing inherently wrong with this approach, designers commonly encounter two types of problems, both resulting from the indiscriminate overall application of the treatment. The first problem is that certain areas where sounds may not need to be muffled are muffled. The second problem is lack of environmental (in this case, acoustical) variety.

The sound in certain places doesn't need to be muted. Lively places need to sound lively. This applies to the casual restaurant or tavern, the sports bar, and the discothéque, among others. Beyond these overall environments, there are partial environments within other, less lively, settings that don't need to be severely muffled. Arrival areas, public corridors, and break areas in office buildings, health care facilities, and other such settings can benefit from a moderate amount of acoustic liveliness. The opposite is also true. Institutional settings, with all those solid, easy to maintain (and loud!) materials can benefit from the incorporation of absorptive materials in some areas to reduce the sound levels. This increases local comfort by reducing loudness in those areas and also enhances the overall environment by providing variety between areas.

If you want to be able to manipulate the acoustics of individual spaces, the one acoustic concept you need to understand and know how to apply is reverberation. **Reverberation time** is the amount of time it takes for sound to decay in space. In environments having hard surfaces, sound will bounce around for a while and take some time

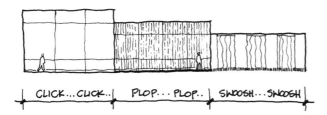

CLICK...CLICK.. | PLOP...PLOP.. | SWOOSH...SWOOSH

Figure 11.20 The sounds produced by materials can be an important contributor to dramatic experiential sequences. In this example, the flooring material of the individual spaces will accentuate or dampen the sound of footsteps. Additionally, the surrounding surfaces can heighten the effect by being more or less reflective/absorptive.

to decay. In these spaces, sound will linger, sometimes producing an echo when it bounces back and forth between two parallel walls. In environments having materials that absorb sound, such as upholstered furniture, curtains, carpet, and acoustic ceiling tiles, a greater amount of sound will be absorbed. Consequently, it will decay rapidly, producing an acoustically muted space.

The other important variable related to reverberation, in addition to absorption, is spatial volume. The greater the spatial volume of a space, the longer the sound will be sustained. Therefore, for acoustically lively areas, think of volume and hard materials. You can use them both or just one. If you need quiet rooms, use soft, sound-absorbing materials and smaller volumes. Since volume manipulations are often difficult to justify in the interior projects most commonly designed, you may often have to rely on absorption manipulations.

The challenge of these seemingly simple acoustic ideas is knowing exactly how to apply them. What is the correct mix of volume and materials, for instance, if you want a moderately lively space? For the designer wanting to explore and experiment with these subtle and tricky aspects of design (and engineering!) it is advisable to work closely with an acoustic consultant until a reasonable amount of familiarity is attained. These types of manipulations, while worthwhile, are also risky. An unsuccessful attempt can have negative consequences and make a client quite upset. It is little wonder, thus, that the tendency is to stay within the safe norms and avoid unnecessary risktaking.

In general, your goal should be to let lively areas be acoustically lively, to ensure that the sound in areas needing quiet is dampened, and to strike an overall healthy balance, appropriate to the type of environment, between the two. With acoustics, as with space and lighting, environmental variety is desirable. The thing to remember is that you can use acoustics to help create experientially rich sequences. Imagine a space, a restaurant entrance for instance, that progresses acoustically in response to footsteps and other acoustic stimuli, from lively, high-pitched tones, to lively and warmer (lower) tones, to a quieter muffled area as you enter the formal dining hall. See the diagram in Figure 11.20.

Other Environmental Factors

We will explore two other environmental factors briefly: the thermal properties of places and the olfactory properties of places. While these originate from sources over which you as the designer exercise relatively little control, certain manipulations are possible to enhance the overall effects produced.

The Thermal Environment

The control of the thermal environment falls under the domain of the mechanical engineer, not the interior designer or architect. The engineer's task is to design mechanical systems that will produce thermally comfortable environments. The problem with the typical solution is the same as with other engineered solutions, namely the tendency to treat entire projects uniformly, with no variety, producing projects of constant, unvarying temperature, humidity, and ventilation. Here we make the same case made for lighting and acoustics: a variety of environmental (in this case, thermal) conditions can make our experience of places richer. However, this advice comes with an important caveat. When it comes to the thermal environment, it is crucial to stay within the accepted comfort zone for that type of environment. Otherwise, the resulting discomfort will overshadow any gains from the variety of conditions produced and is sure to generate many complaints.

There are a few things designers can do to enhance thermal experiences in their projects. They require the assistance of the mechanical engineer. If you want to produce a space that is open and airy, a common request of clients, you could supplement your open space with a genuine airy experience. All you need to do is ask your mechanical engineer to supply extra fresh air ventilation to the room to account for the extra volume. While not always a justifiable request, where it can be implemented, it can result in a very comfortable interior environment because of the higher-than-normal volume of fresh ventilation.

It is sometimes desirable to manipulate the temperature in certain rooms for special reasons. A slightly cold conference room, for instance, will help to keep attendees awake during an early morning meeting. One thing you can do without the help of engineers is to complement the desired thermal character of the room (warm or cold) with materials, colors, and lighting having corresponding connotations. If the goal is warmth, use soft materials, warm colors, and yellowish lighting. If the goal is coldness, use hard, smooth materials, cool colors, and bluish lighting.

People generally enjoy spaces that provide comfort, especially warmth. One possible strategy, especially during climate extremes, is simply to make it possible for at least one important public space in a project to achieve very comfortable thermal properties (i.e., warmth in the winter and coolness in the summer). This could be a major break room or meeting room. This room would then become a popular destination and would acquire a special status because of the comfort associated with it. You could even make the sequence of getting to this area an experience in itself, using not only thermal properties, but also color, lighting, and acoustics to gradually build up the experience until you reach the epicenter of comfort.

The Olfactory Environment

Finally, we wish to say something about the way places smell. This is another variable where the potential interventions by the designer are limited. While certain materials, such as leather and polished wood, have their own peculiar smell, the smells in places are mostly a result of the goods in those places. Many places lack distinct smells, but certain spaces do have strong smells associated with them. These include restaurants, coffee shops, cookie shops, bakeries, soap and perfume shops, flower shops, and even movie theaters. The desirable smells from these places are very much a part of their essence. Consequently, your task as a designer is to take advantage of these natural enhancers. This can be achieved by placing areas with particularly attractive smells in strategic locations in order to attract people, or simply delight passersby. Another possibility is to concentrate, even exaggerate the smells (often through mechanical means) in strategic places to make them acquire a magnetic effect. It is no accident that businesses like cookie stores direct the air from their kitchen exhausts into the public areas

Figure 11.21 One of the main functions of the material palette used in a project is to give it a certain characteristic flavor. The prominent use of stainless steel in (a) produces a refined and clean contemporary look, while the abundant use of wood in (b) produces a formal and dignified look.

outside. Who, after all, can resist the tempting smell of a freshly baked cookie when it is directed at them?

Interior Decorative Elements

Interior decorative elements are exclusively decorative and, thus, play no major functional role in the design. They do, nevertheless, play a crucial role in enriching, and giving expression to interior environments. We could say these are the types of elements that literally dress up a project. Included in this group are finishes, color, pattern, and ornament.

Finishes

You are likely to be fairly familiar with interior finishes by now. Even nondesigners cannot escape them, having to make choices about how to paint the walls and select the rugs and cushions for their homes. Previous design school projects have most likely required the selection of finishes. In school you are likely to use particular finishes because you like the way they look and they are in the family of colors you have decided to use for the project. This is also true in practice, although in practice you become more concerned with the performance properties of the materials.

A major consideration of finish selection is aesthetics. Selections made have a strong impact on the nature of the places you create. They help to determine a stylistic direction for your project, establishing a specific visual character. A project may take on a formal character, or have traditional or modernistic tendencies, because of the choice of finish. Dark woods and heavily patterned

carpets will convey an entirely different character than glass, marble, and stainless steel. Materials allow you to get to a level of stylistic specificity often difficult, or impractical, to achieve by architectural means alone. Compare the two very different looks produced by the two material palettes shown in Figure 11.21.

Beyond this broad overall distinction there are many more choices to be made depending on desired nuance, personal preferences, and other qualifications. In the example of the dark wood and heavily patterned carpet mentioned above, for instance, there are many possibilities. Woods and carpets are available in different varieties that would fit the descriptions of dark and heavily patterned. What is the wood type? What kind of veneer cut is being specified? Is it stained? What finish system are you using for the woodwork? How is the carpet patterned? Is there a motif? What is the size of the repeating patterns? Is it simple or complex? The answers to all these questions will produce a much more specific look for these finishes. They help to define the stylistic direction more precisely and they also force you to think about qualities you may, or may not, want for their own sake, independent of stylistic considerations, such as more or less intricacy or more or less texture.

Materials and Their Finishes

Individual materials have unique inherent qualities. They also acquire other specific qualities based on the way they are manufactured and finished. The hardness of stone, the brittleness of glass, the shine of metals, and the textures of wood are all inherent in materials. Designers need to understand these inherent qualities in order to use these materials appropriately

a   b   c   d

Figure 11.22 Not all woods look the same. In fact, the variety within the world of wood is enormous. One important source of variety is the way wood veneers are sliced. Different cuts will produce different graining effects. Compare the graining characteristics of rotary slicing (a), plain slicing (b), quarter slicing (c), and rift cutting (d).

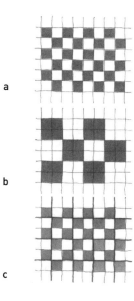

Figure 11.23 Notice the three different effects produced by simple manipulations of tile and grout placement in tile floors. Drawing (a) shows an ordinary checkerboard pattern. In drawing (b), the scale is doubled by changing the size of the squares (while using the same tile size). In drawing (c), two patterns are superimposed on each other, one being the pattern created by the tiles, and the other, the pattern created by the unconventional use of grout between the tiles (shown by the darker lines).

Figure 11.24 The size of the repeating units, the density of repeat, and the contrast of the colors, values, and shapes used all make important contributions to the final effect of a patterned field. The floor in (a) features a dense pattern of small pieces in four different values, producing a rich and busy effect. The floor in (b) features larger units grouped in ways that create subpatterns. Blank spaces between them and less value variation produce a less-busy effect than the one in (a). Floor (c), despite the repetition of the stripes, does not contain identical repeating units. Every stripe is different and the overall size of each unit is much larger than those in the other two examples.

and emphasize their best qualities. Beyond these inherent qualities, materials acquire qualities based on their manufacturing processes and the way in which they are finished. Consequently, the graining of wood will be different depending on how it is cut (Figure 11.22), the texture of carpet will be different depending on how it is constructed, and the sheen level of stone will vary depending on how it is finished.

The effect of finishes will also vary depending on its modularity. A composition with a few large pieces will look and feel very different from one with many small ones. Modular flooring produces different results, depending on the size of the pieces used. It is possible to manipulate the sense of scale by manipulating the pattern of the grout and the tiles (Figure 11.23).

Certain finishes, especially textiles, usually have a pattern. The type of pattern, its size, shape, and content will all affect the final character of the finish. A large floral pattern of vivid, highly contrasting colors may delight some and offend others. A small, abstract, geometric pattern of subdued, low-contrast colors may please many and bore some. The varieties possible are enough to suit every conceivable taste. Patterns and modular arrangements may have more or less uniformity from one piece to the next. The size of the pattern, frequency of repetition, and contrast between adjacent pieces affect the overall look and many different effects are possible. Consider the different effects produced by the three floor patterns shown in Figure 11.24. Texture and pattern are two of the most

Figure 11.25 Texture and pattern can be used to produce subtle or bold results. Compare the understated effect of the stair scene in (a) with the busier effect of the movie theater lobby shown in (b).

important sources of articulation in interior environments. The amount and nature of the texture and pattern used will have a significant impact on the visual character and load level of the environment created (Figure 11.25).

The Feel of Materials

Other than their visual properties, materials have qualities associated with our sense of touch, such as hardness/softness, smoothness/roughness, and warmth/coldness. These are important considerations and we have alluded to some of these before in the context of lighting and thermal qualities. The materials we walk on or otherwise touch are perhaps the most important because we are constantly in physical contact with them. A hard stone floor, a bouncy wood floor, a resilient rubber floor, and a soft, fluffy carpet not only look and sound different, they feel different! Here is one more aspect of design where criteria besides appearance and performance can be incorporated. If you really want to address the sensual aspects of your projects to enhance experience, how about playing with the degree of hardness and texture of the floor finish? The way materials feel when touched (real or imagined) is an important variable for you to explore in design. Using the feel of materials to enrich experience is one of the designer's strategies to create sensual sequences in projects, together with the other modifiers of sequential experience previously discussed.

The temperature of materials and finishes is an interesting consideration. On the one hand are the material's **thermal conduction** properties. Certain materials (such as metals and masonry) tend to absorb the cold or heat around them. The pleasantness of an aluminum bench, for instance, is relative. If the beach is located in a cold room during the winter but exposed to the sun's rays through a window, it can produce a very welcoming and satisfying warmth amidst the cold. If the bench is located in the same room without the benefit of the warming sun or in a sunny, hot room it is likely to become too cold or hot for comfort, especially if experienced with bare skin.

Another aspect related to temperature is a material's ability to breathe, especially in the finishes we sit on or come in physical contact with. A natural textile or leather will breathe and allow air circulation through it while, say, plastic imitating leather will not. You will sweat when exposed directly to the plastic, while the other natural finishes will be more comfortable. Many of us have also experienced this phenomenon in relation to the fabric of the clothes we wear, natural ones being more comfortable than synthetic ones because of their ability to breathe.

Finally, there are the materials we come in contact with through our hands. These are the materials on doorknobs, handrails, and countertops. These also require some consideration and offer opportunities for sensual experience. Other than the relative level of pleasantness associated with the shape and proportions of the element, its temperature and texture will have some influence on the total experience, whether it is turning the doorknob or grabbing the handrail. Here again, the metals will be more thermally volatile than the woods. In terms of texture, the main distinction here is between smooth finishes

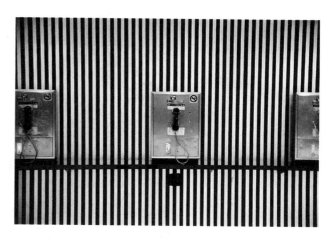

Figure 11.26 Texture, although experienced in more than just visual terms, does often contribute a strong visual statement, as shown here.

and textured ones, whether regularly or randomly textured. Both can be highly pleasurable and can be utilized at the discretion of the designer to achieve the desired effect. The smoothness of a polished metal handrail can produce a very pleasant experience when touched but so can the reassuring effect of the good grip provided by the grainy textural effect on another handrail.

As suggested by the above example, it is clear that texture, in addition to the visual interest it produces (Figure 11.26), can be used favorably on materials that people come in contact with. It can work for us in two ways: by helping us increase users' environmental consciousness, and, as we have seen, by helping us provide pleasant surfaces to come in contact with. The first strategy normally uses floor surfaces. You may have experienced the effect of encountering a highly textured part of a road while driving or of feeling a textured floor close to the platform edge when boarding a train in modern train and subway stations. In both these cases the objective is to alert us to potential nearby danger. When you feel the unusual bumpy texture under your tires or feet, you become more alert and pay more attention to the road, or to the end of the subway platform beyond. You can apply the same strategy even when there is no danger ahead. If you want to increase users' spatial awareness momentarily, you can change the floor texture drastically, making it rough and bumpy. That will wake them up.

Color

We could have included color in our discussion about finishes because most color in interiors comes from the finishes selected for the project. However, color is an element of such power and impact that it deserves separate attention as a physical component of design. Color does a lot more than just decorate and beautify. This is an element that serves to define and articulate, thus contributing clarity and order in design. It is also an element that can have a great impact on our emotions and dictate the mood of a place. Thus, color is also an important instrument for enrichment. Additionally, color can be used in ways that make individuals and groups identify with it, making it invaluable to achieve or reinforce particular expressions.

Much of the color employed in architecture and interiors used to be inherent in the natural materials used for construction. The colors of projects were the colors of the available materials. There are many more choices now. These days, most color is artificial. The colors of paints, plastic laminates, tiles, and textiles are manufactured according to what is fashionable at the time of production. A wide variety of color choices is available, giving designers ample latitude for color selection. There are still many natural materials whose color is inherently determined. Such is the case in wood and stone, for example. The color in most projects is usually a combination of materials with inherent colors and materials with artificial colors.

Associations with Color

Color often has a strong impact on us. This is due to its power to evoke strong emotional responses and to the many associations we make in response to color. Different hues are said to have different effects on humans. Reds, for instance, tend to excite us and make

us tense, while blues and greens have a calming effect. Yellows, on the other hand, excite us differently from reds because of the cheerfulness associated with them. Also important are the color's chroma and value. The greater the intensity of the color, the more it will excite and the darker its value, the more somber a scene will get. The two scenes in Figure 11.27 show how value alone can create dramatic differences in environments. Compare the two very different moods in these two environments.

In addition to the power of color to affect our emotional states, it also influences us through some of the connotations associated with particular colors and their properties. Color brings with it associations with temperature, weight, and gender. We are all familiar with the distinction between cool and warm colors. The blues and greens are considered cool while the reds, oranges, and yellows are considered warm. Similarly, colors can feel heavy (dark colors) or light (light colors), and they can be masculine or feminine (brown and pink, respectively, at least in Western cultures).

Color carries symbolism developed through associations made over time. Therefore, we have colors that are associated with countries (red, white, and blue in the United States), school colors, colors of companies (red Coca-Cola), and colors of organizations and clubs. Whatever the character and spirit of a person or group, whether light and lively, or heavy and somber, it is possible to capture and express it through color.

Behavior of Color

The subject of color has fascinated many people throughout time, from artists to psychologists. A good deal of research has been done about color and certain peculiarities about it have been identified. Other than the ones already mentioned, it has been determined that certain colors seem to advance towards us (warm colors), while others seem to recede and appear further back (cool colors). This, with the relative lightness and darkness of the values used will significantly affect our perception of the size of rooms and spaces. Perhaps one of the most significant findings about color concerns its relativity: our perception of a particular color varies depending on what other color or colors it is seen against. The lightness or darkness of a color, as well as its warmth or coolness, will vary depending on the colors around it.

Using Color

Using color successfully requires sensitivity and appropriate response to existing conditions, knowledge about colors and their behavior, some intuition, and the ability to balance colors harmoniously. With color, what is appropriate in one case is not appropriate in another. It is one of the aspects of design requiring proper congruence between the personality of a project and the choices made. One interesting and challenging aspect of color in interior spaces is that you never see the total effect of your creation until it is all in place. As a designer, you hope that the resulting effect will be good because once all the walls are painted or covered with applied finishes, and once all the furniture is in place with its colorful upholstery, it will be too late to say you've made a mistake and want to make a change.

Context and Suitability

A great measure of the success of a color scheme in a project is dependent on the correspondence between the choices made and the physical context. Although there are many contexts with different levels of immediacy and influence, we want to focus first on what we could call **regional flavor**. We discussed the influence of the regional context in Chapter 9. Here we expand on that discussion, because color is one of the main ways designers seek good correspondence between a project and its regional context.

Some places, because of the physical characteristics of their landscape and/or regional or local cultures, develop their own native color palette. The coast, the desert, and the forest all have inherent colorings that suggest strongly what goes and doesn't go well with them. The colors of Florida are different from the colors of New Mexico or the colors of the American prairie. The colors of New Mexico, for instance, are affected by both the landscape character of the Southwest, but also by the Native American cultural influences of the region. The landscape and architecture are characterized by the soft and cool earth tones of adobe, the sunbaked masonry units traditionally used for construction.

The architecture of the Southwest tends to blend with the desert background on which it sits. Doors, windows, and other architectural features are often painted with accent colors, such as white or blue, to add contrast and detail. Inside, textiles developed from the Native American traditions expand the palette, featuring white, grays, reds, and black. A local color palette has developed from these influences and projects done in the region, and while you are not obligated to follow these colors literally, you should at least understand the local palette as a point of departure.

Other than regional flavor, color responds to the context of the ebb and flow of ever-changing tastes and fashions. Every period in time has its own colors. The Victorian interiors of the nineteenth century replaced the light and airy color schemes of Georgian rooms with schemes featuring multichromatic, dark colors that made them formal and somber. The colors of the fifties were cheerful; sometimes light, often bold. Pastels were popular and colors such as pink, green, and turquoise became widely used. Also popular in interiors were the reds, oranges, and yellows of autumn as the colors of outdoor materials were brought in to add warmth and texture.

Theory and Application

Any designer serious about the meaningful use of color in interiors must study color and become well acquainted with color theory. Theory of color, especially a good grasp of color harmony, is always a good point of reference. We do offer some words of caution about the use of color harmony systems, about the blind belief in the properties of color, and about the existing knowledge of colors' effects on humans.

One thing you should know about color harmony systems is that, while they are helpful in design, any color combination can be made to work if the right combinations and proportions are used. While most of the basic properties of color you learned about in color theory classes have been shown to be true, it is possible to create effects that will contradict them. One example is the notion that warm colors advance and cool colors recede. Paul Zelanski and Mary Pat Fischer stress that "any color can be brought forward or pushed back in space by the visual clues to spatial organization given with it."[2]

Furthermore, while much is known about how color affects us, we must recognize, as Sinclair Gauldie has expressed, that color psychology, "is a debatable land into which the psychologist himself ventures with caution, and only the painter, being guided by intuition and not accountable to science, can feel sure of his steps."[3] Whether the painter can be truly sure of his steps or not, is itself debatable. The point is that, with color, there are no definite rules. The requirements of each project are so particular, and the effects of different color combinations so many, that on the one hand, each project will have hundreds of approaches that are wrong, but dozens that will work, some better than others. It is up to the designer to select which one to use.

Not only is it enough to have the right color palette for a project, the exact colors used and the way they are combined will also determine the success of the application. The point here is that the way colors in a composition will interact is affected by the relative sizes of color areas, their location, lighting conditions, the texture given to color, and what is placed next to what. It is particularly important to remember that the application of color in space is vastly different from its use on a piece of canvas or paper. In architectural space, the colors of a composition are sometimes touching, other times not touching but on the same side of the room, and at times on opposite sides of the room! Just because two colors that are supposed to work together are in the same room does not guarantee they will achieve harmony. Their proportions and positions relative to one another have to be worked out in order for the application to be successful.

Color Strategies

Color is an important design tool. Many design strategies can be implemented successfully through the use of color. A few specific strategies follow.

- Use strong color to create focal areas. Accent colors and contrasting ones will stand out. Particularly effective are saturated vivid colors. Whether used alone or to reinforce an articulated or specially designed area, the use of strong color will ensure that it will be noticed.
- Use contrast to divide sections of the same surface. This strategy can be particularly effective in projects that feature trim. By using contrasting colors (amount of contrast to suit the job) between the wall plane and the trim (base, frames, casings, and moldings) each element can be made to stand out strongly.
- Use contrast to enhance the effect of low-relief articulations and details. By using subtle color or value changes, the three-dimensionality of the composition can be emphasized, especially for parts occurring on different planes.
- Use uniform coloring to simplify the appearance of a dense and complex space. While some color variety is possible, if there are many pieces and objects

in a room and too many colors used, the result can be chaotic.

- Use varied color schemes to make plain spaces more interesting. This strategy is the opposite of the one above. Here, a varied and multichromatic approach can transform an otherwise plain and boring room into a rich and expressive one.

- Use color to unify projects and parts of projects. Color is a powerful unifying element. Whether a surface, a room, or an entire project, color can unify or fragment it. Color can be used to unify similar elements by color coding. An example would be the use of the same color for all the project's exposed mechanical ducts. Color can also emphasize rooms as units. You could paint individual rooms with different colors to distinguish them while using consistency of chroma or value to ensure some unity for the entire composition as a project. You could also just use consistent coloring throughout the project with, perhaps, different color accents in key areas to emphasize them.

- If variety is achieved by other elements, then unify through color. Conversely, if you unify through other design elements, then you can achieve variety through your color selections.

Dangers and Rewards

The assertive use of colors in interiors carries potential risks but also potential rewards. As mentioned earlier, it is useful to compare the application of color with the playing of a highly sensitive musical instrument. In the hands of a skilled performer the loud sounds produced by the musical instrument will be a welcome experience, but in the hands of an amateur the only two possibilities are noise (not good) or the faint playing of simple patterns (not as offensive, although not quite satisfying). Perhaps due to the inherent risks involved, many interior projects lack much color. While simplicity certainly has its place in some applications of design, it is tempting to speculate that many designers shy away from using color assertively because it is hard to do well. As Allen Tate and C. Ray Smith have warned us, "if the colors of an interior are derived from a simple sequence, a designer risks little, but also tends to accomplish little."[4]

Excessive use of color can be as undesirable as too much restraint. Too much color in enclosed spaces can feel like an attack on our senses. Too much variety in color can also be disturbing, especially if used in large chunks. Edith Wharton and Ogden Codman, Jr. explain this with a useful comparison: "a multiplicity of colors produces the same effect as a number of voices talking at the same time. The voices may not be discordant, but continuous chatter is fatiguing in the long run."[5]

Color is a highly aesthetic component of design. You should make a point of learning how to select aesthetically pleasing color schemes. The power of color is such that no matter how successfully all the other aspects of a project are designed and executed, if a project has unappealing colors it will be disliked despite all its other virtues. Perhaps one of the greatest pieces of advice we can give related to the selection of color schemes for interiors is the virtue in discarding unnecessary colors. An otherwise good color scheme with one or two colors too many contributes little and harms much.

The subject of color has been studied extensively by artists and scholars alike and enjoys a fairly abundant literature. Color, as we all understand intuitively, is an extremely important qualifier of built environments. It is, in fact, an ever-present component of any visual experience. Colors carry connotations and are associated with particular attitudes and moods. When it comes to design, especially interior design, color is one of the major determinants of identity. Determining which colors are appropriate for a specific project is, largely, a search for colors appropriate for the particular identity of a client or project.

The work of Shigenobu Kobayashi and the Nippon Color & Design Research Institute (NCD) in Japan is particularly significant among the great body of literature about color. The extensive work of Kobayashi and the Institute links color with its perceived connotations related to identity and personal style and presents it all in a highly useable framework. Their focus is on application, and this makes their work useful to interior designers, who are constantly faced with questions such as, what color should I use to convey an image both delicate and fashionable? or an image that is bright and casual?

"Ours is an age of increasing sensitivity to color," says Kobayashi. "But what meanings are conveyed by the colors that surround us in everyday life? If we could grasp their real meanings, perhaps we would be able to use them more effectively. The first step toward a more effective use of color is to systematize and classify colors through key words that express their meanings and through images that express the differences between them."[1] This is not too difficult to do for single colors, but becomes tricky when colors are used in combination. Kobayashi and his colleagues therefore sought to classify not only single colors, but also color combinations in a systematic way and to link them to their associated meanings. They devised the Color Image Scale, a database for the systematic classification of color combinations.

The scale uses 130 basic colors, from which more than one-thousand three-color combinations were assembled. Additionally, colors were matched with a collection of 180 adjectives covering the entire array of people's perceptions of their connotations and moods. From this information, profiles were prepared for each of the 130 colors and particular color combinations using each color, presenting the images connoted by each one of the single colors and each combination.

The 130 colors cover the entire color spectrum, and include 120 chromatic colors and 10 tones of gray. Chromatic colors are divided into 10 hues (red, yellow-red, yellow, green-yellow, green, blue-green, blue, purple-blue, purple, and red-purple), and each hue is, in turn, subdivided into 12 tones, grouped into the general categories of vivid tones, bright tones, subdued tones, and dark tones.

Colors and their combinations are positioned within a three-dimensional image scale consisting of three interrelated axes: the warm-cool axis, the hard-soft axis, and the clear-gray axis (Figure C11.1). Not only are certain hues (e.g., red) considered warm and others (e.g., blue), cool, but within each hue there is a range from warmest to coolest. The second axis, soft-hard, contains elements of shared human experience related to the relative sense of weight, brightness, and tactility of colors. It is fundamentally linked to weight. In terms of color, this is manifested by the general paleness or deepness of the color. The third axis, clear-gray, is concerned with the amount of gray in a hue or tone.

A key word image scale was developed based on the adjectives people associated with each color and color combination. Descriptors were placed on the three-dimensional scale corresponding with the position of the colors associated with them. Figure C11.2 shows a two-dimensional representation of the key word scale. As Kobayashi explains, "broadly speaking the key words in the warm-soft area of the scale have an intimate feeling, and convey a casual image, while those in the warm-hard section have a dynamic character. The key words in the cool-soft section have a clear feeling and suggest a good sense of color, while those in the cool-hard section convey an image of reliability and formality."[2] This is of course, an oversimplification as there are dozens of descriptors in each of the four quadrants. To make the scale easier to understand, similar key words were grouped under more general headings using categories from fashion, such as casual, elegant, and chic. A graphic representation of the scale with just these general image categories is shown in Figure C11.3. It defines the regions occupied by each of the 16 categories.

The next thing Kobayashi and his associates did to facilitate the practical use of their system was to define eight basic lifestyles associated with particular preferences of colors and adjectives. He explains, "Through the interplay of word and color images in the image scales, we can detect a general pattern in the differences between people's sensitivities. From the differences in individual patterns, we can get a feeling for different kinds of lifestyles. So, in practical terms, when you are creating a new product you can make use of the connections between words, colors, and objects."[3] The eight basic lifestyles are derived from the dominant image categories. The lifestyles are: casual, modern, romantic, natural, elegant, chic, classic, and dandy. They are briefly described below.

Casual Lifestyle (key words: youthful, flamboyant, merry, enjoyable, vivid): This lifestyle is cheerful and easygoing and has an open and happy image. Preference is for vivid and clear colors, with strong and bright tones. People associated with this style are young, such as college students and people in their early twenties.

Modern Lifestyle (key words: urban, rational, sharp, progressive, metallic): The feeling of this group is cool and urbane, with a clear-cut, functional, sharp image. Neutral colors and sharp contrasts are favored. A key color is black. Vivid colors are sometimes used as an accent to create a bold effect. People associated with this lifestyle are young city dwellers who are particular about function and design.

Romantic Lifestyle (key words: soft, sweet, innocent, dreamy, charming): This style is characterized by a feeling of delicacy and sweetness. It is popular with young women. The predominant color qualities are softness, sweetness, and dreaminess. The main color combinations are light pastel tones and white. The colors used are clear.

Natural Lifestyle (key words: natural, tranquil, intimate, simple and appealing, generous): This lifestyle enjoys a natural, warm, simple appearance, with a heartwarming image. Rich, natural materials are preferred, artificial ones are disliked. The main colors are shades of beige, ivory, and yellow-green. People who aim for a cheerful, relaxed, and comfortable feeling belong in this group.

Elegant Lifestyle (key words: refined, graceful, delicate, fashionable, feminine): This group displays a taste for subtlety, a nonchalant style, and a sense of balance and charm. Refinement, tenderness, and calm further describe the image of this group. Grayish colors predominate and color combinations used are subtle gradations. Belonging in this group are women with a sense of gentleness, delicacy, and overall quality.

Chic Lifestyle (key words: sober, modest, simple, quiet and elegant, subtle): This group is characterized by a preference for the sober, calm, quiet, and sophisticated. They enjoy atmospheres that are quiet and polished, with an air of simple elegance. Urban, intelligent, sophisticated adults belong in this group, which has a cooler image than that of the elegant type. Sober, grayish colors predominate, with combinations displaying subtle differences of tones and grayish colors being preferred.

Classic Lifestyle (key words: traditional, classic, mature, tasteful, heavy and deep): An image of authenticity is at the heart of this type. Preferences are toward the elaborate, decorative, and formal. Preferred colors are hard and grayish, with brown, black, olive green, burgundy, and gold used widely. Belonging in this group are older, conservative people who aspire to tradition and authenticity.

Dandy Lifestyle (key words: placid, quiet, sophisticated, sound, dignified, strong, robust): This lifestyle is characterized by a self-possessed tone, stability, masculinity, and quiet sophistication. This type is simpler and cooler in feel than the classic. Preferences are toward hard colors such as brown, navy blue, or dark gray, used in combination with calm, grayish colors. Belonging in this group are adults, predominantly masculine, and with an inclination towards hard and neat atmospheres.

These insightful, research-derived lifestyle categories are the closest thing we have seen to a typology of tastes. Their potential for providing designers with useful insights about people and their taste preferences are enormous. As Kobayashi puts it when referring to his system: "I believe that this classification of colors based on images is the key to understanding the way in which color combinations are perceived, and that this system opens a path to the future, when sensitivity to color will continue to grow."[4]. We couldn't agree more.

The information presented here summarizes discussion in the books *Color Image Scale* and *Colorist*, both by Kobayashi. These two books, as well as his *A Book of Colors*, are highly recommended.

[1] Kobayashi, Shigenobu. *Color Image Scale*, (Kodansha International: New York, 1990) p. 2.

[2] Ibid., p. 12

[3] Ibid., p. 17

[4] Ibid., p. 2

Figure C11.1 The three axes of Kobayashi's model: warm-cool, soft-hard, and clear-grayish.

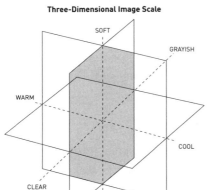

Source: From Colorist *by Shigenobu Kobayashi, published by Kodansha International Ltd. Copyright © 1998 by Shigenobu Kobayashi.*

Figure C11.2 Two-dimensional representation of the key word scale showing key word and their location according of the characteristics of colors associated with them.

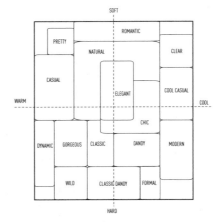

Source: From Color Image Scale *by Shigenobu Kobayashi, published by Kodansha International Ltd. Copyright © 1990 by Nippon Color & Design Research Institute, Inc.*

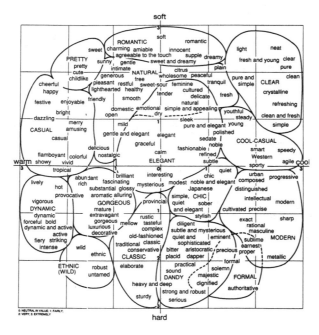

Figure C11.3 Two dimensional representation of just the 16 general categories and their location on the chart according to the characteristics of the colors associated with them.

Source: From Colorist *by Shigenobu Kobayashi, published by Kodansha International Ltd. Copyright © 1998 by Shigenobu Kobayashi*

Figure 11.28 Details give character to the various elements of the environment. Example (a) shows a thoughtful detail that incorporates rich materials, lighting, and signage, and adds interest to an otherwise plain column. Example (b) shows simple but crisp detailing applied to an office door and frame. Example (c) features a series of decorative pilasters of unique shape and rich material.

Ornament and Detail

Ornaments and special details are important decorative treatments that supply richness and expression to projects. They both share the goal of embellishing a project by supplying articulation and relief in particular styles and expressions at a usually small and human scale. The basic difference between the two is that ornamentation usually involves the addition of some object or decorative feature to a project's space or surface, while detailing is usually an inherent part of the construction of an element, only at a smaller, more detailed level.

Ornamentation was used almost without exception in architecture and interior design until the advent of modernism, when, all of a sudden, some considered it a crime to use applied decoration. Instead, a new interest developed in accentuating the inherent expressions of materials and showing structure and its many intersections truthfully and honestly. Today, patterned materials, accessories, graphics, and artwork have become substitutes for the kind of elaborate ornamentation used in the past. Beginning around the mid-1970s there was a renewed interest in ornamentation, at least among some designers. Since then, the level of interest has fluctuated but the practice of ornamentation remains a powerful way to articulate and embellish space and surfaces. Detailing, however, continues to flourish as one of the main ways designers define the style and character of a project.

Detailing requires the shaping and articulation of construction components in ways that express a particular stylistic tendency. All styles have their proper way of expression. The detailing of an old Victorian-style room and its components is vastly different from the detailing of a minimalist modern room and its components. The materials are different, the number of parts are different, the joints are different, and the shapes are different.

The detailing of the smaller parts of projects serves to give a project a unique style and character. Details often do this more convincingly than the main volumes and shapes of a project, which often remain fairly neutral. They all must work together though, and require proper compatibility and consistency of approach. Whether a room or a project ends up being light-handed or heavy-handed, formal or informal, modern or traditional, it will owe much of those qualities to the type of detailing used.

Detailing takes design intent to a smaller scale and develops it more intensely. There are many types of details in interiors. They include intersections of wall planes with ceiling and floor planes, the articulation of columns and other freestanding or protruding elements, changes in levels at the ceiling and floor, doors and frames, casework, relief, molding, reveals, custom-designed furnishings and fixtures, and so on. All these, and many others, need to be given proper expression according to the design vocabulary of the project.

Above all, detailing implies making some element of the built environment special due to the treatment it is given. Figure 11.28 shows examples of three normally ordinary building elements, a sign, a door, and a pilaster, transformed into specially crafted elements through thoughtful detailing. Special detailing can also be used to make freestanding, sculptural elements stand out. Figure 11.29 shows a nicely detailed building directory, and a very expressive and sculptural-looking freestanding sales kiosk. Details show concern for de-

Figure 11.29 Freestanding elements in space often require thoughtful detailing. The building directory shown in (a) is a good example of a little design project unto itself. The skillful integration of materials, shapes, and information give it a strong design presence. Similarly, the eyewear kiosk shown in (b) integrates material, pattern, shapes, graphics, and merchandise to achieve a unique and stylish look.

Figure 11.30 Good details are everywhere in design. Intersections present special detailing opportunities, like the intersection of the column, ceiling, and sign shown in (a). Also, railing systems, and other enriching sculptural fabrications like the ones shown in (b), present opportunities to add enrichment and expression to projects.

sign. Nice detailing implies that care has been taken in the crafting of the objects and other elements of a project. Not every aspect of a project has to stand out as a highly articulated detail but many parts present opportunities for refinement through detailing, especially if they occur in visible, prominent locations like the guardrail system/sculptural screen device and the column/ceiling/sign intersection shown in Figure 11.30.

Designers create many architectural elements and miscellaneous objects in projects; others are selected from available products. They have to ensure that there is proper compatibility between the detailing of specified products (designed and produced by others) and that of the elements custom designed by the designer for the project. The detailing will rarely be identical but it seldom needs to be. Proper compatibility is all that is required.

The art of detailing is one that takes time to cultivate and master. Young designers need to be encouraged to practice it conscientiously and often. There is nothing as sad as a well-conceived space with well-chosen finishes and furnishings but lacking the richness provided by conscientious detailing, even if minimalistic and subtle.

Other Considerations

Protagonists of Place

In addition to all the elements discussed in this chapter there are two other important ingredients in the mix of interior places and the life that unfolds within them. These are the goods and the people supported by our designs. Designers do not control these two components; they react and respond to them. In the process of daily life, humans perform rituals involving other humans and goods. It is the role of design to support and enhance these rituals in order to make them more comfortable and meaningful than they otherwise would be.

The goods of retail stores are the merchandise sold in them. The goods in restaurants are the food items sold in them. The goods in factories are the products fabricated in them. The goods in offices are the pieces of in-

Figure 11.31 Most interior places feature physical goods exhibited, exchanged or consumed in them. In a store it's the merchandise (a), in a deli it's the meats and other consumables (b).

Figure 11.32 The main protagonists of place are, of course, the users. They themselves become part of the scene, adding their physical features, personalities, and behaviors.

formation produced and communicated in them. These goods and the processes behind them (selling, fabricating, communicating) are at the heart of each entity designers provide services to. Understanding, facilitating, and expressing those essences are part of the design task. The goods themselves have a physical presence and often become prominent parts of the visual environment. The nature, size, and packaging of merchandise in a store, for example, can actually dominate the visual field in a store. Figure 11.31 shows the goods in a delicatessen sandwich shop and a gift shop. As you can see, they have their own visual presence and their arrangement requires careful planning and response.

The people who use the spaces we design are also a crucial part of both the drama that unfolds in these places and the look and character of the place. They are the "performers" and come equipped with general scripts according to the role they will perform. While the nature of the scripts is generally known, its specifics are unpredictable. Nevertheless, enough is known about the basic behaviors typically associated with a place to design a responsive solution. The de-

signer of the scene shown in Figure 11.32 knew the basic behaviors involved in the process of checking in at an airplane terminal gate while waiting to board a plane and planned accordingly.

Scripts are similar to sport events where the players, the arena, and the spectators come together, knowing there is going to be a game but not knowing what the specific outcome will be. The designer does not have much control over the people, their attire, or the scripts to be played but responds to them with the goals of facilitating, enriching, and inspiring. People and goods are really the protagonists of the play; the interior environment represents the stage and the props, themselves crucial elements for a smooth and successful play.

Truthfulness and Illusion

Designers have a great deal of power as they play the role of creator for the interior environments they design. With this comes the responsibility to use and manipulate aspects of the physical world in particular ways, depending on preferences and conditions. One interesting point of debate is the role of the designer in reinforcing reality. An important question that emerges from this is: Should designers portray natural physical phenomena truthfully and honestly, or is it okay to manipulate it for effect? Steen Eiler Rasmussen and others have argued for the value of presenting physical phenomena as they are, to correspond with what is natural.[6] If a room has a large volume and hard surfaces, then it has to be, in essence, an acoustically lively room, according to our previous experiences of similar rooms. Sounds will bounce around and linger. The use of excessive sound absorption via carpet and acoustic tile to dampen the sound will produce an unnatural effect. Although all the visual cues are saying, "This is a loud room," the room does not behave accordingly, and we get the sense that there is something wrong with it.

Rasmussen argues the same way for light and color. If a room has a northern exposure, all the natural lighting it receives is diffuse, cool lighting. That is part of the reality of northern rooms. Why alter it? Treatments for that room should, he believes, respect and reinforce its inherent quality. Consequently, lighting and colors should be compatible with the cool natural coloring of the room. Yellowish artificial lighting and warm colors will look out of place and take away from the northern character of the room. The basic premise seems to be to let the room be what it is.

These concerns bring up an interesting point about the merits of being truthful and honest when representing reality. Is it always necessary to be truthful though, especially in the design of interiors, where comfortable conditions often require the manipulation of natural properties, such as daylighting, color, and acoustics? Is it better to have a natural, northern room with inherently lively acoustics, or are the warmth of incandescent lighting and the comfort of quiet footsteps reasons enough to change it, against its natural tendencies? These are difficult questions. This is a good topic for discussion with your peers. What do you think?

Total Environmental Wholeness

Throughout this book, we have been discussing many aspects of design individually, with a special emphasis on the spatial aspects of interior design. This, obvi-ously, is not the way things are presented to you in the real environment. We have presented them as individual topics in order to isolate them and facilitate their understanding. In reality, all these concepts and elements work together, simultaneously, complementing and affecting each other. This brings up the notion of wholeness. The many parts of a project need to both solve the design challenges they are meant to and provide some of the order, enrichment, and expression we have been advocating here. They also need to be perceived as a total unity, one group of many different parts that work cohesively together as a system of specific and consistent intentions. Additionally, they need to be resolved perceptually to achieve a satisfying balance and an overall sense of perceptual correctness.

Beyond this, another type of wholeness should also be conveyed. This is what we call **total environmental wholeness**, the resulting wholeness of environment, occasion, and people operating smoothly and effectively as one indivisible unity. This is the kind of effect achieved when people experience environment, people, and behavior seamlessly as one. On such occasions, environment, people, and actions blend together harmoniously, blurring the perceptual edges that separate them normally, while retaining their inherent, individual characteristics.

Mastery

Your goal as a designer should be to become the best you can be and to truly make a difference in people's lives through the environments you design. There are many levels of competence. It is possible to be a good space planner with a good sense of color and produce clear, efficient, and colorful projects for the enjoyment of all. That alone would make you a fairly competent designer.

What we have been advocating throughout this book goes beyond that. When you try to transcend the limitations of efficient projects with nice finishes and attempt to provide more, then you get into a whole different level of design. It is possible to contribute more to the experiential qualities of projects through thoughtful attention to details in planning and execution. A proper and fitting response to the basic design problem starts the process. If, in addition to a good functional and efficient plan, you can also foster an appropriate sense of order, provide enriching experiences, capture the essence of the organization in the project's expression, and get all the elements used balanced and unified without either lack or excess, you will be designing at a very high level.

Although so much of interior design is concerned with high style and sophistication, it is also important to know how to produce goodness and wholeness for all projects, regardless of their budget and level of sophistication. Poetic dwelling is possible for all budgets, even if it takes greater effort in some cases than others. Not every project is intended to appear in a glossy design magazine. Even those not destined to be fashion statements can be special. To move and inspire its users, a project's quality must be apprehended spontaneously, without intellectual effort; a few simple, unpretentious elements, well placed and arranged, a nice and engaging flow, a detail here and there, a glimpse, a surprise and voilà, you have touched people's emotions.

CASE STUDY
Graphics, Colors, and Materials Providing Expression: Galter Medical Pavilion
Design Firm: Eva Maddox Associates

The Galter Medical Pavilion Project is an excellent example of expression in design. It is a 185 thousand square foot ambulatory health facility that is part of the Swedish Covenant Hospital in Chicago. In addition to the many practical design problems associated with a project like this, there were two crucial and challenging design objectives the owners and designers wished to address. The first one was establishing a distinct identity while embracing the multicultural philosophy of the community-based hospital. The patient population alone spoke 27 different languages. The other principal design objective was to visibly reinforce the hospital's holistic approach to healing, an approach that embodies body, mind, and spirit. In general, a special effort was made to create a facility that felt alive and to celebrate the rich cultural heritage of the surrounding community.

The design solution makes abundant use of graphic patterns, symbols, and signs. The challenge was to come up with symbols that would be understood by the diverse body of patients and staff and that would not be offensive to any one group. The designers used religion, culture, heritage, and nature as inspiration when developing the pattern identity and signage vocabulary.

Shapes, materials, colors, and patterns were selected carefully in order to communicate fitting and desir-

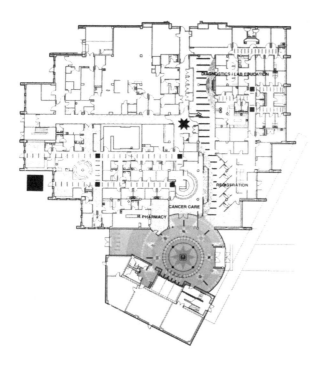

Figure CS11.1 Among other duties, the large circular pattern in the reception area serves to add cohesiveness to a geometrically complex area of the building as seen on this partial floor plan.

Figure CS11.3 View of public corridor area showing blue banding on the floor and blue informational signage.

able messages. Circular patterning was used recurrently throughout the facility. It is symbolic of the Judeo-Christian heritage of the hospital and of the circle as a continuum of life. The strong circular geometry and overall patterning in the first floor entry area is also a good example of this kind of patterning performing multiple duties. In addition to making a powerful first impression; establishing an image of open-

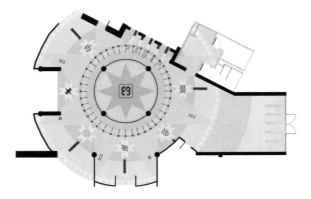

Figure CS11.2 The floor pattern is rich in meaning and visually cheerful and attractive. Superimposed on the circle are layers of meaning: the circle of Christianity, multicultural symbols, and directional indicators.

ness, warmth, and professionalism; and supplying rich symbolism, the assembly also serves to center, organize, and unify an otherwise geometrically complex, and disorienting, part of the building (Figure CS11.1). At a more detailed level, iconic graphics on the floor serve to direct patients and visitors to their target destinations (Figure CS11.2).

The materials and colors used draw from common characteristics of the Swedish tradition. Brick, so common in Swedish construction, is used on the exterior and also inside the lobby, elevator lobbies, and restrooms. The blond finish used for the woodwork throughout is also characteristically Scandinavian. Blue and yellow, the predominant hues of the project, are taken from the Swedish flag. Yellow is used extensively in the lobby, where the patterned terrazzo flooring and the extensive blond wood paneling contribute much to the overall friendliness conveyed by the space. Blue is used as directional signage inside on the floor (as stripes), on accent vertical surfaces, and on general signage throughout (Figure CS11.3).

Color and graphics are used throughout to create easy-to-identify pathways and to highlight key points of service. They communicate at various levels, ranging from direct identification via text to iconic communication via signs associated with different floors and, at the same time, different elements such as wind, rain, and water. The iconic vocabulary consists of simple but memorable symbols, featuring simple shapes such as spirals, stars, and waves (Figure CS11.4). These appear stenciled, painted, or inlaid on both vertical and horizontal surfaces throughout the project. See Figure CS11.5.

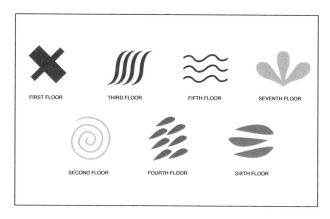

FIRST FLOOR

THIRD FLOOR

FIFTH FLOOR

SEVENTH FLOOR

SECOND FLOOR

FOURTH FLOOR

SIXTH FLOOR

Figure CS11.4 The iconic vocabulary is simple but memorable.

Figure CS11.5 View of reception area showing the prominent use of graphics on the floor.

What is truly remarkable about this project is the seamless integration of architecture, interior design elements, finishes, and graphics to create a clear, cheerful, and dignified environment that expresses meanings connected to its user population and a certain attitude about their holistic and friendly way of conducting business.

Review

Summary

Space and its components do not occur in a vacuum. The effects of space are modified and complemented by texture, light, pattern, and color, not to mention such non-visual contributors as sounds, thermal qualities, and smells. All these factors together add up to the total experience of interior space.

Ambient elements contribute much to users' moods and sense of comfort in the environment. The brightness level, the size and number of light fixtures, and their distribution in space produce countless variations and effects. Light can enhance form but it can also reduce perception of three-dimensionality if used incorrectly.

Light can create or accentuate focal points or emphasize an entire segment of wall or ceiling. Furthermore, attention can be directed to a specific area in space through the use of contrast between the space and adjoining surfaces and areas. Light is also a good space modifier to use to create engaging sequences.

In addition to artificial light, daylight is an important modifier of interior spaces. Designers have to make important choices about the location of specific rooms, functions, and objects in relation to windows. Additionally, the selections made for window treatments and other light-blocking elements near the perimeter have significant effects on the qualities of a room.

Hearing is the second most prominent human sense. The acoustic properties of spaces can produce subtle effects in interior environments. The common tendency is to add sound-absorptive materials to dampen the noise level, but designers need to remember that certain spaces are meant to be acoustically lively and that acoustic variety can help produce enriching experiences.

Two other nonvisual ambient elements are important in modifying place. Although, the thermal environment is not under the full control of interior designers, with the cooperation of the project's mechanical engineer, spaces can be made purposefully colder or warmer for variety and effect. With the thermal environment, though, it is imperative to stay within the client's comfort zone. The final ambient element is smell. With smell, the object is not to produce particular smells but to respond to the desirable existing smells produced in a given environment. Accentuating and directing positive and meaningful smells in places like restaurants, perfume shops, and cookie shops is a powerful way of highlighting some of the pleasant qualities associated with those places.

Interior elements serving, primarily decorative functions include finishes, colors, ornaments, and details. The finish palette chosen for a project is often one of the principal determinants of its stylistic direction. Finishes require much attention, both individually and collectively. Variables include the inherent qualities and connotations of individual materials and the subtle variations produced by the methods of fabrication, cutting, or finishing. Materials also have qualities associated with our tactile sense, such as their relative hardness, texture, and temperature.

Color is one of the most important elements in interiors. It is so prominent visually that it can contribute much to the enhancement of order, enrichment, and expression in the interior environment. Color has the power to evoke strong emotions in people. We also develop learned associations with colors. Different colors have specific associations with temperature, weight, gender, groups, and even countries.

Using color in interiors requires proper knowledge of its properties, as well as a sense of what is appropriate for a given client, program, and existing physical context. While color theory has good information to offer regarding the effects of color and the ways of achieving color harmony, it is crucial for designers to realize that all the rules can be broken. The exact colors used, the relative size of colored areas, their location in relation to each other, their texture, and the lighting conditions all come into play to produce infinite effects depending on the combinations used.

Ornament and detail are to interior design what short detailed strokes are to a painting. Together they add up to give the final piece much of its flavor. Ornamentation involves the application of some nonstructural decorative embellishment to all of a design or part of it. Detailing is inherent in the fabrication of a piece, whether a wall, a light fixture, or a cabinet. Together with the materials and the furniture, details play a major role in establishing the visual character of a place.

Goods and people are two important ingredients of a place not controlled by the designer. They tend to have a reciprocal effect on design and affect the total experience of place. The merchandise at the store, the food at the restaurant, the clerk, the waiter, and the office receptionist all become important components of the scene and the drama that unfolds in it.

Chapter Questions

1. What factors of lighting contribute to the mood of a space?
2. What type of lighting arrangement is best for enhancing three-dimensional form? Why?
3. What types of lighting arrangements are not good enhancers of three-dimensional form? Why?
4. Name three different strategies to create focal areas with light
5. How can light be used to create an interesting sequence? Give an example.
6. Name three things designers can do to respond to and use daylight for effect.
7. Which acoustic concept is particularly important in relations to the acoustic properties of individual spaces?

8. What manipulations in interiors help to dampen sound in a space?

9. What manipulations in interiors help to produce acoustically lively spaces?

10. Give one example of how a designer can manipulate the thermal environment for effect.

11. Give one example of how to take advantage of the pleasant smells inherent in a project type.

12. How does the pattern modularity of finish materials affect the look produced?

13. Name three ways to use the textural qualities of finishes for effect.

14. Name five compositional considerations related to color that can be manipulated for effect.

15. How can color be used to counteract the effects of dense and complex spaces?

16. How can color be used to counteract the effects of plain spaces?

17. What are some of the dangers related to color application?

18. How does detailing relate to the rest of the interior environment?

19. What did this chapter refer to as the "goods" in a space?

20. Are there instances when you think it is appropriate to contradict the natural, inherent properties of places by, for example, making a north-facing room warm and cozy, instead of letting it reflect the natural coolness of northern light? Explain your answer.

Endnotes

1 Unwin, Simon. *Analysing Architecture*, (Routledge: London, 1997) p. 25.

2 Zelanski, Paul, & Mary Pat Fischer. *Design Principles and Problems*, (Harcourt Brace College Publishers: Fort Worth, 1996) p. 238.

3 Gauldie, Sinclair. *The Appreciation of the Arts: Architecture*, (Oxford University Press: London, 1972) p. 139.

4 Tate, Allen, & Ray C. Smith. *Interior Design in the 20th Century*, (Harper and Row: New York, 1986) p. 152.

5 Abercrombie, Stanley. *A Philosophy of Interior Design*, (Harper and Row: New York, 1990) p. 113.

6 Rasmussen, Steen Eiler. *Experiencing Architecture*, (MIT Press: Cambridge, 1993) pp. 218–219, 223, 235–236.

APPENDIX 1

Eighteen Alternatives to the Carpet Border

There is a tendency among many designers, especially but not exclusively novices, to resort to the same solution when attempting to add interest to the floor (usually the carpet) of a room such as a conference room. That solution is what we call "the proverbial carpet border" and is usually manifested by a band around the room. It could be thought of as framing around the room and comes from a tendency many people have to always put a frame around things. Our aim here is to give you some alternatives to this common but limiting tendency.

Figure A1.1a–c shows three common variations of the proverbial carpet border: the simple band around the room (Figure A1.1a), the band with accents on the corners (Figure A1.1b), and the band with hexagon-like ends (Figure A1.1c). These are simplistic, not very sophisticated, but show a desire to add pattern to an otherwise homogeneous flooring. Our first three alternatives are shown in Figure A1.1d–f. Their aim is still to define a rectangular area centered in the room but they accomplish it by using different means: defining the desired area by a rectangle with a contrasting color or value (Figure A1.1d), with a field of stripes (Figure A1.1e), or with a field of squares (Figure A1.1f).

Figure A1.1g–i, in turn, provides three variations to the ones just presented. In Figure A1.1g the colors or values are reversed to accentuate the perimeter instead of the rectangle. We recognize this may be considered another case of the proverbial border. Figure A1.1h is

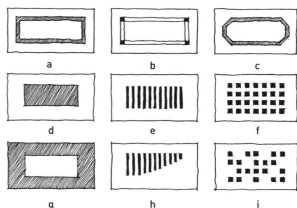

Figure A1.1 Basic carpet borders: rectangular band (a), rectangular band with accent on four corners (b), band with angled ends (c), dark rectangle on light field (d), stripes (e), field of aligned squares (f), light rectangle on dark field (g), progressively shorter stripes (h), random squares (i).

similar to Figure A1.1e except the shape defined by the lines is no longer a rectangle (one side progresses diagonally). In Figure A1.1i, the squares, unlike the regularly spaced ones in Figure A1.1f, are fragmented from a regular and dense center to a dispersed perimeter.

The approach to our design challenge is handled differently in Figure A1.2. The six alternatives shown here are variations on a common theme. These do not attempt to define a rectangular area in the space. The approach here is irregular and asymmetrical. In Figure A1.2a a wide strip is provided along one of the long ends of the room. Figure A1.2b is similar but the strip is along one of the short sides. Meanwhile, Figure A1.2c features a combination of the previous two,

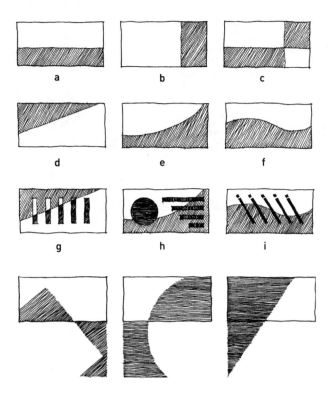

a   b   c

d   e   f

g   h   i

Figure A1.2 Alternatives to borders: wide band along long side (a), wide band along short side (b), combination of a and b (c), corner diagonal field (d), sweeping curve (e), undulating curve (f), corner diagonal with stripes (g), sweeping curve with circle and uneven stripes (h), undulating curve with diagonal stripes and accents (i).

Figure A1.3 Patterns that go beyond the borders: angled rectangle (a), curve (b), diagonal (c).

having strips along one long and one short side with a contrasting intersecting area at the corner. Figure A1.2d–f features more irregular approaches using diagonal (Figure A1.2d) and curvilinear (Figure A1.2e and f) shapes. Notice the differences produced by the two curvilinear solutions. The different radii and orientation of the curves produce quite different effects.

Figure A1.2g–i provides three more variations. They become more complex. These add a layer of shapes on top of the patterns shown in Figure A1.2 d–f. The added shapes clearly become figures on a two-toned field. Figure A1.2g adds a series of stripes. The two other solutions add uneven stripes and a large circle (Figure A1.2h), and diagonal stripes and points (Figure A1.2i).

Finally, Figure A1.3 shows an entirely different approach. Here, the conception of the context is expanded. The area to which a pattern is applied is no longer confined by the boundaries of the original space (even if they are walls). The resulting shapes within the room (or space) are a segment of a larger pattern that continues beyond the space. This is a powerful design device

useful to unify spaces in projects where it is okay to go beyond the borders. The variations shown are three of the many possible. Figure A1.3a shows what appears to be one end of a rectangle. A segment of a curve is shown in Figure A1.3b. In Figure A1.3c, a diagonally shaped strip starts narrow inside the room and moves out, while getting progressively wider. Notice that in these cases it is not necessary to complete (i.e., close) the shape. By just showing enough of it, the mind can read the shape. These applications work best when it is possible to see the shape continuing from one side to the other. Therefore, in cases where the two sides are separated by a wall, it is a good idea to use glass or have an opening near the point where the inside and outside meet so the effect can be perceived.

Nine Alternatives to the Checkerboard Pattern

When it comes to a modular pattern with tile, nothing is as popular as the checkerboard pattern. While not an unattractive pattern, it has become the default pattern for many designers. Creating patterns with tile is one of the most enjoyable and, potentially, creative design activities possible. It is necessary, however, to move beyond the checkerboard pattern. The possibilities are endless. Here are nine ideas for starters.

Figure A1.4 shows the well-known and widely used checkerboard pattern. You are likely to be familiar with it. Contrasting tiles are alternated horizontally and vertically to create a textured field. A popular alternative to the checkerboard pattern is one that places diamonds (or diagonal squares) at the intersec-

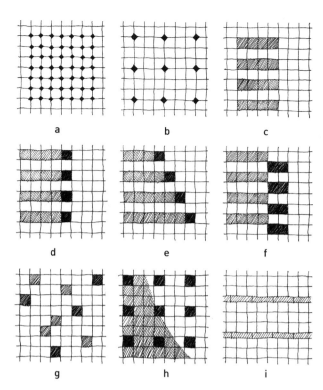

Figure A1.5 Alternatives to the checkerboard pattern: diamond (or inverted square) at each joint (a), diamond (or inverted square) at wider spacing (b), even parallel bands (c), even parallel bands with accents at ends (d), uneven parallel bands with accents at ends (e), even parallel bands with short accent bands at in-between spaces (f), random squares (g), evenly spaced squares over two-toned field with curve (h), bands of contrasting width and finish (i).

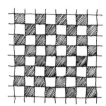

Figure A1.4 The checkerboard pattern

tions of tiles. These can be placed at every intersection (Figure A1.5a) or at wider intervals (Figure A1.5b). These two patterns, like the checkerboard, normally occur uniformly throughout—that is, the entire area is treated the same.

Patterns created with tiles do not necessarily have to be uniform throughout the entire area. Nor do they have to be of the alternating type (black tile, white tile, black tile). It is possible to create lines with tiles by placing several tiles next to each other on a contrasting field. These can be simple uniform bands as shown in Figure A1.5c or they can have accent pieces at the ends as shown in Figure A1.5d. The next two patterns show variations of this idea. In Figure A1.5e the length of the strips vary, getting uniformly longer to create a diagonal slant. In Figure A1.5f, the accent pieces at the ends are two tiles wide and they are shifted to occur on the in-between strips.

A random pattern is used in Figure A1.5g. In a random pattern, accent tiles are placed as if they had been sprinkled on the floor from above. The density can vary. Accent tiles can have a prominent presence or be sparse. Also the density does not need to be uniform throughout. This strategy relies on a painterly eye to achieve good results. The pattern in Figure A1.5h shows two things. First, it is possible to spread apart a uniform pattern of squares. When you do that, they read more as figures than the background. The other thing that takes place in that pattern is the division of the background into a light and a dark zone that meet along a curved line.

Finally, Figure A1.5i illustrates the fact that you are not required to keep the same tile module throughout.

Although the field probably needs to be composed of uniform pieces for practicality, accent bands can be of a contrasting size. It is even possible to use contrasting finishes of the same color tile (or stone) for subtle differentiation. A layout that uses narrow bands of a roughly textured stone against a smoother field of larger tiles can be quite pleasing. The subtle tone-on-tone effects produced by the variations between the two sizes and finishes can produce a restrained, elegant effect.

One last note: remember that just because the majority of tile and stone available commercially is 12" × 12" does not mean that you have to accept this size as a given. This is one example where optimal practical size does not equal the optimal perceptual size. While the 12" square module looks fine in some applications (mostly residential), the module looks out of scale in many commercial applications where an 18" × 18" or a 24" × 24" module would better com-

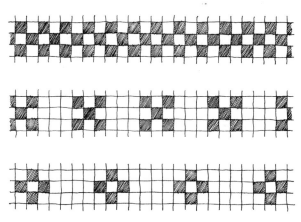

Figure A1.7 Checkerboard band (a), four corners plus center (b), cross pattern (c).

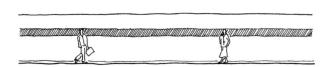

Figure A1.6 Elevation of band on the wall

plement the scale of the space. Similarly, many instances call for the use of smaller modules such as 8" × 8", 4" × 4", and small mosaic tiles. In some projects it is even possible to have the installer cut tiles to a custom size. You may, for instance, want to use rows of 12" × 3" strips. In that case, the installer (or factory) would cut 12" × 12" pieces into four strips to meet your specifications. Cutting tiles requires additional labor and expense and is, obviously, out of the question for low-budget projects. However, it is done frequently on high-end projects.

Six Variations of the Eye-Level Decorative Tile Band

The eye-level decorative tile band has limited applications but is seen frequently in places such as public restrooms and hallways. It usually occurs in places with a field of tile, although it can also be set into a drywall wall as an accent. It is another example of the type of application that gives designers a chance to create meaningful expression, and yet they often resort to simplistic solutions. The application requires some length of uninterrupted wall (Figure A1.6). Although it is normally placed somewhere around eye level, there is no reason it couldn't be done on the upper section of walls in cases where the wall is seen from a distance, as a focal feature.

Figure A1.7 shows three examples of simple patterns. Figure A1.7a, the checkerboard, is well known and needs no elaboration. It is not the most imaginative pattern but it is playful in a simple way and serves to engage

the mind. Figure A1.7b and c are similar to each other. They both use a repeating pattern spaced regularly. The pattern itself fits in a square defined by nine tile spaces (three vertical and three horizontal). Figure A1.7b consists of four corners and a center. Figure A1.7c consists of a top, bottom, left, and right. These patterns, although not very imaginative either, are seen frequently and provide some interest along the band.

We recognize that designers seldom have much time to devote to such tasks as designing tile patterns. However, it is possible to achieve interesting effects without much more effort than that required to do the simple patterns above. Five reminders shall serve to multiply the patterns you can do quickly. They are:

1. Not all accent pieces have to be of the same color or value.
2. You can combine pieces to create lines.
3. Rhythm intervals can vary.
4. You can combine pieces to create a contrasting background.
5. You can combine the horizontal and the vertical.

Figure A1.8a features a simple pattern featuring a rhythm of aligned short light lines and dark points. It is not complex, yet displays the ability of the designer to think in more than one modality simultaneously (points and lines). The pattern shown in Figure A1.8b highlights a background band by using a contrasting tone. It also shows an example of a simple irregular interval of accent pieces (alternating single and paired accent pieces). Figure A1.8c features long lines and paired dark accent pieces. In this pattern, vertical

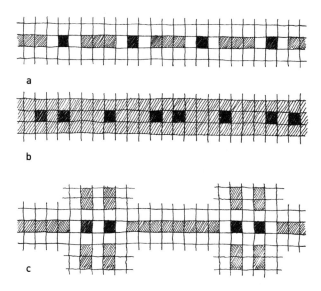

a

b

c

Figure A1.8 Line, square, line (a), contrasting with irregular intervals of single and paired square (b), line, pair of squares, line, plus vertical bands (c).

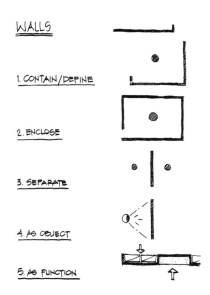

WALLS

1. CONTAIN/DEFINE

2. ENCLOSE

3. SEPARATE

4. AS OBJECT

5. AS FUNCTION

Figure A1.9 The many functions of walls: contain (a), enclose (b), separate (c), as object (d), as function (e).

bands intersect the horizontal band. The exact location of vertical bands would have to be determined to suit the circumstances of the application. They can occur regularly or at strategic locations. Our example shows them coinciding with the locations of the paired accent pieces.

These are just a few of the possibilities to get you started. Using the five reminders above, it is possible to create many different combinations of background, lines, and points using different lengths, tones, and intervals. Give them a try.

Walls, Ceilings, and Columns

In the course of designing interior space, designers are always having to deal with walls, ceilings, and columns. Floors are also one of the enclosing surfaces, although floors have limited opportunities for articulation. They simply need to be flat and even so everyone, regardless of physical ability, can move unimpeded from place to place. Walls, ceilings, and columns, on the other hand, present opportunities for articulation.

It is common for the novice designer to think of walls as something that happens when you need a room, of ceilings as something you need in order to hide ugly mechanical ductwork and suspend lights from, and of columns as things that are just there and about which you can do nothing. Well, that is just part

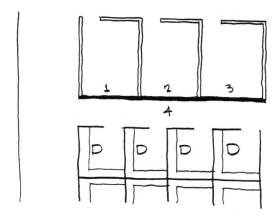

Figure A1.10 Walls have many sides. The dark wall shown is seen independently from three offices and from the open area outside the offices.

of the story. There is much more to these important spatial elements.

Walls do more than just enclose rooms. They also contain, define, separate, decorate, and can actually do work for you (Figure A1.9). Most individual walls are experienced as at least two, frequently more, realities. The darkened wall shown in Figure A1.10 is experienced as four different realities; three individual ones from inside the three rooms, and one from the other side of the offices. In other words, that particular wall could potentially have four totally different expressions! Since walls have, not one but two sides, proper consideration must be given to the appearance and effect of each side. Although walls normally conform to the thickness produced by the particular combination

THE 2 SIDES OF WALLS

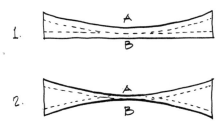

Figure A1.11 Walls have two sides. They may be straight, angled, curved, wide, or narrow.

EXPRESSIVE WALLS.

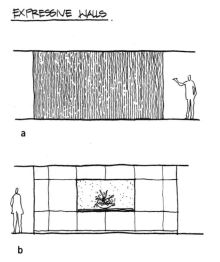

Figure A1.13 Walls can be expressive through surface treatment (a), or articulation and content (b).

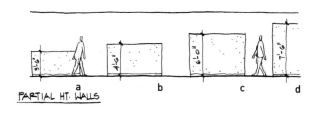

PARTIAL HT. WALLS

Figure A1.14 Walls are not always full-height. Partial-height walls however, come in many heights.

WALLS

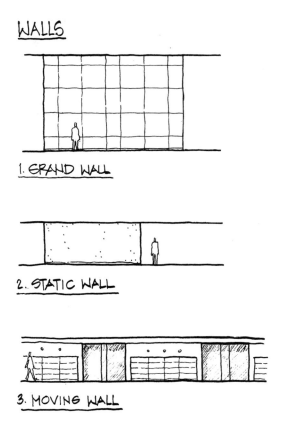

1. GRAND WALL

2. STATIC WALL

3. MOVING WALL

Figure A1.12 Some of the many types of walls: the grand wall (a), the static wall (b), the moving wall (c).

of the materials used and their widths and thicknesses, not all walls need to be of uniform depth. That's right! Either one, or both, sides of the wall can take off and expand to meet your design intentions (Figure A1.11).

Walls embody different personalities according to the roles they assume (Figure A1.12) and the treatment given them by the designer (Figure A1.13). They certainly do not have an obligation to extend to the ceiling (at least the non-structural walls normally used in interiors). So, they can be of any height and shape you want. Different heights create different conditions (Figure A1.14), as do different shapes (Figure A1.15). You can even put a wall to work for you. Figure A1.16 suggests just a few of the many possibilities.

Some walls do have to extend all the way to the ceiling (or beyond) to meet particular enclosure and privacy requirements. Even in many of those cases, however, it is possible to maintain some visual continuity and light penetration through the use of glass. Even when privacy is required, a modest amount of glass can be used to achieve continuity between sides

WALLS - SHAPES/FORMS

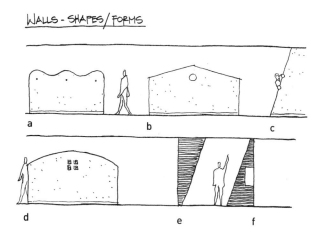

Figure A1.15 Some of the many shapes walls can assume: undulating (a), gable (b), diagonal end (c), semicircular (d), tilted (e).

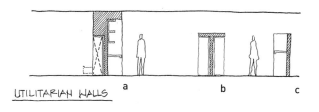

UTILITARIAN WALLS

Figure A1.16 Walls can be utilitarian and incorporate files (b), work counters (c), or both (a).

TRANSPARENCY

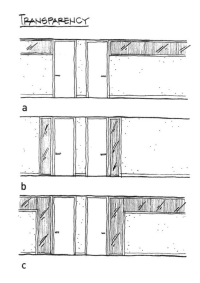

Figure A1.17 Walls can let light from the perimeter in through clerestory glass bands (a), sidelights (b), or both (c).

Figure A1.18 Large areas of glass can be subdivided minimally (a), moderately (b), or extensively (c).

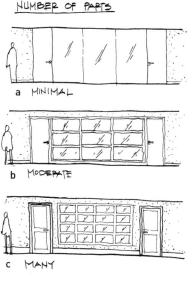

NUMBER OF PARTS

a MINIMAL

b MODERATE

c MANY

Figure A1.19 The weight of the trim framing window walls can be minimal (a), light (b), or heavy (c).

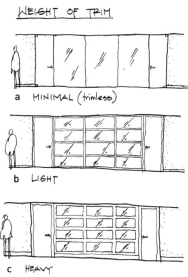

WEIGHT OF TRIM

a MINIMAL (trimless)

b LIGHT

c HEAVY

Figure A1.20 Ceiling height variations can produce many different effects.

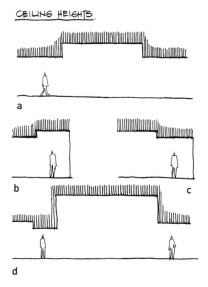

CEILING HEIGHTS

(Figure A1.17). Glass can also cover large areas to produce major connections between sides. The detailing of how this happens, by the way, presents opportunities for many different design expressions. The way glass panels are subdivided creates different looks with their own personalities (Figure A1.18) as do the weight and material of the trim used (Figure A1.19).

CEILING ARTICULATION

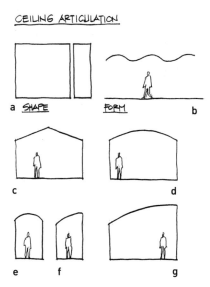

a SHAPE   FORM   b

c   d

e   f   g

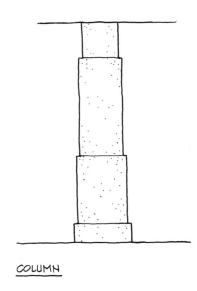

COLUMN

Figure A1.21 The articulation of the ceiling is one of the designer's main tools. Ceilings can be subdivided to define areas (a), undulated (b), gabled (c), or vaulted (d) and (e). Shapes don't always have to be completed symmetrically. It is possible to have, for instance, partial vaults (f) and (g).

Figure A1.24 Columns can be articulated by varying the widths of their different sections. There are, of course, many other ways of articulating columns.

COLUMNS

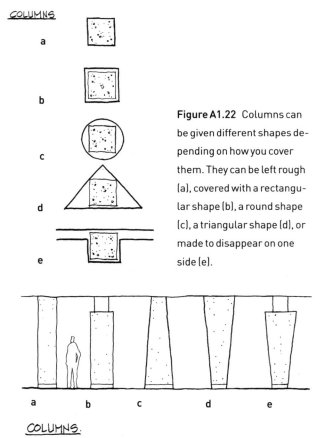

a

b

c

d

e

Figure A1.22 Columns can be given different shapes depending on how you cover them. They can be left rough (a), covered with a rectangular shape (b), a round shape (c), a triangular shape (d), or made to disappear on one side (e).

Ceilings can also perform expressive functions. In addition to the many effects that can be produced by ceiling height variations (Figure A1.20), the shape of ceilings can also be expressive. As Figure A1.21 shows, undulating ceilings, shallow gables and vaults (half and full) are some of the possibilities.

Finally, structural columns, while present and impractical to remove, offer opportunities for expression. Depending on how you cover them (shapes and materials used) different effects can be produced. Figure A1.22 shows different approaches in plan, while Figure A1.23 displays different shapes in section. The fact that other effects are possible through detailing and articulation is suggested by the telescoping column shown in Figure A1.24.

a   b   c   d   e

COLUMNS.

Figure A1.23 The shape of covered columns can assume many shapes: fully covered and full height (a), partial height (b), leaning (c), and (d), or spreading and partial height (e).

APPENDIX 2

Considerations for Office Design

Resolving an office design project requires a good understanding of the many units in the office, their roles, and their relationship to each other. The first step of any office design solution is to carefully place all elements for optimal function. The second step is to organize these into a coherent system of open and enclosed areas. Below we present some useful considerations about the organization of open and enclosed areas. Afterwards we will share a useful conceptual model for space planning based on the kind of work people do.

Office design projects normally take place within the shell of an office building in a business district (usually downtown) or an office park. Typical floors consist of a core (usually somewhere near the center of the floor) containing elevators, exit stairs, mechanical and electrical rooms, and restrooms, with open space around it, which is leased to businesses.

Solids and Voids

One of the most important design tasks for office projects is the previously mentioned disposition of solids (enclosed spaces) and voids (open spaces). Private offices, conference rooms, storage rooms, coffee rooms, and copy/supplies rooms are enclosed spaces. We will consider the first two "people rooms" and the others "service rooms." Additionally, we have open spaces. These include corridors and common open areas with systems furniture.

Offices vary widely. Some offices (e.g., law firms) are very hierarchical and consist mostly of enclosed private offices. Other offices (e.g., a customer service center) consist of mainly open space with systems furniture. Below, we consider various generic office design scenarios within a hypothetical office building shell, and point out some important planning considerations.

Figure A2.1 shows four different schemes within the same building shell. Figure A2.1a and b are for offices requiring many private offices along the perimeter, such as in the case of a law firm. There are three main things we want to point out. First, if at all possible, leave certain areas open to the exterior to allow natural light into and views out from the space. You don't need a lot of them, just a few well-placed ones will do the trick. Second, don't use window space for service rooms. Put those inside and try to integrate them with the core. The core is a solid mass that is already there. In cases like these, it often makes sense to grow the core by continuing its shape outward (as shown at the ends) or by creating a carefully conceived appendix that sticks out (as shown along one side in Figure A2.1b). The third thing we want to point out is the need for articulating long walls. Where you have long stretches of walls, as in these examples, they will appear flat and monotonous unless you articulate the plane to provide variety. The guidelines given in these two examples are not so much exact prescriptions of how to do it, as just reminders to do something to articulate these long planes.

Figure A2.1c and d show two schemes for a very different kind of project: the mostly open project. This type of project may require a few enclosed offices but usually has some requirements for the usual service

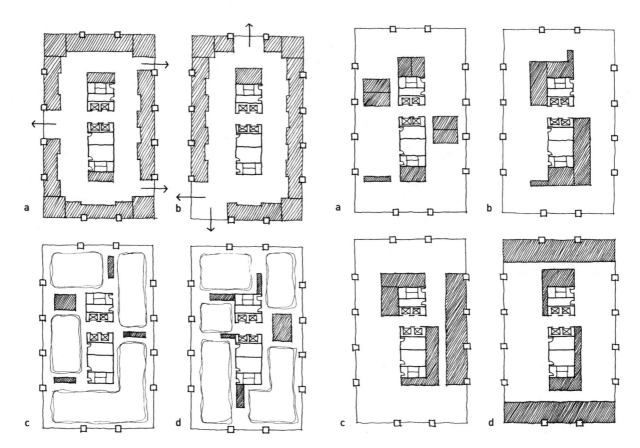

Figure A2.1 Solids and voids in perimeter-office-heavy scenarios (a) and (b), and mostly open scenarios (c) and (d).

Figure A2.2 Solids and voids in scenarios with a moderate number of internal offices and rooms (a) and (b), and scenarios with moderate numbers of perimeter offices (c) and (d).

rooms (or spaces). The problem with the mostly open plan is its tendency to have too much openness, making it perceptually uncomfortable, disorienting, and potentially monotonous. A useful strategy is to use the few required rooms or service areas to subdivide the floor into more manageable neighborhoods. Figure A2.1c shows free-floating elements. It features a floating room and a few narrow service walls. These don't need to be full height, but should be tall enough to achieve separation between the areas. They may incorporate files, work counters, coffee areas, copy areas, and so on. Figure A2.1d shows a similar approach but, in this case, many of the elements are attached to the core at strategic locations. Notice how in these two schemes, the floor is divided into four or five areas of more comfortable sizes and proportions than if the entire floor was left open.

Now we will consider cases that feature a balanced mix of open and enclosed areas. We start with two cases requiring a few people rooms along the perimeter. In other words, there are just a few of those rooms,

but they have to be on the perimeter, by the windows. In these cases, a useful strategy is to group the offices and put them all on one or more sides, so that the other sides can remain fully open. See Figure A2.2. The idea is to let the open areas have significant uninterrupted exposure to natural light and views. Notice that service areas are still incorporated as attachments to the core. As seen in Figure A2.2a and b, their size, proportion, and location produce different leftover open spaces.

Figure A2.2c and d show two schemes with balanced open and enclosed areas where the enclosed spaces don't have to be on the perimeter. The scheme in Figure A2.2c incorporates all the rooms (people and service) into the core. It is possible, as shown, to extend fin walls beyond the main shape if one desires to give an open area a better spatial definition. Finally, Figure A2.2d shows a scheme featuring two floating blocks consisting of back to back (although they could just as well be single) rows of offices. Their strategic placement in this case also utilizes these masses as

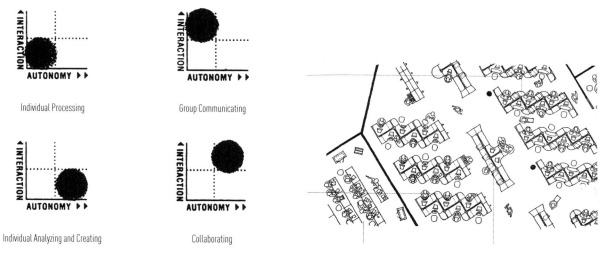

Figure A2.3 Four work processes: low interaction/low autonomy (a), high interaction/low autonomy (b), low interaction/high autonomy (c), high interaction/high autonomy (d).

Figure A2.4 The look of an individual processing work setting

space dividers. The service areas in this scheme are attached to the ends of the core and there is a floating dividing wall that may incorporate some utilitarian function.

Work Processes and Space Planning

Most office projects have some open areas that utilize systems furniture. In fact, many projects almost exclusively consist of open planning. Open space planning does not consist of generic rows of equal cubicles stretching over vast open areas in buildings, although we have seen examples like that. Open space planning has become quite sophisticated, with strategies and customizations to cater to every conceivable working process. Steelcase, the giant systems furniture manufacturer, provides us with a useful model for thinking about work processes and devising appropriate corresponding design solutions.

The model considers the work a person or group performs in terms of two variables: interaction and autonomy. Somebody's work may require much interaction with others or it may be solitary, individual work. It may also range from the autonomy the worker has over such things as to how, when, and where the work is done. Putting the two variables together along vertical and horizontal axes we can see the four possible combinations (Figure A2.3). These define four different types of work approaches requiring different design responses. A designation has been given to each of the four work processes. They are described below.

Individual Processing (Low Interaction, Low Autonomy)

This type of work involves pragmatic, repetitive tasks like inputting data, preparing reports, filing, and doing repetitive telephone tasks. It's individual, steady, and repetitive work. Required individual work spaces are usually compact, with some but not much privacy. The overall space density is usually high. Telemarketing and customer service centers are good examples of this work process. Figure A2.4 shows a generic example of an office area planned using this type of approach.

Group Communicating (High Interaction, Low Autonomy)

This type of work process, unlike the one above, requires the sharing, transferring, and/or exchange of information. Although the key word is sharing, workers and groups still require a certain amount of privacy. Also, workers are not sharing the entire time. Their work could be described as individual work with frequent exchanges. In these cases, it is crucial to understand the extent of the physical sharing in order to optimize the balance between openness and enclosure. Figure A2.5 shows an open area planned to facilitate

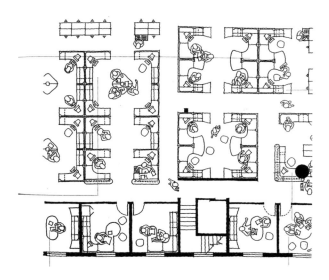

Figure A2.5 The look of a group-communicating work setting

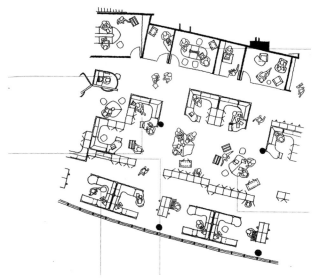

Figure A2.6 The look of a collaborating work setting

interactions among groups of four and between one group and adjacent ones.

Individual Analyzing and Creating (Low Interaction, High Autonomy)

This type of work is individual and intense. It's strategic, cerebral, and focused and requires an environment that facilitates concentration (i.e., privacy). It normally implies a private office, although it is possible to create conditions favorable for this kind of work with systems furniture by using tall privacy panels and locations away from the main flow.

Collaborating (High Interaction, High Autonomy)

This type of work also requires cerebral analysis and creative thinking, except a good amount of it is done with others. You could think of it as group problem solving. Not all the work is done in groups, though. Consequently, this type of work requires both individual privacy and one or more spaces to come together. Figure A2.6 shows a team area that features both individual work stations and a prominent central space where one or more groups can come together.

These distinctions between different work processes give us important insights that we can use to better design individual open areas. These open areas often accommodate varied and complex work requirements and become small microcosms in themselves. Using

the proper type of individual workstation, team clusters, and relationship between teams or clusters are all imperative to enhance the productivity of the office.

Twenty Retail Store Partis

Store design offers some of the best opportunities for creativity and expression in the design field. The main goal of stores is to present merchandise in such a way that makes shoppers want to buy. Crucial design aspects are the effective display of merchandise, the use of interior design to reinforce a particular image or identity, and the effective movement of people through the store.

It is possible to produce, even for a small store space, a wide variety of expressions just by varying the placement and orientation of fixtures and other space elements. Below, we present 20 different parti diagrams for a small retail store. The goal is not to give you specific models to copy but to present examples of the basic typological possibilities for you to study in order to develop the kind of thinking that will help you come up with powerful organizational ideas for your store projects. Keep in mind that generating a strong scheme is only the first step in designing a store and that there are many important design features at smaller scales, such as the materials used, the way they

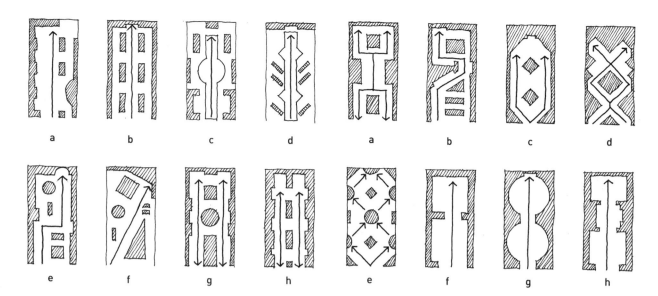

Figure A2.7 Eight store partis: linear asymmetrical (a), linear symmetrical (b), linear, strongly defined and symmetrical with dominant center (c), linear, strongly defined and symmetrical with two nodes (d), two-segment offset (e), diagonal (f), prominently occupied central axis (g), occupied central axis (h).

Figure A2.8 Eight more store partis: straight-angle hybrid (a), straight and diagonal hybrid (b), diagonal and straight combination (c), diagonal (d), diagonal bounce scheme (e), two-compartment off-center (f), two circular compartments (g), three rectangular compartments (h).

are detailed, the fixtures used, and their exact placement. Nevertheless, a strong scheme is crucial to the design of any store. Without one, no matter how beautiful the materials, the detailing, and everything else, the design is not likely to work well as a whole.

Figure A2.7 shows the first eight diagrams. A2.7a–d features organizations with central, linear circulation. The circulation in Figure A2.7a and b is determined by the available central space left by the placement of displays and fixtures. Figure A2.7a is asymmetrical and the circulation spine is just left of center. Figure A2.7b is perfectly symmetrical and is strongly defined by the regularly placed fixtures on either side. Figure A2.7c and d are also central schemes. The central spine on these is defined not by leftover central space but by some architectural device, such as the floor material and/or the shape of the ceiling above. The shapes of these spines are the main components of these two schemes. Everything else is organized around this dominant central organizational element. Notice that other than the linear aspect of circulation these two schemes expand to create nodes, a central circular one in Figure A2.7c and two square (rotated) ones in Figure A2.7d.

The two schemes shown in Figure A2.7e and f feature looser, less formal, central spaces. In Figure A2.7e, circulation is not straight and axial like the

ones before, but is offset around the center of the store and moves to the left side, from which it continues towards a focal end at the rear of the store. Movement in Figure A2.7f is diagonal from front to back with objects and displays also placed diagonally on either side of, and helping to define, the circulation spine. Figure A2.7g and h feature, not circulation, but displays along a central axis. Circulation occurs on either side, along the space defined between the linear central displays and the wall displays. They are very similar except that, in Figure A2.7g, the central fixtures are dominant, while in Figure A2.7h, they complement the sides rather than imposing dominance.

Eight more schemes are shown in Figure A2.8. Figure A2.8a–c are hybrid schemes. Figure A2.8a proceeds from a central display with circulation to either side, to central circulation, and then back to a central display with circulation around it. Meanwhile, Figure A2.8b is a combination of linear asymmetrical movement along the left side and a diagonally oriented central area. Figure A2.8c combines symmetrical diagonal movement in the front and back with linear two-sided circulation in the central zone. The next two diagrams feature diagonal bounce schemes. These force you to move diagonally from featured area to featured area. Figure A2.8d is organized around a main central element and features many pockets

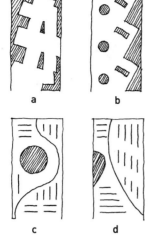

Figure A2.9 Four inflected partis: diagonal/straight combination (a), saw tooth (b), undulating curve (c), sweeping curve (d).

strategically placed along the side walls. Figure A2.8e is organized around a series of focal points, both along the center and the two side walls.

The next three schemes are examples of compartmentalized space. In these, the store is subdivided into explicit compartments, almost like rooms. Figure A2.8f is a simple two-compartment scheme with circulation along one side. Figure A2.8g and h are both symmetrical and axial with circulation occurring down the middle. Figure A2.8g features two circular compartments with a transition passage at the center of the store. Figure A2.8h is a three-compartment arrangement featuring a small central compartment.

The geometry of schemes, of course, can be inflected. Schemes can be curved, angled, or otherwise inflected as long as the move is compatible with the identity of the store. The four diagrams shown in Figure A2.9 are examples of inflected schemes. Figure A2.9a is angled on one side and straight on the other. Figure A2.9b features both angles and free-floating shapes prominently. Figure A2.9c and d are curvilinear. Figure A2.9c features an undulating compound curve around a central dominant circular shape. Figure A2.9d features one sweeping curve along one side and a smaller opposite curvilinear element anchored on the side wall.

The approaches presented above (central linear circulation, central linear displays, loosely organized centers, hybrids, diagonal schemes, compartmentalized schemes, and inflected schemes) are not all the possible approaches but they cover a fair amount of them. The actual interpretation, articulation, and exe-

cution of each approach, however, is subject to infinite variation. That's part of the beauty of design. Not only do you have many approaches to choose from to solve a design problem, but you can customize each of them to suit the specific needs of a project.

The Art of Table Layout in Restaurants

Two realities operate simultaneously in restaurants: the back-of-the-house reality and the front-of-the-house reality. On the one hand, restaurants are like factories, requiring the assembly of products from raw materials that come in periodically. The creations are made on demand and on the spot requiring great organization and efficiency. On the other hand, there is the front-of-the-house experience. Above all, this experience should be pleasant. Although it is clear that the highlight of the experience is the meal itself, all the surrounding factors help to shape the total experience. Sights, sounds, and smells are some of the important environmental contributors. Themes and styles transport patrons to a temporary reality with a very special mood and character.

Designers have little control over such aspects as the quality of the food or how courteous and expedient the service is in a restaurant. They do, however, enjoy great influence over the ambiance of the place. Thoughtful composition, sensitive and well-conceived lighting, and appropriate detailing are some of the ingredients for success. Hopefully this book has given you some ideas about how to use strategies to achieve particular effects. As we have stated before, success re-

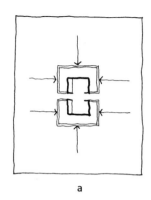 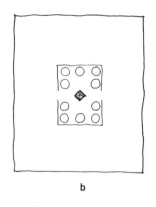 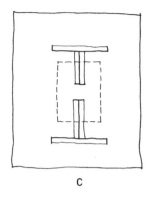

Figure A2.10 Three ways to treat a center zone: no seating but a solid and/or accent feature (a), central seating zone (b), dividing elements central zone (c).

a　　　　　　　　　　　b　　　　　　　　　　　c

quires both good ideas and good execution. You should plan to devote much time to these matters. It is not these that we want to highlight here. Instead we want to address a more mundane, but very important aspect of restaurant design: seating. The goal is to help you with this often time-consuming task so that you can produce a layout quickly and move on to more intricate tasks of the design, such as developing the theme and mood through detailing, color, lighting, and so on.

We begin by considering the two types of possible spaces in which you have to do your layout: the narrow space and the wide space. The first one implies a linear type of arrangement and has several possible layouts, depending on the actual width of the space. The second one presents more options and requires some preliminary decision making. With narrow spaces you can pretty much go at it and start your layout; however with wide spaces having a central zone you have to decide what you are going to do with the center. Figure A2.10 shows your three basic choices. You may put something other than seating in the middle, such as a mass with waiter stations and/or decorative or focal elements (e.g., planters, fountains, etc.), as shown in Figure A2.10a. Your second choice is to have a central seating area, in turn surrounded by narrower, perimeter areas (Figure A2.10b). Your third choice is to eliminate the center through the addition of one or more dividing elements (e.g., linear partial-height walls or planters, and so on). The solution shown in Figure A2.10c is an example of this approach and divides the room into four zones, one per side.

Before we begin looking at layout ideas, let's take a moment to reflect on the limited number of seating zones and table types. There are only two types of seating zones: perimeter and open. Perimeter seating is against a wall or some other boundary. Open seating, as the name implies, is in the open. Table types for perimeter seating include the booth, the two- or four-person against-the-wall table, and the two- or four-person against-the-wall table/banquette combination. You can also, of course, use one of the open-seating table arrangements along the perimeter. Open-seating table arrangements include the round table for four or more, the angled (usually 45 degrees) square table for four, the nonangled square table for two or four, and the nonangled rectangular table for four (seating on long sides). Those are pretty much the possibilities. There are, however, many possible ways of combining perimeter and open seating. The layout you choose depends on the proportions given by the space (or created intentionally by you through subdivision), the mix of tables desired for the restaurant, and your own preferences.

We give our layout ideas below, starting with narrow arrangements. Figure A2.11 shows six layouts consisting of two parallel perimeter walls (no central zone). The layouts in Figure A2.12 feature a center row between two parallel perimeters. Figure A2.13 shows layouts with a central zone of two rows. In Figure A2.14, a partial-height, dividing island is used along the center, thus subdividing the overall space into two narrow spaces. The environment still reads as one room because the center divider is low. The island reads as an object in the middle.

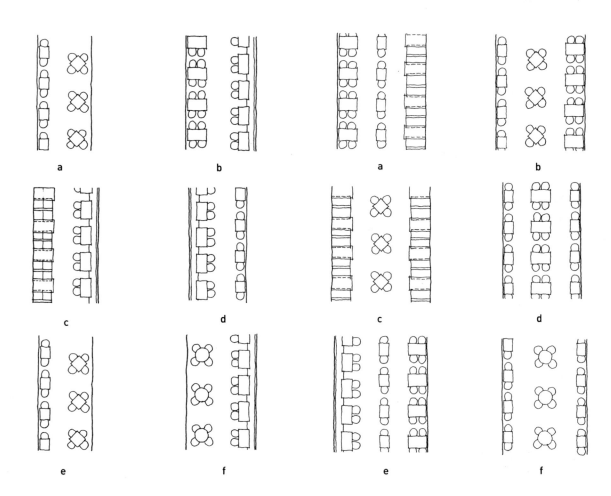

Figure A2.11 Variations of two parallel perimeters with central aisle.

Figure A2.12 Variations of two parallel perimeters with central row of tables.

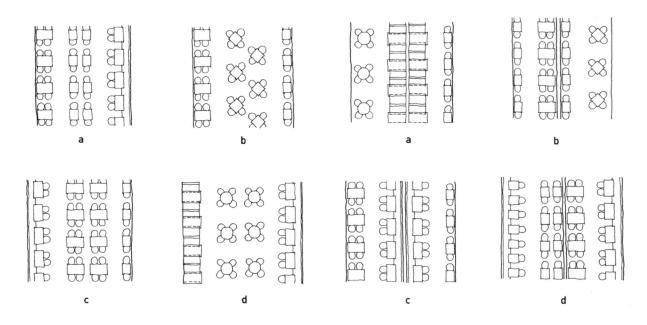

Figure A2.13 Variations of two parallel perimeters with double central rows of tables.

Figure A2.14 Variations of two parallel perimeters with central island.

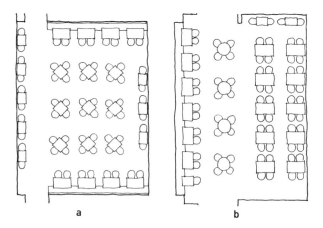

a   b

Figure A2.15 Schemes involving zones: perimeter with tables for two/ mixed zone (a), perimeter with banquettes/row of round tables/zone of tables for four (b).

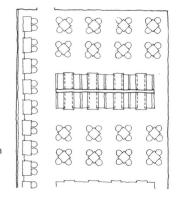

Figure A2.16 Perimeter with banquettes plus large zone subdivided by central island.

Figure A2.15a features a perimeter on the left and a zone on the right. Notice that it is no longer one or two rows of tables in the open but a larger area that reads as a zone. The layout in Figure A2.15b is slightly different. From left to right, it reads as a perimeter/single row/zone arrangement. Finally, Figure A2.16 shows how a large central zone can be subdivided into smaller regions. Whenever possible, avoid very large, undivided zones with a sea of tables. Sitting at one of the center tables is not a very pleasant experience. One feels lost in the middle. In a restaurant it is reassuring to feel anchored against, or at least close to, a wall column or some other element with anchoring properties.

NAME INDEX

 A

Aalto, Alvar, 141–142

Abercrombie, Stanley, 5, 81, 154

APCOA/Standard Parking Office project, 179–181

Appleton, Jay, 211, 212

Arnheim, Rudolf, 225–226, 228

B

Benedikt, Michael, 251–252

Berlyne, Daniel, 176

C

Ching, Francis, 59

Codman, Ogden, 315

Color Image Scale, 316

Crozier, Ray, 176

D

Doane Pet Care Company Headquarters project, 217–218

Duchossois Center for Advanced Medicine, 144–147

E

El Dorado Grill, 253–255

Eva Maddox Associates, 323

F

Farnsworth House, 67

Fibonacci, Leonardo, 274

Fischer, Mary Pat, 314

G

Galter Medical Pavilion Project, 323–324

Gary Lee Partners, 290

Gauldie, Sinclair, 314

German Pavilion, 67

Gibson, James J., 115

Glass House, 67

Graves, Michael, 250

 H

Heimsath, Clovis, 101

Hildebrandt, Grant, 212

HLM Design, 144

Husseri, Edmund, 50

 J

Jencks, Charles, 225, 226

Johnson, Philip, 67

 K

Kahn, Louis, 141–142

Kaplan, Rachel, 176–177

Kaplan, Stephen, 176–177

Kobayashi, Shigenobu, 316–318

L

Le Corbusier, 44, 186, 274

Leupen, Bernard, 154

Linville Architects, 253

Linville, Ed, 253

Lorenz, Konrad, 211

Lynch, Kevin, 42, 44, 47, 52, 54, 159, 160

M

Mehrabian, Albert, 32

Meiss, Pierre Von, 157

Mekus Studios, 179

Moore, Charles, 95, 115

Mount Angel Abbey Library, 141–142

N

Nippon Color & Design Research Institute (NCD), 316

Norberg-Schulz, Christian, 42, 47, 50–52, 156, 160

P

Passini, Romedi, 156, 160

Pelli, Cesar, 93, 101, 249, 252

Phillips Exeter Library, 141–142

Porphyrios, Demetri, 250–251

SUBJECT INDEX

Character concepts, 123, 282. *See also* Expression

Checkerboard pattern alternatives, 330–332

Circular space, 72

Circulation systems, 43–47, 81–83. *See also* Arrival space; Nodes; Paths

    activity manipulation in, 200

    axial, 82

    building, 97

    building surroundings, 95

    components of, 43

    design opportunities, 26, 30

    enrichment of, 16, 192, 200–213

    events in, 202–203

    example, medical clinic, 201–202

    exploration in, 201

    free movement, 82–83

    heart of, 44

    linear, 81

    loop, 81–82

    movement assessment in, 201–202

    network, 83

    order and, 156, 161

    organization models based on, 81–83

    patterns in, 97

    radial, 82

    safety in, 201

    side-trips in, 29

    user perceptions of, 201–202

Clarity, content/intention, 139

Classical approach, 84

Classical architecture, 250–251

Clear intersection, 165

Clients. *See also* Identity

    defined, 100

    good, 101

    requirements from, 109–110

    role of, 100–101

Clinics. *See* Medical facilities

Closedness, 233–234

Closure, 289

Clustering, 164

Coherence, 177

Coherent schemes, 125–126

Collative variables, 176

Color, 311–315. *See also* Modifying elements

    application of, 314

    associations with, 312

    behavior of, 312

    classification system, 316–318

    context of, 313

    emotional effect of, 311–312

    excessive, 315

    figure-ground segregation and, 289

    harmony systems, 313–314

    image/lifestyle and, 316–318

    mood effect of, 316

    regional impact of, 312, 313

    risks/rewards of, 315

    strategies, 314–315

    suitability of, 313

    symbolic content of, 312

    theory of, 313–314

    using, 312, 314

Columns

    design alternatives for, 336

    as open barriers, 48

    placement of, 61

Common enclosure

    promoting understanding with, 164

    unity and, 282

Communication. *See also* Expression

    formal properties of, 224

    interpretation of, 223–226

    symbolic content of, 224, 226

Compartmentalized plans, 74

Complementary composition, 282

Complexity

    ambiguity and, 176, 198–199

    arousal and, 176

    arrangements and, 195

    clarity from, case study, 144–147

    commentary on, 249–250

    as enrichment strategy, 192–196

    with groupings, 195

    mystery and, 177–178

    order and, 175, 176–178, 193

    with patterns, 195

    perceptual hierarchy and, 288

    as preference predictor, 177–178

    research on, 176–178, 192–193

    simplicity vs., 286

    size and, 195

    spatial composition, 194–195

    surface articulation, 193–194

    system overlapping, 195–196

    tension with, 198

    variables, 176–178

difficulty of, 5

emotion and, 4–5

history, 7

intuition and, 5

levels of, 26, 37

mastery of, 322–323

truthfulness/illusion in, 321–322

Design concepts. *See also* Ideation; Organization systems; Organizational concepts (ideas)

character, 123, 282

defined, 121–123

function and, 121

hierarchy of, 122–123

main, 122–123

misconceptions about, 122–123

Designer control, 35–36, 37–38. *See also*

Activity manipulation

clients and, 100–101

disclosure, 75

enrichment, 189–190

exterior orientation, 76–77

focus, 77

focus responsibility, 76

movement, 74

people and, 320–321

permeability, 73–74

relief, 75, 77–78

of sequences, 158

situational factors and, 35

space size, 69–70

Designers

attitude of, 247

creative power of, 321–322

design difficulty and, 5

dominant trait, 4

emotion and, 4–5

excellence as, 9

intuition of, 5

mastery by, 322–323

personal expression of, 246–248

personal style of, 246–247, 249–252

philosophies of, 249–252

requirements for, 5–6

sophisticated expression of, 247–248

Design intention

clarity of, 139

defined, 8

design problems and, 8

enrichment as, 37, 189–190

strategy and, 8–9

Design knowledge, 7–8

current trend of, 7, 231–232

historical, 7

notebook/photos for, 8

research and, 7–8

travel for, 8

Design opportunities

exit space, 30

secondary activity, 29

side trip area, 28–29

target activity area, 28

waiting area, 26

Design principles, 11–17

Design problems. *See also* Project, understanding

defined, 8

understanding, 13–14

Design program

coherent schemes and, 125

expressing necessities of, 233–234

omitted items from, 14

schemes for, 124–126

Design strategies, 5, 8–9

Design studio

critical questioning and, 6–7, 14

importance of, 6–7

perspective and, 7

review/critique in, 6

Design synthesis, 263–265. *See also* Resolution

floor plan resolution, 264

plan refinement, 264–265

process of, 263–264

Destinations, 42–43, 47

arriving at, 27–28

centers as, 43

departing, 29–30

domains as, 42–43

enrichment of, 192, 213–216

events en route to, 202–203

grounding, 214–215

moving toward, 26

personal connection in, 215–216

relief in, 216

task facilitation in, 214–216

Detailing, 319–320

case study, 253–255

effects of, 319–320

identification with, 52

interpretation of, 223–226

legibility of, 177

mental maps of, 158

mystery of, 177

natural features, 95

olfactory, 307–308

people and, 32–33, 320–321

place and, 12–13

pleasure from, 32–33

predictability in, 187

sensory load of, 36–37

situational factors and, 30–36

stability of, 191

surrounding, 34, 94–96

thermal, 306–307

wholeness of, 322

Equilibrium. *See* Balance

Eurythmy, 266

Events

building activity, 23–30

enrichment with, 16, 202–203

levels of, example, 21–23

theater visit, example, 21–23

transition, 202–203

user activity, example, 21–23

Excellence, 9

Exits, moving toward, 30

Exploration, 201

Expression, 221–257. *See also* Modifying
elements

arrival space and, 44, 160–161, 191

articulation and, 128

clarity of, 225–226

closedness as, 233–234

connectedness as, 234

contextual factor, 230–232

cultural, 231

current norms/conventions of, 7,
231–232

defined, 16–17, 223

design assembly, 232–233

of designer, 246–248

as design message, 223–224,
225–226

as design principle, 16–17

first-level, 127–128

formal properties of, 224, 232–233

furnishings and, 54, 227–228

historic, 230–231

of identity, 234–246

inflection and, 128

interpretation of, 223–226

landmarks and, 55

meaning of, 225–226

openness as, 233–234

overview, 222–223

of owner/user personality, 16–17

programmatic necessity, 233–234

regional, 231

segregation as, 234

spectrum of, 226–228

symbolic content of, 189–190, 224,
226, 229, 247–248

of universal experience,
228–230

Extension

consistency vs., 283–284

continuity and, 283–284

defined, 283

overlapping and, 284

repetition vs., 284

Externalizing approaches

conceptual sketches, 132

descriptive scenarios, 131–132

diagrams, 132

verbal, 130–132

visual, 132

Extremes, 196

F

Facility types, 14

Fibonacci Series, 274

Figurative architecture, 250

Figure-ground articulation, 288–289

Finishes, 308–311. *See also* Color

feel of, 310–311

inherent, 308–310

modularity and, 309

patterns and, 309–310

texture and, 309–311

Fit, 121–122

contextual, 155

functional, 155

proper, order and, 155–156

Floor plans

enrichment of, case study, 290–291

holistic view from, 158

Inspiration, 130

Intention. *See* Design intention

Interest, order and, 186

Interior context, 97

Interior designers. *See* Designers

Internal players

    clients, 100–101

    users, 101–102

Interpenetrated spaces, 80

Interpretation, 223–226

    cultural impact on, 225

    of design expression, 223–226

    experiencer background and, 224–225

    inherent expression and, 225

    learned associations and, 225

    meaning and, 225–226

    message strength and, 225–226

    spontaneous meaning and, 225

    visual codes and, 225

Intersection, clear, 165

Intimate scale, 71

J

Joining spaces, 79–80

Journal, design idea, 8

L

Landmarks, 54–55, 162

Layouts, as messages, 227

Learned associations, 225

Legibility. *See also* Disclosure; Orientation; Project understanding, promoting

    of boundaries, 173–174

    of closed corridors, 169–170

    defined, 168

    of enclosed spaces, 168–170

    factors affecting, 168

    increasing, with place elements, 160–162

    order and, 175

    orientation and, 157

    in various enclosure schemes, 170–175

    visibility and, 168–170

Libraries, 105–106, 141–142

Lifestyle. *See also* Identity

    categories of, 317–318

    color/image and, 316–318

Lighting, 297–304. *See also* Modifying elements

    animation with, 302

    boldness of, 197

    brightness of, 298, 299–301

    creating foci with, 299–302

    daylight, 303–304

    form enhancement with, 298–299

    judging success of, 298

    mood effect of, 297–298

    planning, 302, 304

    quality of, 298

    source types, 301–302

    of space, 301

    straight-on, 299

    texture enhancement with, 299

Linear systems, 81

Load level

    environmental balance and, 36–37

    high/low, 36–37

    predicting responses to, 32–33

    preferences, 242–243

    texture/pattern impact on, 310

Location context, 93–94

Loop systems, 81–82

Loose approach, 84

Loosely defined space, 63

Low-load environment, 36–37

M

Main concepts, 122–123

Main paths, 45

Masses

    enclosed, 170–173

    irregular-shaped, 172–173

    multiple enclosed, 171–172

    novelty with, 196, 197

    open plans and, 170–173

    single enclosed, 170–171

Mass, in diagrams, 60

Materials

    breathability of, 310

    feel of, 310–311

    finishes of, 308–310

    patterns in, 309–310

    preferences, 243

    textile, 309

    texture of, 309–311

thermal conduction of, 310

wood, 309

Meaning

inherent expression and, 225

interpretation and, 225–226

of objects, 159–160

spontaneous, 225

Medical facilities

approaching, 24

arriving at, 24, 25

case studies, 144–147, 323–324

circulation example, 201–202

departing, 29–30

destination, arriving at, 27–28

relief in, 76

secondary activities, 29

space in, 41

waiting areas for, 25, 26

Membership

age group, 235, 237

background and, 236–237

identification with, 235

status, 235–236, 237

Messages. *See* Expression

Mobility patterns, 78

Modern approach, 84

Modifying elements, 295–327. *See also*
Color; Lighting

acoustics, 304–306

ambient, 297–308

decorative, 308–320

design opportunities, 26

design principle, 17

detailing, 319–320

effects of, 17

finishes, 308–311

olfactory environment, 307–308

ornamentation, 319–320

overview, 296–297

thermal environment, 306–307

Modulation

defined, 193

path enclosure, 206

surface, 193–194, 206

surface relief, 194

Modulator system, 274

Monumental scale, 70

Mood. *See also* Identity

color affecting, 316

lighting affecting, 297–298

sensory load and, 36–37

Movement. *See also* Circulation systems;
Sequences

designer control of, 74

efficient, 201

free, 82–83

organization systems and, 135

Multinuclear organization, 135

Mystery, complexity and, 177–178

N

Needs. *See also* Human needs

privacy, 114, 233–234

understanding, 13–14

Negative space, 69

Neighborhood

within building, 110–111

outside building, 95

Network systems, 83

Nodes, 46–47. *See also* Circulation systems

centers vs., 46

defined, 46

as enhancers, 46–47

in functional diagrams, 138

manipulating activity with, 199–200

order and, 161

organizing, 135

paths and, 46–47

Novelty

arousal through, 176

as enrichment strategy, 196

extremes for, 196

reducing regularity for, 187

tension with, 198

O

Objects, 53–55

affordances and, 115–116

complexity of, 195

focal, 76

furnishings, 53–54, 227–228

grouping of, 195

identity of, 159

imageability of, 159, 162

landmarks, 54–55, 162

meaning of, 159–160

placement of, 61

scale of, 195, 267–271

shape of, 195

structure and, 159, 160

suspended, 61

Occasion, 31

Offices. *See also* Activities, in buildings

  activity manipulation in, 200

  balancing atmosphere of, 36

  case studies, 179–181, 217–218, 290–291

  central service cores and, 98–99

  design considerations for, 337–340

  disclosure examples, 74

  entry sequence examples, 109–110

  focus in, 76

  goods in, 320–321

  neighborhood (module) in, 110–111

  paths in, 45

  project commonalities, 104

  relief in, 76

  solids/voids in, 337–339

  space features, examples, 98–100

  space planning in, 339–340

  stimulation levels for, 33

  work process design in, 339–340

Olfactory environment, 307–308

Openings, 64, 208–210

Openness, expression with, 233–234

Open plans, 74, 170–175

  boundary shape, 173–174

  case study, 217–218

  with irregular-shaped mass, 172–173

with multiple enclosed masses, 171–172

with one enclosed mass, 170–171

with partial-height elements, 174–175

with partially obscured boundary, 172

Opportunity vs. safety, 211–213

Order, 15–16, 153–183

  advantages of, 15

  architectonic, 156, 265

  arrival space and, 44, 160–161

  balance of, 15–16, 186

  as basic human need, 15, 156

  case study on, 179–181

  centers and, 160

  circulation systems and, 156, 161

  complexity and, 175, 176–178, 193

  connectors and, 161–162

  designing for, 160–175

  as design principle, 15–16, 154–155

  domains and, 160

  of economy, 155–156

  edges and, 161–162

  ends and, 161–162

  enrichment and, 186, 187–192

  first-level, 126–127

  furnishings and, 54

  identity and, 159

  interest and, 186

  kinds of, 155–157

  legibility and, 175

  meaning and, 159–160

  nodes and, 161

optimal level of, 155–156, 176, 187

organization principle for, 157

orientation and, 156–157, 158–160

paths and, 161

place elements and, 160–162

project understanding from, 162–175

proper fit and, 155–156

research on, 176–178

simple geometry for, 157

space composition and, 168–175

storage to support, 156

structure and, 159, 160

traits of, 15

variety and, 186, 187

visual harmony and, 156

Organizational concepts (ideas), 5–6, 14–15, 122–136. *See also* Design concepts; Ideation

  character concepts vs., 123, 282

  coherent schemes for, 125–126

  defined, 123

  descriptive scenarios and, 131–132

  as design principle, 14–15

  first-level enrichment, 127–128

  first-level order, 126–127

  into floor plans, 124–125, 264

  generating, 128–136

  goals of, 123–128

  main concept and, 122–123

  purpose of, 15

  quick approach for, 143–144

  responsive schemes for, 125–126

  stages of, 15, 128–133

interior physical, 34

natural features, 95

Suspended objects, 61

Symbolic content

of admittance/rejection, 229

of ascending/descending, 229

of color, 312

of communication, 224, 226

of constraint/freedom, 229

defined, 224

designer sophistication and, 247–248

of form, 189–190

of iconic signs, 226

spontaneous, 226

universal experiences with, 228–230

Symbols. *See* Diagram graphics

Symmetrical composition, 275–278

central axis/approach correspondence in, 277

characteristics of, 275

complex, 277–278

focal point of, 276–277

purity of, 278

Symmetry, 275–278

defined, 266

figure-ground segregation and, 289

Synergy, 114–115

Synthesis. *See* Design synthesis

System overlapping, 195–196